a reason for Science

Hands-On Activities With Scripture Values

TEACHER GUIDEBOOK

ISBN #1-58938-222-6

Published by The Concerned Group, Inc.

700 East Granite • PO Box 1000 • Siloam Springs, AR 72761

Authors **Dave & Rozann Seela**
Publisher **Russ L. Potter, II**
Senior Editor **Bill Morelan**
Project Coordinator **Lauren Aloha**
Proofreader **Ginger Macfarlan**
Illustrators **Steven Butler**
Josh Ray
Preston Toombs

Printed on recycled paper in the United States

For more information about **A Reason For**® curricula, write to the address above, call, or visit our website.

www.areasonfor.com

800.447.4332

TABLE OF CONTENTS

*"A sound grounding in science strengthens many of the skills that people use every day, like solving problems creatively, thinking critically, working cooperatively in teams, using technology effectively, and valuing life-long learning."**

**National Science Education Standards*, 1999 Washington, D.C.: National Academy Press. (p. ix)

A NEW PARADIGM

A Reason For® Science was designed for children, the handiwork of an infinite God — young minds created with an unlimited capacity to think, to learn, and to discover!

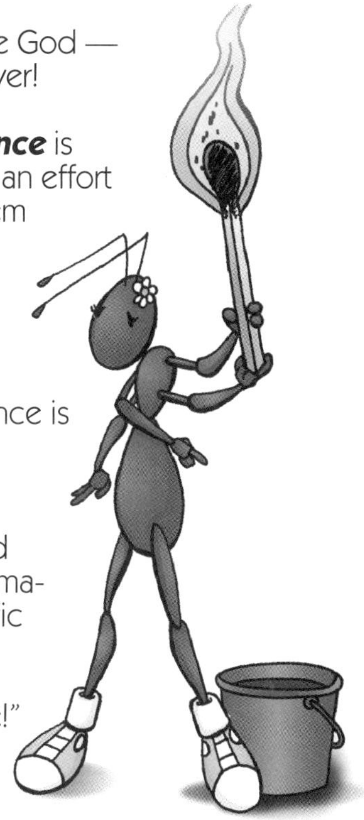

Because of this emphasis on children and how they learn, ***A Reason For® Science*** is based on a different paradigm from the traditional textbook approach. Why? In an effort to address standards and accountability, many of today's science textbooks seem to get learning backwards. They focus primarily on building a knowledge base, assuming students will later attach meaning to memorized facts. The problem is that few elementary students master information presented this way because they simply never become engaged with the material.

By contrast, ***A Reason For® Science*** is based on the premise that learning science is an *active* process. It's "something children do, not something done to them."[2]

According to the **National Science Education Standards**, ". . . active science learning means shifting emphasis away from teachers presenting information and covering science topics. The perceived need to include all the topics and information . . . is in direct conflict with the central goal of having students learn scientific knowledge with understanding."[3]

To paraphrase William Butler Yeats, "Teaching is not filling a pail. It's lighting a fire!"

INQUIRY-BASED LEARNING

A Reason For® Science is designed to teach basic **Life, Earth,** and **Physical Science** concepts through fun, hands-on activities. Its focus is to make learning both fun and meaningful.

But hands-on activities by themselves are not enough. To truly master a concept, students must have "minds-on" experiences as well! This means actively engaging the material through a variety of activities such as group discussion, problem solving, and journaling. It also requires thought-provoking questions that help develop higher-level cognitive skills. The weekly format of ***A Reason For® Science*** is designed to reflect this inquiry-based model.

According to the **National Science Education Standards**, "Inquiry is central to science learning. When engaging in inquiry, students describe objects and events, ask questions, construct explanations, test those explanations against current scientific knowledge, and communicate their ideas to others . . . In this way, students actively develop their understanding of science by combining scientific knowledge with reasoning and thinking skills."[4]

Since different students achieve understanding in different ways and to different degrees, the flexible format of ***A Reason For® Science*** also encourages multiple learning styles and allows for individual differences. Activities challenge students to develop their own unique skills, and encourage them to come up with creative solutions.

NATIONAL STANDARDS

National standards referred to in ***A Reason For® Science*** come from the **National Science Education Standards**[1]. More specifically, they reflect the "K-4 Science Content Standards" (p.121 - 142) and "5-8 Science Content Standards" (p. 143 - 172).

The Teacher Guidebook includes a list of content standards that relate to each individual lesson. References are based on the NSES alphabetic format, plus a numeric code to indicate the bulleted sub-topic. For example, **C1** in a fourth grade lesson would indicate Content Standard **C** and sub-topic **1**. (A detailed description of this content standard can be found on pages 127 - 229 of the **Standards**.)

As noted above, lower grade and upper grade standards are found in different sections of the book. A **C1** reference for a third grade lesson, for example, would be found on page 127 (characteristics of organisms). By contrast, a **C1** reference for a seventh grade lesson would be found on page 155 ("structure and function in living systems").

METHODOLOGY

Master teachers know that a science curriculum is much more than information in a textbook. It has to do with the way content is organized and presented in the classroom. It is driven by underlying principles, and by attitudes and beliefs about how learning occurs. It is expressed in the practices and procedures used in its implementation.

In other words, textbooks don't teach science — *teachers* do!

That's why it's important for you to understand how this curriculum is designed to be used, and how you can enhance the learning process in your classroom.

Concepts, Not Content

The needs of children in elementary school are very different from high school students, especially when it comes to science education. The presentation of the Periodic Table provides a good example. High school students may find it useful to memorize each element, its atomic weight, and its position on a chart. By contrast, elementary school students must first understand the concept of such a table. What is it? How is it used? Why is it arranged this way? Has it always looked like this? How (and why) has it changed over time? Such an approach leads to a foundational understanding of a concept, rather than a body of memorized "facts" that may change over time.*

As Nobel prize winner, Dr. Richard Feynman, once said, "You can know the name of a bird in all the languages of the world, but when you're finished, you'll know absolutely nothing whatever about the bird . . . (that's) the difference between knowing the name of something and knowing something!"

* *For example, less than 30 years ago many students were still being taught the "fact" that matter only has three states (solid, liquid, gas). But in 1970, Hannes Alfven won the Nobel prize for identifying a fourth state of matter (plasma). There are many such examples in education — including the Periodic Table charts themselves, which are being replaced in many places by a 3D computer model that offers new insights into relationships between elements.*

Multi-Sensory Learning

In addition to focusing on concepts instead of just content, ***A Reason For® Science*** uses a multi-sensory approach to learning that supports multiple learning styles.

Visual events include watching teacher demonstrations, studying diagrams and illustrations, and reading summaries. **Auditory** events include participating in group discussions with team members, listening to teacher directions and explanations, and hearing the unique sounds associated with the activities. **Kinesthetic** events include tactile interaction with activity materials, hands-on experimentation, and taking notes, writing answers, and drawing diagrams in individual Student Worktexts.

Omitting any of these components can significantly weaken the learning process, especially for children with specific learning disabilities.

Student-Driven, Teacher-Directed

As long-time educators, the authors of this series recognize that many elementary teachers don't consider themselves "science people." Therefore, this series avoids unnecessary technical jargon, and deals with complex interactions in simple, easy-to-understand language that's reinforced with concrete, hands-on activities.

The Teacher Guidebook is designed to give you the confidence that you need to teach science effectively. In addition to the usual answer keys and explanations, it includes several sections just for teachers.

"Additional Comments" offers tips and techniques for making each lesson run smoothly. "Teacher to Teacher" provides expanded science explanations to increase your understanding. "Extended Teaching" presents a variety of extension ideas for those who wish to go further.

During the first year, we strongly recommend that you try every activity a day or two in advance. Although most activities are relatively simple, this added practice will give you a better feel for any potential problems that might arise.

Most of all, remember that one of the primary goals of this series is to make science FUN for the participants. And that includes you, too!

COMPONENTS

The following are some of the key components in this series:

Letter to Parents

Positive communication between home and school is essential for optimum success with any curriculum. The "Letter to the Parents" (page 3, Student Worktext) provides a great way to introduce ***A Reason For® Science*** to parents. It covers the lesson format, safety issues, connections with national standards, and the integration of Scripture. Along with the opening sections of this Guidebook, the parent letter provides information you need to answer common questions about the series.

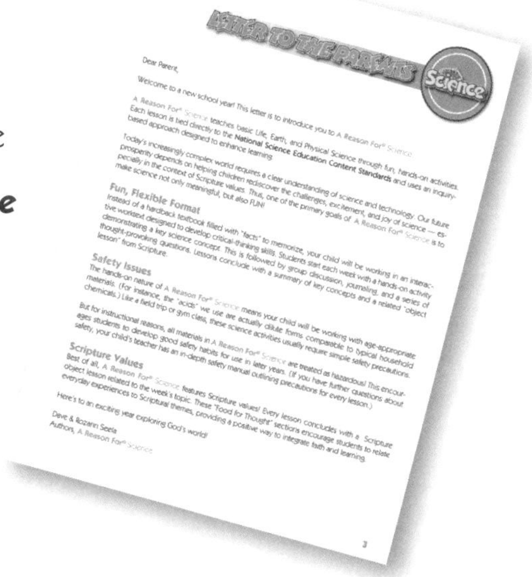

LETTER TO THE PARENTS

Dear Parent,

Welcome to a new school year! This letter is to introduce you to A Reason For® Science.

A Reason For® Science teaches basic Life, Earth, and Physical Science through fun, hands-on activities. Each lesson is tied directly to the **National Science Education Content Standards** and uses an inquiry-based approach designed to enhance learning.

Today's increasingly complex world requires a clear understanding of science and technology. Our future prosperity depends on helping children rediscover the challenges, excitement, and joy of science — especially in the context of Scripture values. Thus, one of the primary goals of A Reason For® Science is to make science not only meaningful, but also FUN!

Fun, Flexible Format

Instead of a hardback textbook filled with "facts" to memorize, your child will be working in an interactive worktext designed to develop critical-thinking skills. Students start each week with a hands-on activity demonstrating a key science concept. This is followed by group discussion, journaling, and a series of thought-provoking questions. Lessons conclude with a summary of key concepts and a related "object lesson" from Scripture.

Safety Issues

The hands-on nature of A Reason For® Science means your child will be working with age-appropriate materials. (For instance, the "acids" we use are actually dilute forms comparable to typical household chemicals.) Like a field trip or gym class, these science activities usually require simple safety precautions.

But for instructional reasons, all materials in A Reason For® Science are treated as hazardous! This encourages students to develop good safety habits for use in later years. (If you have further questions about safety, your child's teacher has an in-depth safety manual outlining precautions for every lesson.)

Scripture Values

Best of all, A Reason For® Science features Scripture values! Every lesson concludes with a Scripture object lesson related to the week's topic. These "Food for Thought" sections encourage students to relate everyday experiences to Scriptural themes, providing a positive way to integrate faith and learning.

Here's to an exciting year exploring God's world!

Dave & Rozann Seela
Authors, A Reason For® Science

3

Student Research Teams

A Reason For® Science was created to model the way scientific study works in the adult world. Students are divided into "research teams" to work through activities cooperatively. Ideally, each research team should be composed of three to five students. (Fewer students per team makes monitoring more difficult; more students per team minimizes participation opportunities.) The best groupings combine students with different "gifts" (skills or abilities), complimentary personalities, etc. — the same kinds of combinations that make effective teams in the corporate or industrial world.

In addition, ***A Reason For® Science*** encourages collaboration between the different teams, again modeling the interactions found in the scientific community.

Individual Student Worktexts

Although students collaborate on activities and thought questions, the Student Worktexts provide opportunities for individual reaction and response. The importance of allowing students to write their own response to questions, keep their own notes, and journal about their individual experiences cannot be underestimated. (While collaboration is essential in the scientific community, no true scientist would neglect to keep his/her own personal notes and records!)

Individual Student Worktexts also provide teachers with an objective way to monitor student participation and learning throughout the school year.

Materials Kits

Quality materials are an integral part of any "hands-on" curriculum. ***A Reason For® Science*** offers complete, easy-to-use Materials Kits for every grade level. With some minor exceptions*, these contain all the materials and supplies needed by one research team for an entire school year. The materials for each team come packaged in an attractive, durable storage container. You can choose to restock consumable portions of the Kit from local materials, or purchase the convenient Refill Pack.

Personal Science Glossary

A glossary is a common component in many science textbooks, yet students rarely use traditional glossaries except when assigned to "look up" a word by the teacher. Since words and terms used in elementary science are not highly technical, this activity is better served by referring students to a standard dictionary.

A more effective approach to helping students learn science words at this level is to encourage them to develop and maintain a **personal science glossary**. This can be a plain spiral-bound notebook with one page (front and back) dedicated to each letter of the alphabet. Throughout the school year, students continually add new words and definitions — not only from their own reading and research, but from the findings of their team members as well.

** To help minimize expenses, kits do not include common classroom supplies (pencils, paper, etc.) and a few large items (soft drink bottles, cans, etc.) that are easily obtained by the teacher. Kit and non-kit materials needed for each lesson are clearly marked in this Teacher Guidebook.*

SAFETY ISSUES

When using hands-on science activities, teachers must be constantly aware of the potential for safety problems. Even the simplest activities using the most basic materials can be dangerous when used incorrectly. **Proper monitoring and supervision is required at all times!**

Although the publisher and authors have made every reasonable effort to ensure that all science activities in ***A Reason For® Science*** are safe when conducted as instructed, neither the publisher nor the authors assume any responsibility for damage or injury resulting from implementation.

It is the responsibility of the school to review available science safety resources and to develop science safety training for their teachers and students, as well as posting safety rules in every classroom.

An excellent source of science safety information is the Council of State Science Supervisors at: http://www.csss-science.org/safety. The CSSS website offers a FREE, downloadable safety guide, "Science and Safety, Making the Connection." This booklet was created with support from the American Chemical Society, the Eisenhower National Clearinghouse for Mathematics and Science Education, the National Aeronautics and Space Administration, and the National Institutes of Health.

To support appropriate safety instruction, every ***A Reason For® Science*** Student Worktext includes a special section on safety. In addition to the safety precautions above, it is strongly recommended that every teacher verify all students clearly understand this information *before* beginning any science activities.

ASSESSMENT METHODS

Authentic assessment is an important part of any quality curriculum. ***A Reason For® Science*** offers a duel approach to assessment. First, participation, understanding, and higher-level thinking skills and can be assessed by periodically collecting and reading students' responses to the essay-style questions in the Student Worktext.

Second, this Teacher Guidebook provides black-line masters for a "weekly quiz" (see page 163). These quizzes offer a more traditional assessment based on fact acquisition. Questions are similar to the type that students might face on any standardized test.

In addition, you can use both these methods to create a customized quarterly or yearly assessment tool. Simply select a combination of true/false and multiple choice questions from the quizzes and essay-style questions from the Student Worktext.

SCRIPTURE CONNECTION

Integrating faith and learning is an essential part of a quality religious education. A unique component of ***A Reason For® Science*** is the incorporation of Scripture Object Lessons into every unit. As students discover basic science principles, they are encouraged to explore various spiritual connections through specific Scripture verses.

Since some school systems may prefer one Scripture translation to another, Scriptures are referenced by chapter and verse only, rather than direct quotations in the text.

CREATIONISM

Many people (including many notable scientists) believe that God created the universe and all the processes both physical and biological that resulted in our solar system and life on Earth.

However, advocates of "creation science" hold a variety of viewpoints. Some believe that Earth is relatively young, perhaps only 6,000 years old. Others believe that Earth may have existed for millions of years, but that various organisms (especially humans) could only be the result of divine intervention since they demonstrate "intelligent design."

Within the creation science community, there are dozens of variations on these themes, even within the specific denominational groups. Instead of promoting a specific view, the authors of this series have chosen to focus on the concept that "God created the Heavens and the Earth," and leave the specifics up to the individual school. Creationism is a faith-based issue.* As such, schools are strongly urged to have a clear position on this topic, and an understanding of how that belief is to be conveyed to their students.

** For that matter, so is the theory of evolution.*

[1] *National Science Education Standards*, 1999 Washington, D.C.: National Academy Press. (p. ix)
[2] *Ibid.* (p. 2)
[3] *Ibid.* (p. 20)
[4] *Ibid.* (p. 2)

This Teacher Guidebook . . .

is based on a simple, easy-to-understand format. Lessons throughout the series follow the same pattern, so once you're familiar with the format for one lesson, you can find information quickly for any other lesson. The samples on the following pages explain the purpose of each section.

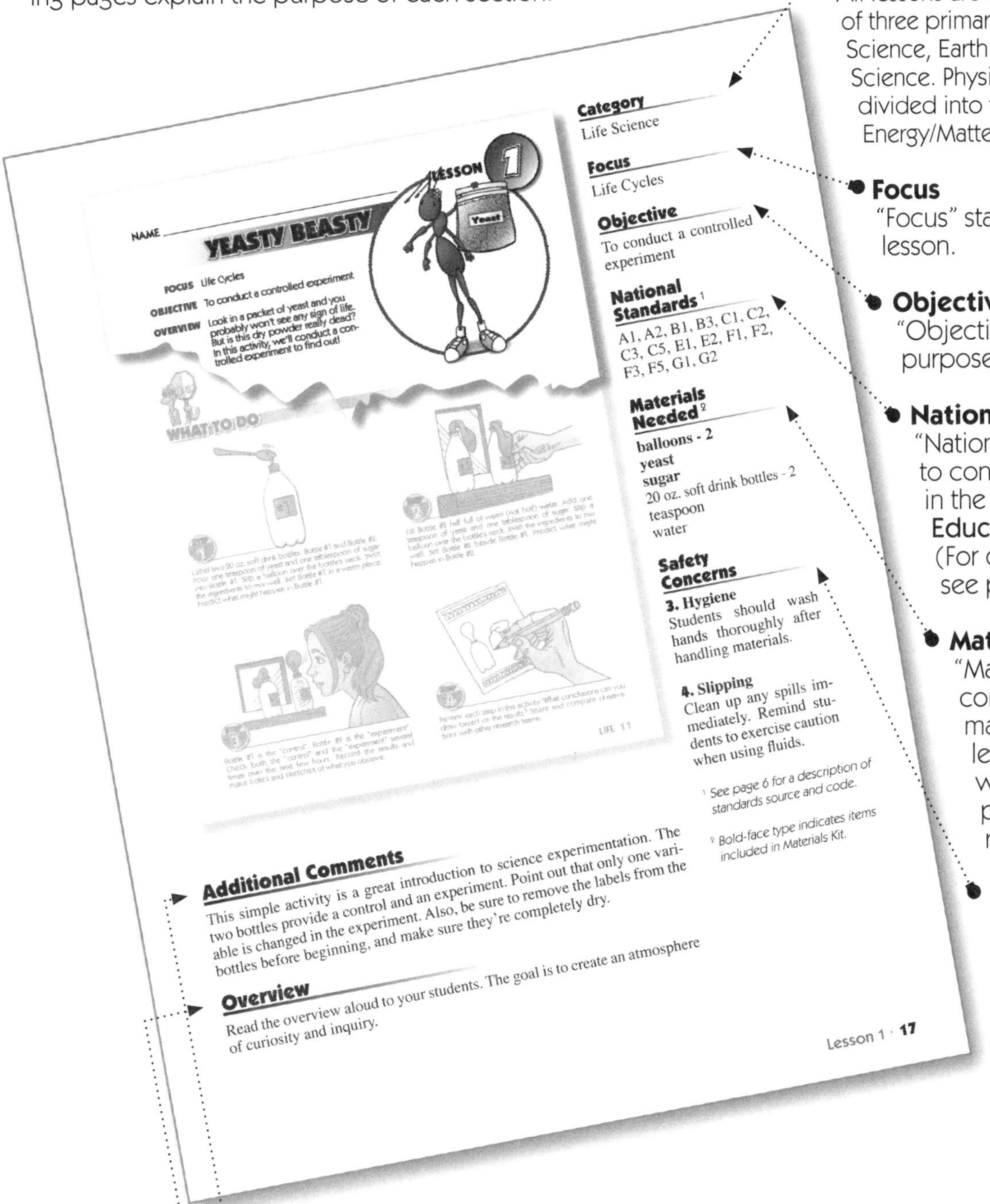
NAME

LESSON 1

YEASTY BEASTY

FOCUS Life Cycles

OBJECTIVE To conduct a controlled experiment

OVERVIEW Look in a packet of yeast and you probably won't see any sign of life. But is this dry powder really dead? In this activity, we'll conduct a controlled experiment to find out!

WHAT TO DO

LIFE 11

Category
Life Science

Focus
Life Cycles

Objective
To conduct a controlled experiment

National Standards [1]
A1, A2, B1, B3, C1, C2, C3, C5, E1, E2, F1, F2, F3, F5, G1, G2

Materials Needed [2]
balloons - 2
yeast
sugar
20 oz. soft drink bottles - 2
teaspoon
water

Safety Concerns
3. Hygiene
Students should wash hands thoroughly after handling materials.

4. Slipping
Clean up any spills immediately. Remind students to exercise caution when using fluids.

[1] See page 6 for a description of standards source and code.

[2] Bold-face type indicates items included in Materials Kit.

Additional Comments
This simple activity is a great introduction to science experimentation. The two bottles provide a control and an experiment. Point out that only one variable is changed in the experiment. Also, be sure to remove the labels from the bottles before beginning, and make sure they're completely dry.

Overview
Read the overview aloud to your students. The goal is to create an atmosphere of curiosity and inquiry.

Lesson 1 · 17

- **Category**
  All lessons are divided into one of three primary categories — Life Science, Earth Science, or Physical Science. Physical Science is further divided into two parts — Forces or Energy/Matter.
- **Focus**
  "Focus" states the topic of the lesson.
- **Objective**
  "Objective" describes the purpose of the lesson.
- **National Standards**
  "National Standards" refers to content standards found in the **National Science Education Standards**. (For details on standards, see page 6.)
- **Materials Needed:**
  "Materials Needed" is a comprehensive list of materials used in the lesson. **Bold-faced** words indicate items provided in the Materials Kit.
- **Safety Concerns:**
  "Safety Concerns" provides details about potential safety hazards. (For more on Safety, see page 9.)
- **Additional Comments:** "Additional Comments" offers tips and techniques for making each lesson run more smoothly.
- **Overview:** The "Overview" provides lesson summaries, thoughts on introducing the lesson, ideas for dealing with materials, and other valuable lesson-specific tips.

What To Do

"What to Do" expands on the Steps found in the Student Workbook. It outlines potential problems, offers alternative procedures, and explains ways to enhance the lesson.

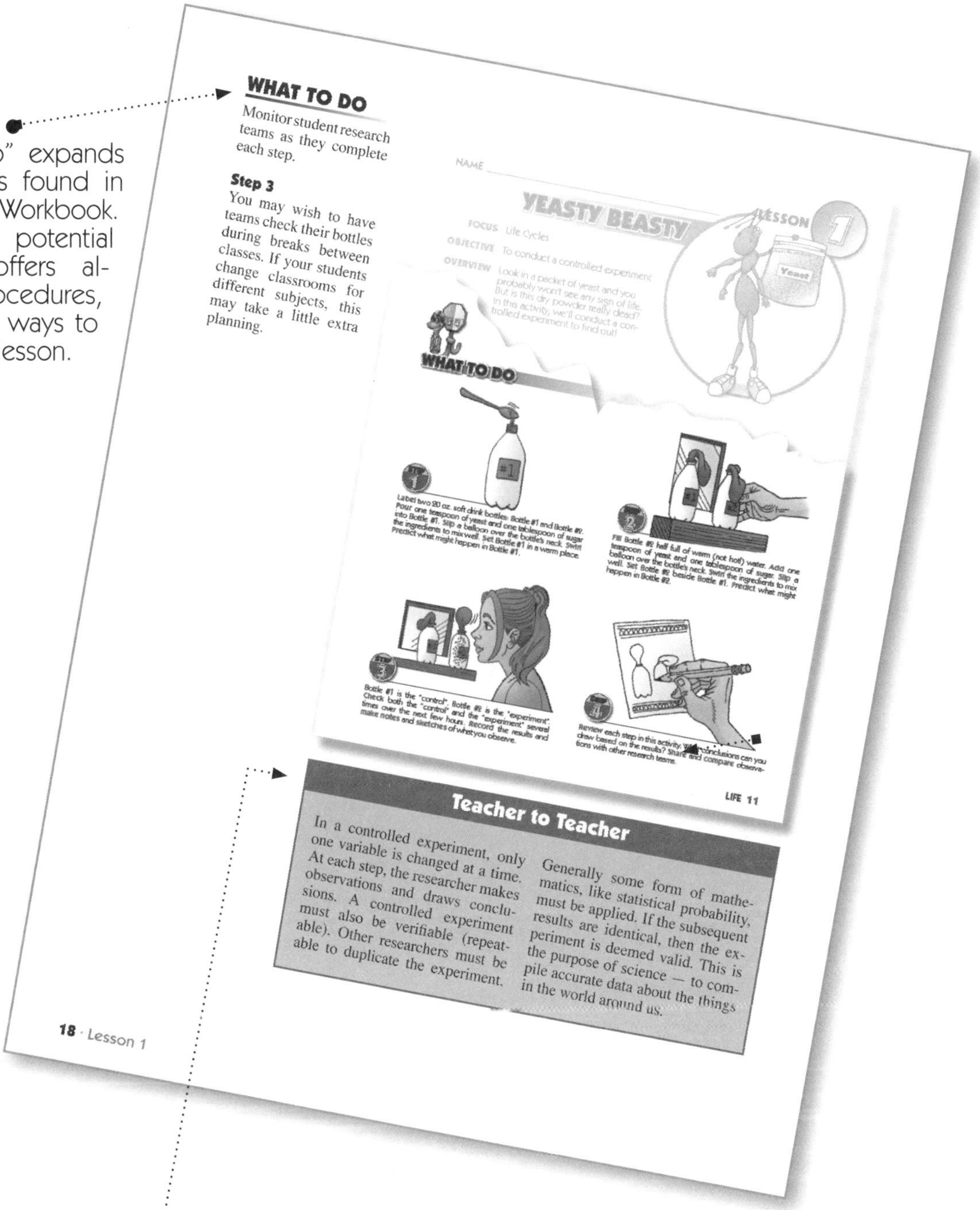

WHAT TO DO

Monitor student research teams as they complete each step.

Step 3

You may wish to have teams check their bottles during breaks between classes. If your students change classrooms for different subjects, this may take a little extra planning.

Teacher to Teacher

In a controlled experiment, only one variable is changed at a time. At each step, the researcher makes observations and draws conclusions. A controlled experiment must also be verifiable (repeatable). Other researchers must be able to duplicate the experiment.

Generally some form of mathematics, like statistical probability, must be applied. If the subsequent results are identical, then the experiment is deemed valid. This is the purpose of science — to compile accurate data about the things in the world around us.

18 · Lesson 1

Teacher To Teacher

"Teacher to Teacher" offers expanded science explanations designed to increase teacher understanding.

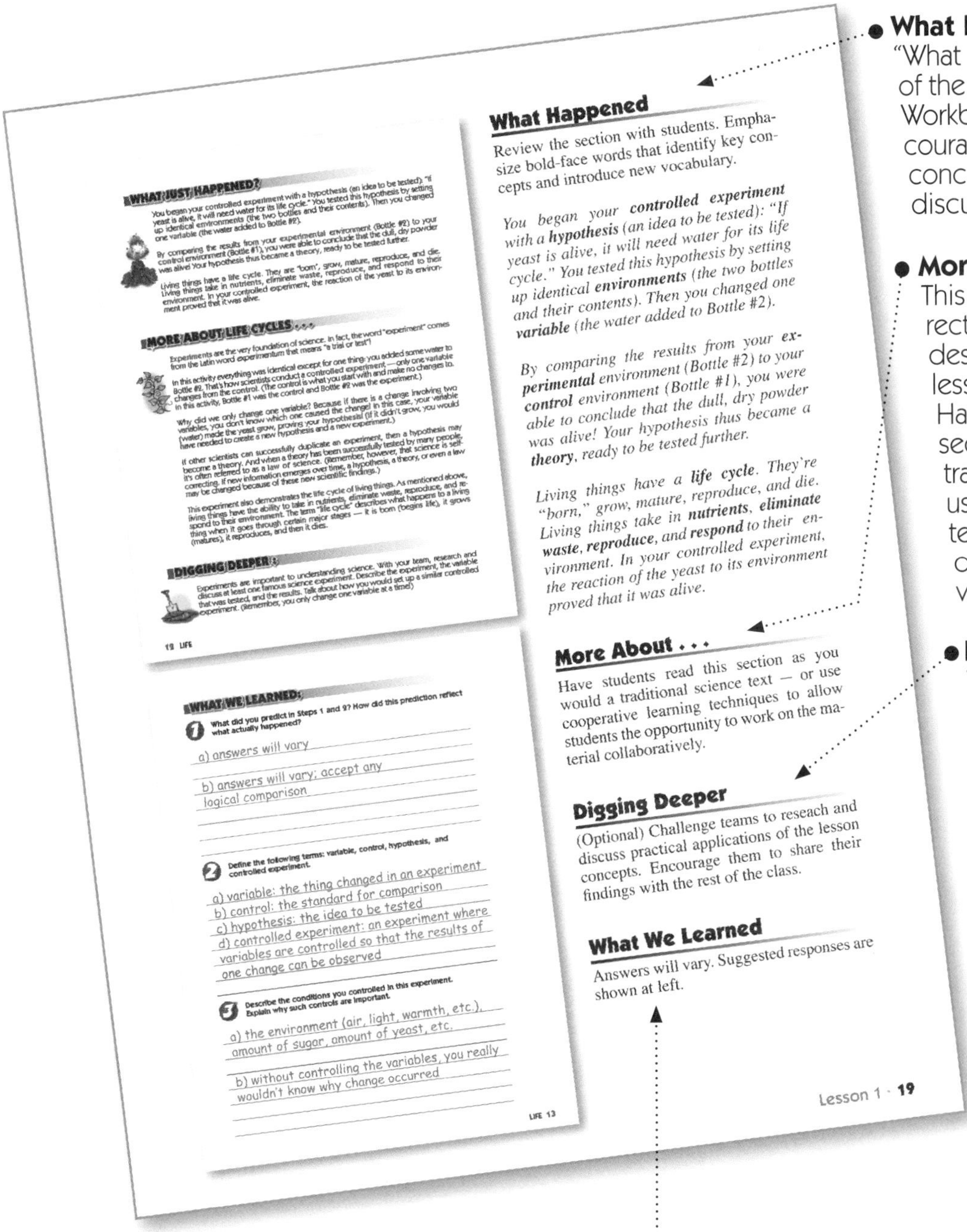

What Happened

"What Happened" is a review of the material in the Student Workbook. Teachers are encouraged to emphasize key concepts with students and to discuss new vocabulary.

More About . . .

This section provides a "direct instruction" component designed to expand the lesson's primary concepts. Have students read this section as you would a traditional science text, or use cooperative learning techniques to allow students the opportunity to work on it collaboratively.

Digging Deeper

This optional activity allows students to show mastery of the lesson's concepts by exploring its practical applications. Its structure also offers a great cross-curricular connection to language arts (doing research in encyclopedias or on the Internet, writing reports, making presentations, etc.).

What We Learned

"What We Learned" provides answer keys for the thought questions found in each lesson. The teacher should encourage students to discuss these questions collaboratively in their teams, then answer the questions individually in their Student Workbooks. This section is also tied directly to one portion of the assessment process (see page 9).

Conclusion
The "Conclusion" is a summary of the key concepts presented in the lesson.

Food for Thought
"Food for Thought" suggests ways to enhance the Scripture Object Lesson. This section provides an important tool for integrating faith and learning.

Journal
"Journal" suggests ways to expand journaling opportunities related to the lesson. The teacher should encourage the students not only to take notes and keep records, but also to make sketches, draw diagrams, and create charts and lists as needed.

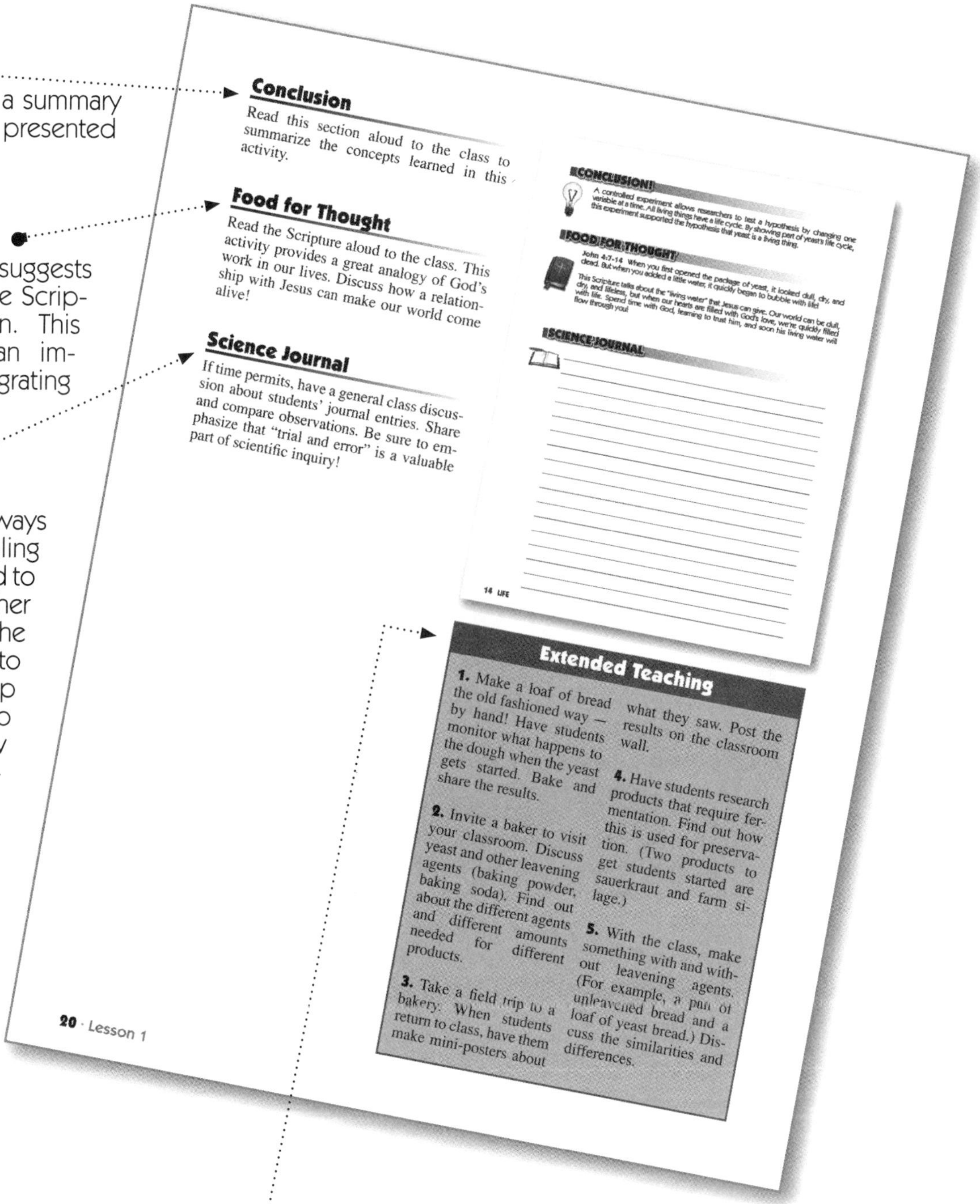

Conclusion
Read this section aloud to the class to summarize the concepts learned in this activity.

Food for Thought
Read the Scripture aloud to the class. This activity provides a great analogy of God's work in our lives. Discuss how a relationship with Jesus can make our world come alive!

Science Journal
If time permits, have a general class discussion about students' journal entries. Share and compare observations. Be sure to emphasize that "trial and error" is a valuable part of scientific inquiry!

Extended Teaching

1. Make a loaf of bread the old fashioned way — by hand! Have students monitor what happens to the dough when the yeast gets started. Bake and share the results.

2. Invite a baker to visit your classroom. Discuss yeast and other leavening agents (baking powder, baking soda). Find out about the different agents and different amounts needed for different products.

3. Take a field trip to a bakery. When students return to class, have them make mini-posters about what they saw. Post the results on the classroom wall.

4. Have students research products that require fermentation. Find out how this is used for preservation. (Two products to get students started are sauerkraut and farm silage.)

5. With the class, make something with and without leavening agents. (For example, a pan of unleavened bread and a loaf of yeast bread.) Discuss the similarities and differences.

20 · Lesson 1

Extended Teaching
"Extended Teaching" presents a variety of extension ideas for those who wish to go further.

Lessons
a reason for...
2

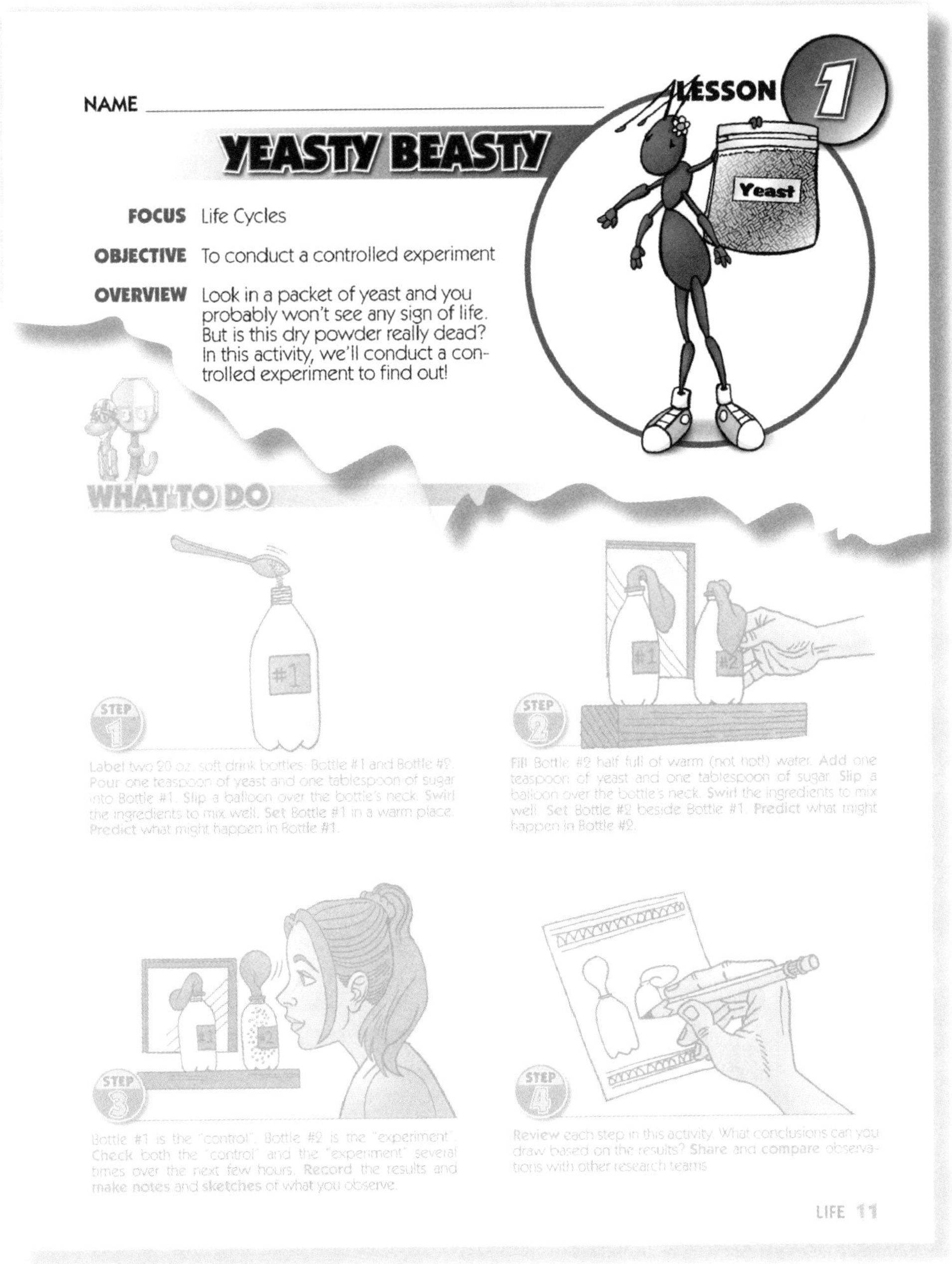
NAME

LESSON 1

YEASTY BEASTY

FOCUS Life Cycles

OBJECTIVE To conduct a controlled experiment

OVERVIEW Look in a packet of yeast and you probably won't see any sign of life. But is this dry powder really dead? In this activity, we'll conduct a controlled experiment to find out!

WHAT TO DO

STEP 1 Label two 20 oz. soft drink bottles: Bottle #1 and Bottle #2. Pour one teaspoon of yeast and one tablespoon of sugar into Bottle #1. Slip a balloon over the bottle's neck. Swirl the ingredients to mix well. Set Bottle #1 in a warm place. Predict what might happen in Bottle #1.

STEP 2 Fill Bottle #2 half full of warm (not hot!) water. Add one teaspoon of yeast and one tablespoon of sugar. Slip a balloon over the bottle's neck. Swirl the ingredients to mix well. Set Bottle #2 beside Bottle #1. Predict what might happen in Bottle #2.

STEP 3 Bottle #1 is the "control". Bottle #2 is the "experiment". Check both the "control" and the "experiment" several times over the next few hours. Record the results and make notes and sketches of what you observe.

STEP 4 Review each step in this activity. What conclusions can you draw based on the results? Share and compare observations with other research teams.

LIFE 11

Category

Life Science

Focus

Life Cycles

Objective

To conduct a controlled experiment

National Standards [1]

A1, A2, C2, C3, C5, G1, G2

Materials Needed [2]

balloons - 2
yeast
sugar
20 oz. soft drink bottles - 2
teaspoon
water

Safety Concerns

3. Hygiene
Students should wash hands thoroughly after handling materials.

4. Slipping
Clean up any spills immediately. Remind students to exercise caution when using fluids.

Additional Comments

This simple activity is a great introduction to science experimentation. The two bottles provide a control and an experiment. Point out that only one variable is changed in the experiment. Also, be sure to remove the labels from the bottles before beginning, and make sure they're completely dry.

Overview

Read the overview aloud to your students. The goal is to create an atmosphere of curiosity and inquiry.

[1] *See page 6 for a description of standards source and code.*

[2] *Bold-face type indicates items included in Materials Kit.*

WHAT TO DO

Monitor student research teams as they complete each step.

Step 3

You may wish to have teams check their bottles during breaks between classes. If your students change classrooms for different subjects, this may take a little extra planning.

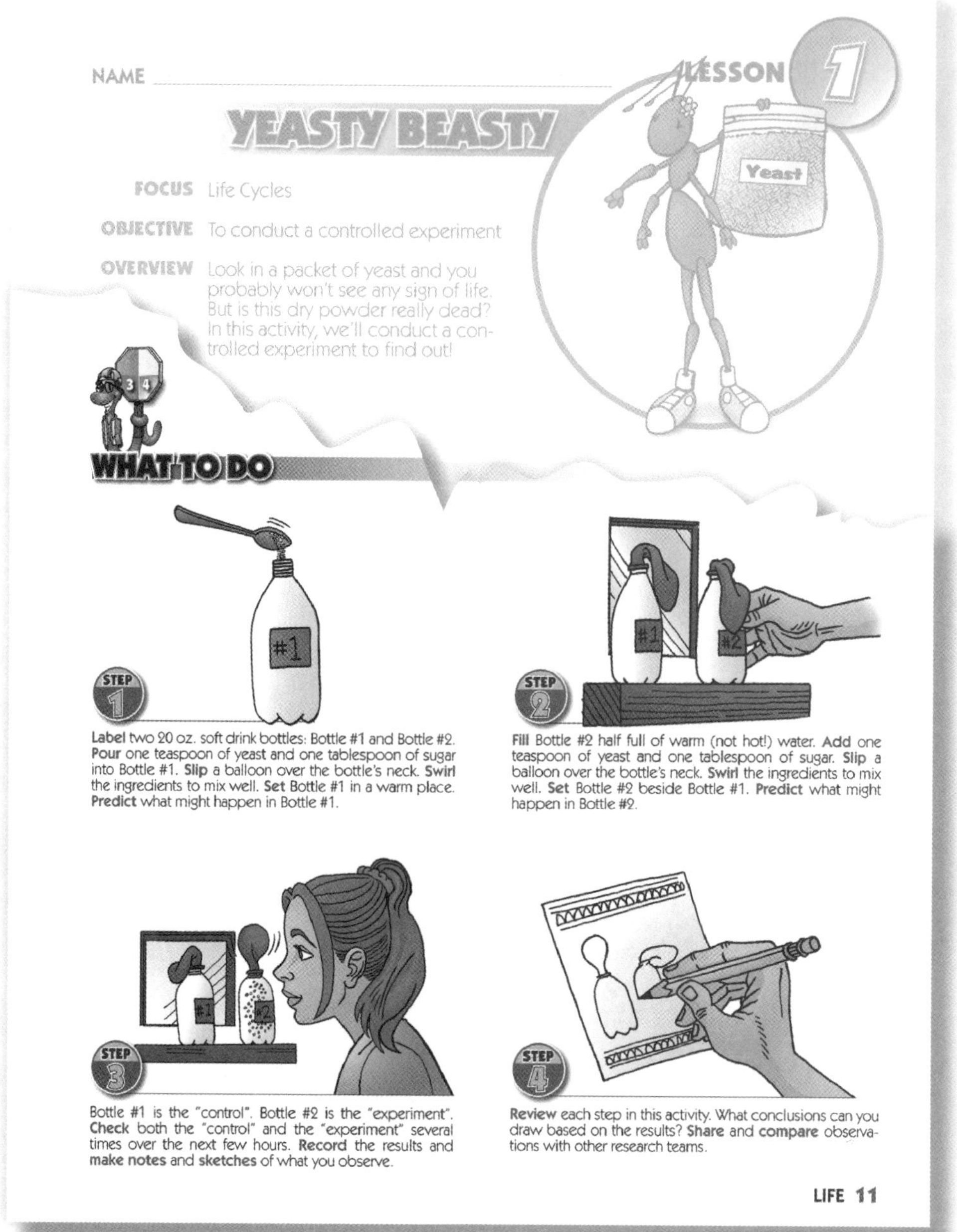

NAME ________________

LESSON 1

YEASTY BEASTY

FOCUS Life Cycles

OBJECTIVE To conduct a controlled experiment

OVERVIEW Look in a packet of yeast and you probably won't see any sign of life. But is this dry powder really dead? In this activity, we'll conduct a controlled experiment to find out!

WHAT TO DO

STEP 1 **Label** two 20 oz. soft drink bottles: Bottle #1 and Bottle #2. **Pour** one teaspoon of yeast and one tablespoon of sugar into Bottle #1. **Slip** a balloon over the bottle's neck. **Swirl** the ingredients to mix well. **Set** Bottle #1 in a warm place. **Predict** what might happen in Bottle #1.

STEP 2 **Fill** Bottle #2 half full of warm (not hot!) water. **Add** one teaspoon of yeast and one tablespoon of sugar. **Slip** a balloon over the bottle's neck. **Swirl** the ingredients to mix well. **Set** Bottle #2 beside Bottle #1. **Predict** what might happen in Bottle #2.

STEP 3 Bottle #1 is the "control". Bottle #2 is the "experiment". **Check** both the "control" and the "experiment" several times over the next few hours. **Record** the results and **make notes** and **sketches** of what you observe.

STEP 4 **Review** each step in this activity. What conclusions can you draw based on the results? **Share** and **compare** observations with other research teams.

LIFE 11

Teacher to Teacher

In a controlled experiment, only one variable is changed at a time. At each step, the researcher makes observations and draws conclusions. A controlled experiment must also be verifiable (repeatable). Other researchers must be able to duplicate the experiment. Generally some form of mathematics, like statistical probability, must be applied. If the subsequent results are identical, then the experiment is deemed valid. This is the purpose of science — to compile accurate data about the things in the world around us.

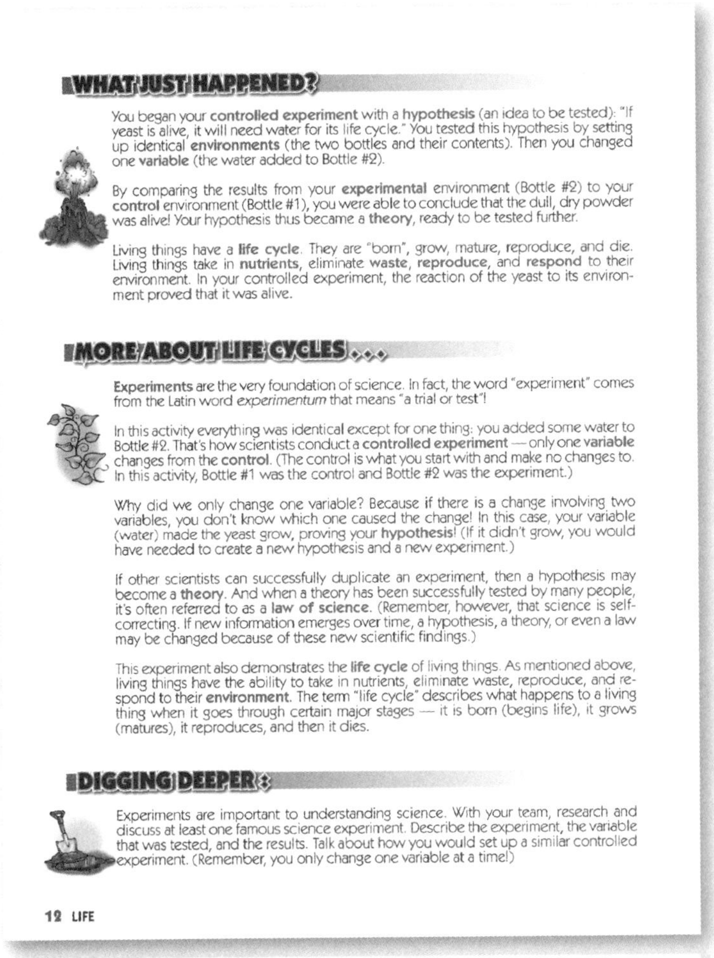

WHAT JUST HAPPENED?

You began your **controlled experiment** with a **hypothesis** (an idea to be tested): "If yeast is alive, it will need water for its life cycle." You tested this hypothesis by setting up identical **environments** (the two bottles and their contents). Then you changed one **variable** (the water added to Bottle #2).

By comparing the results from your **experimental** environment (Bottle #2) to your **control** environment (Bottle #1), you were able to conclude that the dull, dry powder was alive! Your hypothesis thus became a **theory**, ready to be tested further.

Living things have a **life cycle**. They are "born", grow, mature, reproduce, and die. Living things take in **nutrients**, eliminate **waste**, **reproduce**, and **respond** to their environment. In your controlled experiment, the reaction of the yeast to its environment proved that it was alive.

MORE ABOUT LIFE CYCLES . . .

Experiments are the very foundation of science. In fact, the word "experiment" comes from the Latin word *experimentum* that means "a trial or test"!

In this activity everything was identical except for one thing: you added some water to Bottle #2. That's how scientists conduct a **controlled experiment** — only one **variable** changes from the **control**. (The control is what you start with and make no changes to. In this activity, Bottle #1 was the control and Bottle #2 was the experiment.)

Why did we only change one variable? Because if there is a change involving two variables, you don't know which one caused the change! In this case, your variable (water) made the yeast grow, proving your **hypothesis**! (If it didn't grow, you would have needed to create a new hypothesis and a new experiment.)

If other scientists can successfully duplicate an experiment, then a hypothesis may become a **theory**. And when a theory has been successfully tested by many people, it's often referred to as a **law of science**. (Remember, however, that science is self-correcting. If new information emerges over time, a hypothesis, a theory, or even a law may be changed because of these new scientific findings.)

This experiment also demonstrates the **life cycle** of living things. As mentioned above, living things have the ability to take in nutrients, eliminate waste, reproduce, and respond to their **environment**. The term "life cycle" describes what happens to a living thing when it goes through certain major stages — it is born (begins life), it grows (matures), it reproduces, and then it dies.

DIGGING DEEPER:

Experiments are important to understanding science. With your team, research and discuss at least one famous science experiment. Describe the experiment, the variable that was tested, and the results. Talk about how you would set up a similar controlled experiment. (Remember, you only change one variable at a time!)

12 LIFE

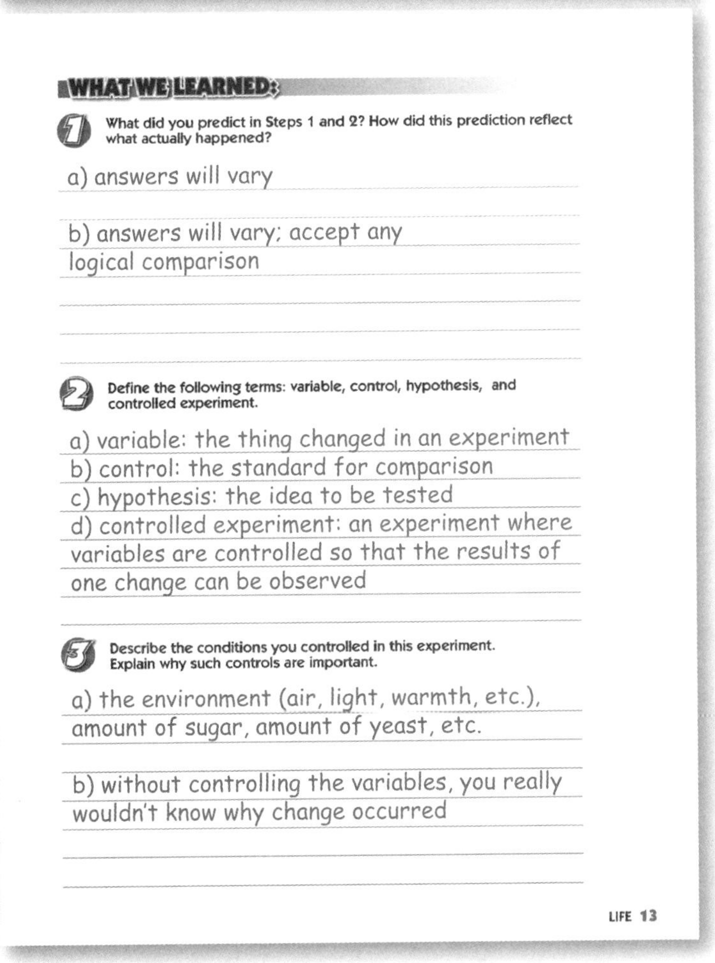

WHAT WE LEARNED:

1 What did you predict in Steps 1 and 2? How did this prediction reflect what actually happened?

a) answers will vary

b) answers will vary; accept any logical comparison

2 Define the following terms: variable, control, hypothesis, and controlled experiment.

a) variable: the thing changed in an experiment
b) control: the standard for comparison
c) hypothesis: the idea to be tested
d) controlled experiment: an experiment where variables are controlled so that the results of one change can be observed

3 Describe the conditions you controlled in this experiment. Explain why such controls are important.

a) the environment (air, light, warmth, etc.), amount of sugar, amount of yeast, etc.

b) without controlling the variables, you really wouldn't know why change occurred

LIFE 13

What Happened

Review the section with students. Emphasize bold-face words that identify key concepts and introduce new vocabulary.

*You began your **controlled experiment** with a **hypothesis** (an idea to be tested): "If yeast is alive, it will need water for its life cycle." You tested this hypothesis by setting up identical **environments** (the two bottles and their contents). Then you changed one **variable** (the water added to Bottle #2).*

*By comparing the results from your **experimental** environment (Bottle #2) to your **control** environment (Bottle #1), you were able to conclude that the dull, dry powder was alive! Your hypothesis thus became a **theory**, ready to be tested further.*

*Living things have a **life cycle**. They are "born," grow, mature, reproduce, and die. Living things take in **nutrients**, **eliminate waste**, **reproduce**, and **respond** to their environment. In your controlled experiment, the reaction of the yeast to its environment proved that it was alive.*

More About . . .

Have students read this section as you would a traditional science text — or use cooperative learning techniques to allow students the opportunity to work on the material collaboratively.

Digging Deeper

(Optional) Challenge teams to reseach and discuss practical applications of the lesson concepts. Encourage them to share their findings with the rest of the class.

What We Learned

Answers will vary. Suggested responses are shown at left.

Conclusion

Read this section aloud to the class to summarize the concepts learned in this activity.

Food for Thought

Read the Scripture aloud to the class. This activity provides a great analogy of God's work in our lives. Discuss how a relationship with Jesus can make our world come alive!

Science Journal

If time permits, have a general class discussion about students' journal entries. Share and compare observations. Be sure to emphasize that "trial and error" is a valuable part of scientific inquiry!

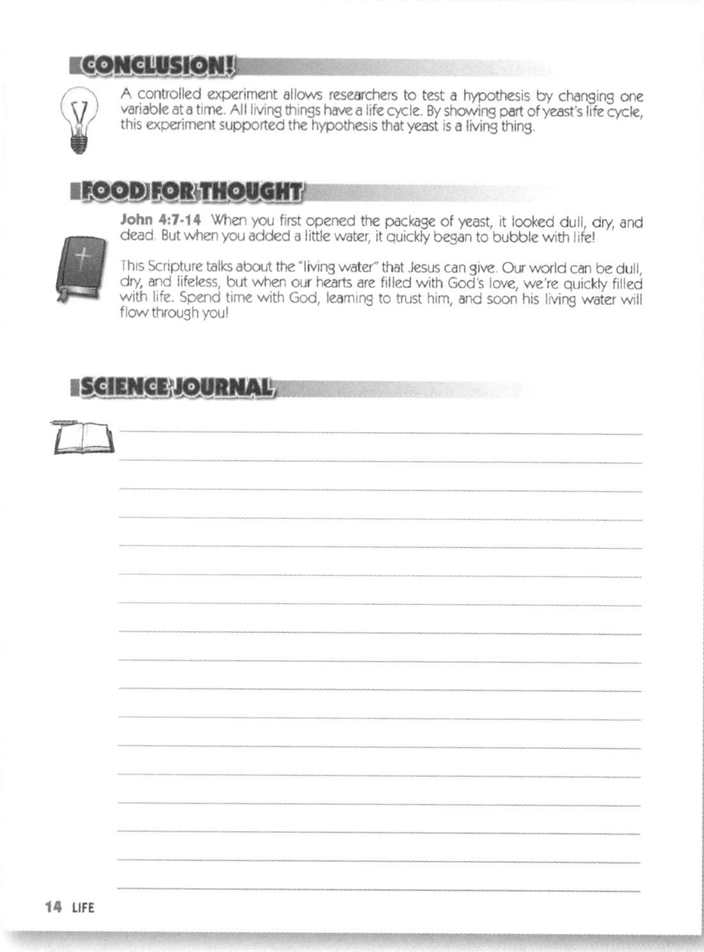

CONCLUSION!

A controlled experiment allows researchers to test a hypothesis by changing one variable at a time. All living things have a life cycle. By showing part of yeast's life cycle, this experiment supported the hypothesis that yeast is a living thing.

FOOD FOR THOUGHT

John 4:7-14 When you first opened the package of yeast, it looked dull, dry, and dead. But when you added a little water, it quickly began to bubble with life!

This Scripture talks about the "living water" that Jesus can give. Our world can be dull, dry, and lifeless, but when our hearts are filled with God's love, we're quickly filled with life. Spend time with God, learning to trust him, and soon his living water will flow through you!

SCIENCE JOURNAL

14 LIFE

Extended Teaching

1. Make a loaf of bread the old fashioned way — by hand! Have students monitor what happens to the dough when the yeast gets started. Bake and share the results.

2. Invite a baker to visit your classroom. Discuss yeast and other leavening agents (baking powder, baking soda). Find out about the different agents and different amounts needed for different products.

3. Take a field trip to a bakery. When students return to class, have them make mini-posters about what they saw. Post the results on the classroom wall.

4. Have students research products that require fermentation. Find out how this is used for preservation. (Two products to get students started are sauerkraut and farm silage.)

5. With the class, make something with and without leavening agents. (For example, a pan of unleavened bread and a loaf of yeast bread.) Discuss the similarities and differences.

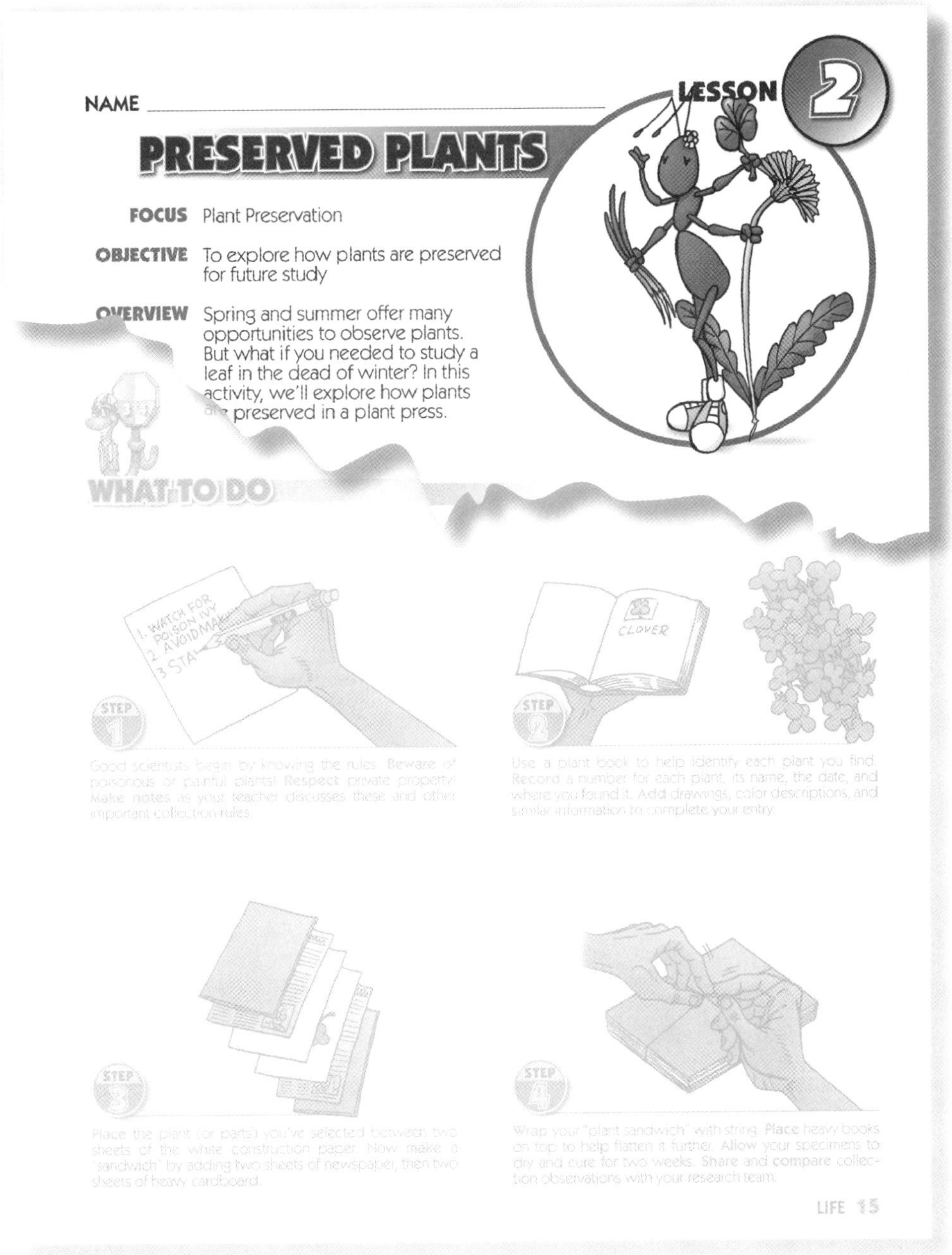
NAME ____________________

LESSON 2

PRESERVED PLANTS

FOCUS Plant Preservation

OBJECTIVE To explore how plants are preserved for future study

OVERVIEW Spring and summer offer many opportunities to observe plants. But what if you needed to study a leaf in the dead of winter? In this activity, we'll explore how plants are preserved in a plant press.

WHAT TO DO

STEP 1 Good scientists begin by knowing the rules. Beware of poisonous or painful plants! Respect private property! Make notes as your teacher discusses these and other important collection rules.

STEP 2 Use a plant book to help identify each plant you find. Record a number for each plant, its name, the date, and where you found it. Add drawings, color descriptions, and similar information to complete your entry.

STEP 3 Place the plant (or parts) you've selected between two sheets of the white construction paper. Now make a "sandwich" by adding two sheets of newspaper, then two sheets of heavy cardboard.

STEP 4 Wrap your "plant sandwich" with string. Place heavy books on top to help flatten it further. Allow your specimens to dry and cure for two weeks. Share and compare collection observations with your research team.

LIFE 15

Additional Comments

Some students may have severe plant allergies. Be sensitive to this issue when planning your collection event. If you have poison oak or poison ivy in your region, help students identify and avoid these plants! You may make your own plant identification books with pictures and descriptions of common plants in your area. Make sure students number each specimen they collect.

Overview

Read the overview aloud to your students. The goal is to create an atmosphere of curiosity and inquiry.

Category

Life Science

Focus

Plant Preservation

Objective

To explore how plants are preserved for future study

National Standards

A1, A2, C1, C5, G1, G2

Materials Needed

plant identification book
white construction paper
newspaper
heavy cardboard
scissors
string or cord
heavy books

Safety Concerns

3. Skin Contact
Remind students to avoid touching poisonous plants

4. Sharp Objects
Remind students to be careful when using scissors.

WHAT TO DO

Monitor student research teams as they complete each step.

Step 1
Rules for collecting: a) avoid poisonous plants b) avoid rare or endangered plants c) avoid private property, nature preserves, and parks e) pick only enough material to preserve f) leave no sign of your visit

Step 2
Encourage students to make rough notes and drawings in a field book (spiral notebook), then transfer them neatly to their journals when they return.

Step 4
Make sure plant presses are stacked where there is good air circulation. Don't place too many in a pile or it will delay drying times.

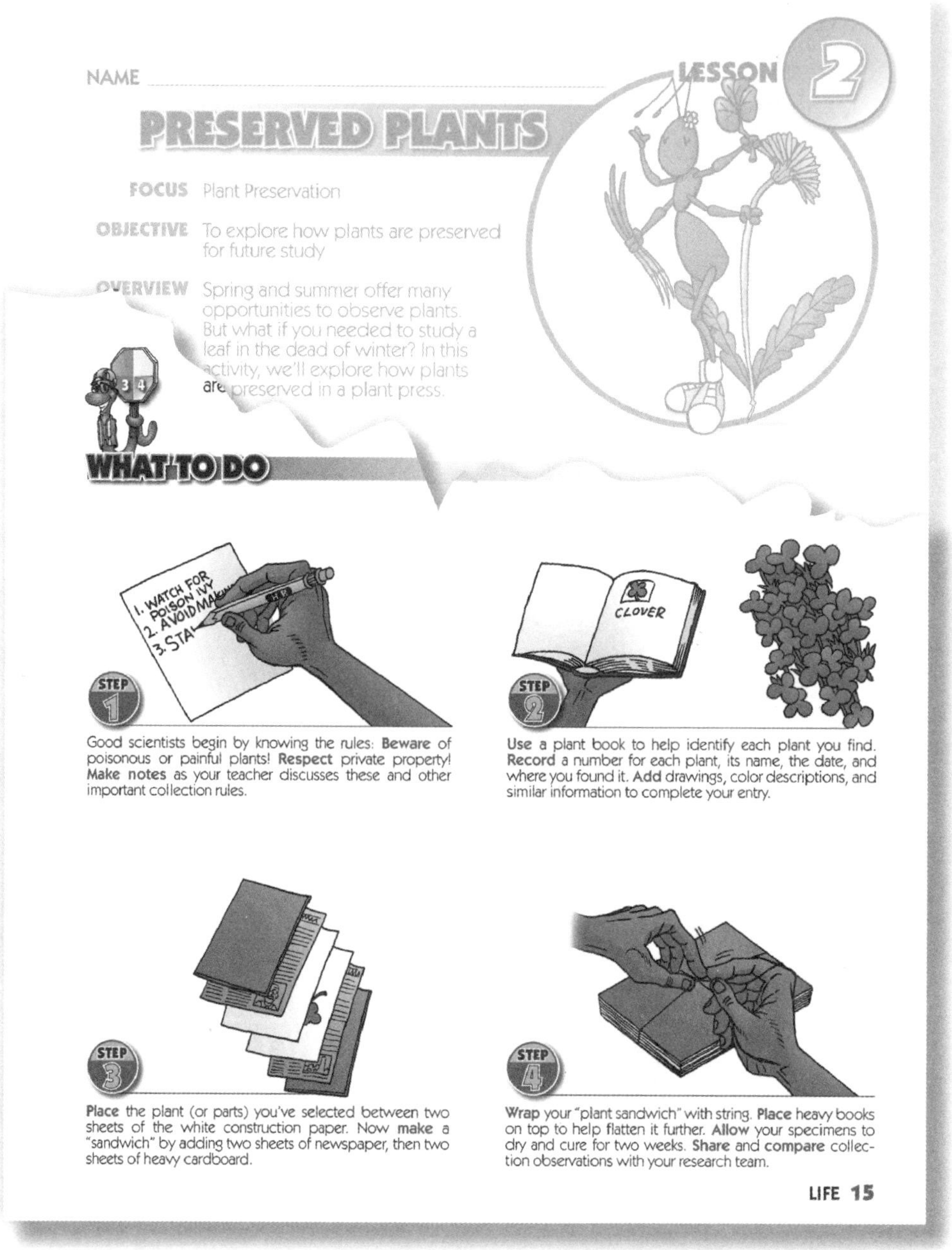

NAME

LESSON 2

PRESERVED PLANTS

FOCUS Plant Preservation

OBJECTIVE To explore how plants are preserved for future study

OVERVIEW Spring and summer offer many opportunities to observe plants. But what if you needed to study a leaf in the dead of winter? In this activity, we'll explore how plants are preserved in a plant press.

WHAT TO DO

STEP 1 Good scientists begin by knowing the rules: **Beware** of poisonous or painful plants! **Respect** private property! **Make notes** as your teacher discusses these and other important collection rules.

STEP 2 **Use** a plant book to help identify each plant you find. **Record** a number for each plant, its name, the date, and where you found it. **Add** drawings, color descriptions, and similar information to complete your entry.

STEP 3 **Place** the plant (or parts) you've selected between two sheets of the white construction paper. Now **make** a "sandwich" by adding two sheets of newspaper, then two sheets of heavy cardboard.

STEP 4 **Wrap** your "plant sandwich" with string. **Place** heavy books on top to help flatten it further. **Allow** your specimens to dry and cure for two weeks. **Share** and **compare** collection observations with your research team.

LIFE 15

Teacher to Teacher

The science of taxonomy names and classifies living things by their characteristics. Taxonomy has been around for a long time. Plants were an important part of early medical practice, so Greek physicians began classifying plants by their medicinal properties. Theophrastus (one of Aristotle's students) could identify over 500 plant species. By the early 1700s, Linnaeus (the originator of the genus/species designations) catalogued nearly 18,000. By the end of that century, Cuvier had listed over 50,000 species! Today biologists estimate that there are hundreds of thousands of separate species in existance.

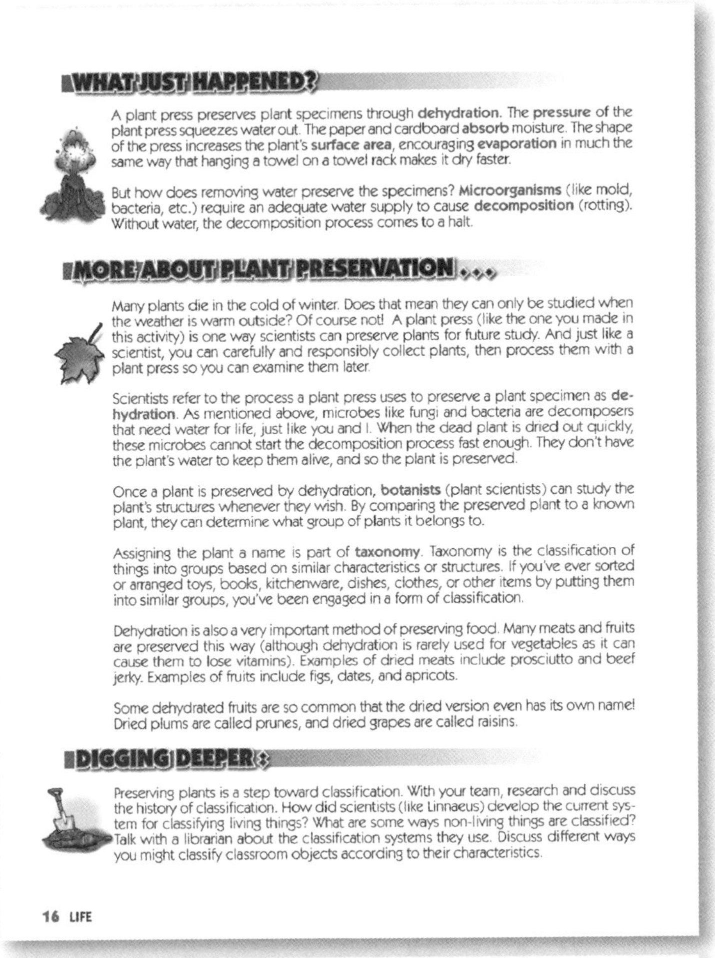

WHAT JUST HAPPENED?

A plant press preserves plant specimens through **dehydration**. The **pressure** of the plant press squeezes water out. The paper and cardboard **absorb** moisture. The shape of the press increases the plant's **surface area**, encouraging **evaporation** in much the same way that hanging a towel on a towel rack makes it dry faster.

But how does removing water preserve the specimens? **Microorganisms** (like mold, bacteria, etc.) require an adequate water supply to cause **decomposition** (rotting). Without water, the decomposition process comes to a halt.

MORE ABOUT PLANT PRESERVATION . . .

Many plants die in the cold of winter. Does that mean they can only be studied when the weather is warm outside? Of course not! A plant press (like the one you made in this activity) is one way scientists can preserve plants for future study. And just like a scientist, you can carefully and responsibly collect plants, then process them with a plant press so you can examine them later.

Scientists refer to the process a plant press uses to preserve a plant specimen as **dehydration**. As mentioned above, microbes like fungi and bacteria are decomposers that need water for life, just like you and I. When the dead plant is dried out quickly, these microbes cannot start the decomposition process fast enough. They don't have the plant's water to keep them alive, and so the plant is preserved.

Once a plant is preserved by dehydration, **botanists** (plant scientists) can study the plant's structures whenever they wish. By comparing the preserved plant to a known plant, they can determine what group of plants it belongs to.

Assigning the plant a name is part of **taxonomy**. Taxonomy is the classification of things into groups based on similar characteristics or structures. If you've ever sorted or arranged toys, books, kitchenware, dishes, clothes, or other items by putting them into similar groups, you've been engaged in a form of classification.

Dehydration is also a very important method of preserving food. Many meats and fruits are preserved this way (although dehydration is rarely used for vegetables as it can cause them to lose vitamins). Examples of dried meats include prosciutto and beef jerky. Examples of fruits include figs, dates, and apricots.

Some dehydrated fruits are so common that the dried version even has its own name! Dried plums are called prunes, and dried grapes are called raisins.

DIGGING DEEPER:

Preserving plants is a step toward classification. With your team, research and discuss the history of classification. How did scientists (like Linnaeus) develop the current system for classifying living things? What are some ways non-living things are classified? Talk with a librarian about the classification systems they use. Discuss different ways you might classify classroom objects according to their characteristics.

16 LIFE

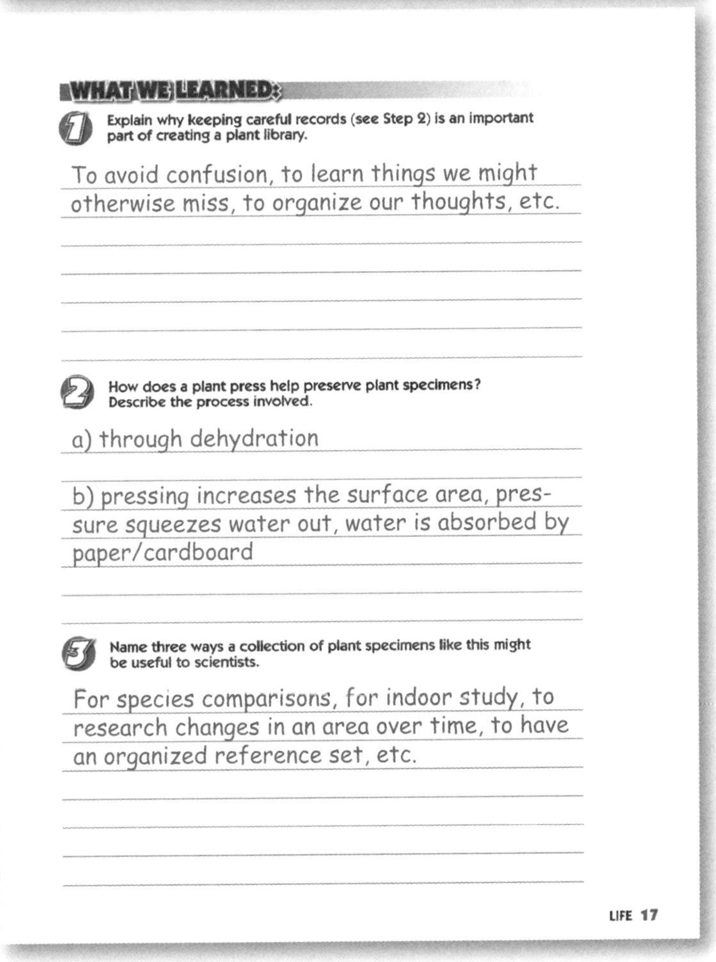

WHAT WE LEARNED:

1. **Explain why keeping careful records (see Step 2) is an important part of creating a plant library.**

   To avoid confusion, to learn things we might otherwise miss, to organize our thoughts, etc.

2. **How does a plant press help preserve plant specimens? Describe the process involved.**

   a) through dehydration

   b) pressing increases the surface area, pressure squeezes water out, water is absorbed by paper/cardboard

3. **Name three ways a collection of plant specimens like this might be useful to scientists.**

   For species comparisons, for indoor study, to research changes in an area over time, to have an organized reference set, etc.

LIFE 17

What Happened

Review the section with students. Emphasize bold-face words that identify key concepts and introduce new vocabulary.

A plant press preserves plant specimens through ***dehydration****. The* ***pressure*** *of the plant press squeezes water out. The paper and cardboard* ***absorb*** *moisture. The shape of the press increases the plant's* ***surface area****, encouraging* ***evaporation*** *in much the same way that hanging a towel on a towel rack makes it dry faster.*

But how does removing water preserve the specimens? ***Microorganisms*** *(like mold, bacteria, etc.) require an adequate water supply to cause* ***decomposition*** *(rotting). Without water, the decomposition process comes to a halt.*

More About . . .

Have students read this section as you would a traditional science text — or use cooperative learning techniques to allow students the opportunity to work on the material collaboratively.

Digging Deeper

(Optional) Challenge teams to reseach and discuss practical applications of the lesson concepts. Encourage them to share their findings with the rest of the class.

What We Learned

Answers will vary. Suggested responses are shown at left.

Conclusion

Read this section aloud to the class to summarize the concepts learned in this activity.

Food for Thought

Read the Scripture aloud to the class. Talk about God's loving care and how he maintains and preserves our lives.

Science Journal

If time permits, have a general class discussion about students' journal entries. Share and compare observations. Be sure to emphasize that "trial and error" is a valuable part of scientific inquiry!

CONCLUSION!

A plant press preserves plant specimens through dehydration. Preservation keeps plants available for future study. Preserved plants can be sorted and classified, adding to our knowledge of plants.

FOOD FOR THOUGHT

Job 10:12 Collecting plants is an interesting way to learn about plants and their classification. A plant press helps us preserve plant specimens for the future.

The short life span of plants reminds us that our life on Earth is all too short compared to eternity. God has an endless future planned for those who trust him. In this Scripture, Job points out that it is God who grants us life, and God's loving care is there to preserve us.

SCIENCE JOURNAL

18 LIFE

Extended Teaching

1. Use the plant press as part of a language arts assignment. The descriptions, drawings, and data make an excellent starting point for an article or report about local plant life.

2. Ask students to research what plants are used for food (wild as well as cultivated). Have them draw pictures and write descriptions, then post the results on a bulletin board.

3. Have each team compile an itemized list (with descriptions) of the specimens in their plant press. Organize the plant presses into a classroom "plant museum."

4. Invite a naturalist to visit your classroom. Discuss local plant life, including any rare or endangered plants that grow in your region. Talk about additional ways to preserve plants for study.

5. Have each team make a map showing where they found each specimen. Compile the maps into a master map of the collection area, showing which plants grow where. Post the map on the classroom wall.

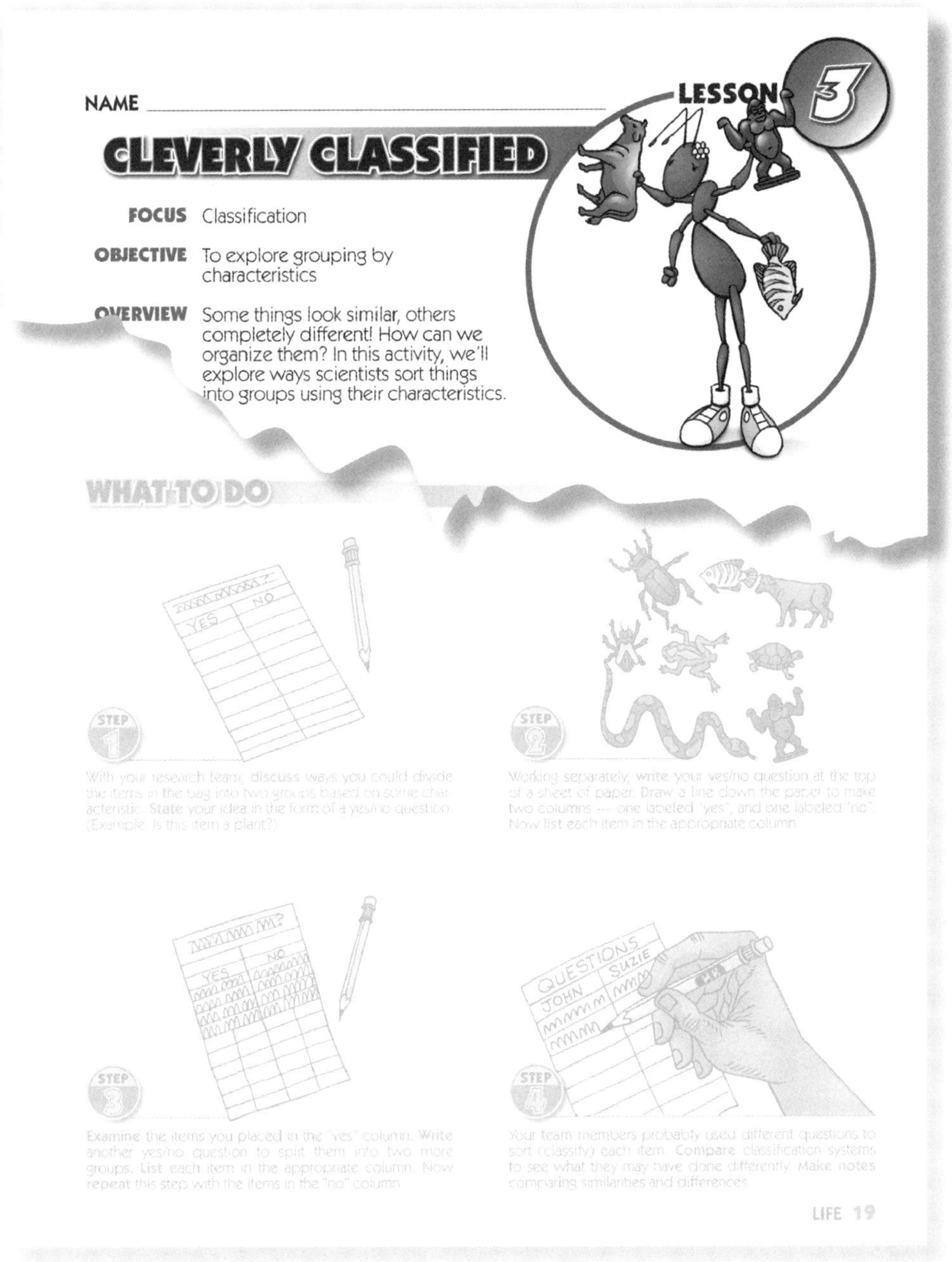

NAME ______________________________

LESSON 3

CLEVERLY CLASSIFIED

FOCUS Classification

OBJECTIVE To explore grouping by characteristics

OVERVIEW Some things look similar, others completely different! How can we organize them? In this activity, we'll explore ways scientists sort things into groups using their characteristics.

WHAT TO DO

STEP 1

With your research team, discuss ways you could divide the items in the bag into two groups based on some characteristic. State your idea in the form of a yes/no question. (Example: Is this item a plant?)

STEP 2

Working separately, write your yes/no question at the top of a sheet of paper. Draw a line down the paper to make two columns — one labeled "yes", and one labeled "no". Now list each item in the appropriate column.

STEP 3

Examine the items you placed in the "yes" column. Write another yes/no question to split them into two more groups. List each item in the appropriate column. Now repeat this step with the items in the "no" column.

STEP 4

Your team members probably used different questions to sort (classify) each item. Compare classification systems to see what they may have done differently. Make notes comparing similarities and differences.

LIFE 19

Category

Life Science

Focus

Classification

Objective

To explore grouping by characteristics

National Standards

A1, A2, C1, C2, C4, C5, F2, G1, G2

Materials Needed

bag of creatures
sheet of paper

Safety Concerns

none

Additional Comments

Student classification lists will be different, depending on what characteristic(s) each student chose to focus on. There is no single "correct" way to complete the first three steps. Comparing lists in Step 4 will help students realize the importance of a "standard" classification list so various researchers can make accurate comparisons.

Overview

Read the overview aloud to your students. The goal is to create an atmosphere of curiosity and inquiry.

WHAT TO DO

Monitor student research teams as they complete each step.

Step 3
After every team completes Step 3, carefully collect and rebag the "creatures" for use next year.

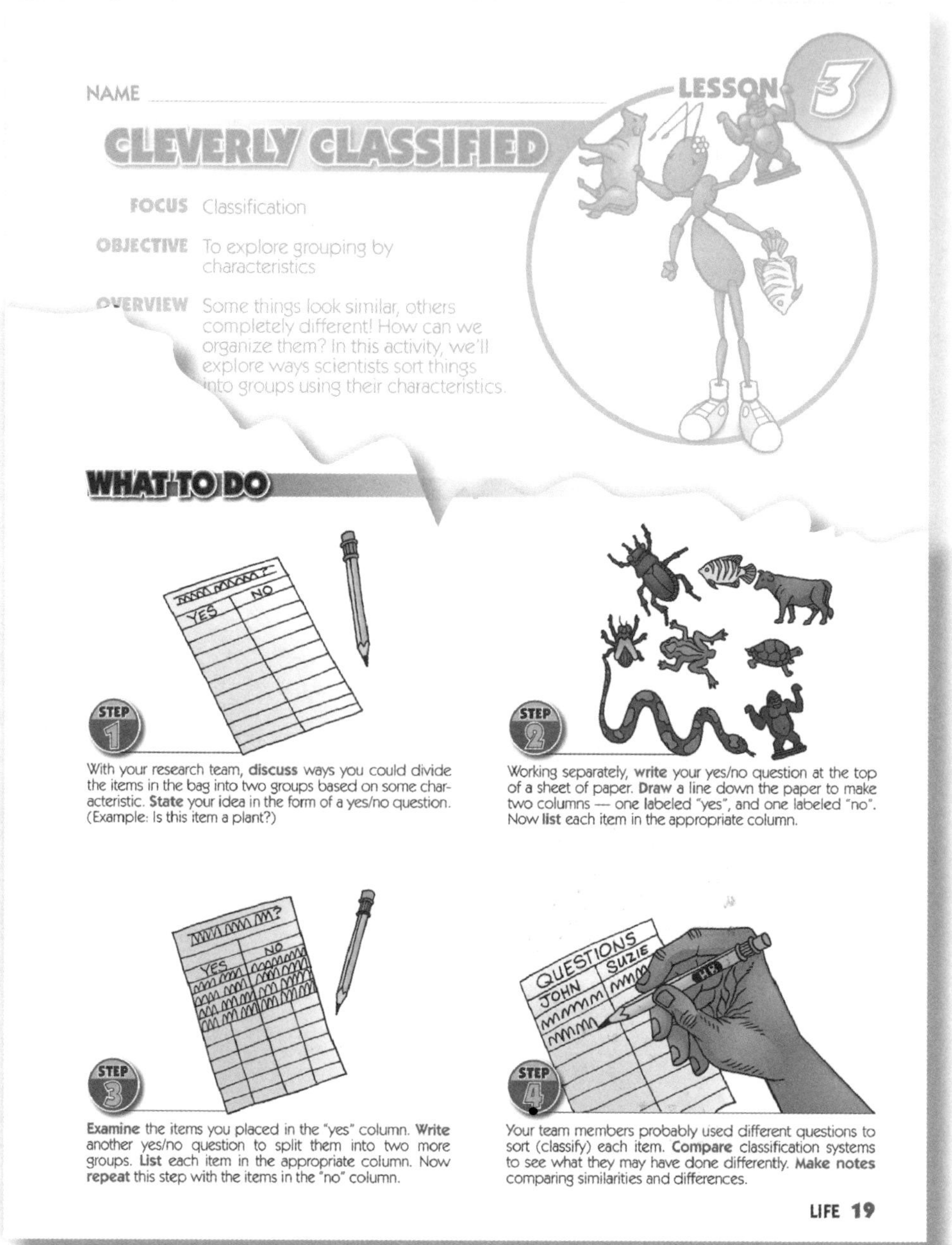

NAME ____________ LESSON 3

CLEVERLY CLASSIFIED

FOCUS Classification

OBJECTIVE To explore grouping by characteristics

OVERVIEW Some things look similar, others completely different! How can we organize them? In this activity, we'll explore ways scientists sort things into groups using their characteristics.

WHAT TO DO

STEP 1 With your research team, **discuss** ways you could divide the items in the bag into two groups based on some characteristic. **State** your idea in the form of a yes/no question. (Example: Is this item a plant?)

STEP 2 Working separately, **write** your yes/no question at the top of a sheet of paper. **Draw** a line down the paper to make two columns — one labeled "yes", and one labeled "no". Now **list** each item in the appropriate column.

STEP 3 **Examine** the items you placed in the "yes" column. **Write** another yes/no question to split them into two more groups. **List** each item in the appropriate column. Now **repeat** this step with the items in the "no" column.

STEP 4 Your team members probably used different questions to sort (classify) each item. **Compare** classification systems to see what they may have done differently. **Make notes** comparing similarities and differences.

LIFE 19

Teacher to Teacher

Living things are sorted into five large groups called kingdoms. Kingdoms are broken into phylum, then orders, then families, then genus, and finally species. For example, human beings are: Animalia (kingdom), Chordata (phylum), Mammalia (class), Primates (order), Hominidae (family), Homo (genus), sapiens (species). Scientists use Latin since it is a "dead" language — no one speaks it today, so it never changes. Note that when writing a genus/species name (like *Homo sapiens*), it is always italicized, the genus is capitalized, and the species is not.

WHAT JUST HAPPENED?

Describing things by their **characteristics** is called **classification**. Sometimes different classification systems are used for different purposes. For instance, to wash your clothes you might sort by color (darks and whites). But when you put your clothes away, you might sort by kind (socks, T-shirts, pants, etc.). Since there were no set **standards** given for this activity, your team members probably used different kinds of classification systems.

However, when scientists sort objects they must use strict classification standards. This allows them to compare their results accurately. Although scientists' classification systems use rigid standards and more complex yes/no questions, the process you used in this activity is essentially the same.

MORE ABOUT CLASSIFICATION . . .

Trying to organize groups of things can be very difficult. At first glance, many things look quite similar. But when you know the right characteristics to look for, you soon discover that there are many small differences that set things apart. Scientists use this kind of close observation to help classify both living and non-living things.

Scientists call this process "taxonomy". Your research team used a variation of taxonomy for the activity on page 19. But as we mentioned above, real taxonomy is a very exact science. Scientists must follow a very strict set of yes/no questions to determine any given creature's place in the overall hierarchy. And all scientists must use the very same rigid and complex questions every time . . . otherwise the answers would not be consistent and the results would not make sense.

When it comes to living things, scientists use six basic categories. The broadest groups are the Kingdoms. A **Kingdom** is organized into different Phylums. A **Phylum** is sorted into different Classes. A **Class** is divided into different Orders. An **Order** is sorted into different Genera. And a **Genus** is divided into various **species**. (Note: As a general rule, all of these categories are capitalized except species.)

For example, the scientific name for a human being is "Homo sapiens". The classification goes like this: Kingdom = Animalia; Phylum = Chordata; Class = Mammalia; Order = Primates; Family = Hominidae; Genus = Homo; and species = sapiens.

However, new technology is complicating the current ranking system. DNA analysis often shows that two organisms, thought to be distant relatives, are actually first cousins! As a result, there's been a lot of rearranging of classifications over the past few years. In fact some scientists now believe that the old Linnaeus system (that dates back over 300 years) is due for a major overhaul.

DIGGING DEEPER:

A **taxonomic key** is a list of "yes/no" questions. Talk about what questions you might use to create a taxonomic key to classify fruit. Discuss the characteristics of different fruits that help set them apart (hairy or smooth, round or long, one seed or many seeds, etc.). Create a taxonomic key to sort apples, bananas, peaches, plums, and grapes. Also try sorting toys, sports cards, clothes, kitchen utensils, etc.

WHAT WE LEARNED:

1. What were the final four groups your classification system created? What characteristics set these groups apart?

answers will vary, but should include logical conclusions

2. Compare your final groups with those of other teams. Describe the similarities and the differences.

answers will vary, but should include logical comparisons

3. Based on what you've learned, why is it important for scientists to use strict classification standards? Why is a system of classifying living things helpful?

a) to maintain the standard; to avoid confusion.

b) so all researchers are studying/discussing the same thing; so the research can be organized; so researchers aren't confused, etc.

What Happened

Review the section with students. Emphasize bold-face words that identify key concepts and introduce new vocabulary.

Describing things by their ***characteristics*** is called ***classification***. Sometimes different classification systems are used for different purposes. For instance, to wash your clothes you might sort by color (darks and whites). But when you put your clothes away, you might sort by kind (socks, t-shirts, pants, etc.). Since there were no set ***standards*** given for this activity, your team members probably used different kinds of classification systems.

However, when scientists sort objects they must use strict classfication standards. This allows them to compare their results accurately. Although scientists' classification systems use rigid standards and more complex yes/no questions, the process you used in this activity is essentially the same.

More About . . .

Have students read this section as you would a traditional science text — or use cooperative learning techniques to allow students the opportunity to work on the material collaboratively.

Digging Deeper

(Optional) Challenge teams to reseach and discuss practical applications of the lesson concepts. Encourage them to share their findings with the rest of the class.

What We Learned

Answers will vary. Suggested responses are shown at left.

Conclusion

Read this section aloud to the class to summarize the concepts learned in this activity.

Food for Thought

Read the Scripture aloud to the class. Discuss the importance of organizing your life to follow God's plan. Challenge students to develop a regular, scheduled devotional time each day.

Science Journal

If time permits, have a general class discussion about students' journal entries. Share and compare observations. Be sure to emphasize that "trial and error" is a valuable part of scientific inquiry!

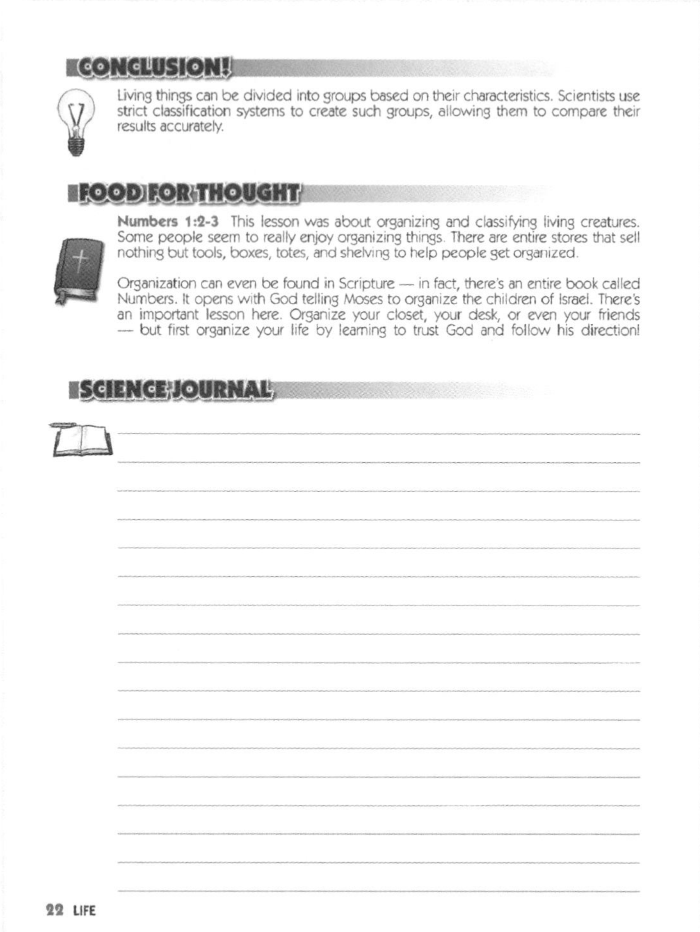

CONCLUSION!

Living things can be divided into groups based on their characteristics. Scientists use strict classification systems to create such groups, allowing them to compare their results accurately.

FOOD FOR THOUGHT

Numbers 1:2-3 This lesson was about organizing and classifying living creatures. Some people seem to really enjoy organizing things. There are entire stores that sell nothing but tools, boxes, totes, and shelving to help people get organized.

Organization can even be found in Scripture — in fact, there's an entire book called Numbers. It opens with God telling Moses to organize the children of Israel. There's an important lesson here. Organize your closet, your desk, or even your friends — but first organize your life by learning to trust God and follow his direction!

SCIENCE JOURNAL

22 LIFE

Extended Teaching

1. Have students bring discarded keys from home (almost everyone has some!). Place the keys in a large container. Challenge students to sort the keys according to characteristics. Save keys for next year.

2. Have each team research the scientific name of a household pet, then find four creatures of the same genus. Make a poster with labeled pictures (genus/species) of all five creatures. Write the genus at the top.

3. Challenge students to apply classification to non-living things. Using an online Latin dictionary (like http://www.arts.cuhk.edu.hk/Lexis/Latin/), make a list of psydo-scientific names for common classroom items. For example, *Ferramenta forfex* indicates the genus "iron tool" and the species "scissors."

4. Discuss the Human Genome Project which is mapping and classifying human chromosomes. Ask different teams to research various aspects of the project and make a report to the class.

5. Have students research how to construct and use a dichotomous key. Have teams use this knowledge to sort a bag of mixed beans. Compare the results. Discuss ways a dichotomous key would be helpful.

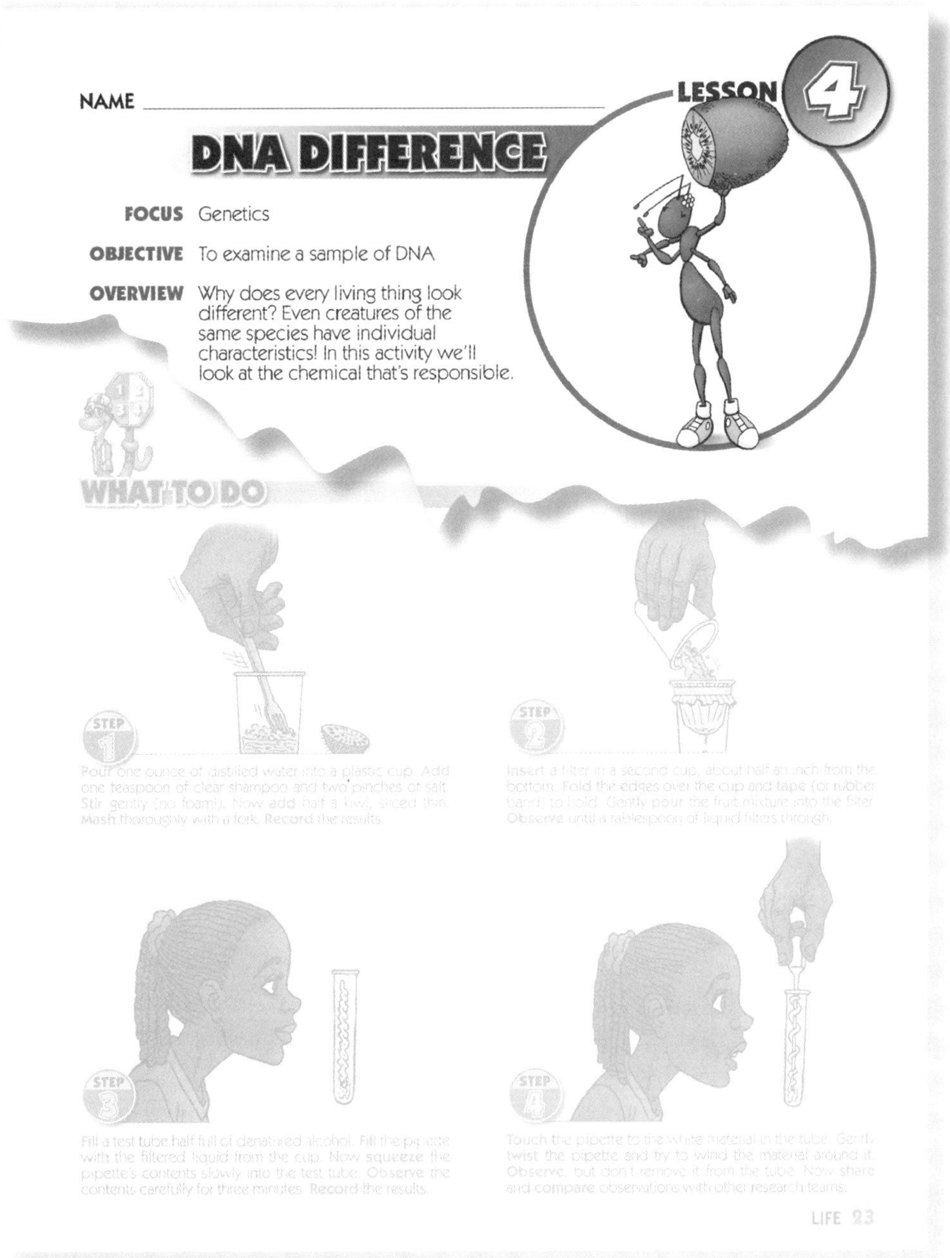

NAME ______________________

LESSON 4

DNA DIFFERENCE

FOCUS Genetics

OBJECTIVE To examine a sample of DNA

OVERVIEW Why does every living thing look different? Even creatures of the same species have individual characteristics! In this activity we'll look at the chemical that's responsible.

WHAT TO DO

STEP 1
Pour one ounce of distilled water into a plastic cup. Add one teaspoon of clear shampoo and two pinches of salt. Stir gently (no foam!). Now add half a kiwi, sliced thin. Mash thoroughly with a fork. Record the results.

STEP 2
Insert a filter in a second cup, about half an inch from the bottom. Fold the edges over the cup and tape (or rubber band) to hold. Gently pour the fruit mixture into the filter. Observe until a tablespoon of liquid filters through.

STEP 3
Fill a test tube half full of denatured alcohol. Fill the pipette with the filtered liquid from the cup. Now squeeze the pipette's contents slowly into the test tube. Observe the contents carefully for three minutes. Record the results.

STEP 4
Touch the pipette to the white material in the tube. Gently twist the pipette and try to wind the material around it. Observe, but don't remove it from the tube. Now share and compare observations with other research teams.

LIFE 23

Additional Comments

To avoid students using knives, peel and slice the kiwi yourself. Use 2 or 3 slices (very thin) for each team. Place the slices in sandwich bags and keep refrigerated until use. You can find denatured alcohol at most hardware stores. (Rubbing alcohol will work, but not very well!) Suave "Daily Clarifying Shampoo" is an inexpensive, readily-available clear shampoo, although other clear shampoos may work equally well.

Overview

Read the overview aloud to your students. The goal is to create an atmosphere of curiosity and inquiry.

Category

Life Science

Focus

Genetics

Objective

To examine a sample of DNA

National Standards

A1, A2, C1, C2, C3, C5, F1, G1, G2

Materials Needed

pipette
test tube
craft stick
plastic cups - 2
plastic fork
coffee filter
salt
rubber band
denatured alcohol
distilled water
clear shampoo
kiwi - sliced
measuring cup

Safety Concerns

1. Goggles/Gloves
Goggles and gloves are recommended whenever students are using chemicals.

2. Open Flame
Denatured alcohol is flammable. Avoid any open flame.

3. Skin Contact
Denatured alcohol can be toxic. Avoid contact with skin.

4. Slipping
Clean up any spills immediately. Remind students to exercise caution when using fluids.

WHAT TO DO

Monitor student research teams as they complete each step.

Step 1

Remind the students that good scientists don't eat their experiments! (Some students find fresh kiwi slices quite tempting.)

Step 3

Remind the students to squeeze the pipette slowly. The contents must be gently added to the test tube. They must hold the test tube steady, keeping the solution as motionless as possible.

Step 4

Sometimes the DNA material winds right up. Other times it has a tendency to clump a bit. The quality of shampoo and type of alcohol will affect the results slightly.

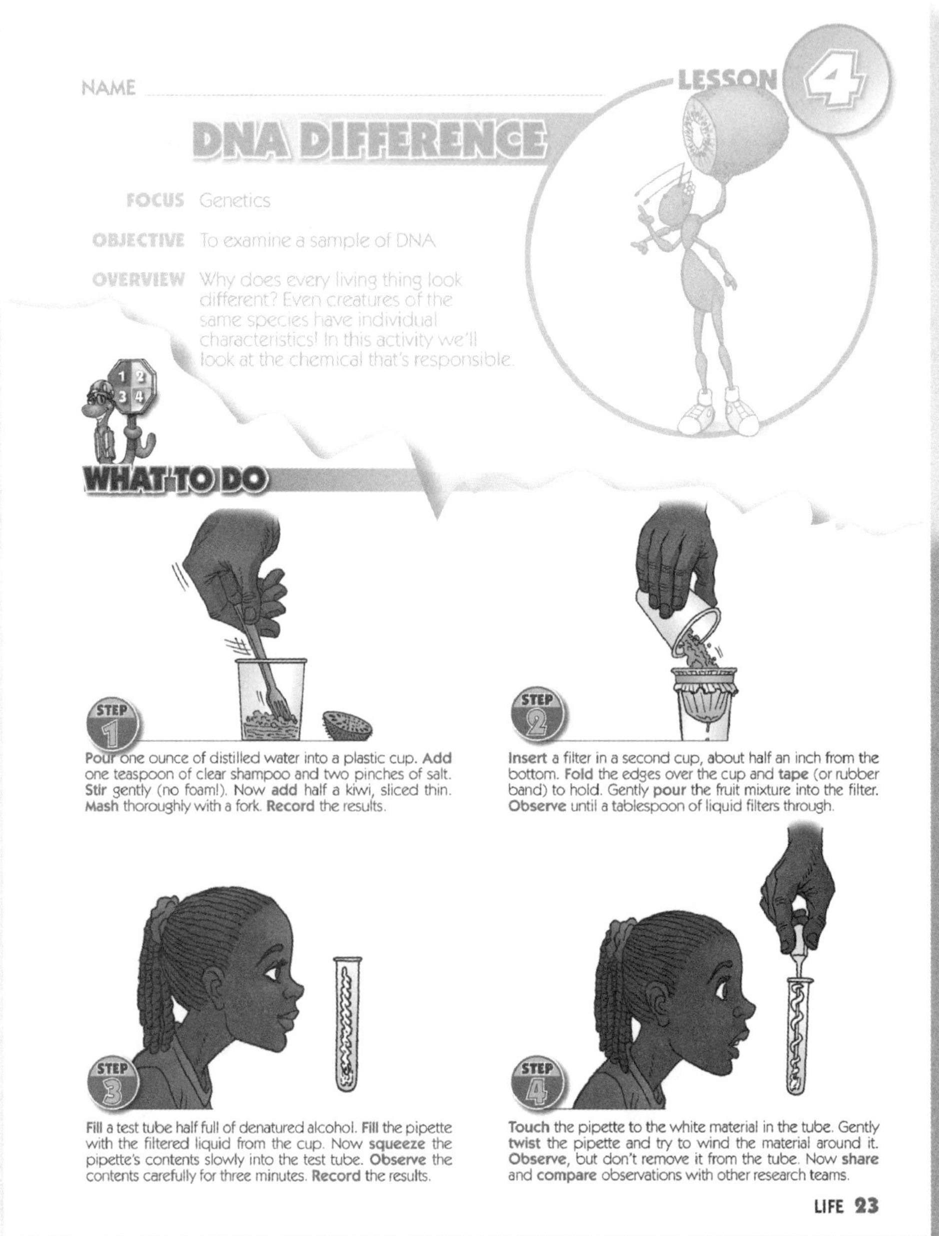

NAME

LESSON 4

DNA DIFFERENCE

FOCUS Genetics

OBJECTIVE To examine a sample of DNA

OVERVIEW Why does every living thing look different? Even creatures of the same species have individual characteristics! In this activity we'll look at the chemical that's responsible.

WHAT TO DO

STEP 1

Pour one ounce of distilled water into a plastic cup. **Add** one teaspoon of clear shampoo and two pinches of salt. **Stir** gently (no foam!). Now **add** half a kiwi, sliced thin. **Mash** thoroughly with a fork. **Record** the results.

STEP 2

Insert a filter in a second cup, about half an inch from the bottom. **Fold** the edges over the cup and **tape** (or rubber band) to hold. Gently **pour** the fruit mixture into the filter. **Observe** until a tablespoon of liquid filters through.

STEP 3

Fill a test tube half full of denatured alcohol. **Fill** the pipette with the filtered liquid from the cup. Now **squeeze** the pipette's contents slowly into the test tube. **Observe** the contents carefully for three minutes. **Record** the results.

STEP 4

Touch the pipette to the white material in the tube. Gently **twist** the pipette and try to wind the material around it. **Observe**, but don't remove it from the tube. Now **share** and **compare** observations with other research teams.

LIFE 23

Teacher to Teacher

DNA is a fascinating chemical. Think of it as a kind of computer program. All the processes that occur are controlled by the instructions hard wired into the original program. DNA is also the only chemical that can replicate itself! When a cell divides, it includes a DNA copy to give the new cell instructions for growth, control, and reproduction. But radiation, ultraviolet light, and even some drugs can cause DNA mutations. Like a computer program, changes in the basic "code" often cause major problems or even fatal errors.

WHAT JUST HAPPENED?

The white material in the test tube is **Deoxyribonucleic Acid**, commonly known as **DNA**. This chemical contains the "blueprints" for making and running a living thing. The DNA you just separated, for instance, contains the unique instructions for making and running a kiwi plant!

All DNA is made from the same **molecules**, but they're arranged in a different pattern. It's like the English language: There are only 26 letters in the alphabet, but look at the millions of words you can make with them! That's why all living things are different. The DNA for every living creature is unique.

MORE ABOUT GENETICS . . .

We started this lesson with the question, *"Why does every living thing look different?"* As you know, even creatures of the same species have individual characteristics that make them unique — different shades of skin or hair, longer ears, a bigger nose, etc.

In this activity, you took steps to isolate and observe the special chemical that causes similarities and differences. DNA, or **Deoxyribonucleic Acid** [dee ock' see rye boh noo klay' ic], contains the "blueprints" for every living thing. All DNA is made from the same type of molecules — they're just arranged in different patterns. Since every arrangement is absolutely unique, life has an almost endless variety!

By combining specific materials in the test tube, you were able to extract the large DNA strands of a kiwi plant. Although kiwi DNA will only produce kiwi plants, minor variations in the DNA can create slight differences from kiwi plant to kiwi plant.

But sometimes DNA can mutate. A mutation is a significant departure in one or more characteristics from the parent organism that is passed on to the next generation. Often these mutations can be harmful. A mutated plant that produces less seeds, for instance, would have difficulty replicating itself in the wild.

However, some mutations are engineered by man. Many of today's food plants contain DNA that has been changed in some way. These changes are designed to create resistance to disease, higher crop yields, or even enhanced vitamin content.

But genetically modified organisms (also called GMOs) are controversial. Although they greatly increase food production in a hungry world, their DNA has been changed in an artificial way. Scientists are currently studying the long-term effects these artificial changes may or may not have on plant diversity and human health.

DIGGING DEEPER:

DNA is arranged in long strands called chromosomes. A chromosome segment with a specific function is called a gene. Some genes are helpful, others are not. Many birth defects are the result of genes passed on by the parents. Research and discuss some human characteristics that are the result of genes (like albinism, color blindness, etc.).

24 LIFE

WHAT WE LEARNED:

1 **What was the purpose of the filter in Step 2? Describe the material left in the filter. Describe the liquid that squeezed through.**

a) to get rid of the pulp.

b) green, lumpy, pulpy

c) mostly clear liquid

2 **What is the common name for Deoxyribonucleic Acid? Describe this unique chemical and what it does.**

a) DNA

b) it's the chemical that contains the blueprints for making and running a living thing

3 **Based on what you've learned, could DNA be helpful in police investigations? How might DNA evidence be used to solve crimes?**

a) yes

b) since DNA is unique, DNA samples could prove someone was at the scene of the crime

LIFE 25

What Happened

Review the section with students. Emphasize bold-face words that identify key concepts and introduce new vocabulary.

The white material in the test tube is ***Deoxyribonucleic Acid,*** *commonly known as* ***DNA****. This chemical contains the "blueprints" for making and running a living thing. The DNA you just separated, for instance, contains the unique instructions for making and running a kiwi plant!*

All DNA is made from the same ***molecules****, but they're arranged in a different pattern. It's like the English language: There are only 26 letters in the alphabet, but look at the millions of words you can make with them! That's why all living things are different. The DNA for every living creature is unique.*

More About . . .

Have students read this section as you would a traditional science text — or use cooperative learning techniques to allow students the opportunity to work on the material collaboratively.

Digging Deeper

(Optional) Challenge teams to reseach and discuss practical applications of the lesson concepts. Encourage them to share their findings with the rest of the class.

What We Learned

Answers will vary. Suggested responses are shown at left.

Conclusion

Read this section aloud to the class to summarize the concepts learned in this activity.

Food for Thought

Read the Scripture aloud to the class. Discuss ways we can reflect the image of God to others.

Science Journal

If time permits, have a general class discussion about students' journal entries. Share and compare observations. Be sure to emphasize that "trial and error" is a valuable part of scientific inquiry!

CONCLUSION!

Deoxyribonucleic Acid is the chemical that contains the blueprints for a living creature. Every creature is unique since the DNA is different for everyone.

FOOD FOR THOUGHT

Genesis 1:26 This activity gave us a glimpse of DNA, one of the basic building blocks God uses to create living creatures. Our DNA determines our physical appearance, our genetic heritage, and even many of our abilities.

This Scripture reminds us that we have another heritage. God made us in his image! We were created to reflect God's love, to share with others, and to take care of the wonderful world God made. The more time you spend getting to know your creator, the better you'll understand his marvelous plans for you.

SCIENCE JOURNAL

26 LIFE

Extended Teaching

1. Have students research DNA. Discover the basic components and structure (shape) of DNA. Explain how DNA resembles a ladder, and what changes occur when it begins to do its work.

2. Have students research cloning. What is it? How does it occur? Point out that humans have used cloning for hundreds of years (grafting plants). Discuss recent developments in cloning.

3. Invite a Christian biologist or geneticist to visit your classroom. Discuss the controversy surrounding animal and human cloning.

4. Have students research diseases carried by DNA (sickle cell anemia, etc.). Find out how the Human Genome Project hopes to counter such diseases. Discuss how a genetic "map" might help fight disease.

5. Have students research illegal drugs and other mutagenic chemicals. How do they cause mutations (changes) in DNA? What are some of the results?

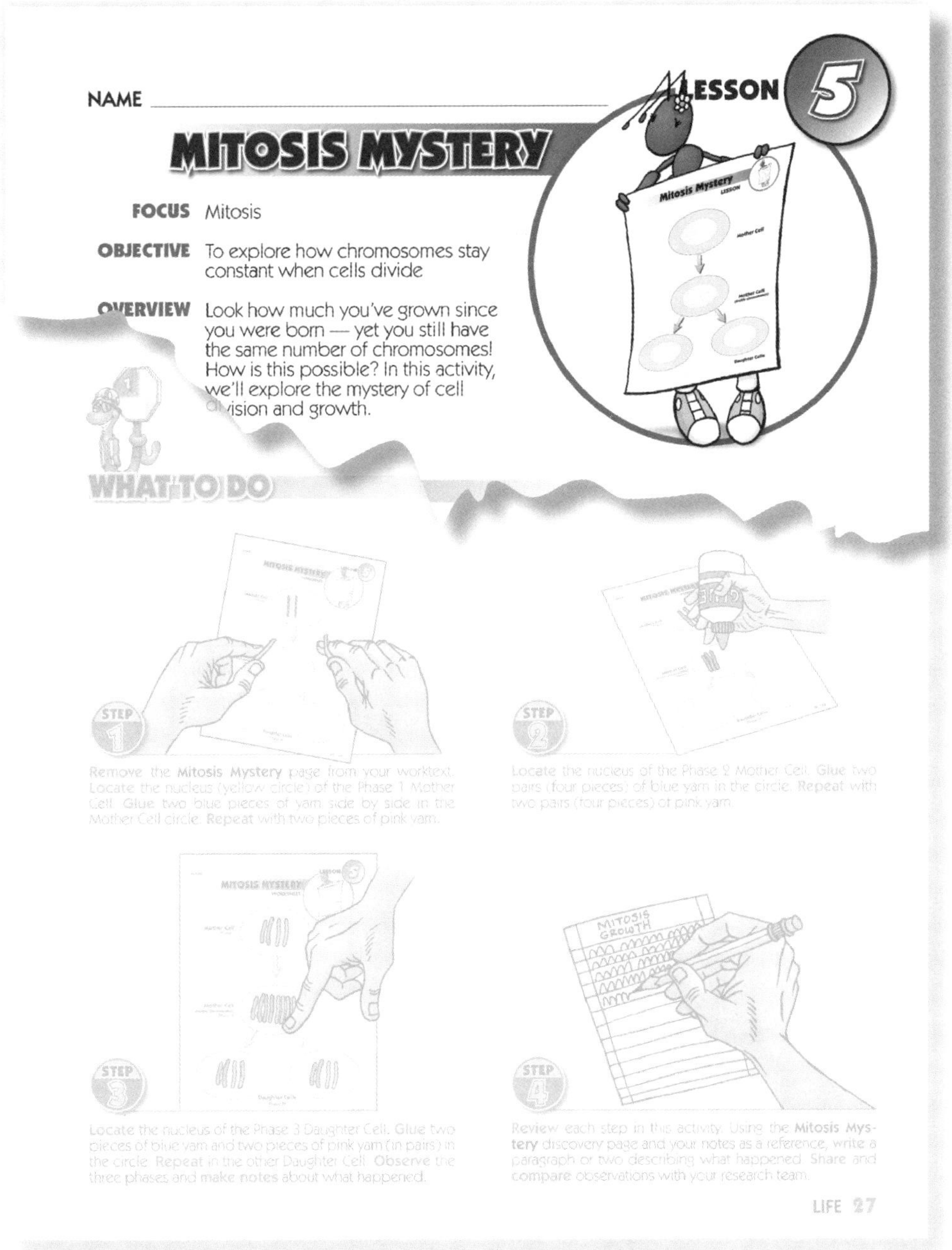

NAME

LESSON 5

MITOSIS MYSTERY

FOCUS Mitosis

OBJECTIVE To explore how chromosomes stay constant when cells divide

OVERVIEW Look how much you've grown since you were born — yet you still have the same number of chromosomes! How is this possible? In this activity, we'll explore the mystery of cell division and growth.

WHAT TO DO

STEP 1: Remove the **Mitosis Mystery** page from your worktext. Locate the nucleus (yellow circle) of the Phase 1 Mother Cell. Glue two blue pieces of yarn side by side in the Mother Cell circle. Repeat with two pieces of pink yarn.

STEP 2: Locate the nucleus of the Phase 2 Mother Cell. Glue two pairs (four pieces) of blue yarn in the circle. Repeat with two pairs (four pieces) of pink yarn.

STEP 3: Locate the nucleus of the Phase 3 Daughter Cell. Glue two pieces of blue yarn and two pieces of pink yarn (in pairs) in the circle. Repeat in the other Daughter Cell. **Observe** the three phases and make notes about what happened.

STEP 4: Review each step in this activity. Using the **Mitosis Mystery** discovery page and your notes as a reference, write a paragraph or two describing what happened. Share and compare observations with your research team.

LIFE 27

Category

Life Science

Focus

Mitosis

Objective

To explore how chromosomes stay constant when cells divide

National Standards

A1, A2, C1, C2, C3, C5, F1, G1, G2

Materials Needed

Mitosis Mystery worksheet *(student worktext, p. 163)*
blue yarn - 10 pieces
pink yarn - 10 pieces
glue or glue stick
scissors

Safety Concerns

1. Sharp Objects
Remind students to be careful when using scissors.

Additional Comments

If you wish to use glue sticks to minimize the mess, have students work on a piece of scrap paper. Lay a piece of yarn on the paper, rub down it with the glue stick, then pick it up and stick it to the worksheet.

Overview

Read the overview aloud to your students. The goal is to create an atmosphere of curiosity and inquiry.

WHAT TO DO

Monitor student research teams as they complete each step.

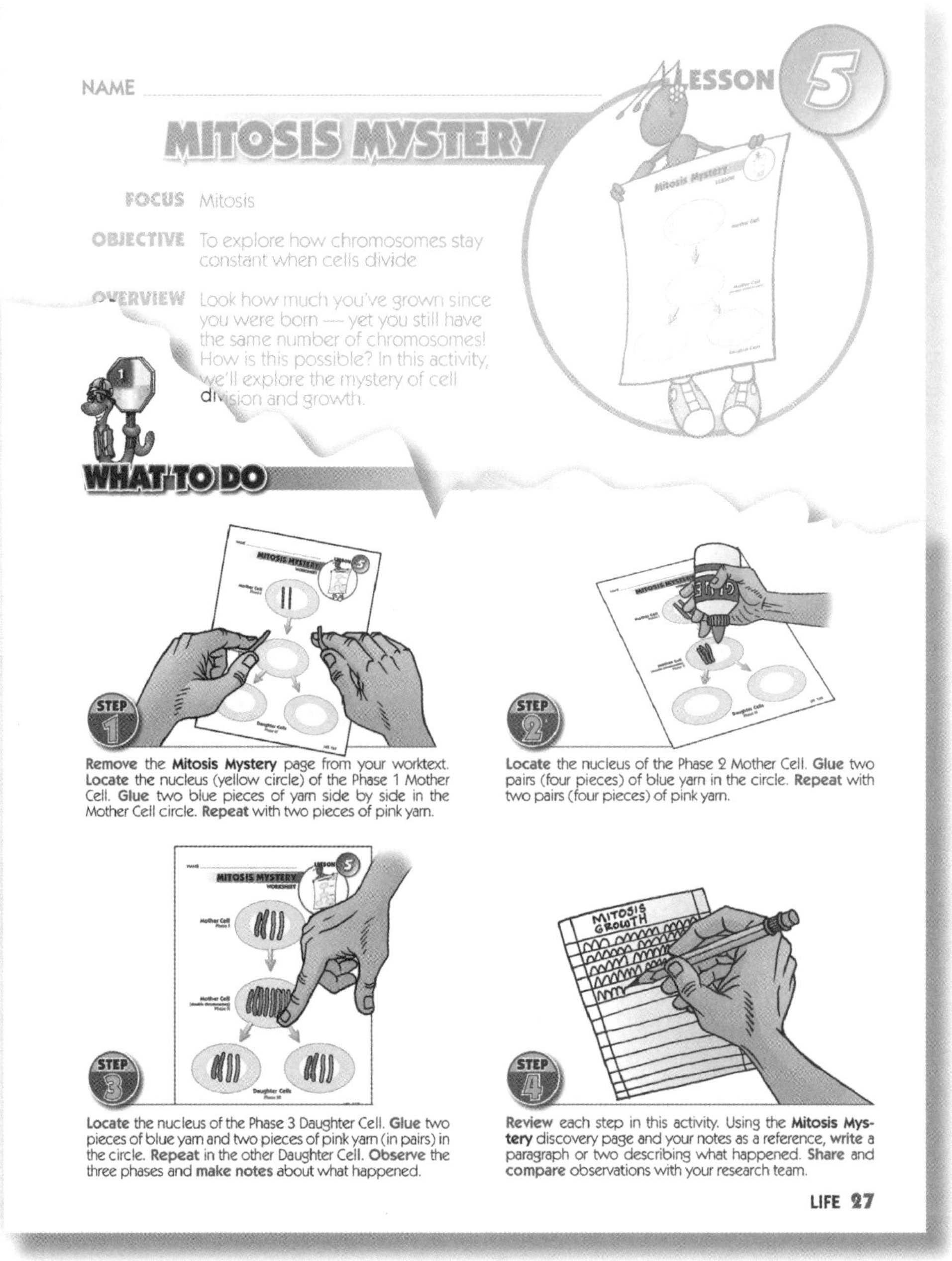

NAME

LESSON 5

MITOSIS MYSTERY

FOCUS Mitosis

OBJECTIVE To explore how chromosomes stay constant when cells divide

OVERVIEW Look how much you've grown since you were born — yet you still have the same number of chromosomes! How is this possible? In this activity, we'll explore the mystery of cell division and growth.

WHAT TO DO

STEP 1

Remove the **Mitosis Mystery** page from your worktext. **Locate** the nucleus (yellow circle) of the Phase 1 Mother Cell. **Glue** two blue pieces of yarn side by side in the Mother Cell circle. **Repeat** with two pieces of pink yarn.

STEP 2

Locate the nucleus of the Phase 2 Mother Cell. **Glue** two pairs (four pieces) of blue yarn in the circle. **Repeat** with two pairs (four pieces) of pink yarn.

STEP 3

Locate the nucleus of the Phase 3 Daughter Cell. **Glue** two pieces of blue yarn and two pieces of pink yarn (in pairs) in the circle. **Repeat** in the other Daughter Cell. **Observe** the three phases and **make notes** about what happened.

STEP 4

Review each step in this activity. Using the **Mitosis Mystery** discovery page and your notes as a reference, **write** a paragraph or two describing what happened. **Share** and **compare** observations with your research team.

LIFE 27

Teacher to Teacher

Cell division (mitosis) is a complicated process. The cell doubles its chromosomes, making identical copies. This is possible because chromosomes are made of DNA. On rare occasions, a chromosome doesn't replicate properly, resulting in a mutation. If the organism lives, each offspring may carry mutated DNA in its programming. Some illegal drugs (like LSD) may cause chromosome breaks, resulting in dangerous health problems.

WHAT JUST HAPPENED?

When a **cell** begins to **divide** (see Step 2), it creates exact copies of its original **chromosomes**. This is the first phase of **mitosis**. When mitosis is complete, the **mother cell** splits into two **daughter cells** (see Step 3). Each daughter cell contains identical copies of the original chromosomes contributed by the parents.

For this activity, we **modeled** a cell with only two sets of chromosomes (four total). Human beings are much more complex, receiving a set of twenty-three chromosomes from each parent (forty-six total).

The primary job of chromosomes is to store information that cells need to help a living creature grow and function. As cells **multiply**, correct chromosome **duplication** and **division** ensures that this process happens correctly. As you can see, mitosis is a critical phase in an organism's life cycle!

MORE ABOUT MITOSIS . . .

You've gotten taller, bigger, stronger, and faster since you were born. That's because you have a lot more cells than you did when you were a baby! But even though you have many more cells, you have exactly the same number of chromosomes in each cell (be they bone, muscle, nerve, or tissue) as you did at the start.

Let's review this important process again: When a cell begins to divide, it creates exact copies of its original chromosomes. This is the first stage of mitosis (also called normal cell division). When mitosis is complete, the mother cell splits into two daughter cells. Each of these daughter cells contains identical copies of the original chromosomes that you got from your parents.

In this activity, we modeled a cell with only two sets of chromosomes (four total). But human beings are much more complex than that. All of us received a set of twenty-three chromosomes from each of our parents (forty-six total). Some living things have more chromosomes than we do; some have fewer. Either way, it's the chromosomes that determine what each living thing is and how it will function.

Chromosomes store the information cells that need to help living things function correctly. Think of them as a complex computer program that helps the organism run properly. As a living thing's cells multiply, correct chromosome duplication and division ensures that the process continues correctly. But if there is a mistake somewhere along the line, the living thing may not survive. Cancer is an example of where mitosis has made a mistake — and the results can be deadly!

As you can see, healthy mitosis is a critical part of any organism's life cycle. It helps us grow, mature, and repair injuries or damage from disease.

DIGGING DEEPER

Abnormalities in mitosis (cell division) can lead to diseases like cancer. Research and discuss some of the possible causes of cancer — tobacco smoke, radiation, chemicals, etc. Talk about some cancer symptoms, treatments, and possible cures.

28 LIFE

WHAT WE LEARNED

1 What did the blue and pink yarn pieces represent? How many chromosomes do human beings receive from each parent?

a) chromosomes

b) 23 from each parent

2 Describe the mitosis process. What happens before the cell divides? Why is this important?

a) answers will vary

b) the mother cell doubles the number of chromosomes

c) otherwise only half the information needed would be available

3 What might happen if something interfered with chromosome duplication during mitosis? What effect might this have on growth?

a) mutated DNA; a damaged chromosome

b) no growth (death), or a damaged growth process

LIFE 29

What Happened

Review the section with students. Emphasize bold-face words that identify key concepts and introduce new vocabulary.

*When a **cell** begins to **divide** (see Step 2), it creates exact copies of its original **chromosomes**. This is the first phase of **mitosis**. When mitosis is complete, the **mother cell** splits into two **daughter cells** (see Step 3). Each daughter cell contains identical copies of the original chromosomes contributed by the parents.*

*For this activity, we **modeled** a cell with only two sets of chromosomes (four total). Human beings are much more complex, receiving a set of twenty-three chromosomes from each parent (forty-six total).*

*The primary job of chromosomes is to store information that cells need to help a living creature grow and function. As cells **multiply**, correct chromosome **duplication** and **division** insures that this process happens correctly. As you can see, mitosis is a critical phase in an organism's life cycle!*

More About . . .

Have students read this section as you would a traditional science text — or use cooperative learning techniques to allow students the opportunity to work on the material collaboratively.

Digging Deeper

(Optional) Challenge teams to reseach and discuss practical applications of the lesson concepts. Encourage them to share their findings with the rest of the class.

What We Learned

Answers will vary. Suggested responses are shown at left.

Conclusion

Read this section aloud to the class to summarize the concepts learned in this activity.

Food for Thought

Read the Scripture aloud to the class. Discuss the story of Abraham and God's promise. Talk about the importance of learning to trust God.

Science Journal

If time permits, have a general class discussion about students' journal entries. Share and compare observations. Be sure to emphasize that "trial and error" is a valuable part of scientific inquiry!

CONCLUSION!

Before dividing, cells duplicate their chromosomes through mitosis. New cells contain identical copies of the original chromosomes. A normal human being has forty-six chromosomes — twenty-three from each parent.

FOOD FOR THOUGHT

Genesis 22:17 Your chromosomes are duplicated every time a new cell is made to repair an injury, fight disease, replace worn parts, or even just help you grow! Every cell in your body came from the original cell created at your conception. The descendants of that cell would be far too numerous to count!

In a time when Abraham believed he would never have even one child, God promised him that his descendants would be too numerous to count. In spite of appearances, Abraham decided to put his trust in God, and entire nations now claim Abraham as their ancestor. Learn to trust in God, for his promises are always true!

SCIENCE JOURNAL

30 LIFE

Extended Teaching

1. Repeat the activity, but use 23 chromosome pairs (46 total) to model human mitosis. You'll need a large sheet of craft paper with huge circles and multiple colors of yarn for the chromosome pairs.

2. Have students research chemotherapy. Discover more about how these potent chemicals are used to treat cancer. Have students give reports about their findings.

3. Have students research how "selective breeding" of animals and plants has improved food production. Have each team make a poster with drawings and descriptions that detail their findings.

4. Invite a cancer survivor to visit your classroom. Discuss treatments and prevention of cancer. Visit the website of the American Cancer Society (www.cancer.org) to learn more.

5. Challenge students to identify the individual stages of mitosis. (A high school or college biology text is a good place to start.) Make bulletin boards with drawings and descriptions outlining these detailed stages.

NAME ____________

LESSON 6

MARVELOUS MEIOSIS

FOCUS Meiosis

OBJECTIVE To explore how cell division creates gametes and determines gender

OVERVIEW We've studied how cells make duplicates of themselves. But what role do chromosomes play in determining if a baby will be a boy or girl? In this activity, we'll explore the answer.

WHAT TO DO

STEP 1 Remove the **Marvelous Meiosis** page from your worktext. **Glue** two pieces of pink yarn in the phase 1 Female Cell. **Glue** one blue and one pink yarn in the phase 1 Male Cell.

STEP 2 Glue four pink yarns in the phase 2 Female Cell. **Glue** two blue yarns and two pink yarns in the phase 2 Male Cell. Now glue two pink yarns in each phase 3 Female Cell, and one blue and one pink yarn in each phase 3 Male cell.

STEP 3 **Glue** one pink yarn in each of the phase 4 Female Gamete cells. **Glue** one blue yarn in two of the phase 4 Male Gamete cells, and one pink yarn in each of the other two.

STEP 4 Pink yarn represents the female "X" chromosomes; blue yarn represents the male "Y" choromosomes. **Add** these designations to your discovery page. **Share** and **compare** results with your research team.

LIFE 31

Category

Life Science

Focus

Meiosis

Objective

To explore how cell division creates gametes and determines gender

National Standards

A1, A2, C1, C2, C3, C5, F1, G1, G2

Materials Needed

Marvelous Meiosis worksheet *(student worktext, p. 165)*
pink yarn - 21 pieces
blue yarn - 7 pieces
glue or glue stick
scissors

Safety Concerns

4. Sharp Objects
Remind students to be careful when using scissors.

Additional Comments

If you wish to use glue sticks to minimize the mess, use the same procedure outlined in "Additional Comments," Lesson 5. Note that the gametes on the worksheet are not to scale. Sperm cells are extremely tiny in comparison to a mature egg cell.

Overview

Read the overview aloud to your students. The goal is to create an atmosphere of curiosity and inquiry.

WHAT TO DO

Monitor student research teams as they complete each step.

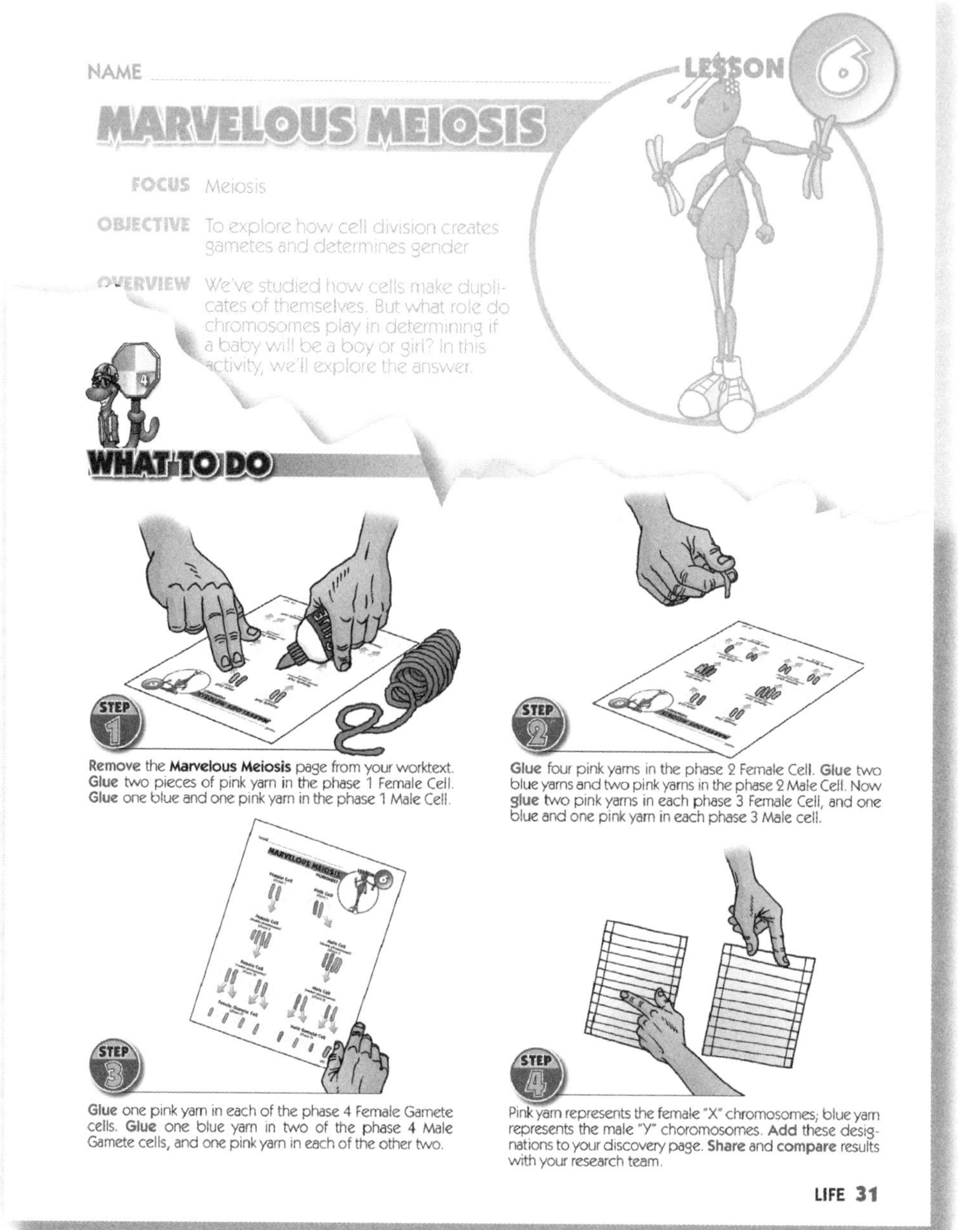

NAME

LESSON 6

MARVELOUS MEIOSIS

FOCUS Meiosis

OBJECTIVE To explore how cell division creates gametes and determines gender

OVERVIEW We've studied how cells make duplicates of themselves. But what role do chromosomes play in determining if a baby will be a boy or girl? In this activity, we'll explore the answer.

WHAT TO DO

STEP 1

Remove the **Marvelous Meiosis** page from your worktext. **Glue** two pieces of pink yarn in the phase 1 Female Cell. **Glue** one blue and one pink yarn in the phase 1 Male Cell.

STEP 2

Glue four pink yarns in the phase 2 Female Cell. **Glue** two blue yarns and two pink yarns in the phase 2 Male Cell. Now **glue** two pink yarns in each phase 3 Female Cell, and one blue and one pink yarn in each phase 3 Male cell.

STEP 3

Glue one pink yarn in each of the phase 4 Female Gamete cells. **Glue** one blue yarn in two of the phase 4 Male Gamete cells, and one pink yarn in each of the other two.

STEP 4

Pink yarn represents the female "X" chromosomes; blue yarn represents the male "Y" choromosomes. **Add** these designations to your discovery page. **Share** and **compare** results with your research team.

LIFE 31

Teacher to Teacher

Scientists describe the number of chromosomes in a cell as haploid, diploid, and tetraploid. Haploid means one set of chromosomes. All gametes produced in meiosis (sex cells) are haploid. Two haploid cells (like a sperm and an egg) join to form a diploid cell (two sets of chromosomes). Most body cells are diploid, containing two sets of chromosomes from each parent. During meiosis and mitosis, each cell doubles the number of chromosomes before splitting. This is the only time during meiosis and mitosis a cell is tetraploid (four sets of chromosomes).

WHAT JUST HAPPENED?

When living creatures **reproduce** by **sexual reproduction**, each parent supplies half the **chromosomes**. To make a **gamete** (sex cell), a **cell** begins by duplicating its chromosomes in regular **mitosis**. But then the cell splits once more in a process called **meiosis.** Meiosis results in a gamete that has only half the normal number of chromosomes. How are the missing number of chromosomes replaced at conception? We'll solve that mystery in our next lesson!

It's important to note that this activity focused only on chromosomes that determine **gender** (sex). There are many other kinds of chromosomes in your body, too. To make things simpler, we only **modeled** splitting the sex chromosomes in this activity. Our next lesson will be more detailed.

MORE ABOUT MEIOSIS . . .

Cells regularly make duplicates of themselves and their chromosomes through the process scientists call mitosis. But some cells undergo a second split (meiosis) that creates a special kind of cell called a gamete. That's what we modeled in this activity.

Like any other new cell, a gamete starts with a parent cell splitting in two through mitosis. But in order to create a gamete, this special cell must split a second time — without retaining all its chromosomes! Scientists call this process meiosis.

The result of meiosis is a special cell that contains only half the normal number of chromosomes. (We'll talk about how the missing chromosomes are replaced during conception in another lesson.)

In this lesson we only focused on the X and Y chromosomes that determine sex. But it's important to remember that there are many other kinds of chromosomes that tag along as well. These additional chromosomes help determine things like hair color, eye color, or height.

Of course, some living things reproduce by asexual reproduction — meaning there are no gametes and no meiosis. For example, single-cell microbes like bacteria simply divide in two using mitosis. Each time bacteria undergo mitosis, they reproduce and make more bacteria that are *identical* to themselves.

But in meiosis, the various chromosomes are separated and reshuffled. That's why you often find people with physical characteristics from one parent or the other or both — but you never find someone who looks *exactly* like their Mom or Dad.

DIGGING DEEPER:

Research and discuss asexual reproduction. How does it differ from sexual reproduction at the cellular level? What are some common living things that reproduce in this fashion (like bacteria)? How can asexual reproduction help ensure their survival?

32 LIFE

WHAT WE LEARNED:

1 **Compare mitosis and meiosis. How are they similar? How are they different?**

a) similar: both involve cells splitting

b) in mitosis, new cells have the same number of chromosomes; in meiosis, new cells have only half the number of chromosomes

2 **What is a gamete? How is it different from a normal cell?**

a) a gamete is a sex cell

b) gametes have only half the usual number of chromosomes

3 **Growth and reproduction are a part of the life cycle of living things. Based on what you've learned, relate these two processes to mitosis and meiosis. Explain your answer.**

mitosis is how cells duplicate to produce growth or repair; meiosis is how cells duplicate for reproduction

LIFE 33

What Happened

Review the section with students. Emphasize bold-face words that identify key concepts and introduce new vocabulary.

When living creatures ***reproduce*** *by* ***sexual reproduction****, each parent supplies half the* ***chromosomes****. To make a* ***gamete*** *(sex cell), a* ***cell*** *begins by duplicating its chromosomes in regular* ***mitosis****. But then the cell splits once more in a process called* ***meiosis****. Meiosis results in a gamete that has only half the normal number of chromosomes. How are the missing number of chromosomes replaced at conception? We'll solve that mystery in our next lesson!*

It's important to note that this activity focused only on chromosomes that determine ***gender*** *(sex). There are many other kinds of chromosomes in your body, too. To make things simpler, we only* ***modeled*** *splitting the sex chromosomes in this activity. Our next lesson will be more detailed.*

More About . . .

Have students read this section as you would a traditional science text — or use cooperative learning techniques to allow students the opportunity to work on the material collaboratively.

Digging Deeper

(Optional) Challenge teams to reseach and discuss practical applications of the lesson concepts. Encourage them to share their findings with the rest of the class.

What We Learned

Answers will vary. Suggested responses are shown at left.

Conclusion

Read this section aloud to the class to summarize the concepts learned in this activity.

Food for Thought

Read the Scripture aloud to the class. Talk about the wonderful things that God has created. Discuss our responsibility to take care of the world God made for us.

Science Journal

If time permits, have a general class discussion about students' journal entries. Share and compare observations. Be sure to emphasize that "trial and error" is a valuable part of scientific inquiry!

CONCLUSION!

Cells duplicate chromosomes through mitosis. During meiosis, some cells divide even further to produce gametes (sex cells) for reproduction. Because of meiosis, gametes have half the usual number of chromosomes.

FOOD FOR THOUGHT

Genesis 1:22 Meiosis and mitosis reflect the ongoing process of growth and reproduction in a life cycle. Without these two processes, life as we know it would soon grind to a halt.

Creation was a time of amazing growth and reproduction. God blessed the world and the result was an amazing and abundant variety of life! Scripture tells us that God was pleased with his creation. Even after centuries of sin and destruction, the world still reflects God's marvelous work. Look at the natural things around you, enjoy them, and don't forget to thank God.

SCIENCE JOURNAL

34 LIFE

Extended Teaching

1. As they divide, chromosomes shuffle around a little. Children look similar, but not identical to their parents. Challenge students to find and list characteristics they have that are similar to a parent or grandparent.

2. Birth defects are caused by genetic factors like damaged chromosomes. But environmental factors (poor diet, drinking, smoking) can also cause birth defects. Have students research these causes and report their findings.

3. Teenage pregnancy is a serious problem in our society. Have students research how teen pregnancy impacts people's lives. Discuss abstinence and ways to avoid pre-marital sex.

4. Have students research the number of babies born each year to unmarried women. What affect does this have on society? What problems are these type of single parent families more likely to encounter?

5. Oogenesis is the process in which egg cells are produced. Have students research egg production in different creatures. Discover the difference (size, purpose, etc.) between egg cells and polar bodies.

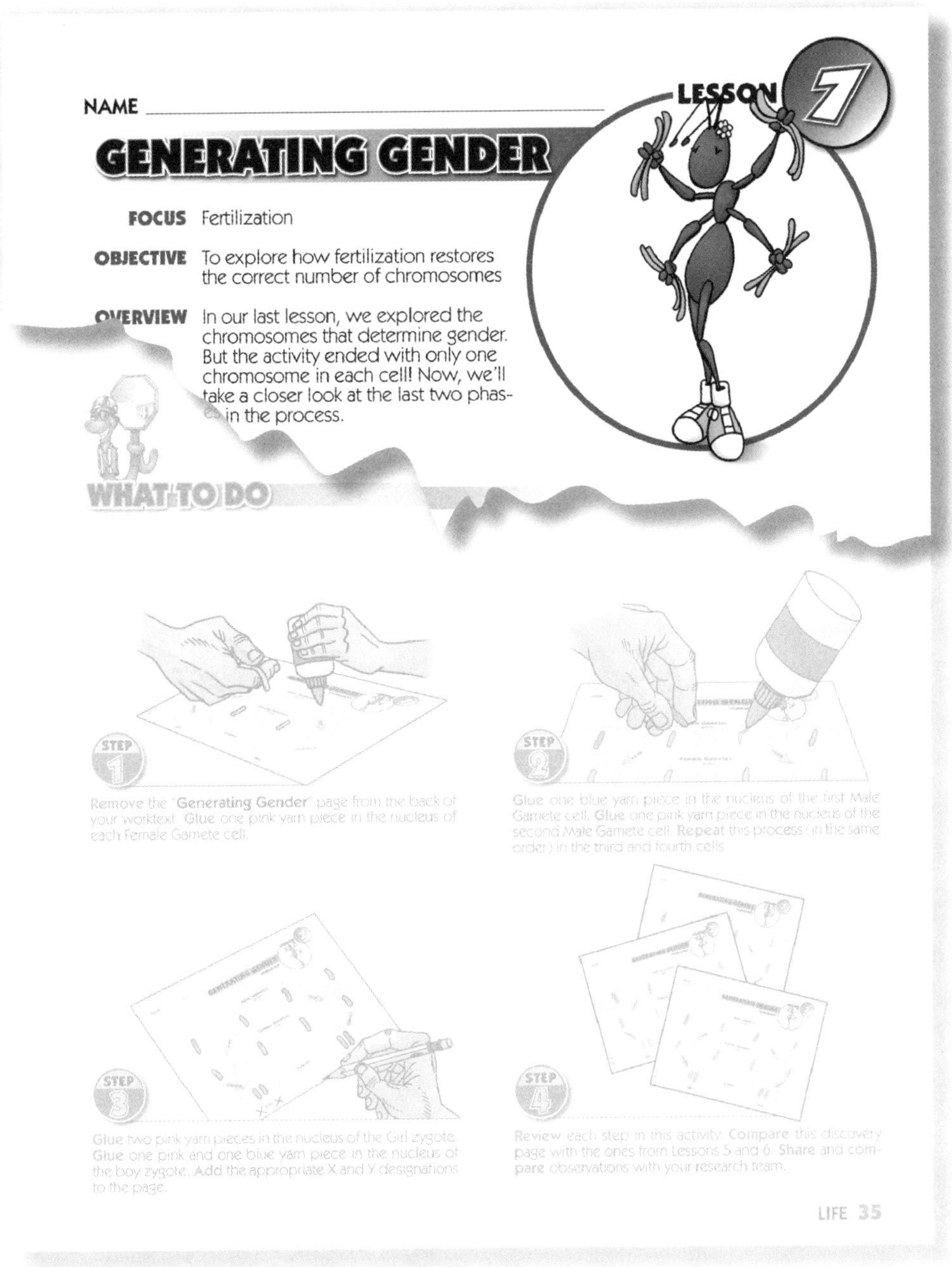
NAME

LESSON 7

GENERATING GENDER

FOCUS Fertilization

OBJECTIVE To explore how fertilization restores the correct number of chromosomes

OVERVIEW In our last lesson, we explored the chromosomes that determine gender. But the activity ended with only one chromosome in each cell! Now, we'll take a closer look at the last two phases in the process.

WHAT TO DO

STEP 1 Remove the "**Generating Gender**" page from the back of your worktext. **Glue** one pink yarn piece in the nucleus of each Female Gamete cell.

STEP 2 **Glue** one blue yarn piece in the nucleus of the first Male Gamete cell. **Glue** one pink yarn piece in the nucleus of the second Male Gamete cell. **Repeat** this process (in the same order) in the third and fourth cells.

STEP 3 **Glue** two pink yarn pieces in the nucleus of the Girl zygote. **Glue** one pink and one blue yarn piece in the nucleus of the boy zygote. **Add** the appropriate X and Y designations to the page.

STEP 4 **Review** each step in this activity. **Compare** this discovery page with the ones from Lessons 5 and 6. **Share** and **compare** observations with your research team.

LIFE 35

Category

Life Science

Focus

Fertilization

Objective

To explore how fertilization restores the correct number of chromosomes

National Standards

A1, A2, C1, C2, C3, C5, F1, G1, G2

Materials Needed

Generating Gender worksheet *(student worktext, p. 167)*
blue yarn - 3 pieces
pink yarn - 9 pieces
glue or glue stick
scissors

Safety Concerns

4. Sharp Objects
Remind students to be careful when using scissors.

Additional Comments

If you wish to use glue sticks to minimize the mess, use the same procedure outlined in "Additional Comments," Lesson 5.

Overview

Read the overview aloud to your students. The goal is to create an atmosphere of curiosity and inquiry. There is no more miraculous or interesting process in science than the creation of a new human being!

WHAT TO DO

Monitor student research teams as they complete each step.

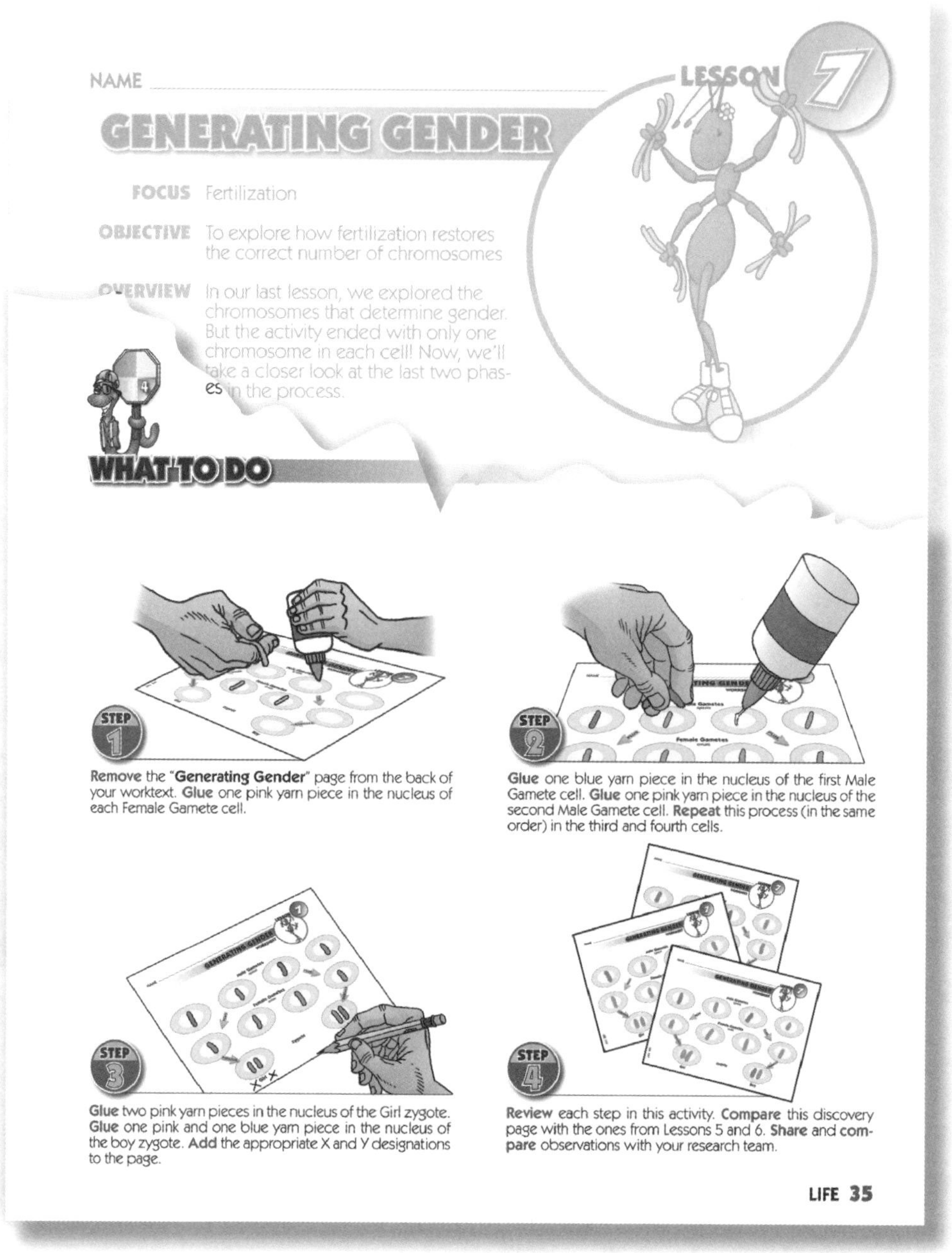
NAME

LESSON 7

GENERATING GENDER

FOCUS Fertilization

OBJECTIVE To explore how fertilization restores the correct number of chromosomes

OVERVIEW In our last lesson, we explored the chromosomes that determine gender. But the activity ended with only one chromosome in each cell! Now, we'll take a closer look at the last two phases in the process.

WHAT TO DO

STEP 1

Remove the "**Generating Gender**" page from the back of your worktext. **Glue** one pink yarn piece in the nucleus of each Female Gamete cell.

STEP 2

Glue one blue yarn piece in the nucleus of the first Male Gamete cell. **Glue** one pink yarn piece in the nucleus of the second Male Gamete cell. **Repeat** this process (in the same order) in the third and fourth cells.

STEP 3

Glue two pink yarn pieces in the nucleus of the Girl zygote. **Glue** one pink and one blue yarn piece in the nucleus of the boy zygote. **Add** the appropriate X and Y designations to the page.

STEP 4

Review each step in this activity. **Compare** this discovery page with the ones from Lessons 5 and 6. **Share** and **compare** observations with your research team.

LIFE 35

Teacher to Teacher

The role of chromosomes in determining gender was first discovered less than 100 years ago by Dr. Nettie Stevens. Her early work on sex determination was based on experiments with beetles, and her findings were first published as a Carnegie Institute report in 1905.

The discovery not only ended long-standing debate over whether sex was based on heredity or embryonic influence, but also showed the first firm link between a heritable characteristic and a particular chromosome.

WHAT JUST HAPPENED?

Human beings have a total of forty-six **chromosomes**. Two of these chromosomes are the ones that determine **gender** (sex). In females, both chromosomes are the same. Scientists call them **X** chromosomes. In males, one chromosome is different. Scientists call it a **Y** chromosome.

During **fertilization**, the combination of sperm and egg creates a special cell called a **zygote**. A baby's gender depends on how the chromosomes in the **gametes** (sex cells) are combined in the zygote. Two X chromosomes produce a girl. One X and one Y produce a boy.

Keep in mind that these are only two chromosomes out of many. The zygote receives forty-four additional chromosomes to complete the forty-six each human needs.

MORE ABOUT FERTILIZATION . . .

When cells split and the chromosome number stays the same, it's called mitosis. When cells split and the chromosome number is cut in half, it's called meiosis. Meiosis is the process that makes the sex cells called gametes.

During fertilization (**conception**), the combination of gametes (sex cells) called **sperm** (male) and **egg** (female) combine to form a special cell called a zygote. In this activity we discovered that two very specific chromosomes in those cells are what determine a baby's gender (sex).

In females, both these chromosomes are the same. Scientists refer to them as the X chromosomes. But in males, there is a second type of sex chromosome. Scientists call it the Y chromosome. In most mammals, an XX chromosome combination produces a female, and an XY combination produces a male. (In other living things, gender is determined by more complex combinations and conditions.)

It's important to remember that human beings have a total of forty-six chromosomes. Every human being must have exactly that number to be normal. It takes the complete "computer program" of forty-six chromosomes to help a human being grow and develop correctly.

If a baby is born with extra chromosomes or too few, it can have serious problems. Down syndrome is a type of birth defect in which a baby has an extra chromosome number 21. Children with Down syndrome often have varying degrees of mental retardation, characteristic facial features, and can also have heart defects. Babies that are born with an extra number 18 or 13 chromosome have multiple birth defects. They usually die in the first months of life.

DIGGING DEEPER:

Research and discuss mutations and the environmental factors that can cause them. Talk about known causes of birth defects and how they can be prevented. If you have time, research how chromosomes affect other living things (like seedless watermelons). These complex combinations and conditions can be quite interesting.

36 LIFE

WHAT WE LEARNED:

1. **What is a gamete? What is a zygote? How many chromosomes does a complete zygote have?**

a) a sex cell

b) a fertilized sex cell

c) 46

2. **What kind of sex chromosomes does an egg cell have? What kind of sex chromosomes does a sperm cell have? Explain your answer.**

a) just X chromosomes

b) X or Y chromosome

c) eggs come from females, so only X is available; sperm comes from males, so both X and Y are available

3. **What sex chromosome combination creates a baby boy? What sex chromosome combination creates a baby girl?**

a) an X and a Y chromosome

b) two X chromosomes

LIFE 37

What Happened

Review the section with students. Emphasize bold-face words that identify key concepts and introduce new vocabulary.

Human beings have a total of 46 ***chromosomes****. Two of these chromosomes are the ones that determine* ***gender*** *(sex). In females, both chromosomes are the same. Scientists call them* ***X*** *chromosomes. In males, one chromosome is different. Scientists call it a* ***Y*** *chromosome.*

During ***fertilization****, the combination of sperm and egg creates a special cell called a* ***zygote****. A baby's gender depends on how the chromosomes in the* ***gametes*** *(sex cells) are combined in the zygote. Two X chromosomes produce a girl. One X and one Y produce a boy.*

Keep in mind that these are only two chromosomes out of many. The zygote receives forty-four additional chromosomes to complete the forty-six each human needs.

More About . . .

Have students read this section as you would a traditional science text — or use cooperative learning techniques to allow students the opportunity to work on the material collaboratively.

Digging Deeper

(Optional) Challenge teams to reseach and discuss practical applications of the lesson concepts. Encourage them to share their findings with the rest of the class.

What We Learned

Answers will vary. Suggested responses are shown at left.

Conclusion

Read this section aloud to the class to summarize the concepts learned in this activity.

Food for Thought

Read the Scripture aloud to the class. Discuss how staying close to God can help us gain the time and wisdom to use this special gift correctly. Talk about the kinds of problems that can occur when God's plan is not followed.

Science Journal

If time permits, have a general class discussion about students' journal entries. Share and compare observations. Be sure to emphasize that "trial and error" is a valuable part of scientific inquiry!

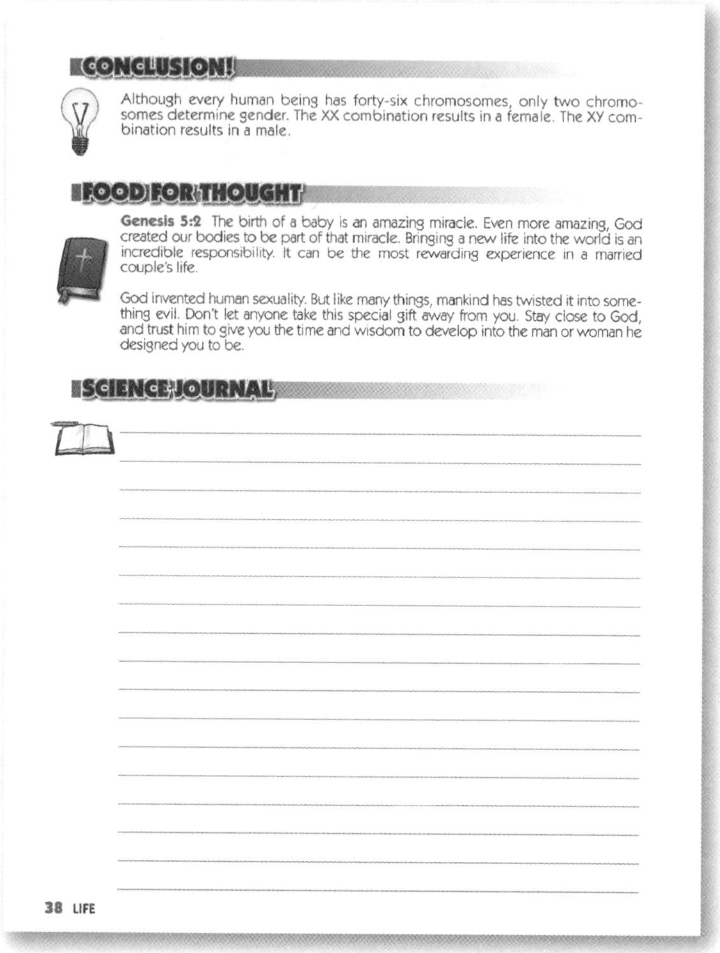

CONCLUSION!

Although every human being has forty-six chromosomes, only two chromosomes determine gender. The XX combination results in a female. The XY combination results in a male.

FOOD FOR THOUGHT

Genesis 5:2 The birth of a baby is an amazing miracle. Even more amazing, God created our bodies to be part of that miracle. Bringing a new life into the world is an incredible responsibility. It can be the most rewarding experience in a married couple's life.

God invented human sexuality. But like many things, mankind has twisted it into something evil. Don't let anyone take this special gift away from you. Stay close to God, and trust him to give you the time and wisdom to develop into the man or woman he designed you to be.

SCIENCE JOURNAL

38 LIFE

Extended Teaching

1. Sometimes there are deviations in the chromosome pattern. Have students research Klinefelter Syndrome (XXY) and Turner's Syndrome (X). How are they similar? How are they different?

2. Have students research Down's Syndrome. What chromosome number deviation causes this condition?

3. Assign each team one of the syndromes listed above. Have them make a poster with drawings and descriptions of the various chromosome patterns involved.

4. Ask students to research the "Barr Body." What does its presence indicate? How is it used as a determiner in tests done for the Olympics?

5. Have students research anabolic steroids. What affect do these chemicals have on the human body? Why is their use dangerous?

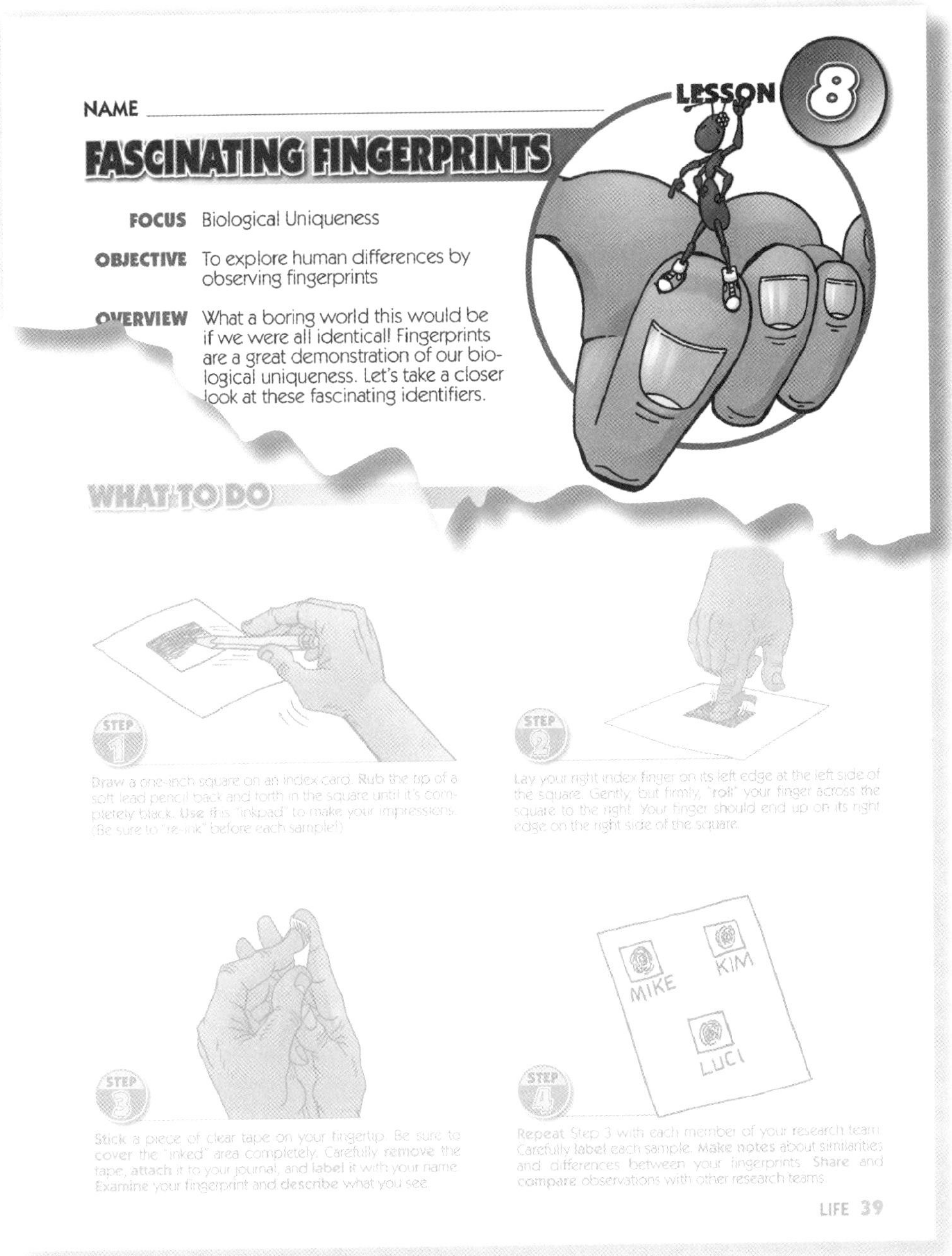

NAME ________________________________

LESSON 8

FASCINATING FINGERPRINTS

FOCUS Biological Uniqueness

OBJECTIVE To explore human differences by observing fingerprints

OVERVIEW What a boring world this would be if we were all identical! Fingerprints are a great demonstration of our biological uniqueness. Let's take a closer look at these fascinating identifiers.

WHAT TO DO

STEP 1

Draw a one-inch square on an index card. **Rub** the tip of a soft lead pencil back and forth in the square until it's completely black. **Use** this "inkpad" to make your impressions. (Be sure to "re-ink" before each sample!)

STEP 2

Lay your right index finger on its left edge at the left side of the square. Gently, but firmly, "**roll**" your finger across the square to the right. Your finger should end up on its right edge on the right side of the square.

STEP 3

Stick a piece of clear tape on your fingertip. Be sure to cover the "inked" area completely. Carefully **remove** the tape, **attach** it to your journal, and **label** it with your name. **Examine** your fingerprint and **describe** what you see.

STEP 4

Repeat Step 3 with each member of your research team. Carefully **label** each sample. **Make notes** about similarities and differences between your fingerprints. **Share** and **compare** observations with other research teams.

LIFE 39

Category

Life Science

Focus

Biological Uniqueness

Objective

To explore human differences by observing fingerprints

National Standards

A1, A2, C1, C2, C5, F1, F5, G1, G2

Materials Needed

3x5 index card
soft lead pencil
clear adhesive tape
magnifying glass (optional)

Safety Concerns

none

Additional Comments

This activity can be messy. Allow sufficient time for clean up afterward. Too much or too little pencil rubbing affects the quality of the fingerprint images. Students need a bit of practice to discover the right amount of graphite needed. If you feel fingerprinting may raise privacy issues in your school, collect and destroy all index cards when the activity is finished.

Overview

Read the overview aloud to your students. The goal is to create an atmosphere of curiosity and inquiry. Fingerprints are a fascinating area for study!

WHAT TO DO

Monitor student research teams as they complete each step.

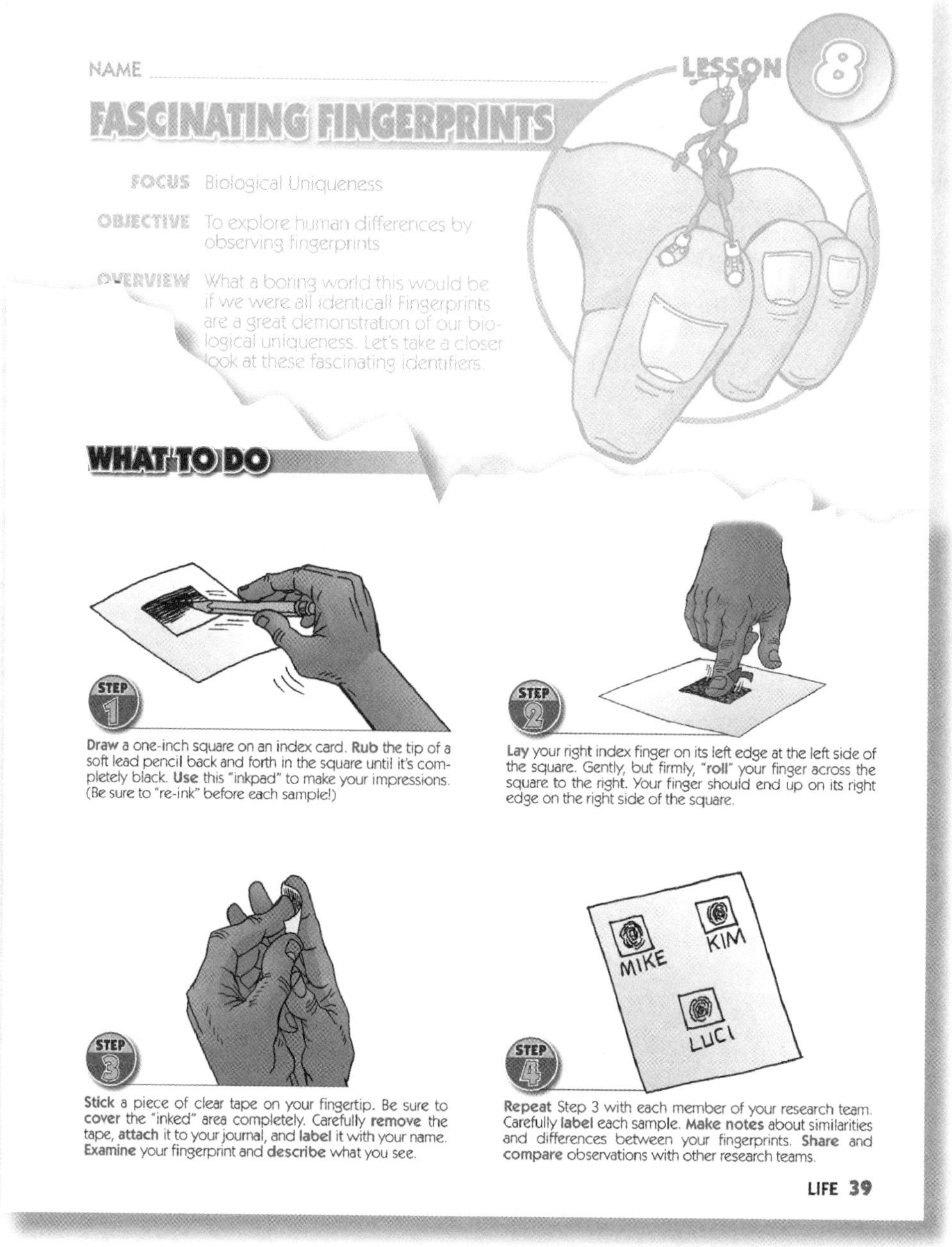

NAME ....

LESSON 8

FASCINATING FINGERPRINTS

FOCUS Biological Uniqueness

OBJECTIVE To explore human differences by observing fingerprints

OVERVIEW What a boring world this would be if we were all identical! Fingerprints are a great demonstration of our biological uniqueness. Let's take a closer look at these fascinating identifiers.

WHAT TO DO

STEP 1

Draw a one-inch square on an index card. **Rub** the tip of a soft lead pencil back and forth in the square until it's completely black. **Use** this "inkpad" to make your impressions. (Be sure to "re-ink" before each sample!)

STEP 2

Lay your right index finger on its left edge at the left side of the square. Gently, but firmly, "**roll**" your finger across the square to the right. Your finger should end up on its right edge on the right side of the square.

STEP 3

Stick a piece of clear tape on your fingertip. Be sure to **cover** the "inked" area completely. Carefully **remove** the tape, **attach** it to your journal, and **label** it with your name. **Examine** your fingerprint and **describe** what you see.

STEP 4

Repeat Step 3 with each member of your research team. Carefully **label** each sample. **Make notes** about similarities and differences between your fingerprints. **Share** and **compare** observations with other research teams.

LIFE 39

Teacher to Teacher

Fingerprints were used for signing documents as far back as the ancient Assyrians and Chinese. The first scientific classification of fingerprints was proposed by Purkinje in 1823, but fingerprinting didn't become common until the late 1800s, when Galton developed the ten finger system we still use today. Surprisingly, fingerprints are still considered more accurate than DNA, especially in criminal cases involving identical twins!

WHAT JUST HAPPENED?

When scientists make observations, they look for **patterns**. In the case of your fingerprints, the most easily observed patterns are the loop, the arch, and the whorl. A **loop** is a hump like an upside down U. An **arch** is a loop with a floor to it. A **whorl** is like a loop leaning to one side or the other.

Fingerprints are so unique that they can be used to accurately identify people. If you look at your fingertips closely under a magnifier, you can see little **ridges** (high points) separated by **valleys** (low spots). A fingerprint is actually an imprint of the "ink" (in this case the pencil lead) that stuck to the ridges.

MORE ABOUT BIOLOGICAL UNIQUENESS . . .

Your physical appearance is primarily the result of the chromosome combinations that you inherited from your parents at conception. Chromosomes are long chains of the chemical DNA (Deoxyribonucleic Acid). A human being must have 46 of these DNA chains to grow and develop normally.

The individual "links" on a chromosome chain are called genes. There are many genes on each chromosome. The study of how these genes transfer characteristics from one generation to the next is called **genetics.**

But even though you may share many characteristics with family members (your hair texture, your eye color, your physical build, etc.), the specific combination of your physical traits makes you unique. Every human being on Earth is different — all of us are special creations of God!

Fingerprints are a great example of this biological uniqueness. Simply put, no two people have the same fingerprints. Even though the imprints may have similarities, the loops, arches, whorls, and other patterns are different for every individual — even in the fingerprints of identical twins.

That's why fingerprints can play a very important role in the crime-solving science called **forensics**. Law enforcement agencies regularly rely on fingerprint files as a tool whenever they need to identify people.

For instance, the fingerprint files of the FBI (Federal Bureau of Investigation) contain over 250 million sets of fingerprint cards. If all these cards were placed on top of one another, they would make a stack over 31 miles high. (That's one reason why the government is spending millions of dollars to convert these paper cards to digital images that can be stored and researched on computers.)

DIGGING DEEPER:

Research and discuss the science of genetics and the Human Genome Project. How many genes do human beings have? What specific characteristics do they transmit? What genes are dangerous to those who inherit them? What genes are most helpful?

WHAT WE LEARNED:

1. **Describe the difference between a ridge and a valley. Which shows up as the dark lines in an imprint?**

a) a ridge is a high point; a valley is a low point

b) the ridges

2. **Explain the difference between a loop, an arch, and a whorl. Which pattern does your fingerprint show?**

a) loop is an upside down U; arch is a loop with a floor; whorl is a loop leaning to one side

b) answers will vary, including "none of these"

3. **How do fingerprints demonstrate "biological uniqueness"? How is this helpful to law enforcement agencies and forensic scientists?**

a) no two people have the same fingerprints

b) it can help them identify an individual criminal or victim

What Happened

Review the section with students. Emphasize bold-face words that identify key concepts and introduce new vocabulary.

When scientists make observations, they look for ***patterns****. In the case of your fingerprints, the most easily observed patterns are the loop, the arch, and the whorl. A* ***loop*** *is a hump like an upside down U. An* ***arch*** *is a loop with a floor to it. A* ***whorl*** *is like a loop leaning to one side or the other.*

Fingerprints *are so unique that they can be used to accurately identify people. If you look at your fingertips closely under a magnifier, you can see little* ***ridges*** *(high points) separated by* ***valleys*** *(low spots). A fingerprint is actually an imprint of the "ink" (in this case the pencil lead) that stuck to the ridges.*

More About . . .

Have students read this section as you would a traditional science text — or use cooperative learning techniques to allow students the opportunity to work on the material collaboratively.

Digging Deeper

(Optional) Challenge teams to reseach and discuss practical applications of the lesson concepts. Encourage them to share their findings with the rest of the class.

What We Learned

Answers will vary. Suggested responses are shown at left.

Conclusion

Read this section aloud to the class to summarize the concepts learned in this activity.

Food for Thought

Read the Scripture aloud to the class. Discuss how every individual is unique and how God created each of us for a special purpose. Talk about ways of getting to know God better.

Science Journal

If time permits, have a general class discussion about students' journal entries. Share and compare observations. Be sure to emphasize that "trial and error" is a valuable part of scientific inquiry!

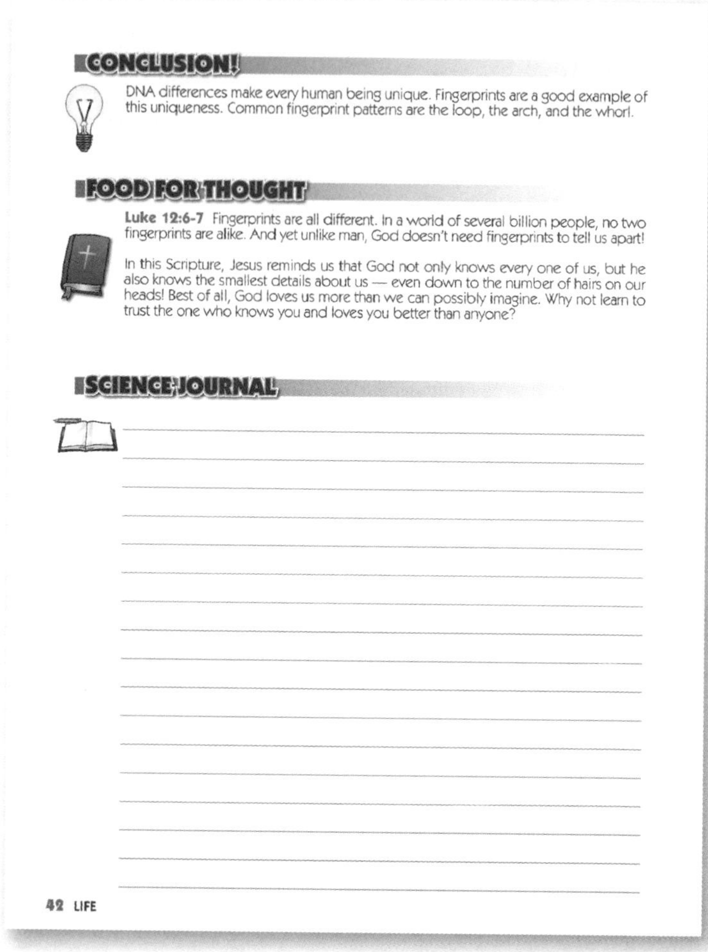
CONCLUSION!

DNA differences make every human being unique. Fingerprints are a good example of this uniqueness. Common fingerprint patterns are the loop, the arch, and the whorl.

FOOD FOR THOUGHT

Luke 12:6-7 Fingerprints are all different. In a world of several billion people, no two fingerprints are alike. And yet unlike man, God doesn't need fingerprints to tell us apart!

In this Scripture, Jesus reminds us that God not only knows every one of us, but he also knows the smallest details about us — even down to the number of hairs on our heads! Best of all, God loves us more than we can possibly imagine. Why not learn to trust the one who knows you and loves you better than anyone?

SCIENCE JOURNAL

42 LIFE

Extended Teaching

1. Use a copy machine to greatly enlarge your fingerprint. Place this on a transparency and project it for the class to see. Using terms from this lesson, discuss the characteristics of this print.

2. Have students determine which fingerprint patterns are the most and least common among their classmates. List the number of each kind. Research the names of the least common patterns.

3. Have students research identical twins. Find out why fingerprints are an even more accurate method for telling the difference between twins than DNA!

4. Invite a detective or a forensic expert to visit your classroom. Discuss the role that biological uniqueness plays in helping them solve crimes.

5. Have students research the term "electronic fingerprints." How does this relate to computer crime and the field of forensics? Compare these unique signatures that computers leave to human fingerprints.

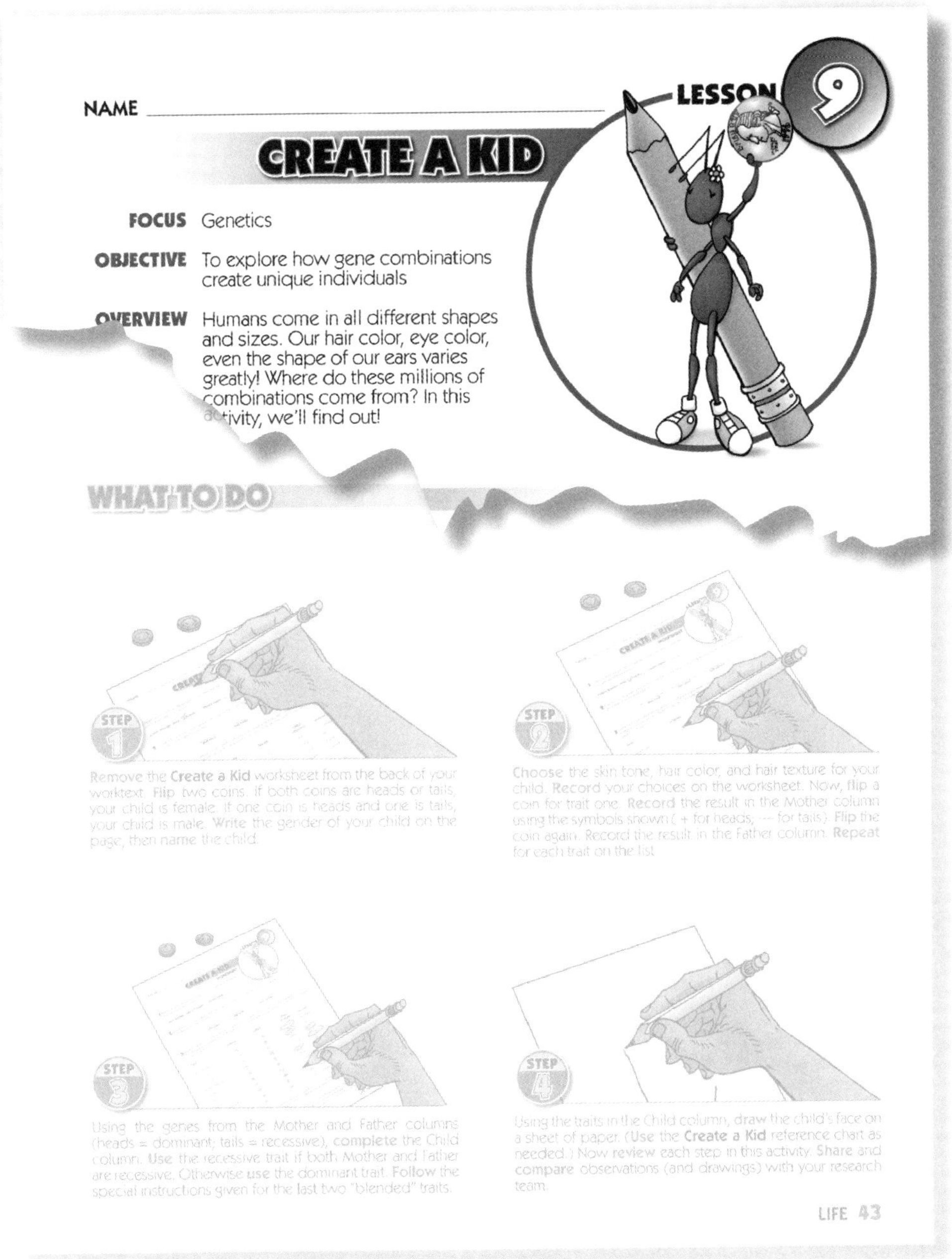
NAME

LESSON 9

CREATE A KID

FOCUS Genetics

OBJECTIVE To explore how gene combinations create unique individuals

OVERVIEW Humans come in all different shapes and sizes. Our hair color, eye color, even the shape of our ears varies greatly! Where do these millions of combinations come from? In this activity, we'll find out!

WHAT TO DO

STEP 1
Remove the **Create a Kid** worksheet from the back of your worktext. **Flip** two coins. If both coins are heads or tails, your child is female. If one coin is heads and one is tails, your child is male. **Write** the gender of your child on the page, then name the child.

STEP 2
Choose the skin tone, hair color, and hair texture for your child. **Record** your choices on the worksheet. Now, flip a coin for trait one. **Record** the result in the Mother column using the symbols shown (+ for heads, — for tails). **Flip** the coin again. Record the result in the Father column. **Repeat** for each trait on the list.

STEP 3
Using the genes from the Mother and Father columns (heads = dominant; tails = recessive), **complete** the Child column. **Use** the recessive trait if both Mother and Father are recessive. Otherwise **use** the dominant trait. **Follow** the special instructions given for the last two "blended" traits.

STEP 4
Using the traits in the Child column, **draw** the child's face on a sheet of paper. (**Use** the **Create a Kid** reference chart as needed.) Now **review** each step in this activity. **Share** and **compare** observations (and drawings) with your research team.

LIFE 43

Category

Life Science

Focus

Genetics

Objective

To explore how gene combinations create unique individuals

National Standards

A1, A2, B1, C1, C2, C5, F1, F4, G1, G2

Materials Needed

Create A Kid worksheet *(student worktext, p. 169)*
Create A Kid reference sheet *(student worktext, p. 171)*
chart
coins - 2
sheet of paper (blank)

Safety Concerns

none

Additional Comments

Human genomes are extremely complicated. Make sure students aren't left with the idea that the design process is this simple or random. This simple activity is only designed to show why people look different. It doesn't begin to show the millions of possible gene combinations!

Overview

Read the overview aloud to your students. The goal is to create an atmosphere of curiosity and inquiry.

WHAT TO DO

Monitor student research teams as they complete each step.

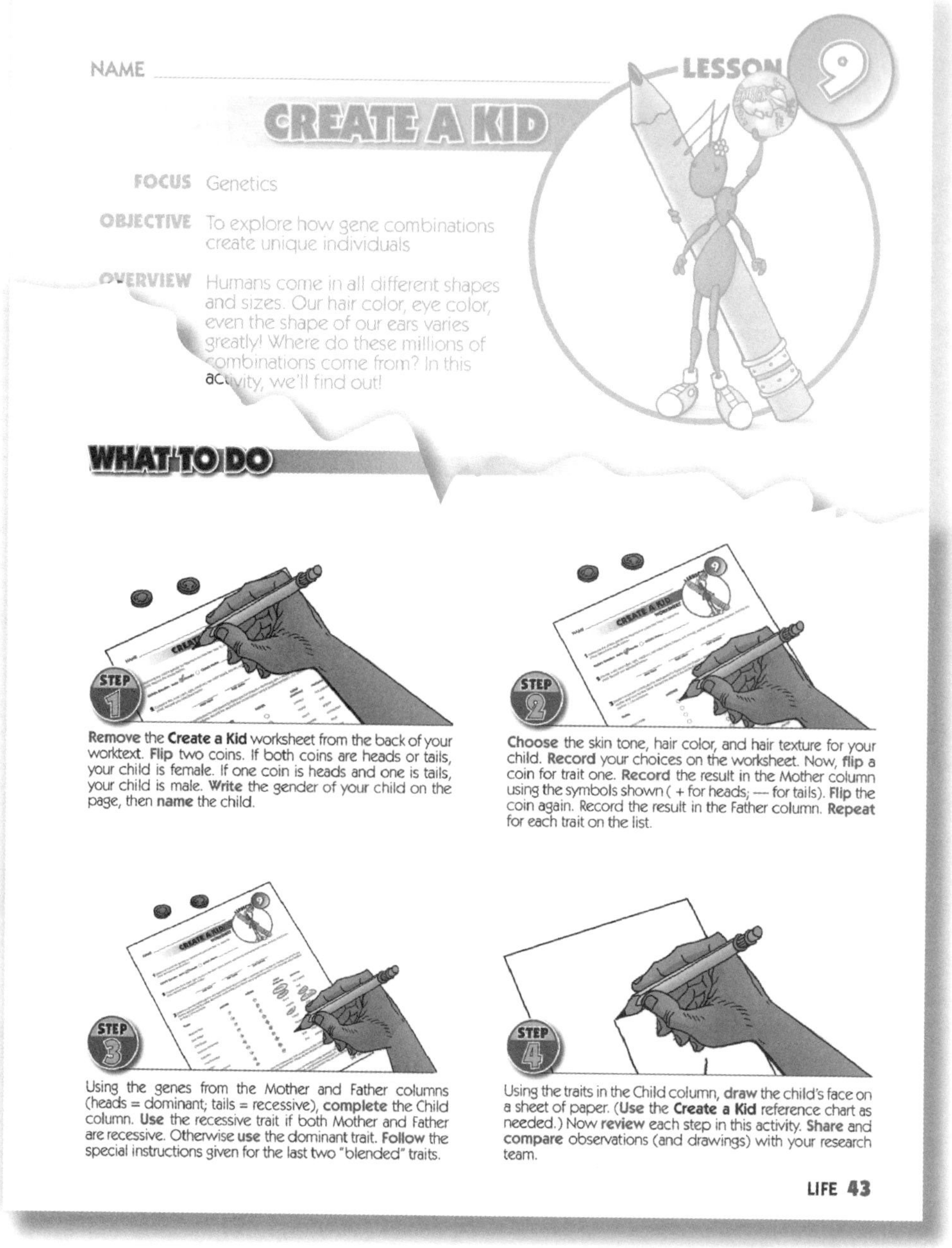

NAME

LESSON 9

CREATE A KID

FOCUS Genetics

OBJECTIVE To explore how gene combinations create unique individuals

OVERVIEW Humans come in all different shapes and sizes. Our hair color, eye color, even the shape of our ears varies greatly! Where do these millions of combinations come from? In this activity, we'll find out!

WHAT TO DO

STEP 1 **Remove** the **Create a Kid** worksheet from the back of your worktext. **Flip** two coins. If both coins are heads or tails, your child is female. If one coin is heads and one is tails, your child is male. **Write** the gender of your child on the page, then **name** the child.

STEP 2 **Choose** the skin tone, hair color, and hair texture for your child. **Record** your choices on the worksheet. Now, **flip** a coin for trait one. **Record** the result in the Mother column using the symbols shown (+ for heads; — for tails). **Flip** the coin again. Record the result in the Father column. **Repeat** for each trait on the list.

STEP 3 Using the genes from the Mother and Father columns (heads = dominant; tails = recessive), **complete** the Child column. **Use** the recessive trait if both Mother and Father are recessive. Otherwise **use** the dominant trait. **Follow** the special instructions given for the last two "blended" traits.

STEP 4 Using the traits in the Child column, **draw** the child's face on a sheet of paper. (**Use** the **Create a Kid** reference chart as needed.) Now **review** each step in this activity. **Share** and **compare** observations (and drawings) with your research team.

LIFE 43

Teacher to Teacher

Scientists once thought there were hundreds of thousands of human genes. But the Human Genome Project (begun in 1990 and completed in 2003) has found approximately 30,000. In the process, they've determined the sequences of roughly three billion chemical base pairs that make up human DNA, stored that information in databases, and improved tools for data analysis. The project has also created a multibillion-dollar biotechnology industry and is fostering development of new medical applications.

WHAT JUST HAPPENED?

Obviously we don't get our looks by flipping a coin, but this activity helps us see how **genes** combine to create a completely unique individual! The actual process is much more complex, of course. As we've seen in our other lessons, God created the marvelous chemical **DNA** which is composed of long strings of information known as **chromosomes.** Humans have 46 chromosomes (23 from each parent) and these play the major role in determining what a child will look like.

Some traits are **dominant**. They appear no matter what other gene is around. Other traits are **recessive**. These show up only when there's no dominant gene in the mix. And some genetic traits lurk quietly in the background for a generation or two, causing some of us to look more like our grandparents than our parents! What an interesting mix God created. Think how boring it would be if we all looked the same.

MORE ABOUT GENETICS . . .

No discussion of genetics would be complete without a look at the work of **Gregor Mendel**, the man often called the "father of modern genetics". Mendel's experiments over 150 years ago still provide the foundation for today's genetic research.

Mendel was born in Austria (a country in central Europe) in 1822. When he turned 21, he joined a monastery famous for philosophy and natural sciences. He was sent to the University of Vienna to study, and 10 years later he returned to the monastery as a teacher. Not long after this, Mendel began to study variations in plants in the monastery's garden. He soon focused on pea plants, and over the years he cultivated and tested almost 30,000 individual plants!

These pea plants had many distinct characteristics (tall, short, smooth, wrinkly, etc.). Mendel isolated individual plants, controlling the parentage of each generation. He quickly discovered that tall plants crossed with short plants do not make medium plants. About 25% of the offspring were short and 75% were tall. He concluded that some genes were recessive and some were dominant. Further experiments yielded two generalizations that later became known as Mendel's **Laws of Inheritance**.

Here's an example: Because you come from two parents, each parent provides half the genes for any given trait. When both genes are dominant (AA), your body expresses that trait. Even if one gene is recessive (Aa), the dominant characteristic will still be expressed . . . but the recessive gene may be passed to a future generation.

Recessive traits can sneak through for years until the right combination occurs. Then if both parents pass along a recessive gene (aa), the recessive trait suddenly reappears. That's why even if your parents both have black hair (dominant), your new baby sister might have the same red hair (recessive) that your great, great grandmother had!

DIGGING DEEPER:

Research and discuss dominant and recessive genes in human beings. Make a list of some of the most common characteristics caused by dominant or recessive genes. Even something as simple as whether a person's earlobes are free-hanging (AA, Aa) or attached (aa) is controlled by genetic combinations!

44 LIFE

WHAT WE LEARNED:

1. Describe the four simple dominant/recessive combinations and their results. (example: mother dominant + father dominant = child dominant)

mother (+) and father (+) = child (+)
mother (+) and father (-) = child (+)
mother (-) and father (+) = child (+)
mother (-) and father (-) = child (-)

2. Compare your child with the children of your team members. How were they similar? How were they different?

answers will vary but should reflect the characteristics discussed in this lesson

3. Based on what you've learned, could you predict which parent a child would more likely resemble if you knew each parent's dominant and recessive genes? Explain your answer.

a) yes, at least to some degree

b) "thick nose" father and "thin nose" mother will probably have "thick nose" child. But gene combinations are too complex to be sure! (That's why question said "likely"!)

LIFE 45

What Happened

Review the section with students. Emphasize bold-face words that identify key concepts and introduce new vocabulary.

*Obviously we don't get our looks by flipping a coin, but this activity helps us see how **genes** combine to create a completely unique individual! The actual process is much more complex, of course. As we've seen in our other lessons, God created the marvelous chemical **DNA** which is composed of long strings of information known as **chromosomes**. Humans have 46 chromosomes (23 from each parent) and these play the major role in determining what a child will look like.*

*Some traits are **dominant**. They appear no matter what other gene is around. Other traits are **recessive**. These show up only when there's no dominant gene in the mix. And some genetic traits lurk quietly in the background for a generation or two, causing some of us to look more like our grandparents than our parents! What an interesting mix God created. Think how boring it would be if we all looked the same.*

More About . . .

Have students read this section as you would a traditional science text — or use cooperative learning techniques to allow students the opportunity to work on the material collaboratively.

Digging Deeper

(Optional) Challenge teams to reseach and discuss practical applications of the lesson concepts. Encourage them to share their findings with the rest of the class.

What We Learned

Answers will vary. Suggested responses are shown at left.

Conclusion

Read this section aloud to the class to summarize the concepts learned in this activity.

Food for Thought

Read the Scripture aloud to the class. God gives each of us unique talents. Discuss this concept with students. For example, hospitality is as much a talent as playing an instrument.

Science Journal

If time permits, have a general class discussion about students' journal entries. Share and compare observations. Be sure to emphasize that "trial and error" is a valuable part of scientific inquiry!

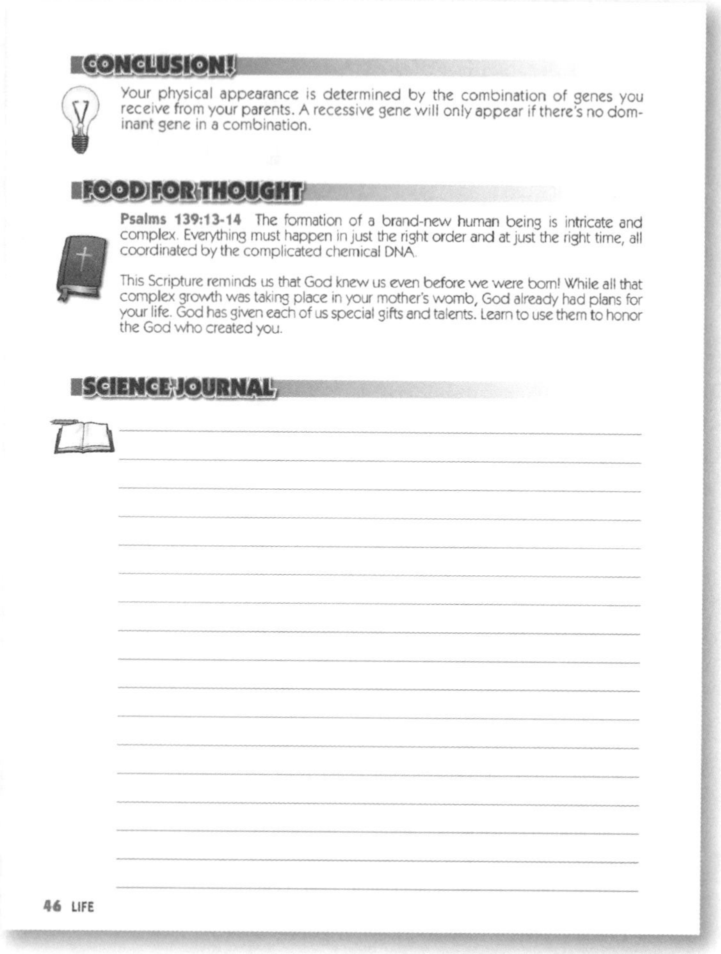

CONCLUSION!

Your physical appearance is determined by the combination of genes you receive from your parents. A recessive gene will only appear if there's no dominant gene in a combination.

FOOD FOR THOUGHT

Psalms 139:13-14 The formation of a brand-new human being is intricate and complex. Everything must happen in just the right order and at just the right time, all coordinated by the complicated chemical DNA.

This Scripture reminds us that God knew us even before we were born! While all that complex growth was taking place in your mother's womb, God already had plans for your life. God has given each of us special gifts and talents. Learn to use them to honor the God who created you.

SCIENCE JOURNAL

46 LIFE

Extended Teaching

1. Have students visit genetic research sites on the Internet. Look for new crops, livestock improvements, disease treatments, etc. Have students write reports or make posters to share their findings.

2. A key person in the history of genetics was a monk named Gregor Mendel. Have students research his experiments with pea plants. Discribe how his research contributed to modern genetics.

3. Genetic engineering has generated a huge amount of press coverage, both positive and negative. Have students research this controversy and share their findings with the class.

4. Have students visit the March of Dimes website (www.modimes.org). Find out how birth defects can be reduced. What kind of research is going on?

5. Challenge students to make bulletin boards on what they've learned about genetics. Topics could include chromosome combinations, genome research, genetic engineering, dominant/recessive traits, etc.

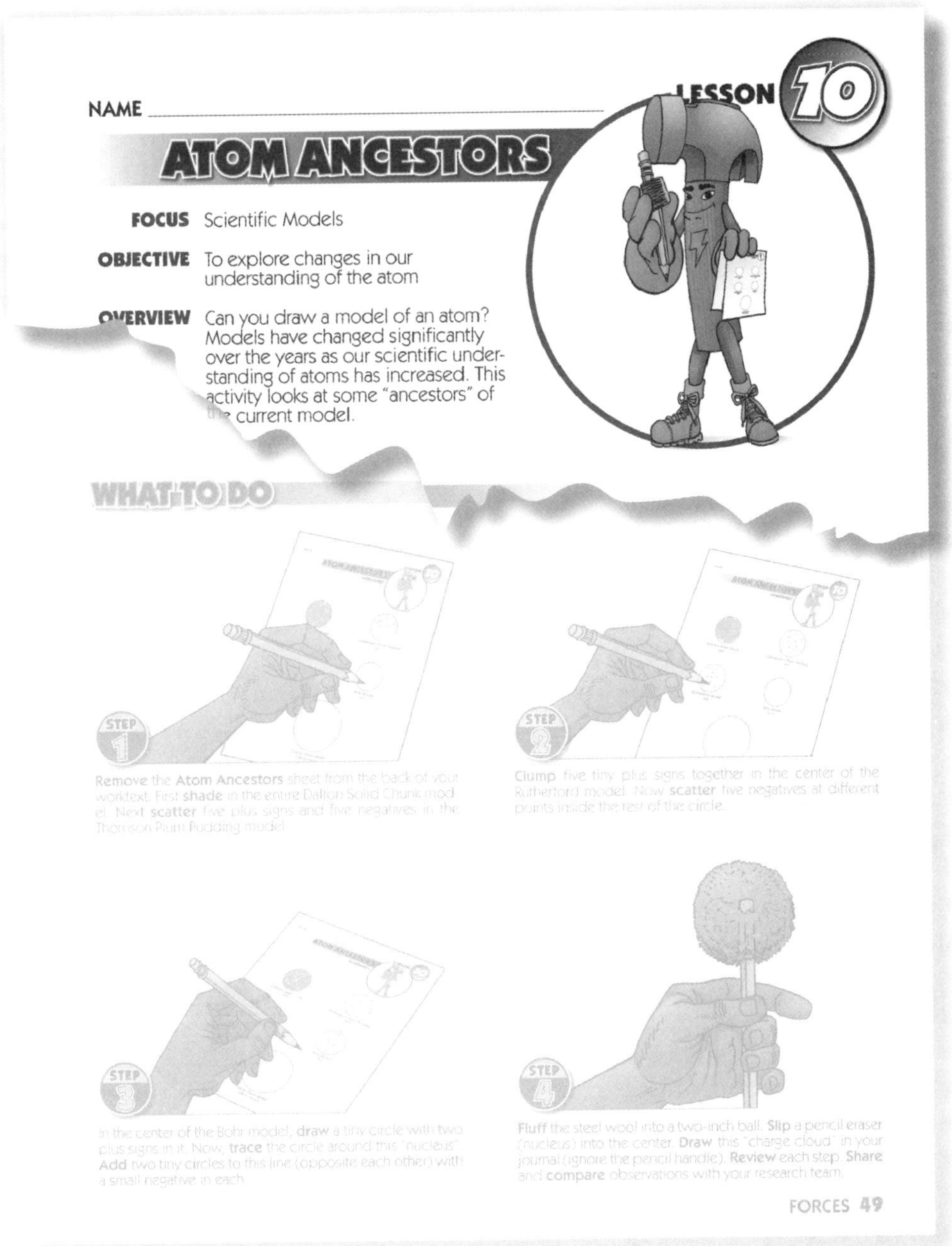

NAME ______________________

LESSON 10

ATOM ANCESTORS

FOCUS Scientific Models

OBJECTIVE To explore changes in our understanding of the atom

OVERVIEW Can you draw a model of an atom? Models have changed significantly over the years as our scientific understanding of atoms has increased. This activity looks at some "ancestors" of the current model.

WHAT TO DO

STEP 1 **Remove** the **Atom Ancestors** sheet from the back of your worktext. First **shade** in the entire Dalton Solid Chunk model. Next **scatter** five plus signs and five negatives in the Thomson Plum Pudding model.

STEP 2 **Clump** five tiny plus signs together in the center of the Rutherford model. Now **scatter** five negatives at different points inside the rest of the circle.

STEP 3 In the center of the Bohr model, **draw** a tiny circle with two plus signs in it. Now, **trace** the circle around this "nucleus". **Add** two tiny circles to this line (opposite each other) with a small negative in each.

STEP 4 **Fluff** the steel wool into a two-inch ball. **Slip** a pencil eraser (nucleus) into the center. **Draw** this "charge cloud" in your journal (ignore the pencil handle). **Review** each step. **Share** and **compare** observations with your research team.

FORCES 49

Category

Physical Science
Forces

Focus

Scientific Models

Objective

To explore changes in our understanding of the atom

National Standards

A1, A2, B1, B2, E1, E2, F5, G1, G2

Materials Needed

Atom Ancestors worksheet *(student worktext, p.173)*
steel wool
pencil (with eraser)

Safety Concerns

none

Additional Comments

Focus on the idea that concepts evolve as our scientific knowledge increases.

Overview

Read the overview aloud to your students. The goal is to create an atmosphere of curiosity and inquiry.

WHAT TO DO

Monitor student research teams as they complete each step.

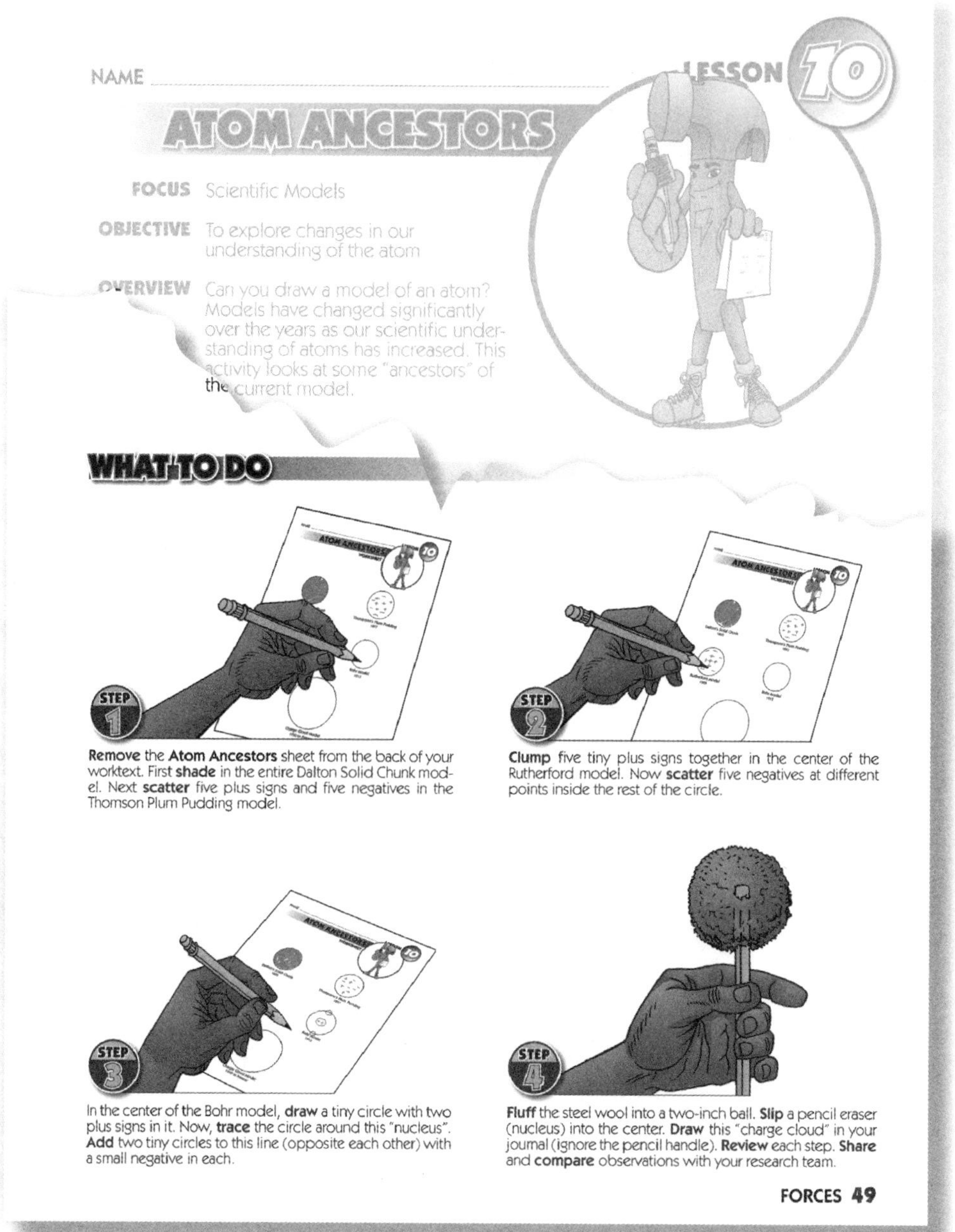

NAME

LESSON 10

ATOM ANCESTORS

FOCUS Scientific Models

OBJECTIVE To explore changes in our understanding of the atom

OVERVIEW Can you draw a model of an atom? Models have changed significantly over the years as our scientific understanding of atoms has increased. This activity looks at some "ancestors" of the current model.

WHAT TO DO

STEP 1 **Remove** the **Atom Ancestors** sheet from the back of your worktext. First **shade** in the entire Dalton Solid Chunk model. Next **scatter** five plus signs and five negatives in the Thomson Plum Pudding model.

STEP 2 **Clump** five tiny plus signs together in the center of the Rutherford model. Now **scatter** five negatives at different points inside the rest of the circle.

STEP 3 In the center of the Bohr model, **draw** a tiny circle with two plus signs in it. Now, **trace** the circle around this "nucleus". **Add** two tiny circles to this line (opposite each other) with a small negative in each.

STEP 4 **Fluff** the steel wool into a two-inch ball. **Slip** a pencil eraser (nucleus) into the center. **Draw** this "charge cloud" in your journal (ignore the pencil handle). **Review** each step. **Share** and **compare** observations with your research team.

FORCES 49

Teacher to Teacher

While the Charge Cloud model reflects the most recent thinking about atoms, scientists continue to study and explore this fascinating area. For instance, we now know that electrons in the "cloud" don't just whiz around randomly. They are arranged in "energy levels" similar to the rungs on a ladder.

What Just Happened?

These **models** represent decades of increased scientific understanding. John Dalton thought **atoms** were solid **particles**. He named them "atomos" after the Greek word for "indivisible". When **positive/negative** characteristics were discovered, J. J. Thomson created the Plum Pudding model. Then in the 1940s, scientists proved atoms are not indivisible. **Atomic energy** (and nuclear bombs) is based on "splitting" atoms.

Later, Ernest Rutherford proved atoms have a positive-charged center, so he arranged **electrons** at random around this center. Neils Bohr created the planetary model, with electrons in neat little orbits called **energy levels**. The most recent atom model, the **charge cloud**, shows a dense positive **nucleus** surrounded by a fuzzy negative "cloud". Energy levels don't follow neat little orbits, but spin around in dozens of directions! As scientific knowledge continues to advance, even more accurate models of the atom may emerge.

More About Scientific Models . . .

It's important to remember that a scientific model is often simply an idea that allows us to better understand how some part of our world works.

Take an atom model, for instance. Even the most recent version is simply a *representation* of what scientists think is happening at the molecular level. It's not an actual picture of protons and neutrons surrounded by electrons, nor is it a larger version of a physical structure that you could ever hold in your hand.

An atom model is simply the *idea* that particles such as protons, neutrons, and electrons exist, and that they tend to behave in certain ways. Since human beings can't touch or see them in our physical world (like we can a baseball or a book), scientists create models to explain behaviors they have observed, and to make predictions about what behaviors might be observed in the future.

In addition, a model can only reflect the knowledge that scientists have at the time they make it. (We can see this in the progression from John Dalton's work to the "charge cloud" model.) As better information becomes available, better models are made to help us increase our understanding of how things work.

The **Periodic Table** is another example of this. Although the concept of organizing the elements began with Laviosier in the 1700s, our modern Periodic Table dates back to Mendeleyev in 1869. Harry Hubbard first published the familiar "standardized" Table in 1924, and that's what you find in most chemistry textbooks today. However, a new version of the "Tables" was developed by Roy Alexander in the mid 1990s. His three-dimensional model (now known as the Alexander Arrangement) more clearly defines the complex interrelationships between the elements.

Digging Deeper:

Research and discuss the Alexander Arrangement and similar scientific models that have evolved over time. Why do models change over time? What things usually lead to a change in a model? How do scientific models help us better understand the way our world works?

50 FORCES

What We Learned:

1 **Describe the Thomson, Rutherford, and Bohr models of the atom. What later discoveries changed each of these models?**

a) Thompson: "plum pudding" of mixed positive/negative charges; Rutherford: atoms have positive centers; Bohr: the planetary model.

b) Thompson: the discovery that atoms are not indivisible; Rutherford/Bohr: acceptance of the charge cloud model

2 **Describe the Charge Cloud model of the atom. How is it similar to earlier models? How is it different?**

a) dense positive nucleus surrounded by fuzzy negative cloud

b) answers will vary depending on what part of earlier models is discussed

3 **Based on what you've learned, why do models change over time? How do these changes enhance scientific understanding?**

a) models change as we learn more

b) more accurate models equal better understanding

FORCES **51**

What Happened

Review the section with students. Emphasize bold-face words that identify key concepts and introduce new vocabulary.

*These **models** represent decades of increased scientific understanding. John Dalton thought **atoms** were solid **particles**. He named them "atomos" after the Greek word for "indivisible." When **positive/negative** characteristics were discovered, J. J. Thomson created the plum pudding model. Then in the 1940s, scientists proved atoms are not indivisible. **Atomic energy** (and nuclear bombs) is based on "splitting" atoms.*

*Later, Ernest Rutherford proved atoms have a positive-charged center, so he arranged **electrons** at random around this center. Neils Bohr created the planetary model, with electrons in neat little orbits called **energy levels**. The most recent atom model, the **charge cloud**, shows a dense positive **nucleus** surrounded by a fuzzy negative "cloud". Energy levels don't follow neat little orbits, but spin around in dozens of directions! As scientific knowledge continues to advance, even more accurate models of the atom may emerge.*

More About . . .

Have students read this section as you would a traditional science text — or use cooperative learning techniques to allow students the opportunity to work on the material collaboratively.

Digging Deeper

(Optional) Challenge teams to reseach and discuss practical applications of the lesson concepts. Encourage them to share their findings with the rest of the class.

What We Learned

Answers will vary. Suggested responses are shown at left.

Conclusion

Read this section aloud to the class to summarize the concepts learned in this activity.

Food for Thought

Read the Scripture aloud to the class. Talk about the importance of continued growth in our spiritual lives. Discuss ways we can increase our personal time with God.

Science Journal

If time permits, have a general class discussion about notes and drawings various students added to their journal pages. Discuss correct and incorrect predictions, and remind students that this "trial and error" process is part of the scientific process.

CONCLUSION!

Scientists use models to enhance understanding. These models change over time to reflect new discoveries.

FOOD FOR THOUGHT

2 Peter 3:18 The first scientists who attempted to describe the atom used all the information at their disposal. As the years went by and scientists continued to study, they learned more and more. Over time, the atom model became more accurate and useful.

Like those scientists, God's children must continue to study and learn. The more time we spend with God, learning to trust in him, the more we will grow in the grace and knowledge of our Lord.

SCIENCE JOURNAL

52 FORCES

Extended Teaching

1. Have each team research one of the scientists in this lesson. Challenge teams to create a poster describing this scientist and his work.

2. Take a field trip to a hospital x-ray lab. Find out how this type of radiation is used to locate problems inside the human body. Have students write a paragraph about one thing they learn.

3. Invite a cancer therapist to visit your classroom. Find out how radiation is used in health care. Have students write a paragraph about one thing they learn.

4. Challenge teams to make three-dimensional historical models of atoms using clay, pipe cleaners, and similar materials. Have each team describe their model to the class.

5. Have teams research the Atomic Energy Commission's website. Challenge them to discover facts about atoms, radiation, and reactors. Make a bulletin board to display their findings.

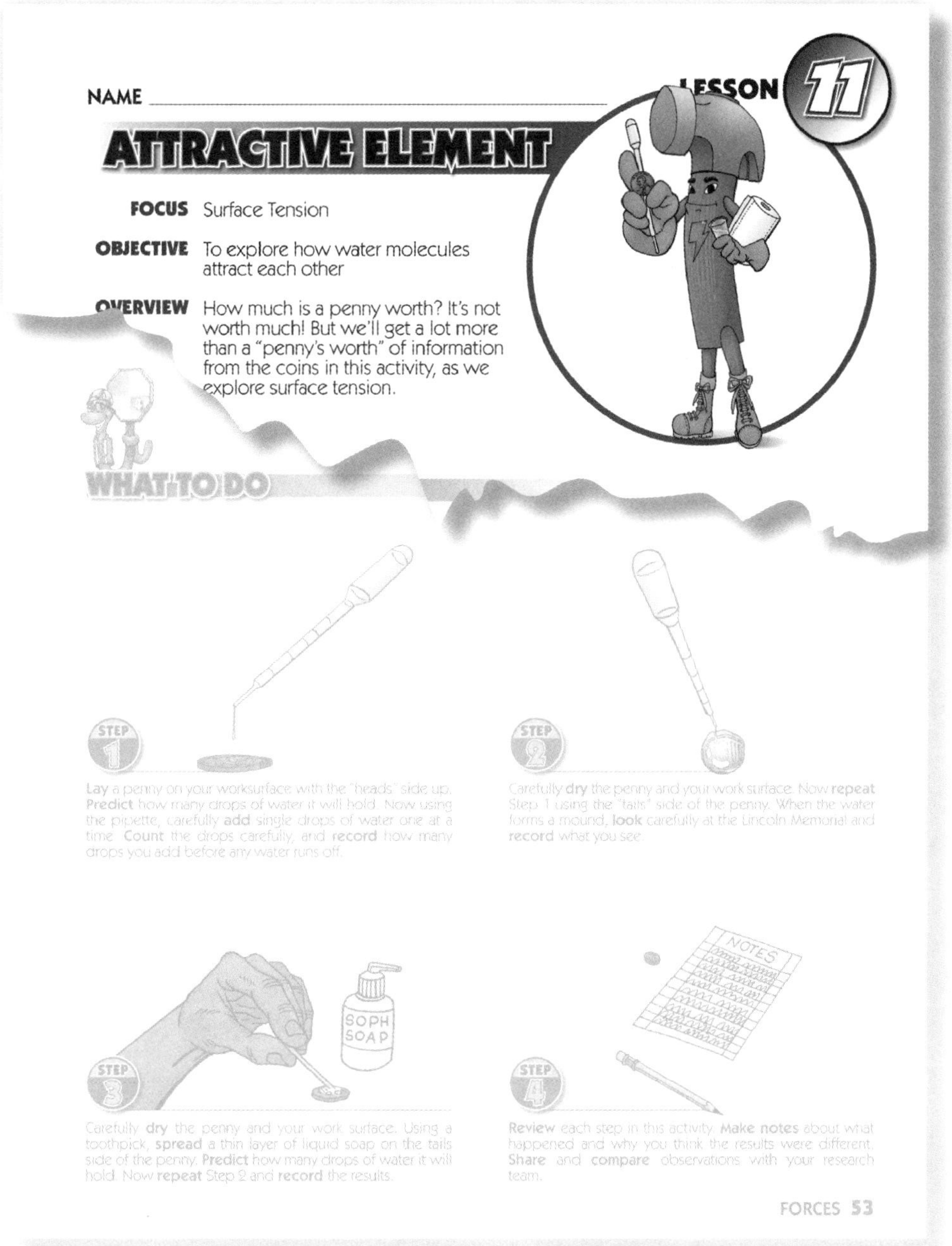
NAME ____________________ LESSON 11

ATTRACTIVE ELEMENT

FOCUS Surface Tension

OBJECTIVE To explore how water molecules attract each other

OVERVIEW How much is a penny worth? It's not worth much! But we'll get a lot more than a "penny's worth" of information from the coins in this activity, as we explore surface tension.

WHAT TO DO

STEP 1 **Lay** a penny on your worksurface with the "heads" side up. **Predict** how many drops of water it will hold. Now using the pipette, carefully **add** single drops of water one at a time. **Count** the drops carefully, and **record** how many drops you add before any water runs off.

STEP 2 Carefully **dry** the penny and your work surface. Now **repeat** Step 1 using the "tails" side of the penny. When the water forms a mound, **look** carefully at the Lincoln Memorial and **record** what you see.

STEP 3 Carefully **dry** the penny and your work surface. Using a toothpick, **spread** a thin layer of liquid soap on the tails side of the penny. **Predict** how many drops of water it will hold. Now **repeat** Step 2 and **record** the results.

STEP 4 **Review** each step in this activity. **Make notes** about what happened and why you think the results were different. **Share** and **compare** observations with your research team.

FORCES 53

Category

Physical Science
Forces

Focus

Surface Tension

Objective

To explore how water molecules attract each other

National Standards

A1, A2, B1, B2, G1, G2

Materials Needed

penny
pipette
toothpick
water
liquid soap
paper towels

Safety Concerns

4. Slipping
There is a potential for spills. Remind students to exercise caution with water.

Additional Comments

This activity provides a good opportunity to work on students' predicting skills. Students may be surprised at how many drops of water can be "piled" onto a coin.

Overview

Read the overview aloud to your students. The goal is to create an atmosphere of curiosity and inquiry.

WHAT TO DO

Monitor student research teams as they complete each step.

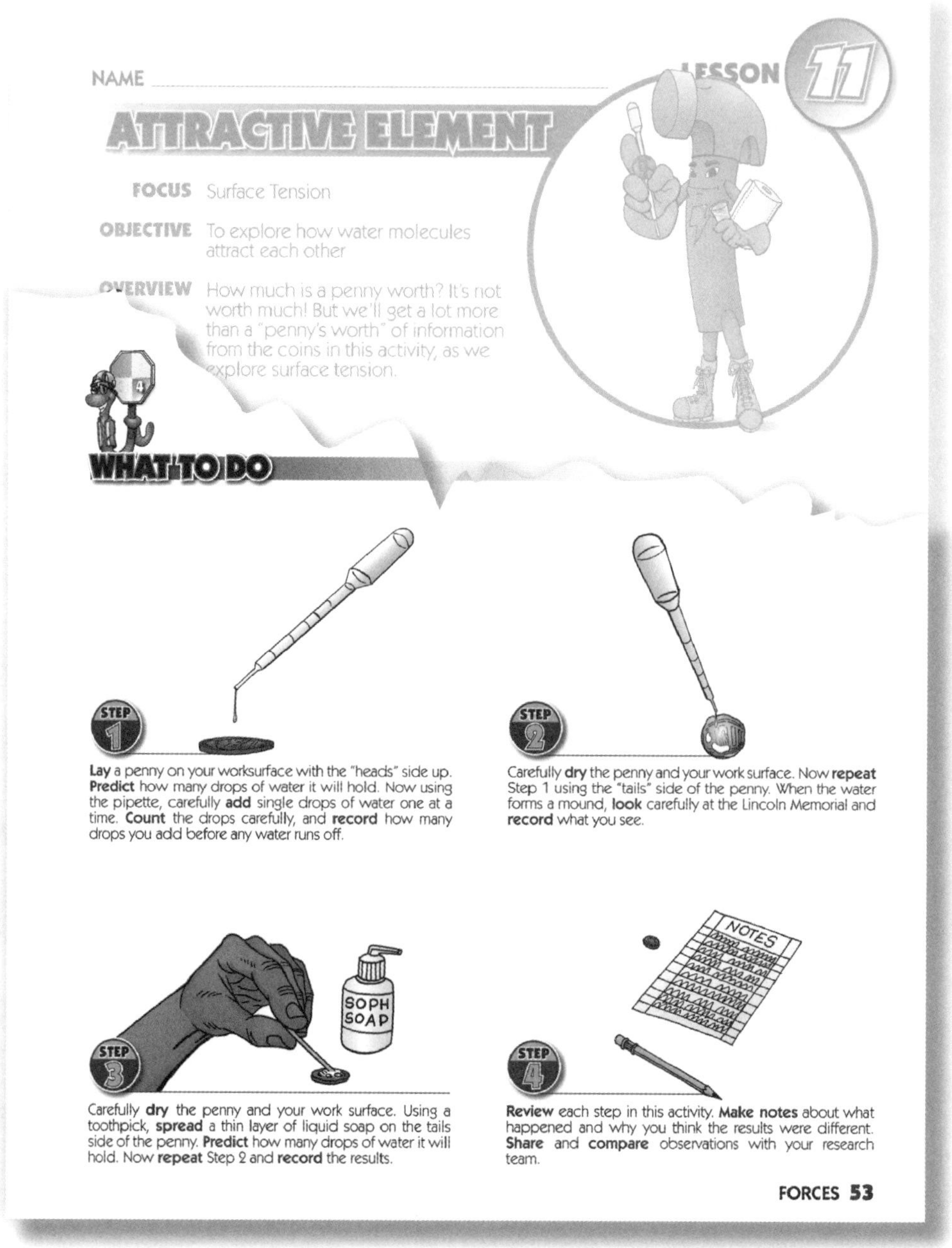

NAME

LESSON 11

ATTRACTIVE ELEMENT

FOCUS Surface Tension

OBJECTIVE To explore how water molecules attract each other

OVERVIEW How much is a penny worth? It's not worth much! But we'll get a lot more than a "penny's worth" of information from the coins in this activity, as we explore surface tension.

WHAT TO DO

STEP 1 **Lay** a penny on your worksurface with the "heads" side up. **Predict** how many drops of water it will hold. Now using the pipette, carefully **add** single drops of water one at a time. **Count** the drops carefully, and **record** how many drops you add before any water runs off.

STEP 2 Carefully **dry** the penny and your work surface. Now **repeat** Step 1 using the "tails" side of the penny. When the water forms a mound, **look** carefully at the Lincoln Memorial and **record** what you see.

STEP 3 Carefully **dry** the penny and your work surface. Using a toothpick, **spread** a thin layer of liquid soap on the tails side of the penny. **Predict** how many drops of water it will hold. Now **repeat** Step 2 and **record** the results.

STEP 4 **Review** each step in this activity. **Make notes** about what happened and why you think the results were different. **Share** and **compare** observations with your research team.

FORCES **53**

Teacher to Teacher

The bond demonstrated in this activity is known as a hydrogen bond. In a hydrogen bond, hydrogen is attracted to neighboring oxygen. Hydrogen bonds hold bunches of water molecules together, but also important cell chemicals like DNA. Surfactants (like soap and detergents) break hydrogen bonds. This was apparent in Step 3, when the penny couldn't hold as much water as before!

WHAT JUST HAPPENED?

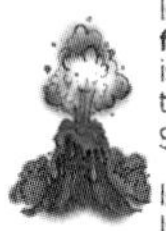

In Step 1 and Step 2, you were able to "pile" the water due to a property called **surface tension**. Surface tension is caused by **water molecules** sticking together. Water is formed from **hydrogen** and **oxygen**. The hydrogen in one water molecule is attracted to the oxygen in another water molecule. This happens over and over (like a group of people grasping hands), creating a **bonding** effect called surface tension.

In an interesting side-effect, the round surface of the water pile formed a **convex lens**. In Step 2, it **magnified** the surface of the penny so you see President Lincoln sitting in his chair!

Beginning in Step 3, however, the water wouldn't pile anymore since the detergent you added interfered with the water molecules' ability to bond together. (That's what makes detergent useful for cleaning!)

MORE ABOUT SURFACE TENSION . . .

A penny may not buy much these days, but in this case it got you a lot of information about surface tension!

Scientists call the bond demonstrated in this activity a **hydrogen bond**. In a hydrogen bond, a hydrogen atom is attracted to another atom. This is usually an atom of oxygen, nitrogen, or fluorine.

As you saw in Step 1, a hydrogen bond can hold thousands of water molecules together, causing the water to pile up in a heap. This is why steam beads up on the bathroom mirror, why rain beads up on a car's windshield, and why water beads up on the hood of a freshly-waxed car. Hydrogen bonds can also affect the shape of raindrops as they fall.

The ability of hydrogen to bond with other atoms also impacts important cell chemicals like DNA. Without hydrogen bonds, genetics as we know it would not exist. Our internal chemistry would no longer function properly and we would die.

Of course, sometimes breaking a hydrogen bond is helpful. As you discovered in Step 3, there are certain materials (like soaps or detergents) that can break hydrogen bonds. Scientists call these materials "**surfactants**".

When a surfactant breaks water's hydrogen bonds, it increases the water's ability to penetrate a material. That's why we use soap to clean our hands or wash the dishes. It helps water penetrate and soften the dirt, and then washes it away.

DIGGING DEEPER:

Research and discuss why water is so important to human survival. What are some of the ways we use water every day? What properties of water make it useful in industry, agriculture, and our homes?

WHAT WE LEARNED:

1 **Describe surface tension. Explain how water's composition makes surface tension possible.**

a) surface tension is caused by water molecules sticking together

b) the hydrogen in one molecule is attracted to the oxygen in another molecule

2 **What were you able to see in the Lincoln Memorial in Step 2? Explain what made this possible.**

a) Lincoln sitting on his chair

b) water acted as a lens

3 **Jumping into a pool "head first" is no problem, but a belly flop really hurts! Based on what you've learned, explain why.**

in a belly flop, a lot more of your body hits the surface and has to break through millions more water molecules

What Happened

Review the section with students. Emphasize bold-face words that identify key concepts and introduce new vocabulary.

*In Step 1 and Step 2, you were able to "pile" the water due to a property called **surface tension**. Surface tension is caused by **water molecules** sticking together. Water is formed from **hydrogen** and **oxygen**. The hydrogen in one water molecule is attracted to the oxygen in another water molecule. This happens over and over (like a group of people grasping hands), creating a **bonding** effect called surface tension.*

*In an interesting side-effect, the round surface of the water pile formed a **convex lens**. In Step 2, it **magnified** the surface of the penny so you see President Lincoln sitting in his chair!*

Beginning in Step 3, however, the water wouldn't pile anymore since the detergent you added interfered with the water molecules' ability to bond together. (That's what makes detergent useful for cleaning!)

More About . . .

Have students read this section as you would a traditional science text — or use cooperative learning techniques to allow students the opportunity to work on the material collaboratively.

Digging Deeper

(Optional) Challenge teams to reseach and discuss practical applications of the lesson concepts. Encourage them to share their findings with the rest of the class.

What We Learned

Answers will vary. Suggested responses are shown at left.

Conclusion

Read this section aloud to the class to summarize the concepts learned in this activity.

Food for Thought

Read the Scripture aloud to the class. Talk about the importance of working together. Discuss ways God's people can support one another.

Science Journal

If time permits, have a general class discussion about notes and drawings various students added to their journal pages. Discuss correct and incorrect predictions, and remind students that this "trial and error" process is part of the scientific process.

CONCLUSION!

Surface tension is caused by water molecules sticking together through hydrogen bonds. Detergent can interfere with this bonding process, breaking surface tension.

FOOD FOR THOUGHT

1 Corinthians 12:12 A single drop of water couldn't accomplish much by itself. But when a lot of drops worked together, amazing things began to happen!

This Scripture reminds us that a church operates in much the same way. As the body of Christ, each of us has a job to do. Alone we can't accomplish very much. But when God's children all work together, amazing things can happen!

SCIENCE JOURNAL

56 FORCES

Extended Teaching

1. Challenge teams to devise an experiment to test the effectiveness of different soaps in cleaning cloths or sponges. Have students write a paragraph on what they discover.

2. Invite an exterminator to your classroom. Have him/her explain why many herbicides and insecticides use soap as a surfactant. Have students write a paragraph about one thing they learn.

3. Have teams research how soil erosion is caused by rain. Challenge teams to create a poster showing how farmers keep rain and wind from carrying soil away.

4. Many aquatic animals have special oil on their feathers or skins to keep water off. Have teams make a bulletin board of these animals showing what happens when this coating is lost.

5. Take a field trip to a grocery store. Have teams create lists of different soaps, detergents and cleaners. Challenge them to explain similarities and differences.

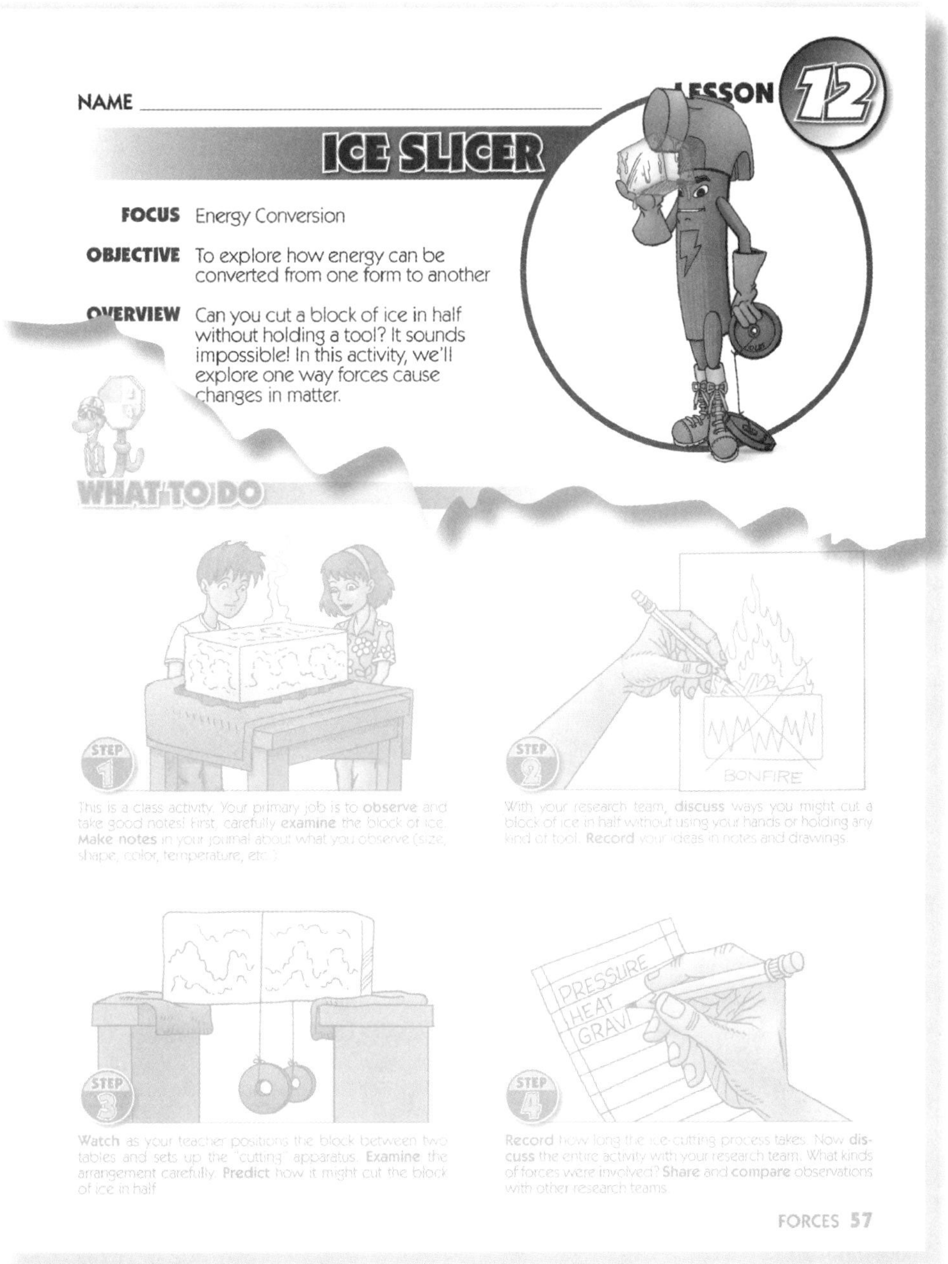
NAME ______________________

LESSON 12

ICE SLICER

FOCUS Energy Conversion

OBJECTIVE To explore how energy can be converted from one form to another

OVERVIEW Can you cut a block of ice in half without holding a tool? It sounds impossible! In this activity, we'll explore one way forces cause changes in matter.

WHAT TO DO

STEP 1

This is a class activity. Your primary job is to **observe** and take good notes! First, carefully **examine** the block of ice. **Make notes** in your journal about what you observe (size, shape, color, temperature, etc.).

STEP 2

BONFIRE

With your research team, **discuss** ways you might cut a block of ice in half without using your hands or holding any kind of tool. **Record** your ideas in notes and drawings.

STEP 3

Watch as your teacher positions the block between two tables and sets up the "cutting" apparatus. **Examine** the arrangement carefully. **Predict** how it might cut the block of ice in half.

STEP 4

PRESSURE
HEAT
GRAVI

Record how long the ice-cutting process takes. Now **discuss** the entire activity with your research team. What kinds of forces were involved? **Share** and **compare** observations with other research teams.

FORCES 57

Category

Physical Science
Forces

Focus

Energy Conversion

Objective

To explore how energy can be converted from one form to another

National Standards

A1, A2, B1, B2, B3, G1, G2

Materials Needed

thin wire
block of ice
weights - 2
tables - 2
pan to catch drips

Safety Concerns

2. Thermal Burn
Ice can "burn" skin with prolonged contact.

4. Slipping
There is a potential for spills. Remind students to exercise caution with water.

Additional Comments

The block of ice should be flat on the top and bottom. Use bricks or barbells for weights and the thinnest wire that will not break. Keep paper towels and a mop on hand in case of spills. Sometimes the ice will re-freeze as the wire cuts through the block! If so, be sure to show students this phenomenon.

Overview

Read the overview aloud to your students. The goal is to create an atmosphere of curiosity and inquiry.

WHAT TO DO

Monitor student research teams as they complete each step.

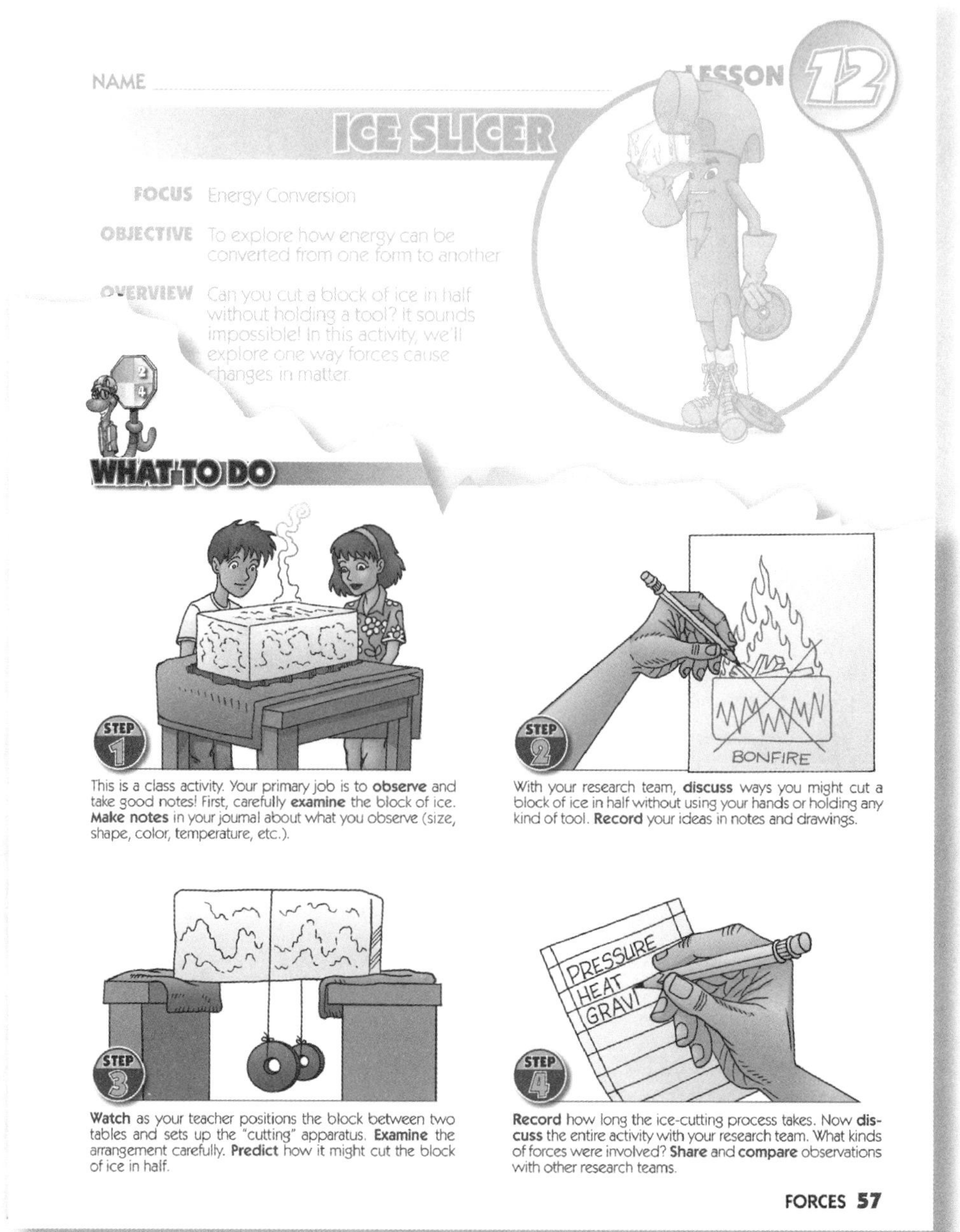

NAME

LESSON 12

ICE SLICER

FOCUS Energy Conversion

OBJECTIVE To explore how energy can be converted from one form to another

OVERVIEW Can you cut a block of ice in half without holding a tool? It sounds impossible! In this activity, we'll explore one way forces cause changes in matter.

WHAT TO DO

STEP 1 This is a class activity. Your primary job is to **observe** and take good notes! First, carefully **examine** the block of ice. **Make notes** in your journal about what you observe (size, shape, color, temperature, etc.).

STEP 2 With your research team, **discuss** ways you might cut a block of ice in half without using your hands or holding any kind of tool. **Record** your ideas in notes and drawings.

STEP 3 **Watch** as your teacher positions the block between two tables and sets up the "cutting" apparatus. **Examine** the arrangement carefully. **Predict** how it might cut the block of ice in half.

STEP 4 **Record** how long the ice-cutting process takes. Now **discuss** the entire activity with your research team. What kinds of forces were involved? **Share** and **compare** observations with other research teams.

FORCES **57**

Teacher to Teacher

The terms force and energy are often used interchangeably — but they're not quite the same thing! Force is a physical quantity which can affect the motion of an object. Any kind of push or pull is a force. By contrast, energy is the capacity for doing "work" (moving an object a distance). In short, force moves an object and energy determines how much it can move.

What Just Happened?

When you lifted the weights, you **opposed** the **force** of **gravity**. Your action gave the weights **potential energy**. By attaching the weights to a wire, you were able to concentrate the potential energy at the point where the wire touched the ice.

As **gravity** began **pulling** down on the weights, a lot of **pressure** built up in this small area. The pressure **converted** the potential energy of the weights into **heat** — a form of **kinetic** (moving) **energy**.

In other words, the potential energy of the weights on the wire was converted into heat energy. This heat changed the ice from a **solid** form (ice) into a **liquid** form (water), cutting a thin slice through the ice in the process.

More About Energy Conversion . . .

Were you surprised that you could cut a block of ice in half without using some kind of power tool? The clever conversion of energy can help us do many seemingly impossible tasks.

In this activity, you converted potential energy into heat energy. The higher you raised the weights, the more potential energy you created. The wire helped you concentrate this potential energy into a very small area, producing your "Ice Slicer".

The blades on an ice skate work much the same way. The weight of the skater is concentrated into a very small area on the ice. This converts the potential energy into heat energy, melting the solid ice that is touched by the blade. That's why ice skaters can move so fast — they're actually sliding along on a thin layer of water that forms between their skate blades and the ice!

There was a lot of **energy conversion** going on in this activity. Your muscles converted the potential energy of your breakfast into the kinetic energy needed to lift the weights. The kinetic energy of lifting the weights was converted into potential energy once they were up in the air. And as you discovered, the wire helped convert this potential energy into the heat energy needed to slice the ice.

Energy conversion is all around us. When gasoline is burned in a car's engine, some of its potential energy is changed into movement. (The rest is converted into heat, friction, sound, and other types of energy that isn't so helpful.) When you use a cell phone, it converts the potential energy stored in the battery into the electrical energy that flows through its circuits. When you run around the playground, you convert the potential energy that was stored in your body (from that sandwich you ate for lunch) into the kinetic energy of movement.

Digging Deeper:

The "Law of Conservation of Energy" states that energy can't be created or destroyed. It can only be changed from one form to another. Research this concept on the Internet. (The U.S. Department of Energy has a great "Energy Kids" section.) Discover and discuss other ways that conversion of energy makes our lives easier.

58 FORCES

What We Learned:

1 Describe the kind of energy that was given to the weights by lifting them off the floor. What was the opposing force?

a) potential

b) gravity

2 Explain how the wire "cut" the ice. Where did the energy come from? What form did it take?

a) answers will vary

b) the pressure of the wire on the ice

c) heat

3 Based on what you've learned, what effect would heavier weights and thinner wire have on the cutting time? Explain your answer.

the wire would cut the ice faster because there is more pressure (weight) on a smaller surface area

FORCES 59

What Happened

Review the section with students. Emphasize bold-face words that identify key concepts and introduce new vocabulary.

*When you lifted the weights, you **opposed** the **force** of **gravity**. Your action gave the weights **potential energy**. By attaching the weights to a wire, you were able to concentrate the potential energy at the point where the wire touched the ice.*

*As **gravity** began **pulling** down on the weights, a lot of **pressure** built up in this small area. The pressure changed the potential energy of the weights into **heat** – a form of kinetic (moving) energy.*

In other words, the potential energy of the weights on the wire was converted into heat energy. This heat changed the ice from a solid form (ice) into a liquid form (water), cutting a thin slice through the ice in the process..

More About . . .

Have students read this section as you would a traditional science text – or use cooperative learning techniques to allow students the opportunity to work on the material collaboratively.

Digging Deeper

(Optional) Challenge teams to reseach and discuss practical applications of the lesson concepts. Encourage them to share their findings with the rest of the class.

What We Learned

Answers will vary. Suggested responses are shown at left.

Conclusion

Read this section aloud to the class to summarize the concepts learned in this activity.

Food for Thought

Read the Scripture aloud to the class. Talk about ways people "get ahead" by doing things that are not right. Discuss why honesty is always the best policy.

Science Journal

If time permits, have a general class discussion about notes and drawings various students added to their journal pages. Discuss correct and incorrect predictions, and remind students that this "trial and error" process is part of the scientific process.

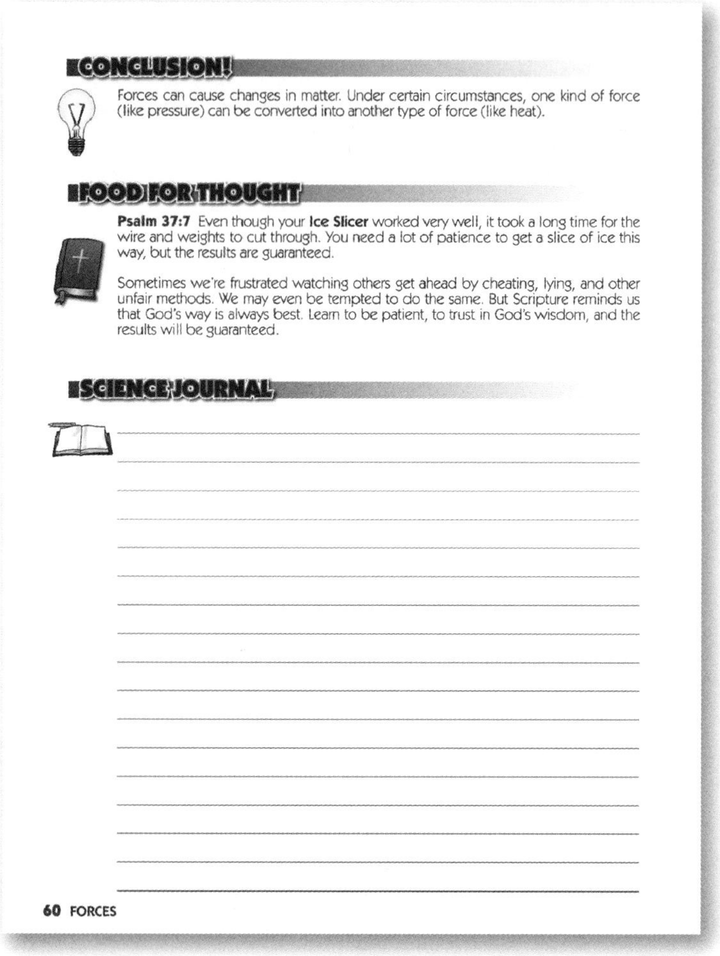

CONCLUSION!

Forces can cause changes in matter. Under certain circumstances, one kind of force (like pressure) can be converted into another type of force (like heat).

FOOD FOR THOUGHT

Psalm 37:7 Even though your **Ice Slicer** worked very well, it took a long time for the wire and weights to cut through. You need a lot of patience to get a slice of ice this way, but the results are guaranteed.

Sometimes we're frustrated watching others get ahead by cheating, lying, and other unfair methods. We may even be tempted to do the same. But Scripture reminds us that God's way is always best. Learn to be patient, to trust in God's wisdom, and the results will be guaranteed.

SCIENCE JOURNAL

60 FORCES

Extended Teaching

1. Repeat this activity outdoors or in a very hot or very cold room. Have students compare the results to the original activity. How are they similar? How are they different?

2. Challenge teams to list examples of changes they've seen in the state of matter. Have them list the beginning state and changed state for each example.

3. Challenge teams to list examples of energy conversion (light to heat, falling water to electricity, etc.). Make a bulletin board depicting the results.

4. Take a field trip to a fire station. Find out how water is transferred from tank trucks through hoses to the fire. Have students write a paragraph about one thing they learn.

5. Invite a backhoe operator to visit your school. Have him/her demonstrate how the hydraulic system transfers energy. Have students write a paragraph about one thing they learn.

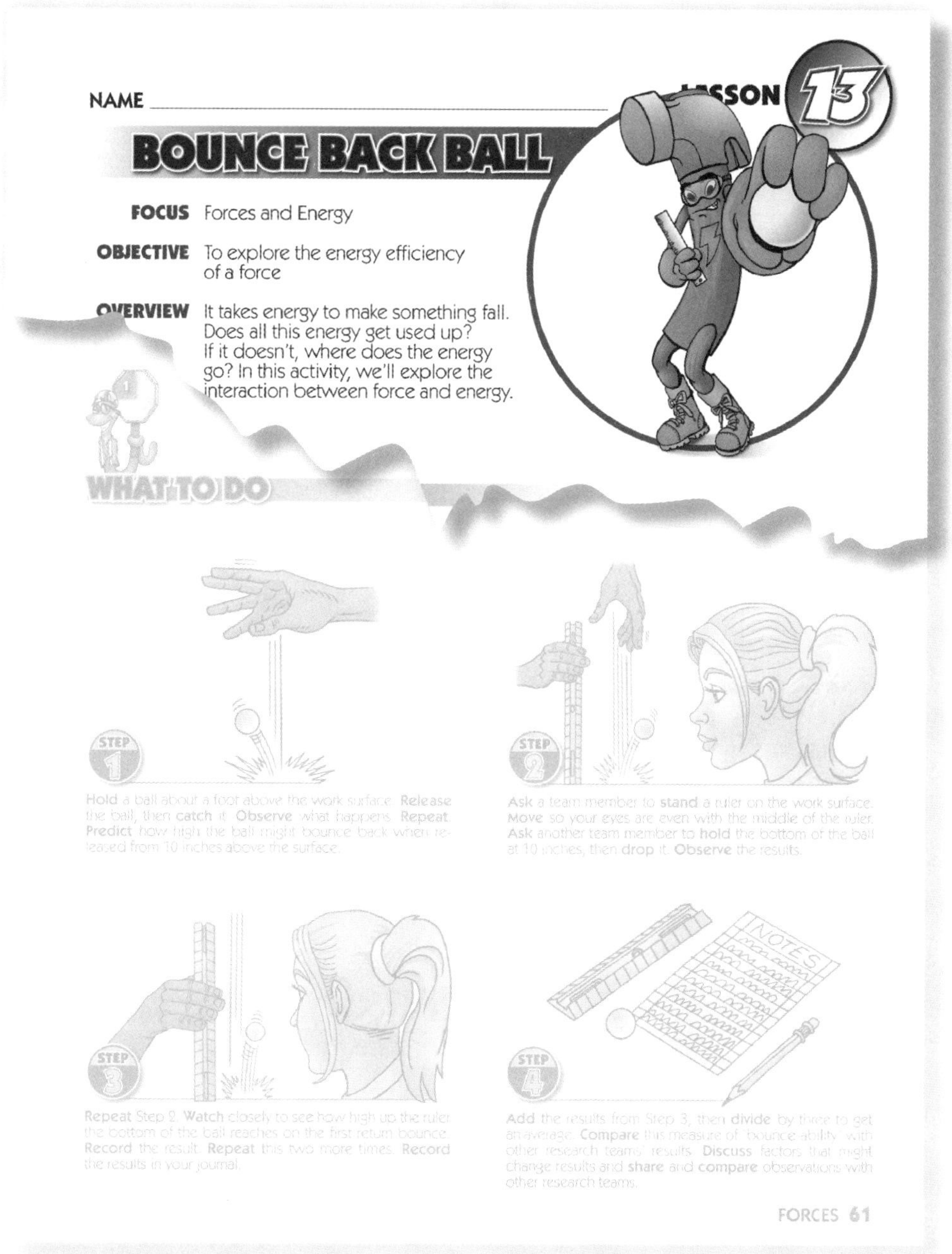
NAME ____________________ LESSON 13

BOUNCE BACK BALL

FOCUS Forces and Energy

OBJECTIVE To explore the energy efficiency of a force

OVERVIEW It takes energy to make something fall. Does all this energy get used up? If it doesn't, where does the energy go? In this activity, we'll explore the interaction between force and energy.

WHAT TO DO

STEP 1
Hold a ball about a foot above the work surface. **Release** the ball, then **catch** it. **Observe** what happens. **Repeat**. **Predict** how high the ball might bounce back when released from 10 inches above the surface.

STEP 2
Ask a team member to **stand** a ruler on the work surface. **Move** so your eyes are even with the middle of the ruler. **Ask** another team member to **hold** the bottom of the ball at 10 inches, then **drop** it. **Observe** the results.

STEP 3
Repeat Step 2. **Watch** closely to see how high up the ruler the bottom of the ball reaches on the first return bounce. **Record** the result. **Repeat** this two more times. **Record** the results in your journal.

STEP 4
Add the results from Step 3, then **divide** by three to get an average. **Compare** this measure of "bounce-ability" with other research teams' results. **Discuss** factors that might change results and **share** and **compare** observations with other research teams.

FORCES 61

Category

Physical Science
Forces

Focus

Forces and Energy

Objective

To explore the energy efficiency of a force

National Standards

A1, A2, B1, B2, B3, E1, E2, F5, G1, G2

Materials Needed

rubber ball
goggles
ruler

Safety Concerns

1. Goggles
Goggles are a reasonable precaution to protect eyes from the bouncing ball.

Additional Comments

A 10 inch starting height is used for easy calculation. A 4 inch bounce, for instance, equals 40% efficiency. Advanced students may wish to test their math skills by trying different heights. The results will *always* be less than 100% unless the ball is *thrown* downward!

Overview

Read the overview aloud to your students. The goal is to create an atmosphere of curiosity and inquiry.

WHAT TO DO

Monitor student research teams as they complete each step.

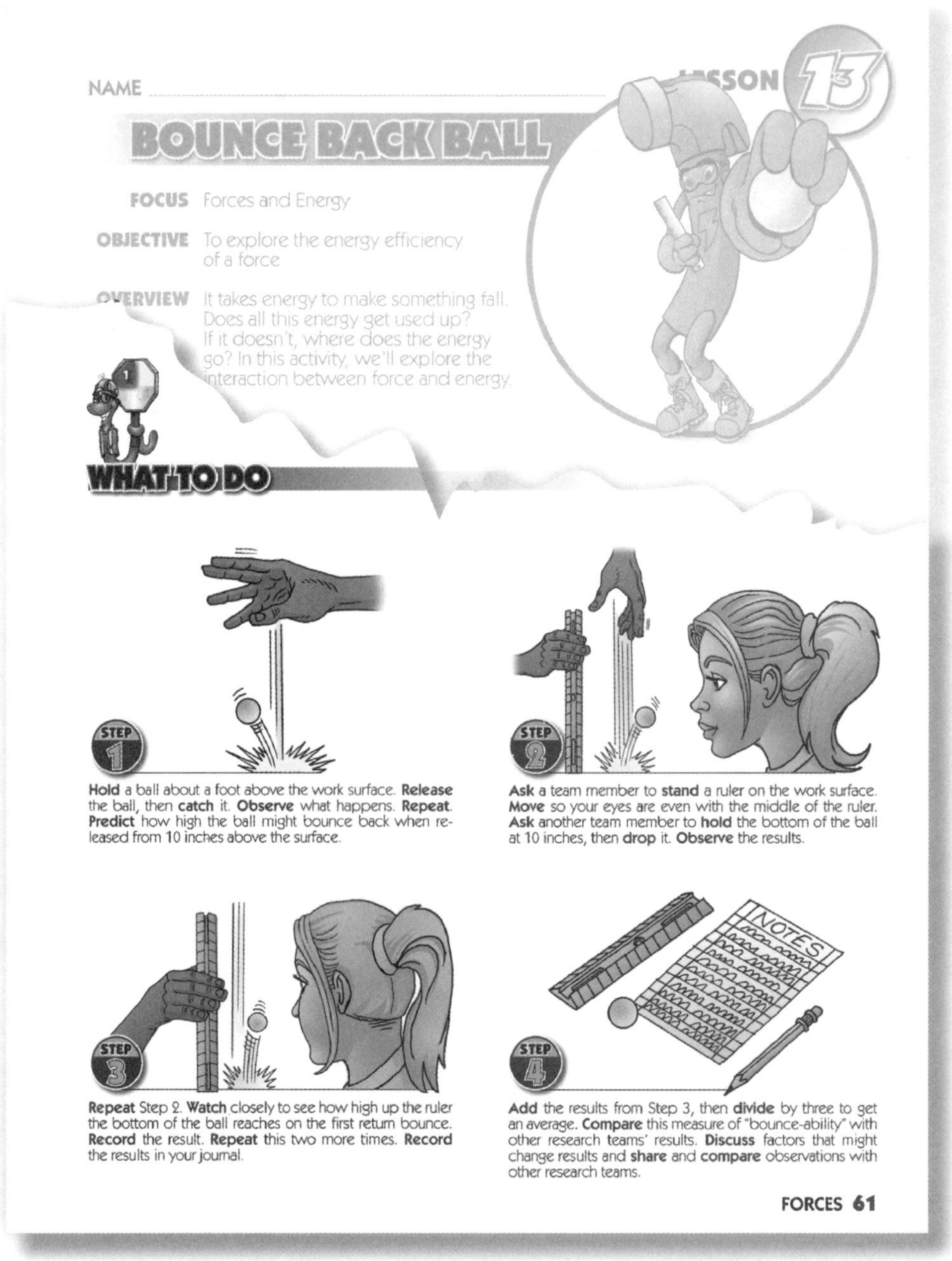

NAME

LESSON 13

BOUNCE BACK BALL

FOCUS Forces and Energy

OBJECTIVE To explore the energy efficiency of a force

OVERVIEW It takes energy to make something fall. Does all this energy get used up? If it doesn't, where does the energy go? In this activity, we'll explore the interaction between force and energy.

WHAT TO DO

STEP 1

Hold a ball about a foot above the work surface. **Release** the ball, then **catch** it. **Observe** what happens. **Repeat**. **Predict** how high the ball might bounce back when released from 10 inches above the surface.

STEP 2

Ask a team member to **stand** a ruler on the work surface. **Move** so your eyes are even with the middle of the ruler. **Ask** another team member to **hold** the bottom of the ball at 10 inches, then **drop** it. **Observe** the results.

STEP 3

Repeat Step 2. **Watch** closely to see how high up the ruler the bottom of the ball reaches on the first return bounce. **Record** the result. **Repeat** this two more times. **Record** the results in your journal.

STEP 4

Add the results from Step 3, then **divide** by three to get an average. **Compare** this measure of "bounce-ability" with other research teams' results. **Discuss** factors that might change results and **share** and **compare** observations with other research teams.

FORCES 61

Teacher to Teacher

Work is defined as the product of force and distance. For example, imagine two people weigh the same and travel the same distance. One walks, the other runs. Even though there are some differences, the amount of work being done is the same.

WHAT JUST HAPPENED?

When you dropped the ball, it didn't bounce all the way back up. Some of the **energy** from its fall was **absorbed** when it hit the work surface. More was drained away by the **resistance** of **friction** and **air**. Energy was also lost in other ways (like the ball flexing). Each time it fell, the ball lost a little more energy and bounced back a little less.

Whenever we put energy into something, we expect to get some of it back. The amount of energy we get back compared to what we put in is the degree of **efficiency**. For example, if you drop a ball from 10 inches and it bounces back five inches, your rate of efficiency would be 50 percent.

Scientists and engineers are constantly on the lookout for new ways to increase the efficiency of every form of technology we use.

MORE ABOUT FORCES AND ENERGY . . .

The "Law of Conservation of Energy" states that energy can't be created or destroyed. It can only be changed from one form to another. But our ball bounced back less and less each time. Isn't that an exception to this law of science? Wasn't some energy lost with each bounce?

The answer is that the word "lost" is a little misleading. The energy didn't just vanish into thin air — it changed into a different form! Let's review what happened.

You gave the ball **potential energy** by holding it in the air. When it was dropped, gravity pulled it down, turning this into **kinetic energy**. When the ball hit the desk, it flattened slightly as its particles squeezed together. This was because some of the kinetic energy the ball had was changed into **elastic potential energy**.

There were other factors at work, too. As the ball fell, the friction of passing through the air changed a tiny amount of kinetic energy into **heat energy**. And even the noise the ball made when it hit the surface of the desk changed some of the energy into **sound energy**. (Yes, sound waves require energy too.)

With all that going on, it's a wonder the ball had any energy left to bounce back at all!

Here's another example: Cars often convert only a small percentage of the energy we put into them into movement. The rest turns into things like heat, light, sound, friction, and so on.

But as we mentioned earlier, scientists and engineers are constantly searching for better ways to increase the efficiency of everything we use. That's why many cars today get much better gas mileage than similar cars did just 20 years ago.

DIGGING DEEPER:

Even though we always get back all the energy we put into something, it is not always in the form we find most useful. Research and discuss the fuel efficiency ratings of various cars. What are some factors that impact gas mileage? What are some ways engineers can change cars to improve fuel efficiency?

WHAT WE LEARNED:

1 **What force pulled the ball down in Step 1? What factors caused it to bounce back a little less?**

a) gravity

b) the resistance of friction and air

2 **Why must the ball be held perfectly still before dropping it? What other factors might impact the results?**

a) if the ball is moving, energy will be added or taken away

b) heat, friction, air resistance, etc.

3 **Based on what you've learned, explain how an "efficiency rating" might help you make comparisons if you were buying an appliance.**

answers will vary, but should reflect logical conclusions

What Happened

Review the section with students. Emphasize bold-face words that identify key concepts and introduce new vocabulary.

When you dropped the ball, it didn't bounce all the way back up. Some of the ***energy*** *from its fall was* ***absorbed*** *when it hit the work surface. More was drained away by the* ***resistance*** *of* ***friction*** *and* ***air****. Energy was also lost in other ways (like the ball flexing). Each time it fell, the ball lost a little more energy and bounced back a little less.*

Whenever we put energy into something, we expect to get some of it back. The amount of energy we get back compared to what we put in is the degree of ***efficiency****. For example, if you drop a ball from 10 inches and it bounces back 5 inches, your rate of efficiency would be 50 percent.*

Scientists and engineers are constantly on the lookout for new ways to increase the efficiency of every form of technology we use.

More About . . .

Have students read this section as you would a traditional science text — or use cooperative learning techniques to allow students the opportunity to work on the material collaboratively.

Digging Deeper

(Optional) Challenge teams to reseach and discuss practical applications of the lesson concepts. Encourage them to share their findings with the rest of the class.

What We Learned

Answers will vary. Suggested responses are shown at left.

Conclusion

Read this section aloud to the class to summarize the concepts learned in this activity.

Food for Thought

Read the Scripture aloud to the class. Talk about God's unlimited power. Discuss examples students have seen of God's power working in their lives or the lives of others.

Science Journal

If time permits, have a general class discussion about notes and drawings various students added to their journal pages. Discuss correct and incorrect predictions, and remind students that this "trial and error" process is part of the scientific process.

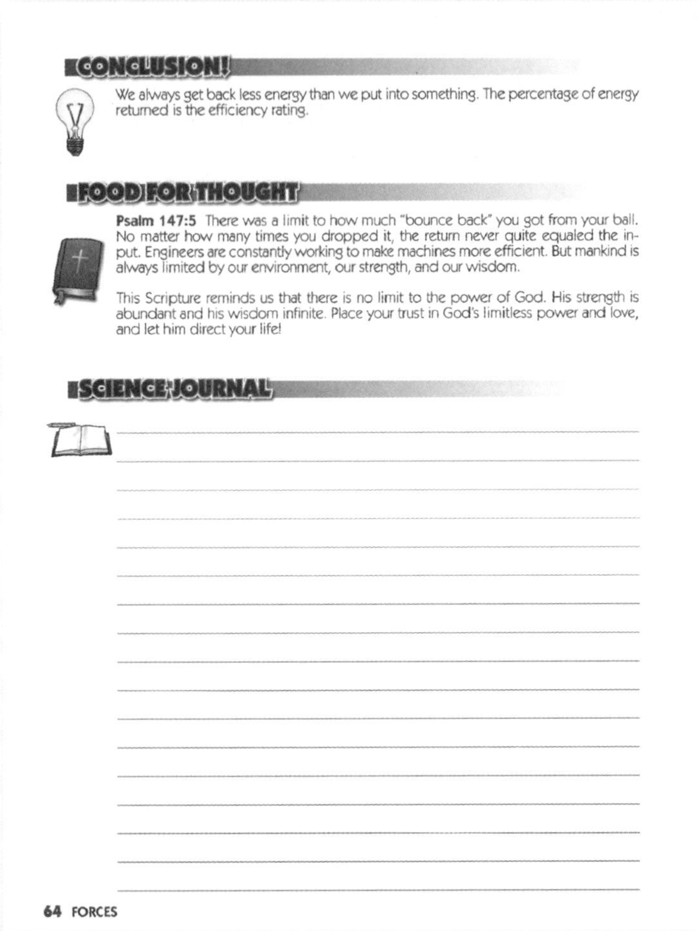

CONCLUSION!

We always get back less energy than we put into something. The percentage of energy returned is the efficiency rating.

FOOD FOR THOUGHT

Psalm 147:5 There was a limit to how much "bounce back" you got from your ball. No matter how many times you dropped it, the return never quite equaled the input. Engineers are constantly working to make machines more efficient. But mankind is always limited by our environment, our strength, and our wisdom.

This Scripture reminds us that there is no limit to the power of God. His strength is abundant and his wisdom infinite. Place your trust in God's limitless power and love, and let him direct your life!

SCIENCE JOURNAL

64 FORCES

Extended Teaching

1. Place a ball in the hot sun and another in the freezer for one hour. Repeat the activity using these two balls. Have students compare the results with the original activity. How are they similar? How are they different?

2. Using the Internet, have students research mileage ratings of different types of vehicles. Challenge each team to create a poster comparing the results of at least three vehicles.

3. Invite an electrician to your classroom. Have him/her talk about ways we can make our homes more energy efficient. Have students write a paragraph about one thing they learn.

4. Take a field trip to a local car repair shop. Have the mechanic share tips on making cars more efficient. Have students write a paragraph about one thing they learn.

5. Have teams list places where work is done by moving objects. Challenge each team to make a presentation to the class about one such location, explaining how the work is accomplished.

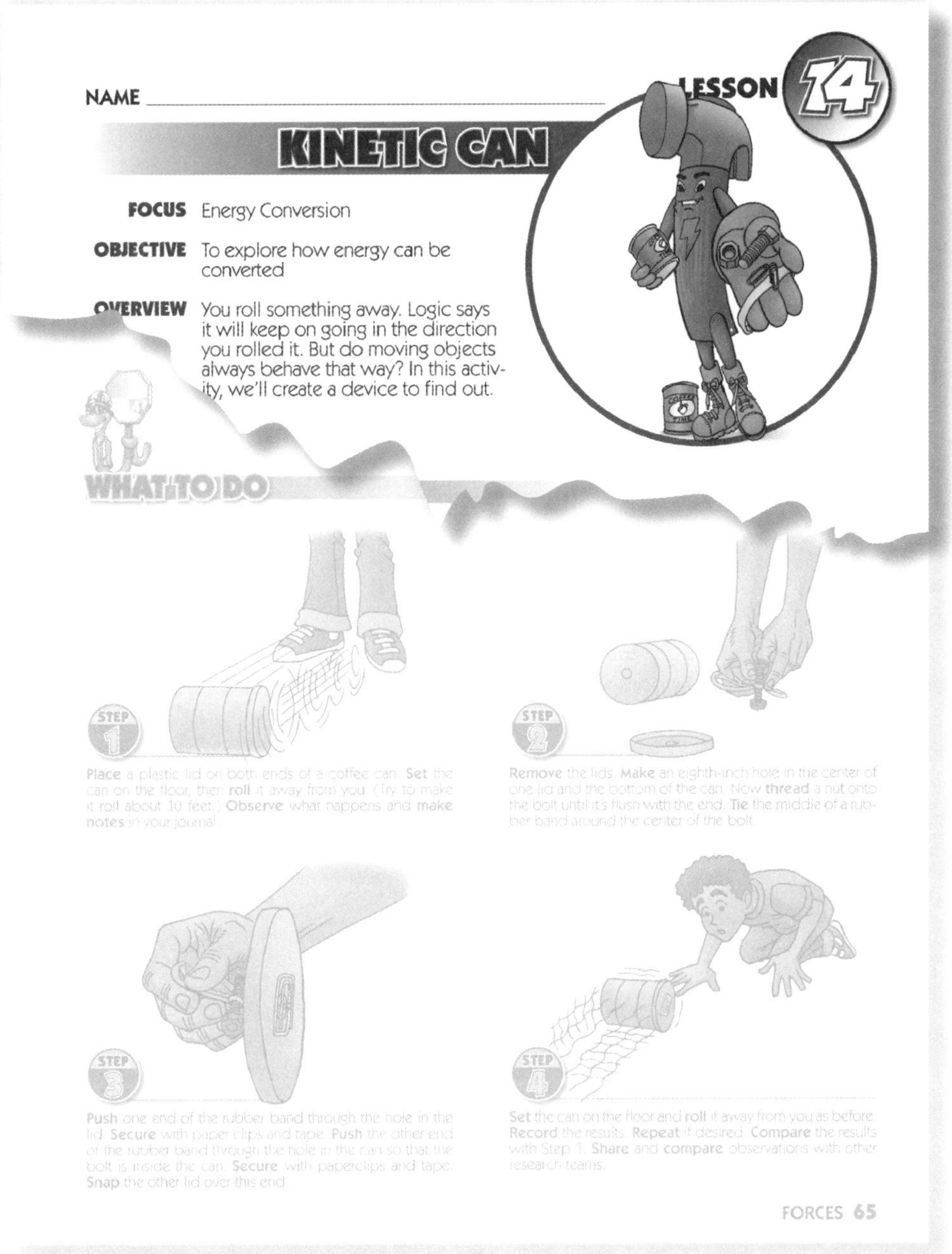

NAME

LESSON 14

KINETIC CAN

FOCUS Energy Conversion

OBJECTIVE To explore how energy can be converted

OVERVIEW You roll something away. Logic says it will keep on going in the direction you rolled it. But do moving objects always behave that way? In this activity, we'll create a device to find out.

WHAT TO DO

STEP 1

Place a plastic lid on both ends of a coffee can. **Set** the can on the floor, then **roll** it away from you. (Try to make it roll about 10 feet.) **Observe** what happens and **make notes** in your journal.

STEP 2

Remove the lids. **Make** an eighth-inch hole in the center of one lid and the bottom of the can. Now **thread** a nut onto the bolt until it's flush with the end. **Tie** the middle of a rubber band around the center of the bolt.

STEP 3

Push one end of the rubber band through the hole in the lid. **Secure** with paper clips and tape. **Push** the other end of the rubber band through the hole in the can so that the bolt is inside the can. **Secure** with paperclips and tape. **Snap** the other lid over this end.

STEP 4

Set the can on the floor and **roll** it away from you as before. **Record** the results. **Repeat** if desired. **Compare** the results with Step 1. **Share** and **compare** observations with other research teams.

FORCES 65

Category

Physical Science
Forces

Focus

Energy Conversion

Objective

To explore how energy can be converted

National Standards

A1, A2, B1, B2, B3, F5, G1, G2

Materials Needed

large rubber band
paperclips - 2
nut and bolt
plastic lid - 2
coffee can
tape

Safety Concerns

4. Slipping
The rolling can may present a tripping hazard. Remind students to use caution.

Additional Comments

For best results, demonstrate this activity before students begin. (You may wish to practice first!) Smooth floors allow the cans to roll best (avoid carpet). Pre-drill all holes in cans and lids. Each can must have two lids or it will not roll straight.

Overview

Read the overview aloud to your students. The goal is to create an atmosphere of curiosity and inquiry.

WHAT TO DO

Monitor student research teams as they complete each step.

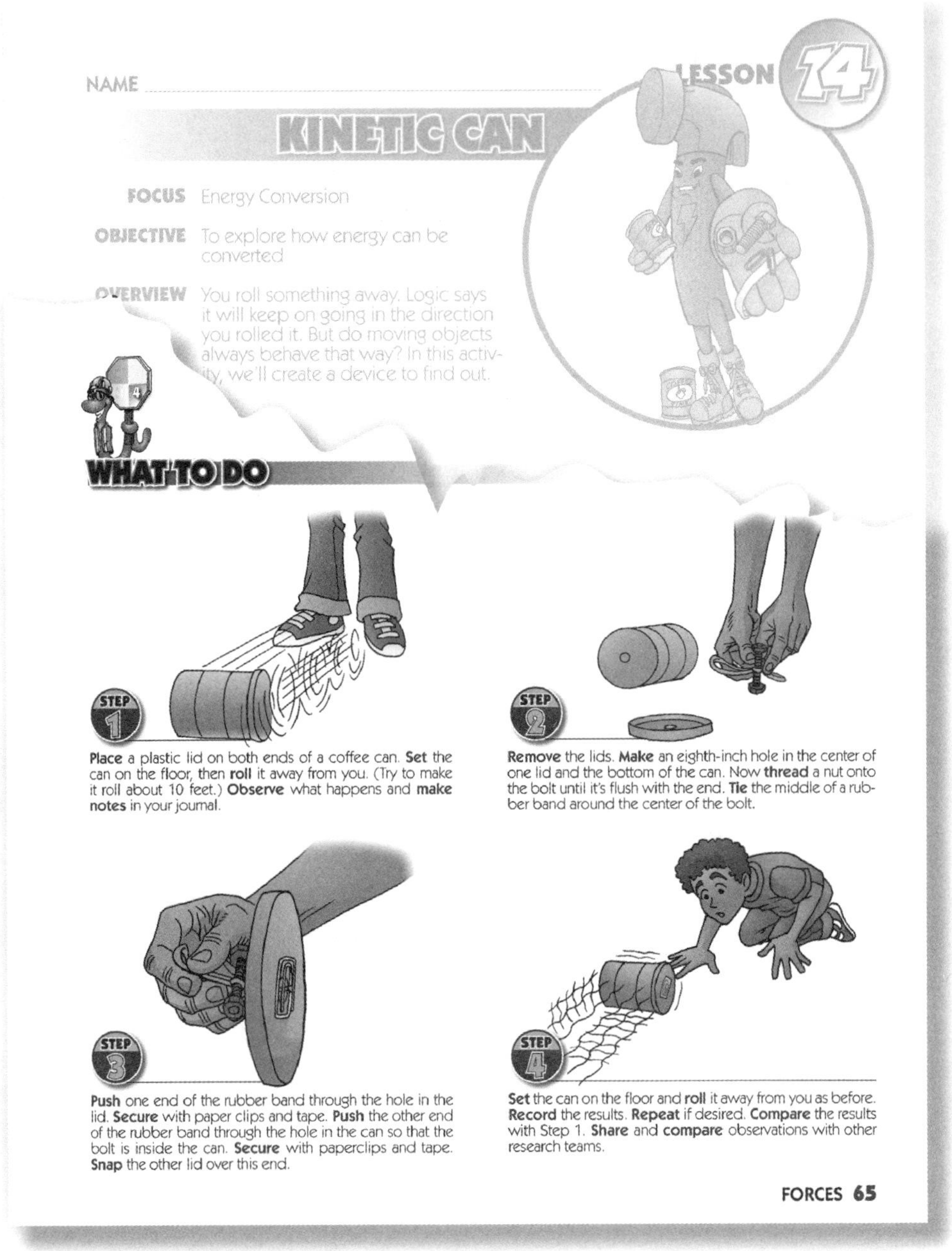

NAME

LESSON 14

KINETIC CAN

FOCUS Energy Conversion

OBJECTIVE To explore how energy can be converted

OVERVIEW You roll something away. Logic says it will keep on going in the direction you rolled it. But do moving objects always behave that way? In this activity, we'll create a device to find out.

WHAT TO DO

STEP 1 **Place** a plastic lid on both ends of a coffee can. **Set** the can on the floor, then **roll** it away from you. (Try to make it roll about 10 feet.) **Observe** what happens and **make notes** in your journal.

STEP 2 **Remove** the lids. **Make** an eighth-inch hole in the center of one lid and the bottom of the can. Now **thread** a nut onto the bolt until it's flush with the end. **Tie** the middle of a rubber band around the center of the bolt.

STEP 3 **Push** one end of the rubber band through the hole in the lid. **Secure** with paper clips and tape. **Push** the other end of the rubber band through the hole in the can so that the bolt is inside the can. **Secure** with paperclips and tape. **Snap** the other lid over this end.

STEP 4 **Set** the can on the floor and **roll** it away from you as before. **Record** the results. **Repeat** if desired. **Compare** the results with Step 1. **Share** and **compare** observations with other research teams.

FORCES 65

Teacher to Teacher

The key to this activity is the conversion of one form of energy to another. As volatile energy prices demonstrate, our culture is dependent on the efficiency of such conversions. But the "Law of Conservation of Energy" states that no energy conversion is ever 100% efficient. Some energy is always lost to friction and other forces. That's why engineers are constantly trying to find ways to improve the efficiency of devices — especially as energy supplies go down, populations go up, and prices begin to soar!

WHAT JUST HAPPENED?

You rolled the can in Step 1 and it moved away. But when you repeated the identical movement in Step 3, the can rolled away — but then it rolled back! What gives?

In Step 1, the can rolled until it ran out of the **kinetic** (moving) **energy** you provided. **Friction** between the can and floor eventually **absorbed** this energy. But in Step 2, the rubber band/bolt arrangement inside **converted** some of the kinetic energy you provided into **potential energy**. The can rolled a short distance, stopped, then rolled back in the opposite direction! The rubber band/bolt arrangement absorbed much of the energy you provided (except what was lost to friction and the rattling sound you heard) and converted it to an **opposing force** that quickly brought the can rolling back toward you.

MORE ABOUT ENERGY CONVERSION . . .

In this activity, you saw that energy can be converted from one form to another. The kinetic energy of the rolling can was converted into potential (stored) energy by the rubber band and bolt arrangement inside. But once the kinetic energy driving the can forward was expended, the potential energy in the twisted rubber band was able to convert back to kinetic energy which drove the can in the opposite direction.

Energy conversion is very important. If energy on Earth could not change from one form to another, life as we know it could not exist. Virtually everything in our world uses energy conversion in some form or another.

For instance, in the natural world, a tree absorbs sunlight (a form of kinetic energy) and converts it into the potential chemical energy of wood. When the wood is cut and dried, this chemical energy is ready to use. Burning a log in the fireplace converts this potential energy into light, sound, and heat.

Most man-made devices also rely on the conversion of energy. Everything from cell phones to cars needs energy conversion in order to function.

When a portable electronic device (like a cell phone or a CD player) is charged, the kinetic energy of electricity is converted into potential energy that is stored inside the battery. When the device is used, the potential energy is converted back into the electric energy that flows through its circuits to make it work.

Here's another example: The gasoline you put into your car has a lot of potential energy. When it is burned in the car's engine, this potential energy is converted into movement, light, and sound. This form of energy conversion is what helps bring you to school, and then takes you back home again!

DIGGING DEEPER:

Energy can be converted in many ways. Research and discuss some of the newer "Earth friendly" technologies for converting energy. (Solar, geothermal, and wind energy systems are a good place to start.) Find out the advantages and disadvantages of each technology you research.

WHAT WE LEARNED:

1 **Describe the device you created in Step 2 and Step 3. Explain how it converts energy.**

a) answers will vary

b) pushing the can gave it kinetic energy, but the bolt inside made the rubber band twist, storing up potential energy

2 **Why did the can behave differently in Step 1 and Step 4? What forces were involved?**

a) Step 1 didn't have the rubber band and bolt arrangement inside; Step 4 did.

b) kinetic energy, potential energy, friction, etc.

3 **Based on what you've learned, how well would this activity work on a floor with thick carpet? Why?**

a) not very well

b) too much friction

What Happened

Review the section with students. Emphasize bold-face words that identify key concepts and introduce new vocabulary.

You rolled the can in Step 1, and it moved away. But when you repeated the identical movement in Step 3, the can rolled away — but then it rolled back! What gives?

*In Step 1, the can rolled until it ran out of the **kinetic** (moving) **energy** you provided. **Friction** between the can and floor eventually **absorbed** this energy. But in Step 2, the rubber band/bolt arrangement inside **converted** some of the kinetic energy you provided into **potential energy**. The can rolled a short distance, stopped, then rolled back in the opposite direction! The rubber band/bolt arrangement absorbed much of the energy you provided (except what was lost to friction and the rattling sound you heard) and converted it to an **opposing force** that quickly brought the can rolling back toward you.*

More About . . .

Have students read this section as you would a traditional science text — or use cooperative learning techniques to allow students the opportunity to work on the material collaboratively.

Digging Deeper

(Optional) Challenge teams to reseach and discuss practical applications of the lesson concepts. Encourage them to share their findings with the rest of the class.

What We Learned

Answers will vary. Suggested responses are shown at left.

Conclusion

Read this section aloud to the class to summarize the concepts learned in this activity.

Food for Thought

Read the Scripture aloud to the class. Talk about times students really put their trust in God. Discuss ways they were blessed, or were able to bless someone through their experience.

Science Journal

If time permits, have a general class discussion about notes and drawings various students added to their journal pages. Discuss correct and incorrect predictions, and remind students that this "trial and error" process is part of the scientific process.

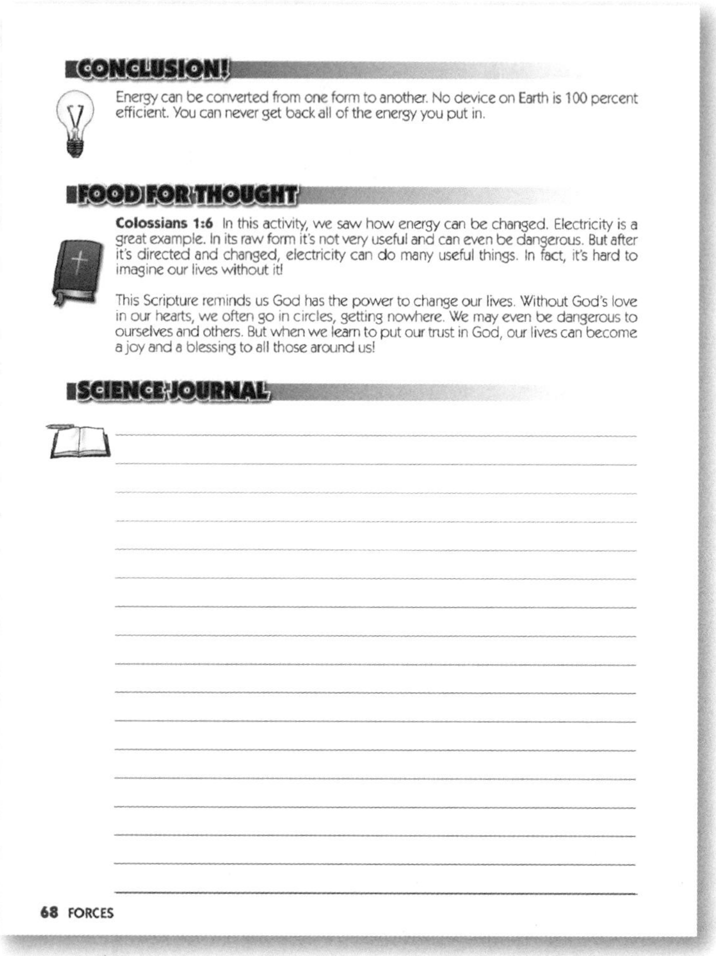
CONCLUSION!

Energy can be converted from one form to another. No device on Earth is 100 percent efficient. You can never get back all of the energy you put in.

FOOD FOR THOUGHT

Colossians 1:6 In this activity, we saw how energy can be changed. Electricity is a great example. In its raw form it's not very useful and can even be dangerous. But after it's directed and changed, electricity can do many useful things. In fact, it's hard to imagine our lives without it!

This Scripture reminds us God has the power to change our lives. Without God's love in our hearts, we often go in circles, getting nowhere. We may even be dangerous to ourselves and others. But when we learn to put our trust in God, our lives can become a joy and a blessing to all those around us!

SCIENCE JOURNAL

68 FORCES

Extended Teaching

1. Challenge teams to design their own "trained can" using different size rubber bands and weights. (A clear container will make it easier for them to see energy conversion happening.)

2. Using the Internet, look up Newton's Laws of Motion. Challenge teams to show how Newton's Laws were used in this activity.

3. Have teams list places where energy is converted. Challenge each team to make a presentation to the class about one such location, explaining how the conversion process works.

4. Take a field trip to an electrical power plant. Find out how electricity is made from falling water, burning coal, or nuclear processes. Have students write a paragraph about one thing they learn.

5. Invite a nutritionist to visit your classroom. Talk about how eating the proper kinds of food can lead to increased energy. Have students write a paragraph about one thing they learn.

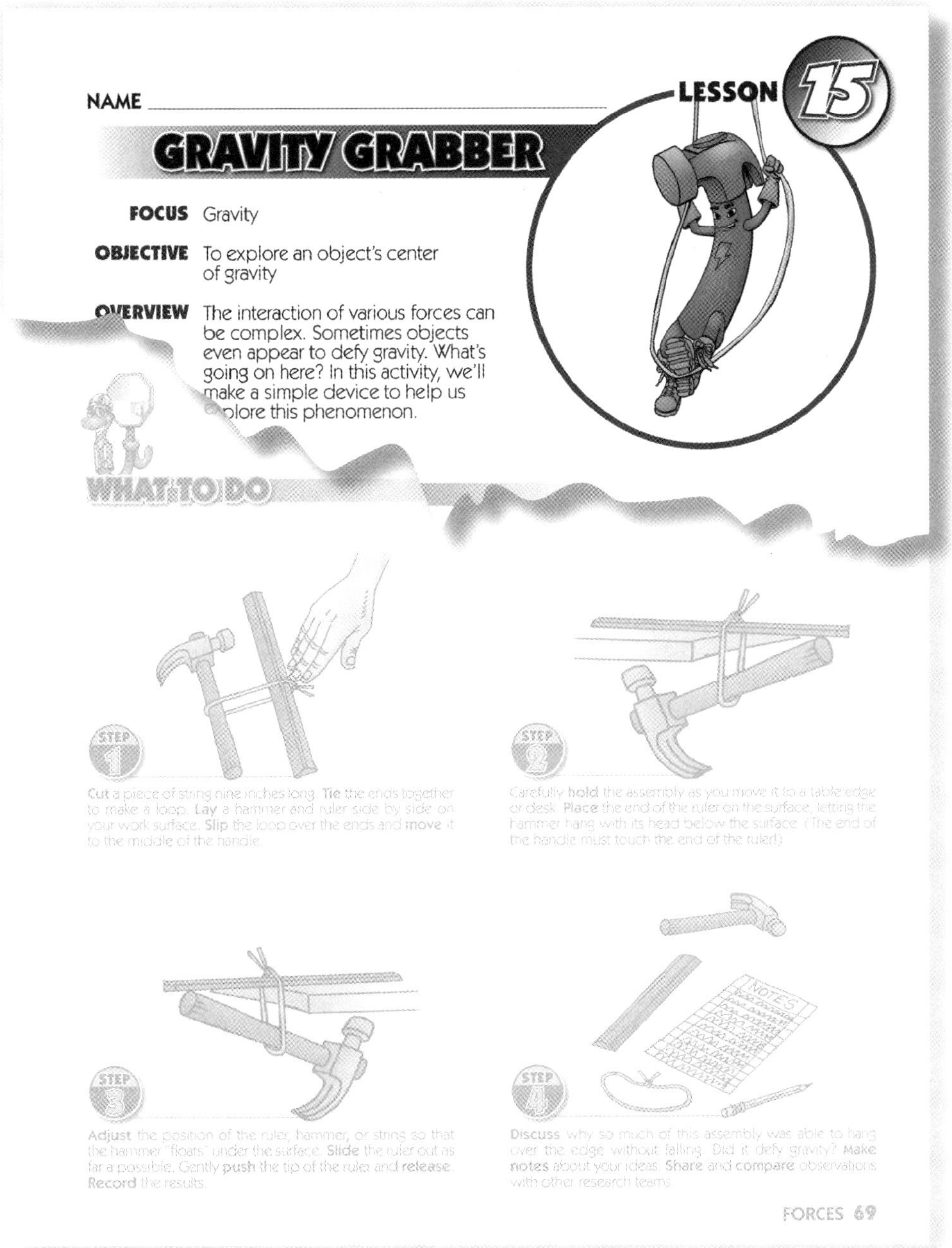

NAME ______________________

LESSON 15

GRAVITY GRABBER

FOCUS Gravity

OBJECTIVE To explore an object's center of gravity

OVERVIEW The interaction of various forces can be complex. Sometimes objects even appear to defy gravity. What's going on here? In this activity, we'll make a simple device to help us explore this phenomenon.

WHAT TO DO

STEP 1

Cut a piece of string nine inches long. **Tie** the ends together to make a loop. **Lay** a hammer and ruler side by side on your work surface. **Slip** the loop over the ends and **move** it to the middle of the handle.

STEP 2

Carefully **hold** the assembly as you move it to a table edge or desk. **Place** the end of the ruler on the surface, letting the hammer hang with its head below the surface. (The end of the handle must touch the end of the ruler!)

STEP 3

Adjust the position of the ruler, hammer, or string so that the hammer "floats" under the surface. **Slide** the ruler out as far a possible. Gently **push** the tip of the ruler and **release**. **Record** the results.

STEP 4

Discuss why so much of this assembly was able to hang over the edge without falling. Did it defy gravity? **Make notes** about your ideas. **Share** and **compare** observations with other research teams.

FORCES 69

Category

Physical Science
Forces

Focus

Gravity

Objective

To explore an object's center of gravity

National Standards

A1, A2, B1, B2, B3, G1, G2

Materials Needed

9 inch string
hammer
ruler

Safety Concerns

4. Other
Remind students to keep toes and fingers away from potentially falling hammers!

Additional Comments

A great way to begin this activity is to tell students you can make a hammer "float"! (It's best to practice this before demonstrating.) Wooden rulers work best for this activity. The work surface must have room underneath for the hammer to swing. With smaller hammers, use shorter string.

Overview

Read the overview aloud to your students. The goal is to create an atmosphere of curiosity and inquiry.

WHAT TO DO

Monitor student research teams as they complete each step.

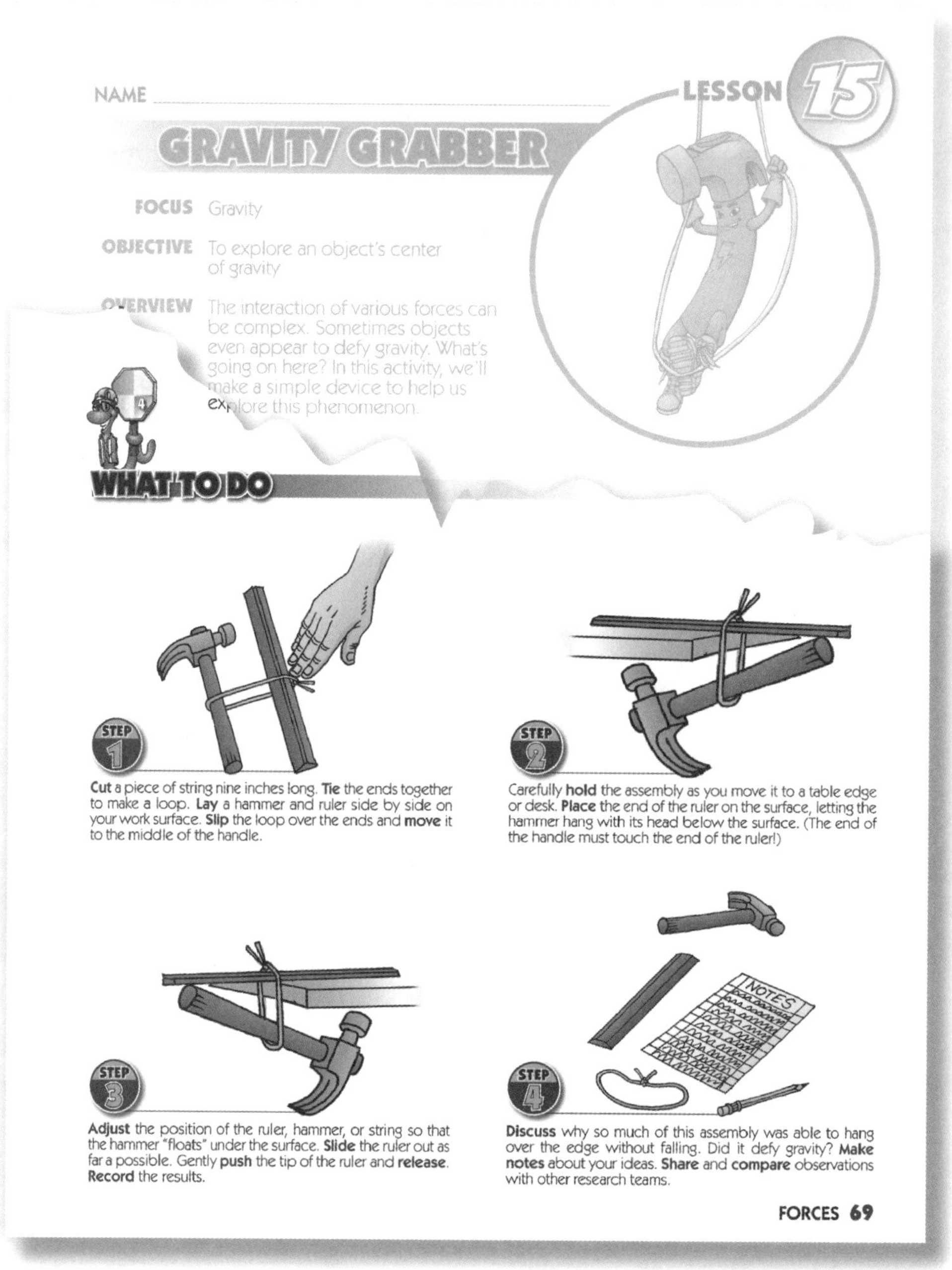

NAME

LESSON 15

GRAVITY GRABBER

FOCUS Gravity

OBJECTIVE To explore an object's center of gravity

OVERVIEW The interaction of various forces can be complex. Sometimes objects even appear to defy gravity. What's going on here? In this activity, we'll make a simple device to help us explore this phenomenon.

WHAT TO DO

STEP 1

Cut a piece of string nine inches long. **Tie** the ends together to make a loop. **Lay** a hammer and ruler side by side on your work surface. **Slip** the loop over the ends and **move** it to the middle of the handle.

STEP 2

Carefully **hold** the assembly as you move it to a table edge or desk. **Place** the end of the ruler on the surface, letting the hammer hang with its head below the surface. (The end of the handle must touch the end of the ruler!)

STEP 3

Adjust the position of the ruler, hammer, or string so that the hammer "floats" under the surface. **Slide** the ruler out as far a possible. Gently **push** the tip of the ruler and **release**. **Record** the results.

STEP 4

Discuss why so much of this assembly was able to hang over the edge without falling. Did it defy gravity? **Make notes** about your ideas. **Share** and **compare** observations with other research teams.

FORCES 69

Teacher to Teacher

Center of gravity has a major affect on torque. For instance, the body proportions of athletes in any given sport are very similar. (This is true regardless of race or gender.) The reason is that the center of gravity of an arm or leg has an impact on the amount and strength of torque available.

WHAT JUST HAPPENED?

In Step 3, the hammer appeared to be floating underneath the table. But don't worry — **gravity** is still alive and well! The key to this illusion lies in the device's **center of gravity**. In order to fall, the center of gravity must be beyond the table's edge.

But in this device, the **mass** (which is a lot like weight) is actually centered near the hammer's head because the head's metal is heavier than the wood in the handle. This shift in the center of gravity kept the device from falling.

By the way, the twisting **force** you felt as you were setting up this device was **torque**. If the device wasn't balanced properly, this torque would have twisted it, making the device fall to the floor.

MORE ABOUT GRAVITY . . .

Sometimes the way forces interact to make things move (or not move) can seem very complicated! In this activity, for instance, the hammer appeared to defy gravity as it "floated" below the table. But once you understood what was taking place, the mystery quickly became clear.

Center of gravity is actually an important concept. It helps explain the movement of many different kinds of objects. For example, when you lift a long object (like a shovel or a ladder), it's a lot easier to pick up and control if you have at least one hand at the center of gravity, instead of grabbing it by one end.

In many sports and athletic competitions, an athlete will move his/her body up or down or from side to side to shift center of gravity. This allows football players to complete difficult tackles, gymnasts to perform handsprings and flips, and ballerinas to engage in beautiful, graceful moves.

Torque is a related force. If an object isn't balanced properly, torque will cause the object to twist or rotate in some fashion. For example, when you start to slip on a patch of ice, you instinctively throw your arms out to the side to "catch your balance". This helps offset torque and (hopefully) keeps you from falling.

Have you ever watched a mechanic balance a tire? That relates to center of gravity and torque, too. A tire is "balanced" when the mass of the tire and wheel is equally distributed. Mechanics balance a tire by adding small weights to the wheel's rim as needed. Out of balance tires create unwanted torque which can make your whole car shake at high speeds! They can also shorten the life of your tires, and cause extra wear and tear on bearings, shocks and other suspension components.

DIGGING DEEPER:

Research and discuss how "center of gravity" and "torque" relate to various sports. For instance, what does center of gravity have to do with kicking a soccer ball, and why does a quarterback spiral a football? If you have time, locate the center of gravity of some non-breakable objects by trying to balance them on your finger.

70 FORCES

WHAT WE LEARNED:

1 **Describe what happened when you pushed on the ruler in Step 3. Why was gravity unable to pull this device down to the floor?**

a) the hammer wobbled, then rebalanced

b) center of gravity was near the hammer's head, not near the middle of it's handle

2 **Define center of gravity, mass, and torque. How are they related in this activity?**

a) the center of an object's mass

b) like weight; the amount of matter present

c) a twisting force

d) see "What Happened" for description

3 **Describe the role of the ruler in this activity. What would happen if the hammer handle and ruler lost contact? Why?**

a) to transfer force

b) the hammer would fall because center of gravity would change

FORCES **71**

What Happened

Review the section with students. Emphasize bold-face words that identify key concepts and introduce new vocabulary.

*In Step 3, the hammer appeared to be floating underneath the table. But don't worry — **gravity** is still alive and well! The key to this illusion lies in the device's **center of gravity**. In order to fall, the center of gravity must be beyond the table's edge.*

*But in this device, the **mass** (which is a lot like weight) is actually centered near the hammer's head because the head's metal is heavier than the wood in the handle. This shift in the center of gravity kept the device from falling.*

*By the way, the twisting **force** you felt as you were setting up this device was **torque**. If the device wasn't balanced properly, this torque would have twisted it, making the device fall to the floor.*

More About . . .

Have students read this section as you would a traditional science text — or use cooperative learning techniques to allow students the opportunity to work on the material collaboratively.

Digging Deeper

(Optional) Challenge teams to reseach and discuss practical applications of the lesson concepts. Encourage them to share their findings with the rest of the class.

What We Learned

Answers will vary. Suggested responses are shown at left.

Conclusion

Read this section aloud to the class to summarize the concepts learned in this activity.

Food for Thought

Read the Scripture aloud to the class. Talk about the importance of staying close to God. Discuss how this allows God's power to work in our lives.

Science Journal

If time permits, have a general class discussion about notes and drawings various students added to their journal pages. Discuss correct and incorrect predictions, and remind students that this "trial and error" process is part of the scientific process.

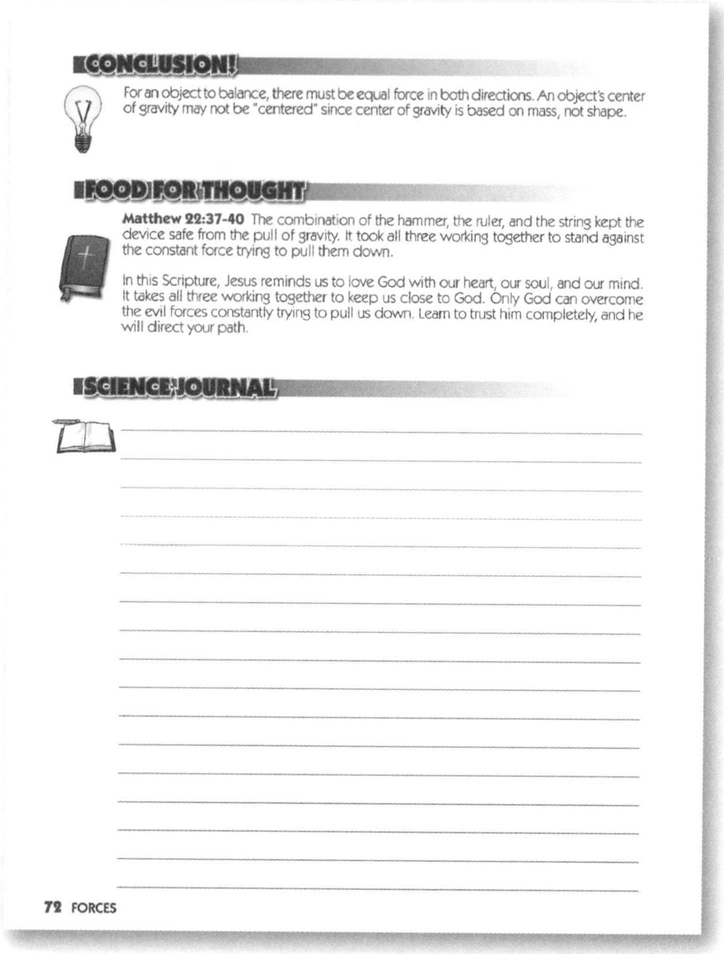

CONCLUSION!

For an object to balance, there must be equal force in both directions. An object's center of gravity may not be "centered" since center of gravity is based on mass, not shape.

FOOD FOR THOUGHT

Matthew 22:37-40 The combination of the hammer, the ruler, and the string kept the device safe from the pull of gravity. It took all three working together to stand against the constant force trying to pull them down.

In this Scripture, Jesus reminds us to love God with our heart, our soul, and our mind. It takes all three working together to keep us close to God. Only God can overcome the evil forces constantly trying to pull us down. Learn to trust him completely, and he will direct your path.

SCIENCE JOURNAL

72 FORCES

Extended Teaching

1. Explore torque in action on the playground with a teeter-totter, swing, merry-go-round, etc. Have teams discuss the results, then have students write a paragraph describing the experience.

2. Have teams discuss torque. Challenge each team to create a poster showing various objects that illustrate torque (bats, arms, golf clubs, hammers, legs, etc.).

3. Invite a college or professional baseball player to visit your classroom. Have him/her explain the best way to hold a bat for maximum force. Discuss how different holds create different torque.

4. Watch a video showing the performance of a tightrope walker. What is the purpose of the long pole? Discuss how center of gravity plays a role in balance.

5. Take a field trip to an architect's studio. Discuss the concept of cantilevering and how it uses center of gravity to create shapes that appear to defy gravity. Have students write a paragraph about one thing they learn.

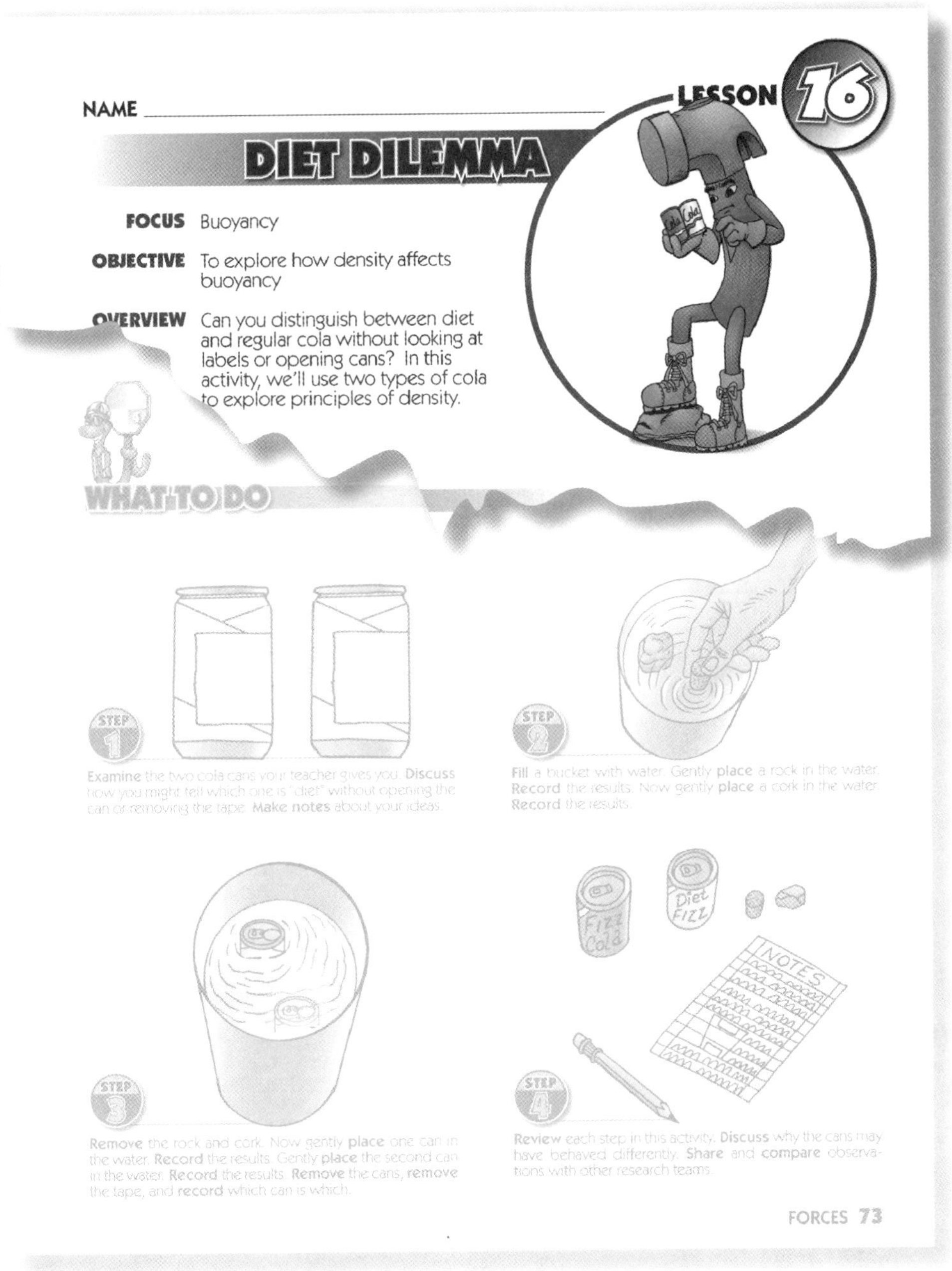

NAME ______________________

LESSON 16

DIET DILEMMA

FOCUS Buoyancy

OBJECTIVE To explore how density affects buoyancy

OVERVIEW Can you distinguish between diet and regular cola without looking at labels or opening cans? In this activity, we'll use two types of cola to explore principles of density.

WHAT TO DO

STEP 1
Examine the two cola cans your teacher gives you. **Discuss** how you might tell which one is "diet" without opening the can or removing the tape. **Make notes** about your ideas.

STEP 2
Fill a bucket with water. Gently **place** a rock in the water. **Record** the results. Now gently **place** a cork in the water. **Record** the results.

STEP 3
Remove the rock and cork. Now gently **place** one can in the water. **Record** the results. Gently **place** the second can in the water. **Record** the results. **Remove** the cans, **remove** the tape, and **record** which can is which.

STEP 4
Review each step in this activity. **Discuss** why the cans may have behaved differently. **Share** and **compare** observations with other research teams.

FORCES 73

Category

Physical Science
Forces

Focus

Buoyancy

Objective

To explore how density affects buoyancy

National Standards

A1, A2, B1, B2, G1, G2

Materials Needed

rock
cork
can diet cola
can regular cola
tape
bucket
water

Safety Concerns

4. Slipping
There is a potential for spills. Remind students to exercise caution with water.

Additional Comments

Cover cola cans with tape in advance. Have students offer ideas on how to tell which one is which without opening them. Most soft drink varieties will work, but it's a good idea to test in advance to be sure!

Overview

Read the overview aloud to your students. The goal is to create an atmosphere of curiosity and inquiry.

WHAT TO DO

Monitor student research teams as they complete each step.

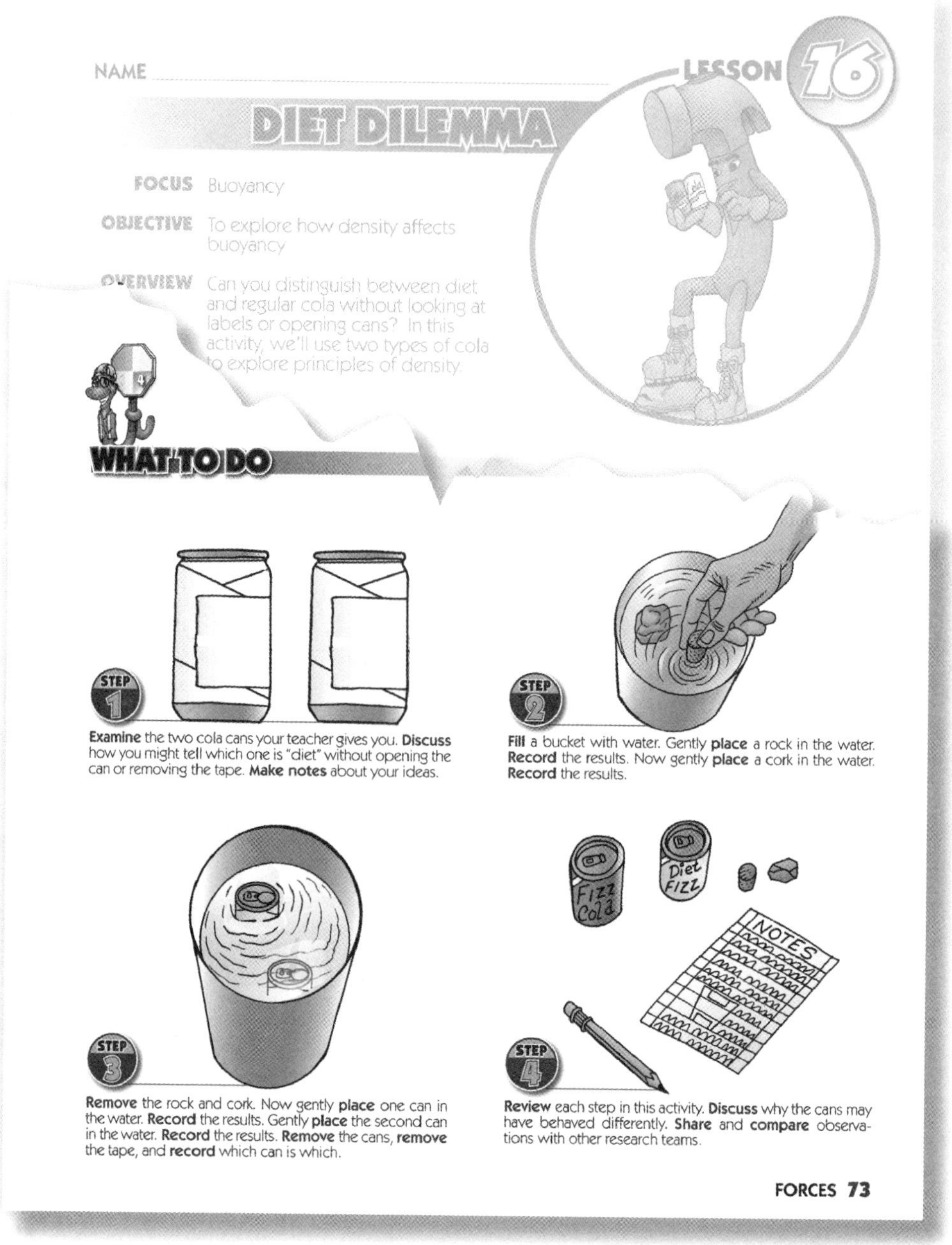

NAME ______

LESSON 16

DIET DILEMMA

FOCUS Buoyancy

OBJECTIVE To explore how density affects buoyancy

OVERVIEW Can you distinguish between diet and regular cola without looking at labels or opening cans? In this activity, we'll use two types of cola to explore principles of density.

WHAT TO DO

STEP 1
Examine the two cola cans your teacher gives you. **Discuss** how you might tell which one is "diet" without opening the can or removing the tape. **Make notes** about your ideas.

STEP 2
Fill a bucket with water. Gently **place** a rock in the water. **Record** the results. Now gently **place** a cork in the water. **Record** the results.

STEP 3
Remove the rock and cork. Now gently **place** one can in the water. **Record** the results. Gently **place** the second can in the water. **Record** the results. **Remove** the cans, **remove** the tape, and **record** which can is which.

STEP 4
Review each step in this activity. **Discuss** why the cans may have behaved differently. **Share** and **compare** observations with other research teams.

FORCES **73**

Teacher to Teacher

Materials float because they are less dense than water. But then, how do huge steel ships float? It's because they displace water with air (which is less dense than water). Poke a hole in the hull however, and the combination of water and dense steel quickly sinks.

WHAT JUST HAPPENED?

Density is the **weight** of a material compared to the weight of another material of the same **volume**. For instance, a block of concrete is more dense than a block of polystyrene (styrofoam®) that's the identical size. In other words, the **pull** of **gravity** is greater on the concrete than on the polystyrene.

Gravity and **buoyancy** are **opposing forces**. Some materials (like cork) are **buoyant** because they are less dense than water. They float. Other materials (like rock) are more dense than water. They sink.

Interestingly enough, the density of regular cola and diet cola is different! Regular cola contains sugar which is more dense than the artificial sweeteners used in diet cola. This density difference is what caused the different behaviors in this activity.

MORE ABOUT BUOYANCY . . .

Density is an important property of matter. Since density is based on the mass (similar to weight*) of a material compared to its volume, scientists have a simple mathematical formula for calculating density. You simply divide the mass by the volume. In mathemetical terms it looks like this:

$$D = m / v$$

So usually, objects that are less dense than water float, and objects that are more dense than water sink.

That's why many old ships were made of wood. Wood makes a great boat because it is less dense than water, and so it floats. Even if a storm breaks the boat into pieces, the pieces still float.

But wait a minute. What about modem ships like oil tankers and aircraft carriers? Aren't they made of steel? And since steel is much more dense than water, how can these huge ships float? It's because the hull of the ship displaces water with air, so the volume of the ship is mostly air (which is less dense than water). But if a hole in the hull lets water get in (replacing all the air), the dense steel ship would quickly sink.

Density helps determine how we use many objects. Fishing bobbers (low density) hold up our bait. An air mattress (low density) lets us relax on the water. Lead shields (high density) protect technicians from powerful X-rays. Concrete (high density) gives strength to the foundations of our buildings.

**Note: Weight depends on the pull of gravity. Take two iron blocks of the same mass, one on Earth and one on the moon. The one on the moon will be lighter, even though the mass of the two blocks is the same.*

DIGGING DEEPER:

Research and discuss how density and buoyancy relate to the things you can find in and around a lake (boat docks, watercraft, anchors, life jackets, fishing gear, etc.). Find out how emerging technology has changed some of these items over the years.

WHAT WE LEARNED:

1 Compare the two cans of cola. How were they similar? How were they different? What made them behave differently in Step 3?

a) answers will vary, but should reflect logical comparisons

b) regular cola is more dense than diet cola

2 Define density, gravity, and buoyancy. How does each of these relate to this activity?

a) the weight of a material compared to another material of equal volume
b) a downward pull
c) an upward push that makes things float
d) see "What Happened" for description

3 Based on what you've learned, could an object float in a swimming pool without touching the surface or bottom? Why or why not?

a) yes

b) depends on the relationship of the object's density to the density of water

What Happened

Review the section with students. Emphasize bold-face words that identify key concepts and introduce new vocabulary.

***Density** is the **weight** of a material compared to the weight of another material of the same **volume**. For instance, a block of concrete is more dense than a block of polystyrene (Styrofoam®) that's the identical size. In other words, the **pull** of **gravity** is greater on the concrete than on the polystyrene.*

***Gravity** and **buoyancy** are **opposing forces**. Some materials (like cork) are **buoyant** because they are less dense than water. They float. Other materials (like rock) are more dense than water. They sink.*

Interestingly enough, the density of regular cola and diet cola is different! Regular cola contains sugar which is more dense than the artificial sweeteners used in diet cola. This density difference is what caused the different behaviors in this activity.

More About . . .

Have students read this section as you would a traditional science text — or use cooperative learning techniques to allow students the opportunity to work on the material collaboratively.

Digging Deeper

(Optional) Challenge teams to reseach and discuss practical applications of the lesson concepts. Encourage them to share their findings with the rest of the class.

What We Learned

Answers will vary. Suggested responses are shown at left.

Conclusion

Read this section aloud to the class to summarize the concepts learned in this activity.

Food for Thought

Read the Scripture aloud to the class. Talk about how outside appearances can be deceiving. Discuss ways we can develop our inner beauty.

Science Journal

If time permits, have a general class discussion about notes and drawings various students added to their journal pages. Discuss correct and incorrect predictions, and remind students that this "trial and error" process is part of the scientific process.

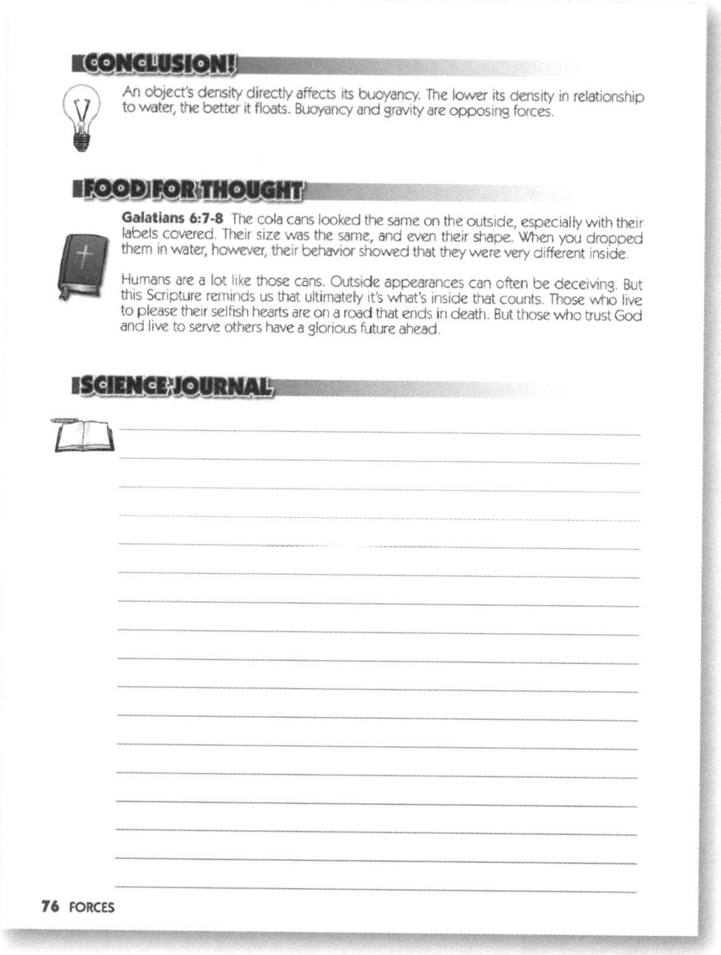

CONCLUSION!

An object's density directly affects its buoyancy. The lower its density in relationship to water, the better it floats. Buoyancy and gravity are opposing forces.

FOOD FOR THOUGHT

Galatians 6:7-8 The cola cans looked the same on the outside, especially with their labels covered. Their size was the same, and even their shape. When you dropped them in water, however, their behavior showed that they were very different inside.

Humans are a lot like those cans. Outside appearances can often be deceiving. But this Scripture reminds us that ultimately it's what's inside that counts. Those who live to please their selfish hearts are on a road that ends in death. But those who trust God and live to serve others have a glorious future ahead.

SCIENCE JOURNAL

76 FORCES

Extended Teaching

1. Repeat this activity using other products that contain natural and artifical sweeteners. Have students compare the results with the original activity. How were they similar? How were they different?

2. Have teams research the Civil War battle between the Monitor and Merrimac — the first battle between "ironclads". Challenge them to explain similarities and differences between these two ships.

3. Take a field trip to a scuba teaching facility. Find out about the equipment used and how it works. Have an instructor demonstrate "neutral" bouyancy. Have students write a paragraph about one thing they learn.

4. Invite an X-ray Technician to visit your classroom. Have him/her explain how the density of lead plays a role in protecting people from dangerous radiation. Have students write a paragraph about one thing they learn.

5. Bring a helium balloon to class. Show it to students, then place it in a refrigerator for a few hours. Bring it back out and monitor changes in buoyancy as it warms back up again.

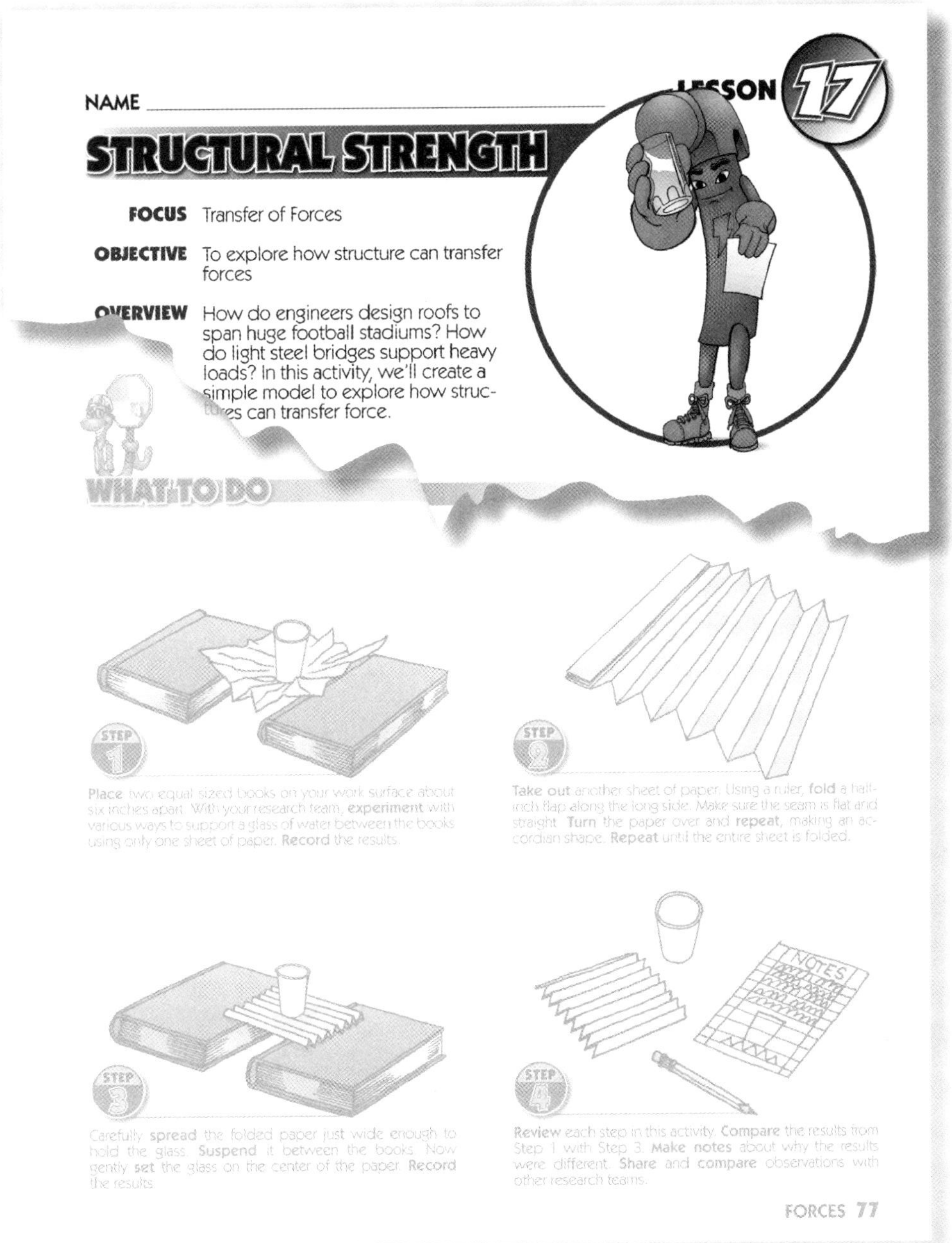

NAME

LESSON 17

STRUCTURAL STRENGTH

FOCUS Transfer of Forces

OBJECTIVE To explore how structure can transfer forces

OVERVIEW How do engineers design roofs to span huge football stadiums? How do light steel bridges support heavy loads? In this activity, we'll create a simple model to explore how structures can transfer force.

WHAT TO DO

STEP 1

Place two equal sized books on your work surface about six inches apart. With your research team, **experiment** with various ways to support a glass of water between the books using only one sheet of paper. **Record** the results.

STEP 2

Take out another sheet of paper. Using a ruler, **fold** a half-inch flap along the long side. Make sure the seam is flat and straight. **Turn** the paper over and **repeat**, making an accordian shape. **Repeat** until the entire sheet is folded.

STEP 3

Carefully **spread** the folded paper just wide enough to hold the glass. **Suspend** it between the books. Now gently **set** the glass on the center of the paper. **Record** the results.

STEP 4

Review each step in this activity. **Compare** the results from Step 1 with Step 3. **Make notes** about why the results were different. **Share** and **compare** observations with other research teams.

FORCES 77

Category

Physical Science
Forces

Focus

Transfer of Forces

Objective

To explore how structure can transfer forces

National Standards

A1, A2, B1, B2, B3, E1, E2, F4, F5, G1, G2

Materials Needed

plastic cup
books - 2
water
paper

Safety Concerns

4. Slipping
There is a potential for spills. Remind students to exercise caution with water.

Additional Comments

To avoid the potential for breakage, be sure to use plastic cups to hold the water.

Overview

Read the overview aloud to your students. The goal is to create an atmosphere of curiosity and inquiry.

WHAT TO DO

Monitor student research teams as they complete each step.

NAME ______________________ LESSON 17

STRUCTURAL STRENGTH

FOCUS Transfer of Forces

OBJECTIVE To explore how structure can transfer forces

OVERVIEW How do engineers design roofs to span huge football stadiums? How do light steel bridges support heavy loads? In this activity, we'll create a simple model to explore how structures can transfer force.

WHAT TO DO

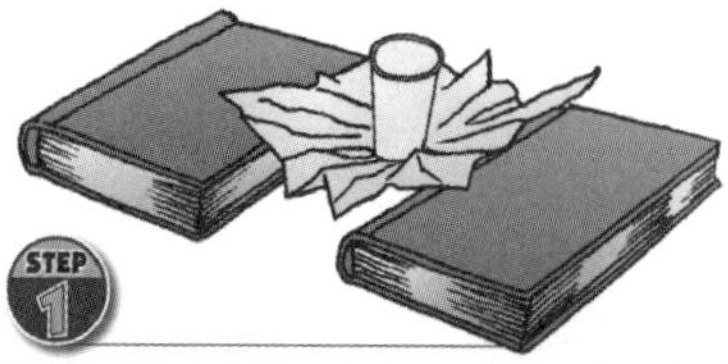

STEP 1

Place two equal sized books on your work surface about six inches apart. With your research team, **experiment** with various ways to support a glass of water between the books using only one sheet of paper. **Record** the results.

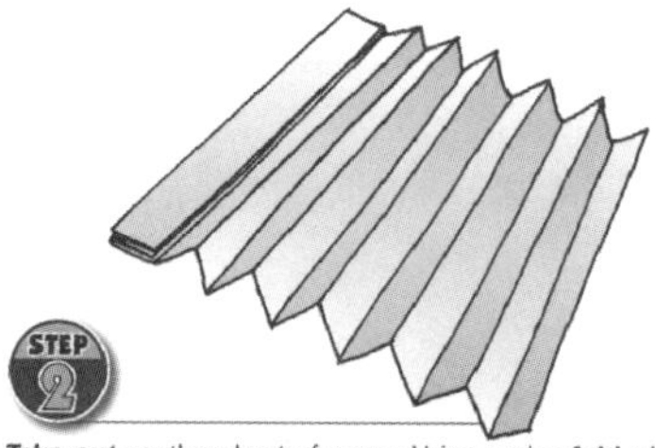

STEP 2

Take out another sheet of paper. Using a ruler, **fold** a half-inch flap along the long side. Make sure the seam is flat and straight. **Turn** the paper over and **repeat**, making an accordian shape. **Repeat** until the entire sheet is folded.

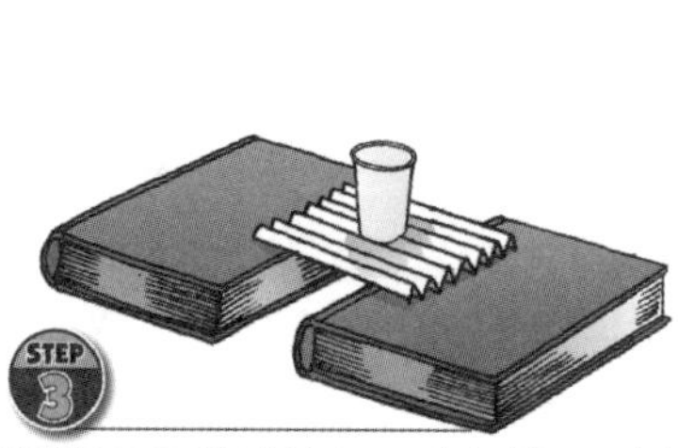

STEP 3

Carefully **spread** the folded paper just wide enough to hold the glass. **Suspend** it between the books. Now gently **set** the glass on the center of the paper. **Record** the results.

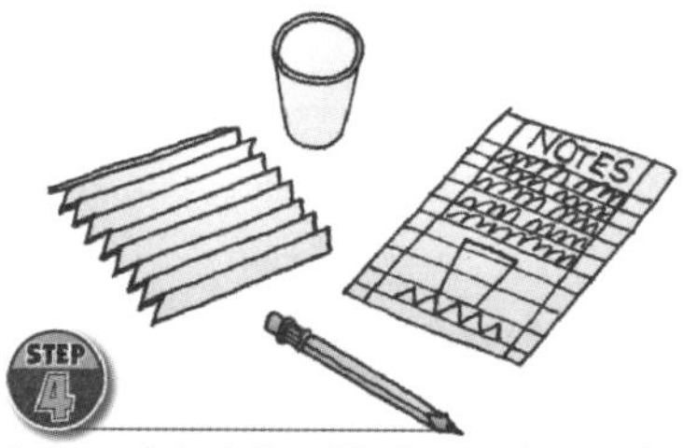

STEP 4

Review each step in this activity. **Compare** the results from Step 1 with Step 3. **Make notes** about why the results were different. **Share** and **compare** observations with other research teams.

FORCES 77

Teacher to Teacher

The "wood" paper is made from is called cellulose. In its original form (a tree) the fibers reinforce each other, giving the wood tremendous strength. But when this wood is ground up, the fibers are separated and realigned. This makes paper much more flexible, but not very strong.

In this activity, we folded a sheet of paper in a way that helped the fibers work together again. This regained some of the original strength. This is the principle applied in making strong cardboard boxes. The corrugations between layers give the material extra strength and support.

WHAT JUST HAPPENED?

To support the glass, you needed some way to **oppose** the **force** of **gravity**. You probably didn't find it in Step 1. A flat sheet of paper doesn't provide much support! The wood fibers in the paper have been made very flat and smooth. This is what makes paper easy to write on. (Imagine trying to write on a piece of bark!)

Originally the **wood fibers** in the tree the paper was made from were quite capable of supporting a glass. By folding the paper into a series of triangles, you regained some of that original strength. The **structure** of the folded paper **transferred** the **weight** of the glass to the books and table, defeating the **pull** of gravity.

By understanding the **transfer of forces**, engineers are able to design structures where relatively light-weight materials will support heavy loads.

MORE ABOUT TRANSFER OF FORCES . . .

Designing structures like bridges and buildings can be a complex task. Engineers must balance the need for strength against the possibility of using too much material. If the materials used are too large or too heavy, constructing the building can be too expensive. But if fewer or lighter materials are used, the building can be unsafe.

However, as you discovered in this activity, the design of a structural support is just as important as its size. The flat piece of paper couldn't even begin to support the glass of water at first. But when it was folded into a series of triangles, it supported the glass easily. (Engineers use a variation of this to design strong, light-weight roof trusses.)

Let's take a closer look at how this really works.

In this activity, the paper truss transferred the downward force of the glass (weight) to the table. The table transferred the force through its legs to the floor. The floor transferred the force to the building's foundation, and the foundation transferred the force to Earth itself. If any one of these components had been unable to transfer the force, it would have failed — and the glass would have fallen!

It is only by understanding how force is transferred that engineers are able to design structures where relatively light-weight materials can support heavy loads.

The next time you walk into a large department store (like a Wal-Mart or Target), look up at the steel trusses supporting the roof. Notice how the trusses rest on huge steel beams. Follow a beam with your eye to the support column or wall that transfers the roof's force to floor, and through the floor to the ground. As you can see, engineers used their understanding of the transfer of forces to design this structure so that it would be safe and useful for a long time!

DIGGING DEEPER:

Research and discuss how the work of engineers impacts our daily lives. Check out some ways their designs relate to sports, entertainment, medical innovations, and even fast food! (The American Society of Civil Engineers has some great links for kids on its website.)

WHAT WE LEARNED:

1 **How did folding the paper in Step 2 change its strength? What did the folded paper allow you to do with the downward force of gravity?**

a) made it much stronger

b) transfer the weight and defeat gravity

2 **If you turned the paper 90 degrees so the folds were parallel with the books, what might happen? Why?**

a) the paper would not support the weight

b) the support goes the wrong direction

3 **Based on what you've learned, explain the phrase, "the longer the bridge, the more difficult the design". How does this statement relate to the forces demonstrated in this activity?**

a) the longer the bridge, the less support it has in the middle; this makes it more difficult to design

b) longer bridges require better designs to overcome the downward pull of gravity

What Happened

Review the section with students. Emphasize bold-face words that identify key concepts and introduce new vocabulary.

To support the glass, you needed some way to ***oppose*** *the* ***force*** *of* ***gravity****. You probably didn't find it in Step 1. A flat sheet of paper doesn't provide much support! The wood fibers in the paper have been made very flat and smooth. This is what makes paper easy to write on. (Imagine trying to write on a piece of bark!)*

Ordinarily the ***wood fibers*** *in the tree the paper was made from were quite capable of supporting a glass. By folding the paper into a series of triangles, you regained some of that original strength. The* ***structure*** *of the folded paper* ***transferred*** *the* ***weight*** *of the glass to the books and table, defeating the* ***pull*** *of gravity.*

By understanding the ***transfer of forces****, engineers are able to design structures where relatively light-weight materials will support heavy loads.*

More About . . .

Have students read this section as you would a traditional science text — or use cooperative learning techniques to allow students the opportunity to work on the material collaboratively.

Digging Deeper

(Optional) Challenge teams to reseach and discuss practical applications of the lesson concepts. Encourage them to share their findings with the rest of the class.

What We Learned

Answers will vary. Suggested responses are shown at left.

Conclusion

Read this section aloud to the class to summarize the concepts learned in this activity.

Food for Thought

Read the Scripture aloud to the class. Talk about God's unlimited power. Discuss ways we can learn to rely on God's power in our lives.

Science Journal

If time permits, have a general class discussion about notes and drawings various students added to their journal pages. Discuss correct and incorrect predictions, and remind students that this "trial and error" process is part of the scientific process.

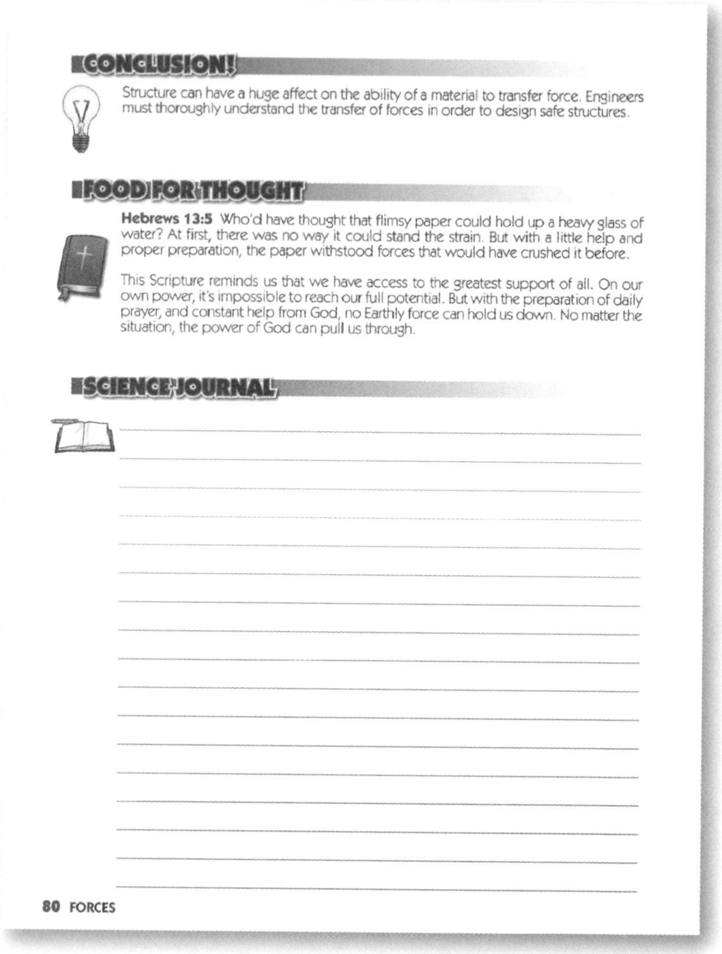

CONCLUSION!

Structure can have a huge affect on the ability of a material to transfer force. Engineers must thoroughly understand the transfer of forces in order to design safe structures.

FOOD FOR THOUGHT

Hebrews 13:5 Who'd have thought that flimsy paper could hold up a heavy glass of water? At first, there was no way it could stand the strain. But with a little help and proper preparation, the paper withstood forces that would have crushed it before.

This Scripture reminds us that we have access to the greatest support of all. On our own power, it's impossible to reach our full potential. But with the preparation of daily prayer, and constant help from God, no Earthly force can hold us down. No matter the situation, the power of God can pull us through.

SCIENCE JOURNAL

80 FORCES

Extended Teaching

1. Repeat this activity using strips of cardboard. Experiment to see which way the corrugations must run. Have students compare the results with the original activity. How were they similar? How were they different?

2. Using the Internet, have teams research the structure of major bridges. What holds them up? Challenge each team to make a presentation to the class describing one of these bridges.

3. Invite a structural engineer or architect to visit your classroom. Talk about how structures are designed to defeat gravity. Have students write a paragraph about one thing they learn.

4. Borrow a lab scale and weigh the paper. Now weigh the glass of water. Comparing these two figures gives you the "strength-to-weight ratio." Have students apply this concept to other combinations.

5. Take a field trip to visit a university engineering lab. Have technicians demonstrate some of their on-going structural experiments. Have students write a paragraph about one thing they learn.

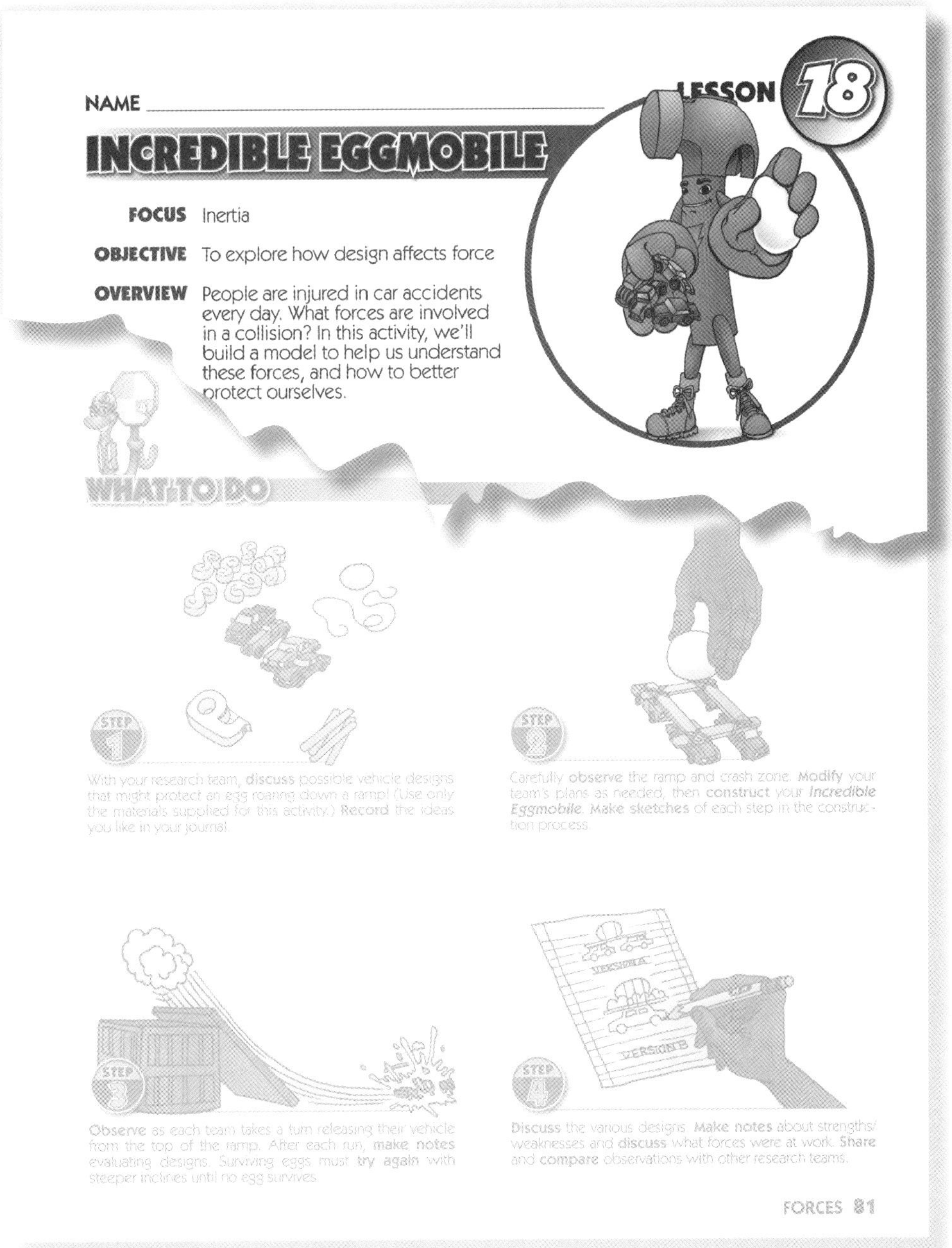
NAME ______________________

LESSON 18

INCREDIBLE EGGMOBILE

FOCUS Inertia

OBJECTIVE To explore how design affects force

OVERVIEW People are injured in car accidents every day. What forces are involved in a collision? In this activity, we'll build a model to help us understand these forces, and how to better protect ourselves.

WHAT TO DO

STEP 1 With your research team, **discuss** possible vehicle designs that might protect an egg roaring down a ramp! (Use only the materials supplied for this activity.) **Record** the ideas you like in your journal.

STEP 2 Carefully **observe** the ramp and crash zone. **Modify** your team's plans as needed, then **construct** your ***Incredible Eggmobile***. **Make sketches** of each step in the construction process.

STEP 3 **Observe** as each team takes a turn releasing their vehicle from the top of the ramp. After each run, **make notes** evaluating designs. Surviving eggs must **try again** with steeper inclines until no egg survives.

STEP 4 **Discuss** the various designs. **Make notes** about strengths/weaknesses and **discuss** what forces were at work. **Share** and **compare** observations with other research teams.

FORCES 81

Category

Physical Science
Forces

Focus

Inertia

Objective

To explore how design affects force

National Standards

A1, A2, B1, B2, B3, E1, E2, F4, F5, G1, G2

Materials Needed

toy cars - 4
craft sticks - 4
packing pellets
string
egg
ramp
tape

Safety Concerns

4. Slipping
Broken eggs create the potential for slipping. Remind students to exercise extra caution.

Additional Comments

Step 3 works best in an outdoor location. (A concrete area that butts up against the building is ideal.) Clean up can easily be accomplished with a hose. Since students are handling eggs, be sure they wash their hands thoroughly with soap and water when finished.

Overview

Read the overview aloud to your students. The goal is to create an atmosphere of curiosity and inquiry.

WHAT TO DO

Monitor student research teams as they complete each step.

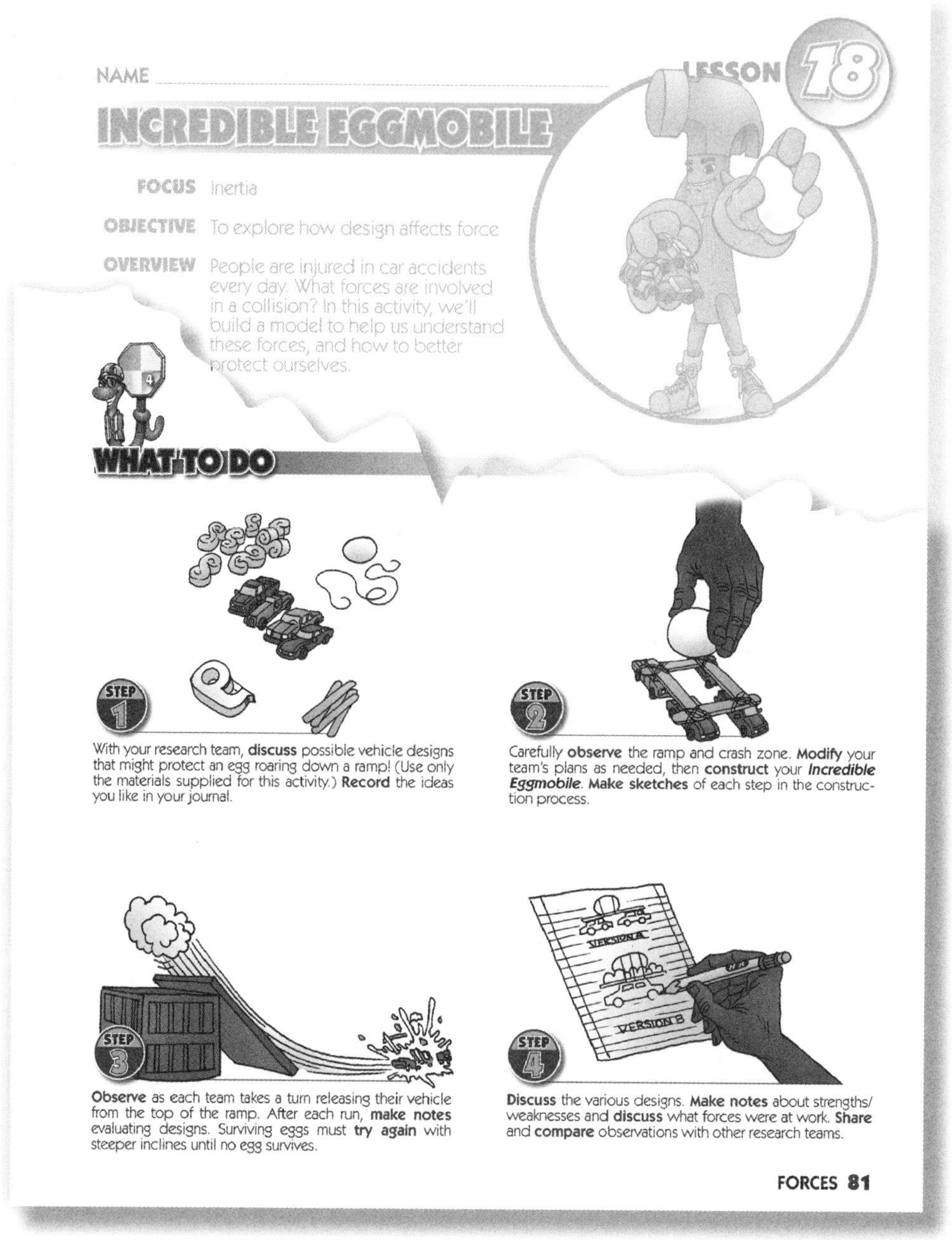

NAME ______________________________ LESSON 18

INCREDIBLE EGGMOBILE

FOCUS Inertia

OBJECTIVE To explore how design affects force

OVERVIEW People are injured in car accidents every day. What forces are involved in a collision? In this activity, we'll build a model to help us understand these forces, and how to better protect ourselves.

WHAT TO DO

STEP 1 With your research team, **discuss** possible vehicle designs that might protect an egg roaring down a ramp! (Use only the materials supplied for this activity.) **Record** the ideas you like in your journal.

STEP 2 Carefully **observe** the ramp and crash zone. **Modify** your team's plans as needed, then **construct** your ***Incredible Eggmobile***. **Make sketches** of each step in the construction process.

STEP 3 **Observe** as each team takes a turn releasing their vehicle from the top of the ramp. After each run, **make notes** evaluating designs. Surviving eggs must **try again** with steeper inclines until no egg survives.

STEP 4 **Discuss** the various designs. **Make notes** about strengths/weaknesses and **discuss** what forces were at work. **Share** and **compare** observations with other research teams.

FORCES 81

Teacher to Teacher

Break open one of the "surviving" eggs and you'll often find that the yolk inside is broken. Even though the shell stopped, the yolk kept moving and collided with the inside of the shell. This process explains some motorcycle injuries. Although the helmet protects the head, the impact may still damage the brain if it collides with the inside of the skull.

WHAT JUST HAPPENED?

By lifting your eggmobile to the top of the ramp you **opposed** gravity, giving your eggmobile **potential energy**. Letting it go turned potential energy into **kinetic** (moving) **energy**. But all this energy had to go somewhere. Part of Newton's **Law of Inertia** states that when an object is moving, it keeps moving until acted on by another **force**. At the end of the ramp, your eggmobile suddenly encountered that force — an immovable wall!

If your eggmobile was well-designed, it was able to **absorb** or **transfer** most of the force with minimal damage to its passenger. But imagine what would have happened if your egg wasn't strapped in? As long as it's attached to the vehicle, it stops when the vehicle stops. But without that attachment, your egg becomes a rapidly moving projectile (probably with tragic results). That's why always wearing your seatbelt is vital to your safety!

MORE ABOUT INERTIA . . .

Newton's First Law (also known as the "Law of Inertia") states that an object in motion tends to stay in motion unless an external force is applied to it. This means that once something is moving it takes some kind of force to stop it.

Cars and trucks are relatively heavy. When you get them moving, there's a lot of force involved. At 70 miles per hour, it takes the average car over 300 feet to come to a complete stop. That's about the length of a football field!

But in a car accident, that force doesn't have the distance to dissipate. It has to go somewhere NOW! That's why car accidents can be fatal. The human body is not designed to absorb that kind of immense force.

Fortunately safety engineers have figured out ways to absorb or transfer much of the energy away from us. Collapsible bumpers, air bags, padded dashes, and soft steering wheels are all designed to help absorb the energy of a car crash.

In addition, many parts of today's cars are designed to crumple or fold in the event of an accident (something like the cushioning you created for your eggmobile). This folding and crumpling also helps transfer even more force away from us.

But in order for these protective devices to work properly, the car's passengers must be wearing their seatbelts! If you're not firmly attached to the car, your body won't stop when the car does. In accordance with Newton's First Law, you will keep moving until some kind of external force stops you — possibly resulting in injury or death.

So be smart, and be safe. Always wear your seatbelt!

DIGGING DEEPER:

Crash test dummies have saved thousands of lives. Research and discuss how these human replicas work, and why they are essential in the development of all types of new vehicles, from family minivans to fighter planes.

82 FORCES

WHAT WE LEARNED:

1. **What kinds of forces are involved in a collision? Why are these forces dangerous to human beings?**

   a) inertia, kinetic energy, etc.

   b) answers should reflect description from "What Happened?"

2. **Based on what you've learned, explain why always wearing a seatbelt is vital to your safety.**

   if you are wearing a seatbelt, then your body will stop when the car stops

3. **If you were to repeat this activity, how might you change your design? Explain how these changes could make your eggmobile safer.**

   answers will vary, but should reflect logical conclusions

FORCES 83

What Happened

Review the section with students. Emphasize bold-face words that identify key concepts and introduce new vocabulary.

*By lifting your eggmobile to the top of the ramp you **opposed** gravity, giving your eggmobile **potential energy**. Letting it go turned potential energy into **kinetic** (moving) **energy**. But all this energy had to go somewhere. Part of Newton's **law of inertia** states that when an object is moving, it keeps moving until acted on by another **force**. At the end of the ramp, your eggmobile suddenly encountered that force — an immovable wall!*

*If your eggmobile was well-designed, it was able to **absorb** or **transfer** most of the force with minimal damage to its passenger. But imagine what would have happened if your egg wasn't strapped in? As long as it's attached to the vehicle, it stops when the vehicle stops. But without that attachment, your egg becomes a rapidly moving projectile (probably with tragic results). That's why always wearing your seatbelt is vital to your safety!*

More About . . .

Have students read this section as you would a traditional science text — or use cooperative learning techniques to allow students the opportunity to work on the material collaboratively.

Digging Deeper

(Optional) Challenge teams to reseach and discuss practical applications of the lesson concepts. Encourage them to share their findings with the rest of the class.

What We Learned

Answers will vary. Suggested responses are shown at left.

Conclusion

Read this section aloud to the class to summarize the concepts learned in this activity.

Food for Thought

Read the Scripture aloud to the class. Talk about the importance of learning to trust God. Discuss ways God is a shield to those who trust Him.

Science Journal

If time permits, have a general class discussion about notes and drawings various students added to their journal pages. Discuss correct and incorrect predictions, and remind students that this "trial and error" process is part of the scientific process.

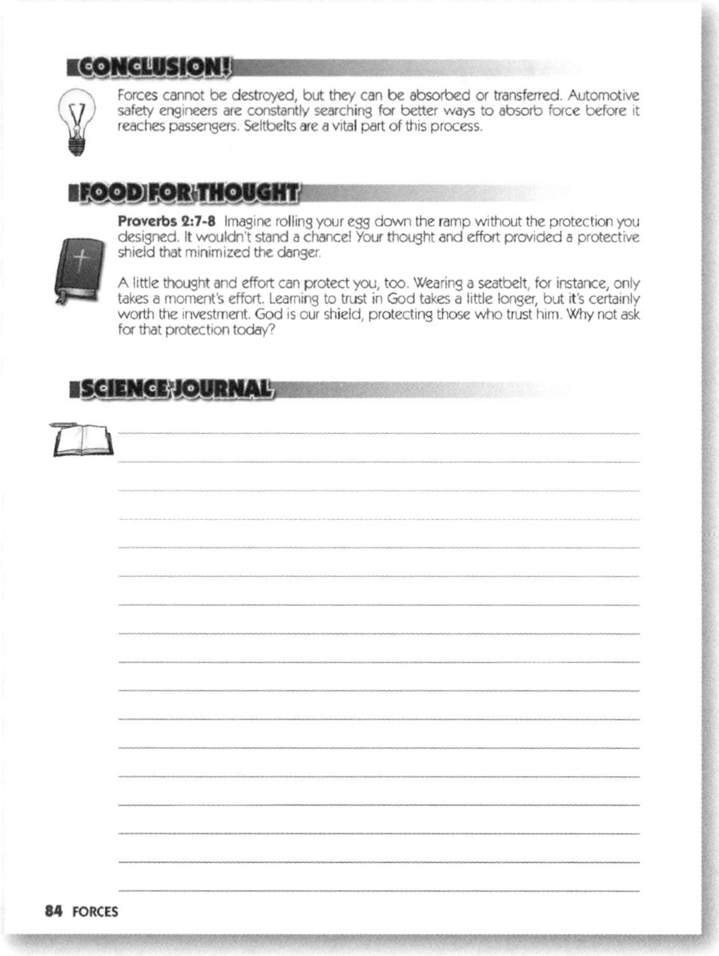

CONCLUSION!

Forces cannot be destroyed, but they can be absorbed or transferred. Automotive safety engineers are constantly searching for better ways to absorb force before it reaches passengers. Seltbelts are a vital part of this process.

FOOD FOR THOUGHT

Proverbs 2:7-8 Imagine rolling your egg down the ramp without the protection you designed. It wouldn't stand a chance! Your thought and effort provided a protective shield that minimized the danger.

A little thought and effort can protect you, too. Wearing a seatbelt, for instance, only takes a moment's effort. Learning to trust in God takes a little longer, but it's certainly worth the investment. God is our shield, protecting those who trust him. Why not ask for that protection today?

SCIENCE JOURNAL

84 FORCES

Extended Teaching

1. Invite a state trooper to visit your classroom. Have him/her talk about the importance of wearing seat belts. Have students write a paragraph about one thing they learn.

2. Using the Internet, have teams research new technologies that are being developed to help paraplegics and quadriplegics. Challenge teams to create a bulletin board depicting their findings.

3. Have teams research different forms of safety equipment. Challenge each team to make a poster showing one kind of safety equipment and how it prevents injuries.

4. Take a field trip to a large sporting goods store. Have the manager demonstrate various kinds of safety equipment from different sports. Have students write a paragraph about one thing they learn.

5. See if a local law enforcement agency can provide videos on seatbelt safety. Show these to your class and have teams discuss the content. Have students write a paragraph about one thing they learn.

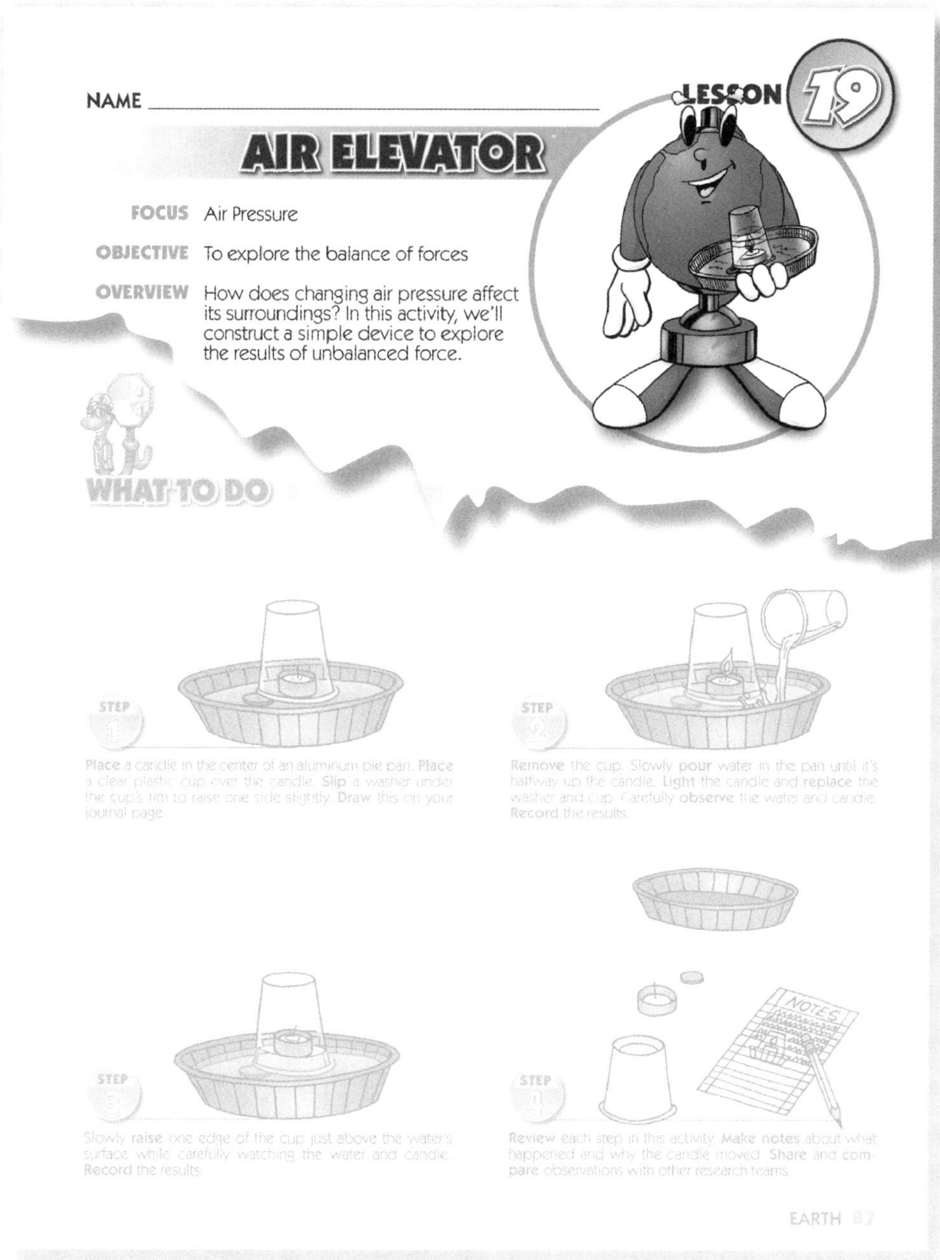

NAME

LESSON 19

AIR ELEVATOR

FOCUS Air Pressure

OBJECTIVE To explore the balance of forces

OVERVIEW How does changing air pressure affect its surroundings? In this activity, we'll construct a simple device to explore the results of unbalanced force.

WHAT TO DO

STEP 1 **Place** a candle in the center of an aluminum pie pan. **Place** a clear plastic cup over the candle. **Slip** a washer under the cup's rim to raise one side slightly. **Draw** this on your journal page.

STEP 2 **Remove** the cup. Slowly **pour** water in the pan until it's halfway up the candle. **Light** the candle and **replace** the washer and cup. Carefully **observe** the water and candle. **Record** the results.

STEP 3 Slowly **raise** one edge of the cup just above the water's surface while carefully watching the water and candle. **Record** the results.

STEP 4 **Review** each step in this activity. **Make notes** about what happened and why the candle moved. **Share** and **compare** observations with other research teams.

EARTH 87

Category
Earth Science

Focus
Air Pressure

Objective
To explore the balance of forces

National Standards
A1, A2, B1, B2, D1, G1, G2

Materials Needed
clear plastic cup
washer
candle
matches
aluminum pie pan
water

Safety Concerns
2. Open Flame
Remind students to exercise caution around the candle flame.

4. Slipping
There is a potential for spills. Remind students to exercise caution.

Additional Comments
You can avoid students handling matches by lighting the candles for them. A lighter wand works well for this. Mixing food coloring with the water will add a little drama.

Overview
Read the overview aloud to your students. The goal is to create an atmosphere of curiosity and inquiry.

WHAT TO DO

Monitor student research teams as they complete each step.

NAME

LESSON 19

AIR ELEVATOR

FOCUS Air Pressure

OBJECTIVE To explore the balance of forces

OVERVIEW How does changing air pressure affect its surroundings? In this activity, we'll construct a simple device to explore the results of unbalanced force.

WHAT TO DO

STEP 1

Place a candle in the center of an aluminum pie pan. **Place** a clear plastic cup over the candle. **Slip** a washer under the cup's rim to raise one side slightly. **Draw** this on your journal page.

STEP 2

Remove the cup. Slowly **pour** water in the pan until it's halfway up the candle. **Light** the candle and **replace** the washer and cup. Carefully **observe** the water and candle. **Record** the results.

STEP 3

Slowly **raise** one edge of the cup just above the water's surface while carefully watching the water and candle. **Record** the results.

STEP 4

Review each step in this activity. **Make notes** about what happened and why the candle moved. **Share** and **compare** observations with other research teams.

EARTH 87

Teacher to Teacher

Forces (either push or pull) are always found in pairs. If a pencil is placed on a desk, gravity pulls the pencil downward, but the mass of the desk pushes back. Since the pencil isn't floating off into space or falling toward the floor, the push/pull of forces between the desk and pencil are equal. Another name for this is an equalibrium.

WHAT JUST HAPPENED?

When you placed the cup over the candle in Step 1, nothing happened. The **force** of the **air pressure** was the same inside and outside the cup. When you placed the cup over the burning candle in Step 2, you trapped air in the cup. The **combustion** process quickly removed the **oxygen** from that air, lowering the air pressure in the cup.

The low air pressure in the cup **pulled**, the high air pressure outside the cup **pushed**, and the water level in the cup moved up until the **forces** inside and outside were **equalized**. (Notice that **movement** only occurred when there were **unbalanced forces**. Once **equilibrium** was achieved, the movement stopped.)

In Step 3, you lifted the edge of the cup, unbalancing the air pressure again. To equalize the forces, the water level (and candle) immediately moved back down.

MORE ABOUT AIR PRESSURE . . .

Air is all around us. In fact, some people describe our lives as "swimming in an ocean of air." As we saw in this activity, this massive ocean of air has pressure, and even though we may not feel it, air pressure can go up or down.

One of the most important ways that air pressure affects our daily lives is its impact on the weather. A high air pressure system is like a huge mountain of air. A low air pressure system is more like a spread-out plain. That's the reason there are very few clouds in a high pressure area — the clouds and rain sort of slide down the slopes of the mountain, and gather in the valleys and plains. And, of course, that's why a low pressure system usually results in clouds or precipitation of some kind.

Scientists use a special tool called a **barometer** to measure air pressure in the atmosphere. Sometimes a weather report (especially on rural radio stations) will refer to the current "barometric pressure" and whether it's "rising" or "falling". That's one way that farmers know what kind of weather to expect. Rising pressure means a period of fair weather is possible; falling pressure often means that rain is on the way. Fishermen tend to appreciate this information, too, since many believe that the best time to fish is when the barometer is falling!

There are many other ways that air pressure affects us, too. Without it, you may not have been able to get to school today since air pressure is what kept the tires on your car or bicycle inflated! Air pressure is also used in industry to power many types of tools and equipment.

And, of course, a certain amount of air pressure is necessary for our lungs to function properly so that we can breathe. That's a very important use indeed!

DIGGING DEEPER:

Air pressure is a very important part of our daily lives. Research and discuss various ways that air pressure affects us. Some areas to explore include weather systems, tools and equipment, and medical devices. Be sure to share your findings with the rest of the class.

88 EARTH

WHAT WE LEARNED:

1. **What force made the water rise in Step 2? What opposing force made the water fall in Step 3? Explain what determined which force won in each step.**

a) lower air pressure

b) gravity

c) the seal determined if gravity or air pressure won

2. **What effect would a hole in the cup have on the air pressure inside? How would this change the results? Why?**

a) it would allow the air pressure to constantly equalize

b) the water wouldn't be pulled up

c) because air pressure would never decrease

3. **Imagine that a candle is glued to the pie pan. Based on what you observed, what would determine whether water or lack of oxygen puts out the flame? Explain.**

a) how quickly pressure equalizes

b) the water will stop rising when the air pressure equalizes; if this happens quickly, water won't reach the flame

EARTH 89

What Happened

Review the section with students. Emphasize bold-face words that identify key concepts and introduce new vocabulary.

*When you placed the cup over the candle in Step 1, nothing happened. The **force** of the **air pressure** was the same inside and outside the cup. When you placed the cup over the burning candle in Step 2, you trapped air in the cup. The **combustion** process quickly removed the **oxygen** from that air, lowering the air pressure in the cup.*

*The low air pressure in the cup **pulled**, the high air pressure outside the cup **pushed**, and the water level in the cup moved up until the **forces** inside and outside were **equalized**. (Notice that **movement** only occurred when there were **unbalanced forces**. Once **equilibrium** was achieved, the movement stopped.)*

In Step 3, you lifted the edge of the cup, unbalancing the air pressure again. To equalize the forces, the water level (and candle) immediately moved back down.

More About . . .

Have students read this section as you would a traditional science text — or use cooperative learning techniques to allow students the opportunity to work on the material collaboratively.

Digging Deeper

(Optional) Challenge teams to reseach and discuss practical applications of the lesson concepts. Encourage them to share their findings with the rest of the class.

What We Learned

Answers will vary. Suggested responses are shown at left.

Conclusion

Read this section aloud to the class to summarize the concepts learned in this activity.

Food for Thought

Read the Scripture aloud to the class. Talk about the importance of a relationship with Christ. Discuss ways we can daily experience His infinite love.

Science Journal

If time permits, have a general class discussion about notes and drawings various students added to their journal pages. Discuss correct and incorrect predictions, and remind students that this "trial and error" process is part of the scientific process.

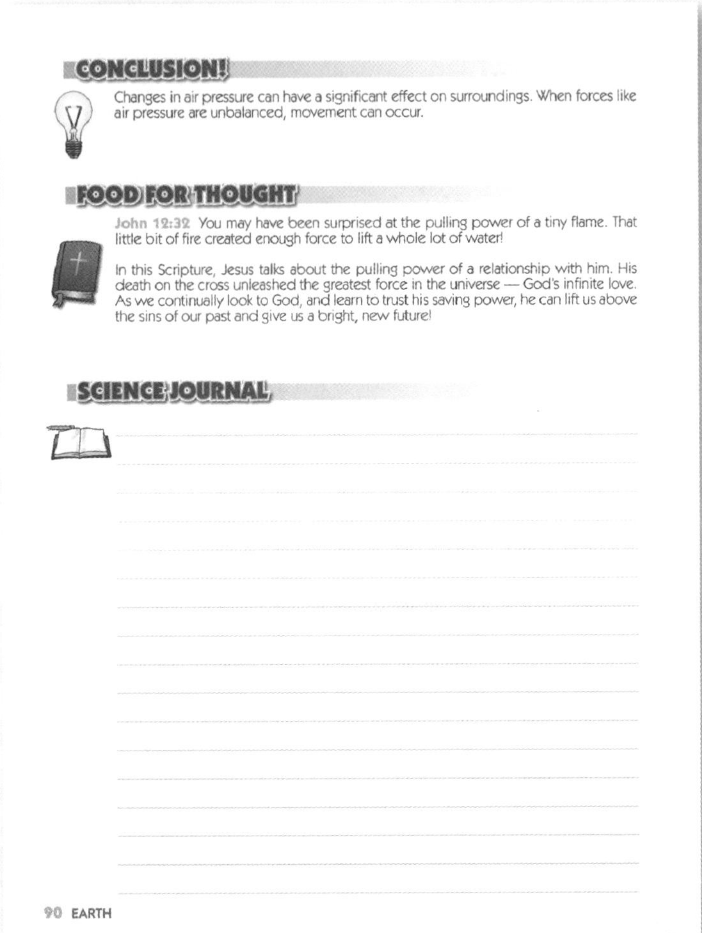

CONCLUSION!

Changes in air pressure can have a significant effect on surroundings. When forces like air pressure are unbalanced, movement can occur.

FOOD FOR THOUGHT

John 12:32 You may have been surprised at the pulling power of a tiny flame. That little bit of fire created enough force to lift a whole lot of water!

In this Scripture, Jesus talks about the pulling power of a relationship with him. His death on the cross unleashed the greatest force in the universe — God's infinite love. As we continually look to God, and learn to trust his saving power, he can lift us above the sins of our past and give us a bright, new future!

SCIENCE JOURNAL

90 EARTH

Extended Teaching

1. Repeat this activity using hot water in the pie pan. Have teams compare the results with the original activity. How are they similar? How are they different?

2. Have teams find examples of push/pull forces around school. Challenge each team to make a poster depicting some of their findings.

3. Using the Internet, have teams research elevator history. Find out how elevators work and how they've changed over time. Challenge each team to contribute a description or drawing to an elevator bulletin board.

4. Invite a scuba diver to visit your classroom. Ask him/her to explain how air pressure plays a role in diving. Discuss "neutral buoyancy." Have students write a paragraph about one thing they learn.

5. Take a field trip to a boat lift distributor. (The yellow pages or www.hydrohoist.com are good sources.) Find out how air pressure is used to raise and lower boats. Have students write a paragraph about one thing they learn.

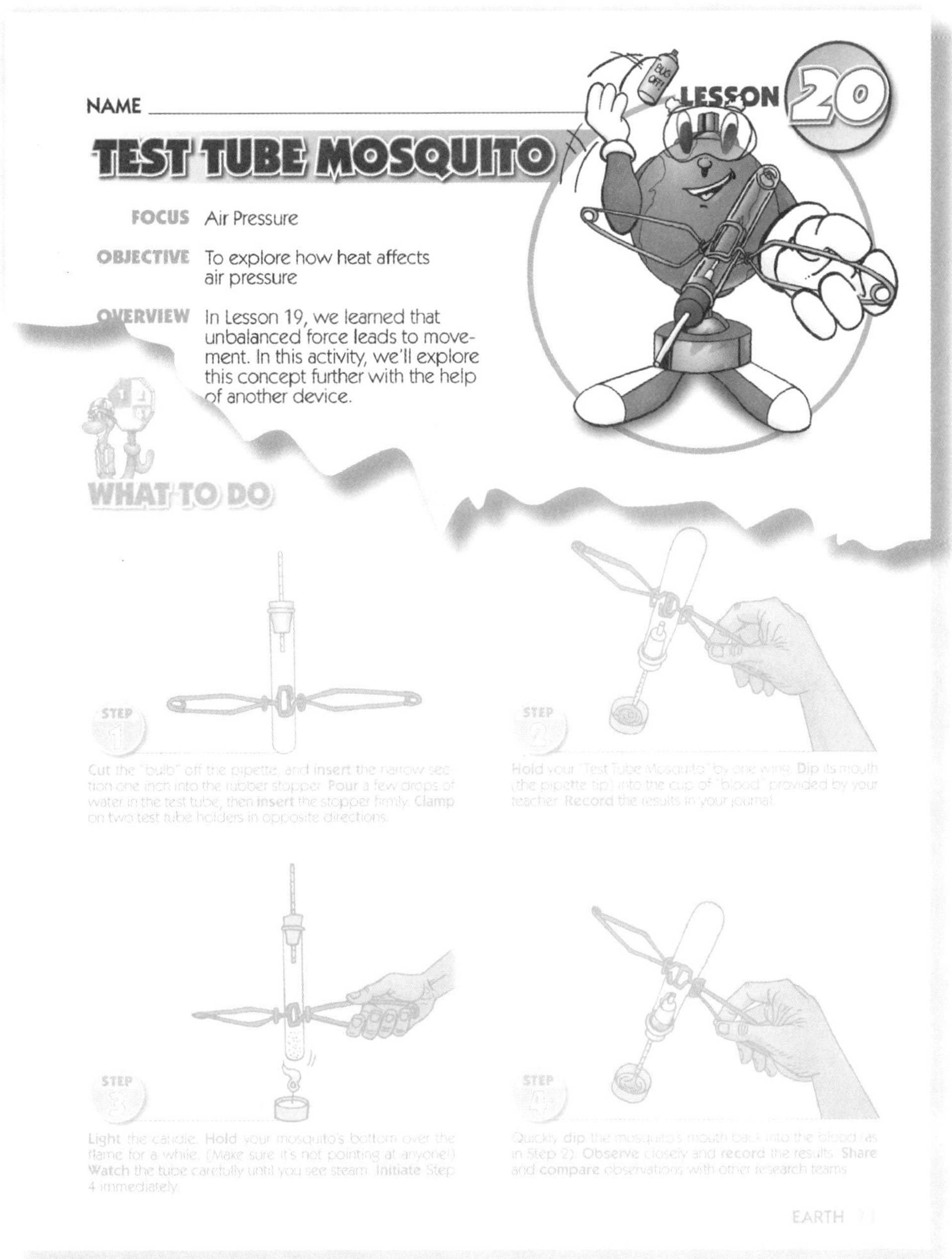
NAME ______________________________

LESSON 20

TEST TUBE MOSQUITO

FOCUS Air Pressure

OBJECTIVE To explore how heat affects air pressure

OVERVIEW In Lesson 19, we learned that unbalanced force leads to movement. In this activity, we'll explore this concept further with the help of another device.

WHAT TO DO

STEP 1 Cut the "bulb" off the pipette, and **insert** the narrow section one inch into the rubber stopper. **Pour** a few drops of water in the test tube, then **insert** the stopper firmly. **Clamp** on two test tube holders in opposite directions.

STEP 2 **Hold** your "Test Tube Mosquito" by one wing. **Dip** its mouth (the pipette tip) into the cup of "blood" provided by your teacher. **Record** the results in your journal.

STEP 3 **Light** the candle. **Hold** your mosquito's bottom over the flame for a while. (Make sure it's not pointing at anyone!) **Watch** the tube carefully until you see steam. **Initiate** Step 4 immediately.

STEP 4 Quickly **dip** the mosquito's mouth back into the blood (as in Step 2). **Observe** closely and **record** the results. **Share** and **compare** observations with other research teams.

EARTH 91

Category

Earth Science

Focus

Air Pressure

Objective

To explore how heat affects air pressure

National Standards

A1, A2, B1, B2, D1, G1, G2

Materials Needed

rubber stopper w/hole
test tube holders - 2
test tube
pipette
candle
red food coloring
water
scissors
matches

Safety Concerns

1. Goggles
Since this activity combines steam and glass, goggles are a reasonable precaution.

2. Open Flame
Remind students to exercise caution around the candle flame.

4. Breakage
Glass test tubes can break. Remind students to exercise caution.

Additional Comments

Depending on student maturity, you may wish to do this as a demonstration only. Test tubes must always be pointed away from people while heating. Lighting candles yourself avoids students handling matches. Make the "blood" ahead of time with red food coloring and water. A few drops of blue will deepen the color.

Overview

Read the overview aloud to your students. The goal is to create an atmosphere of curiosity and inquiry.

WHAT TO DO

Monitor student research teams as they complete each step.

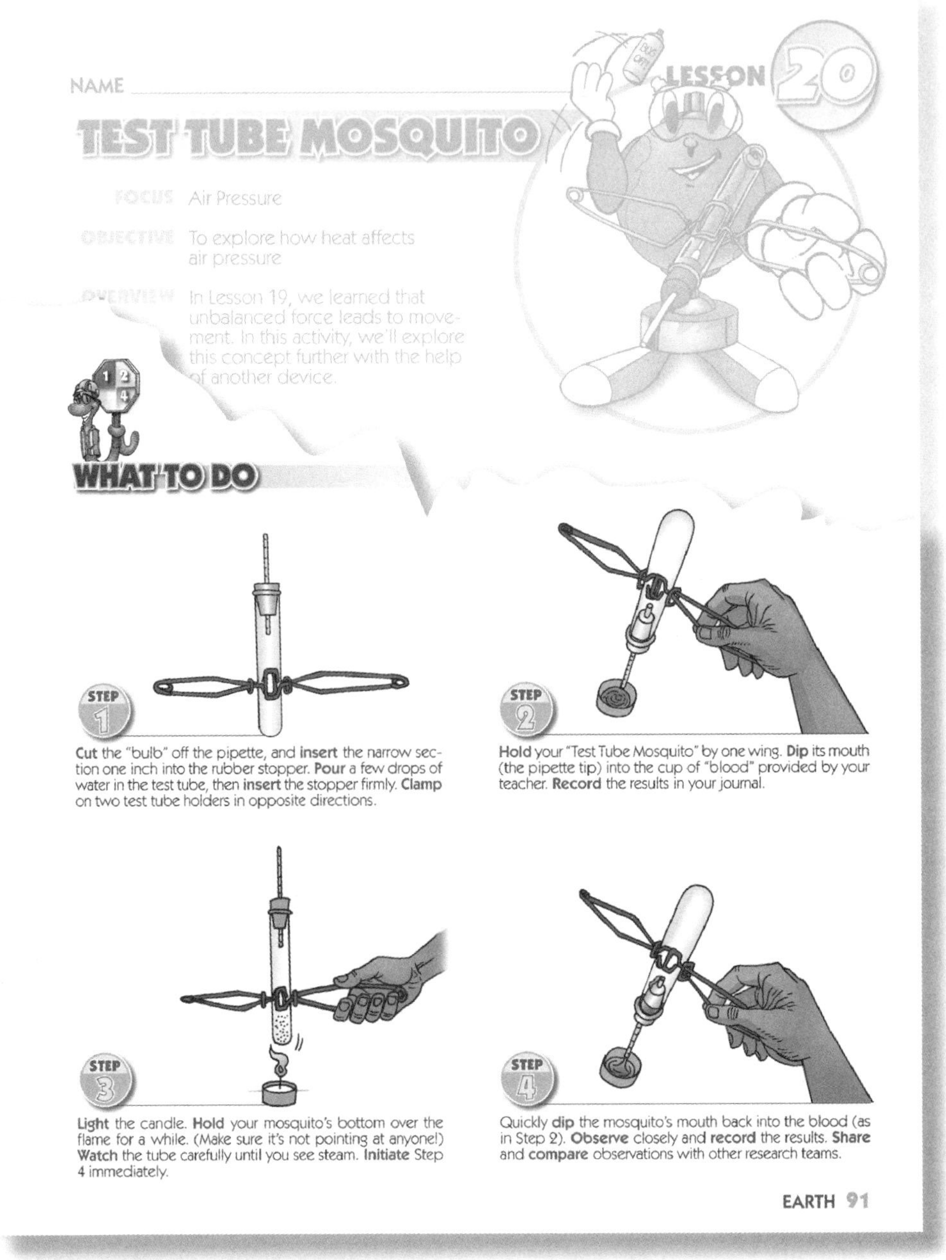

NAME

LESSON 20

TEST TUBE MOSQUITO

FOCUS Air Pressure

OBJECTIVE To explore how heat affects air pressure

OVERVIEW In Lesson 19, we learned that unbalanced force leads to movement. In this activity, we'll explore this concept further with the help of another device.

WHAT TO DO

STEP 1

Cut the "bulb" off the pipette, and **insert** the narrow section one inch into the rubber stopper. **Pour** a few drops of water in the test tube, then **insert** the stopper firmly. **Clamp** on two test tube holders in opposite directions.

STEP 2

Hold your "Test Tube Mosquito" by one wing. **Dip** its mouth (the pipette tip) into the cup of "blood" provided by your teacher. **Record** the results in your journal.

STEP 3

Light the candle. **Hold** your mosquito's bottom over the flame for a while. (Make sure it's not pointing at anyone!) **Watch** the tube carefully until you see steam. **Initiate** Step 4 immediately.

STEP 4

Quickly **dip** the mosquito's mouth back into the blood (as in Step 2). **Observe** closely and **record** the results. **Share** and **compare** observations with other research teams.

EARTH 91

Teacher to Teacher

The Kinetic Theory of Matter states that all particles are in constant motion, and the faster they move, the greater the force generated. In this activity, you used temperature to change the particles' speed. The hotter they got, the faster they moved — eventually generating enough force that some of them left the tube. As the remaining particles cooled, they slowed down and air pressure in the tube fell, pulling water up into the "mosquito."

WHAT JUST HAPPENED?

When you tried to get the mosquito to drink in Step 2, nothing happened. **Air pressure** inside and outside the tube was the same. But when you **heated** the tube in Step 3, you created unequal **forces**. The water and air **molecules** in the steam (water changed from **liquid** to **gas** by boiling) began to race around rapidly, many escaping through the open pipette. When the **heat** was removed, the water molecules **condensed** back into liquid form. The combination of missing air molecules and condensing water molecules created lower air pressure inside the tube.

Normally this low air pressure would **pull** in outside air to **equalize** the pressure — but you placed the only opening in water! Since the low pressure couldn't pull in air, it pulled in the water instead. Combined with the **push** of the higher air pressure outside, it made your "Test Tube Mosquito" take a big drink!

MORE ABOUT AIR PRESSURE . . .

As you discovered in this activity, forces work in pairs. The heat you applied created a pressure difference. The combination of a "push" from high pressure outside and a "pull" from low pressure inside caused the liquid to move into the tube.

Wind is produced by a similar process. The Sun's heat creates pressure differences on Earth's surface. Air is pushed from the high pressure areas and pulled into the low pressure areas. The greater the difference in pressure, the stronger the wind blows.

Wind movement can be very beneficial. Wind circulates air around the planet, helping regulate temperatures by making hot areas cooler and cold areas warmer. Wind can remove excess moisture from clothes drying on a line, or from a field that needs to dry out so it can be planted. A light wind can even keep us cool on a hot day.

In addition, people through the ages have harnessed the force of moving wind to help pump water and grind grain. A modern variation involves using wind to generate electricity. Giant wind turbines convert the kinetic energy of moving wind into the mechanical energy needed to produce electrical current. States with strong, steady winds like California, Texas, and Iowa are leaders in this technology.

Of course, too much wind can be bad. Large storms can cause tremendous financial destruction and loss of human life. The broad winds of a hurricane can exceed 150 miles per hour, with "storm surge" pushing water far inland, causing serious flooding. While much smaller than hurricanes, tornadoes can be even more violent. Tornado winds can occasionally exceed 300 miles per hour, tossing cars around like tin cans. Fortunately, the most violent tornadoes (F4 or F5) are very rare, accounting for less than one percent of recorded tornadoes each year.

DIGGING DEEPER:

Research and discuss the effect of heat on Earth's atmosphere. According to scientists, what impact might an increase in Earth's overall temperature have on global weather patterns? Share and compare the findings of your research team with the information collected by other teams.

92 EARTH

WHAT WE LEARNED:

1 **The heat energy from the candle created an unbalanced force in this activity. Explain how.**

heat made molecules speed up, forcing some out the tube, creating lower air pressure inside

2 **The heat of the Sun can create unbalanced forces on Earth. Explain how this can impact the weather (in both good ways and bad).**

answers will vary, but should reflect concepts like the following: air is pushed from high pressure areas and pulled into low pressure areas; wind movement helps regulate temperature and moisture; too much wind causes large storms and can lead to loss of life and property; etc.

3 **Compare this activity with Lesson 19. What forces were involved? How were these lessons similar? How were they different?**

a) gravity, air pressure

b) similar: both used heat to change air pressure

c) different: different materials

EARTH 93

What Happened

Review the section with students. Emphasize bold-face words that identify key concepts and introduce new vocabulary.

When you tried to get the mosquito to drink in Step 2, nothing happened. ***Air pressure*** *inside and outside the tube was the same. But when you* ***heated*** *the tube in Step 3, you created unequal* ***forces****. The water and air* ***molecules*** *in the steam (water changed from* ***liquid*** *to* ***gas*** *by boiling) began to race around rapidly, many escaping through the open pipette. When the* ***heat*** *was removed, the water molecules* ***condensed*** *back into liquid form. The combination of missing air molecules and condensing water molecules created lower air pressure inside the tube.*

Normally this low air pressure would ***pull*** *in outside air to* ***equalize*** *the pressure – but you placed the only opening in water! Now the low pressure couldn't pull in air, so it pulled on the water instead. Combined with the* ***push*** *of the higher air pressure outside, it made your Test Tube Mosquito take a big drink!*

More About . . .

Have students read this section as you would a traditional science text — or use cooperative learning techniques to allow students the opportunity to work on the material collaboratively.

Digging Deeper

(Optional) Challenge teams to reseach and discuss practical applications of the lesson concepts. Encourage them to share their findings with the rest of the class.

What We Learned

Answers will vary. Suggested responses are shown at left.

Conclusion

Read this section aloud to the class to summarize the concepts learned in this activity.

Food for Thought

Read the Scripture aloud to the class. Talk about God's plans for our lives (see also Jeremiah 29:11). Discuss ways we can learn to rely on God's power and wisdom.

Science Journal

If time permits, have a general class discussion about notes and drawings various students added to their journal pages. Discuss correct and incorrect predictions, and remind students that this "trial and error" process is part of the scientific process.

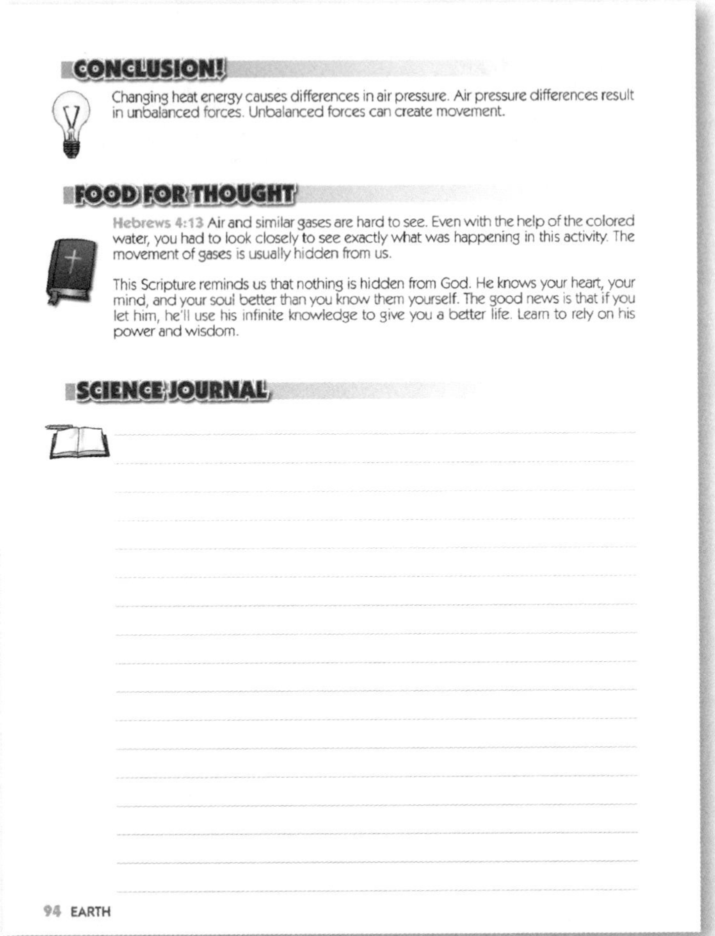

CONCLUSION!

Changing heat energy causes differences in air pressure. Air pressure differences result in unbalanced forces. Unbalanced forces can create movement.

FOOD FOR THOUGHT

Hebrews 4:13 Air and similar gases are hard to see. Even with the help of the colored water, you had to look closely to see exactly what was happening in this activity. The movement of gases is usually hidden from us.

This Scripture reminds us that nothing is hidden from God. He knows your heart, your mind, and your soul better than you know them yourself. The good news is that if you let him, he'll use his infinite knowledge to give you a better life. Learn to rely on his power and wisdom.

SCIENCE JOURNAL

94 EARTH

Extended Teaching

1. Expand Lessons 19 and 20 by having teams discuss what they've learned about air pressure. Challenge each team to create a poster showing examples of air pressure (bicycle tires, air mattresses, etc.).

2. Using the Internet, have teams research steam engines. Find out how they generate force. Challenge each team to contribute material for a class bulletin board on steam engines.

3. Invite a meteorologist to your classroom. Have him/her talk about air pressure and how it relates to the weather. Have students write a paragraph about one thing they learn.

4. Take a field trip to a power plant. Have someone explain how steam is generated and its pressure used to create electricity. Have students write a paragraph about one thing they learn.

5. Mosquitoes and disease are closely linked to the Panama Canal. Have teams research the building of the canal. Find out how disease challenges were overcome. Challenge each team to make a presentation on their findings.

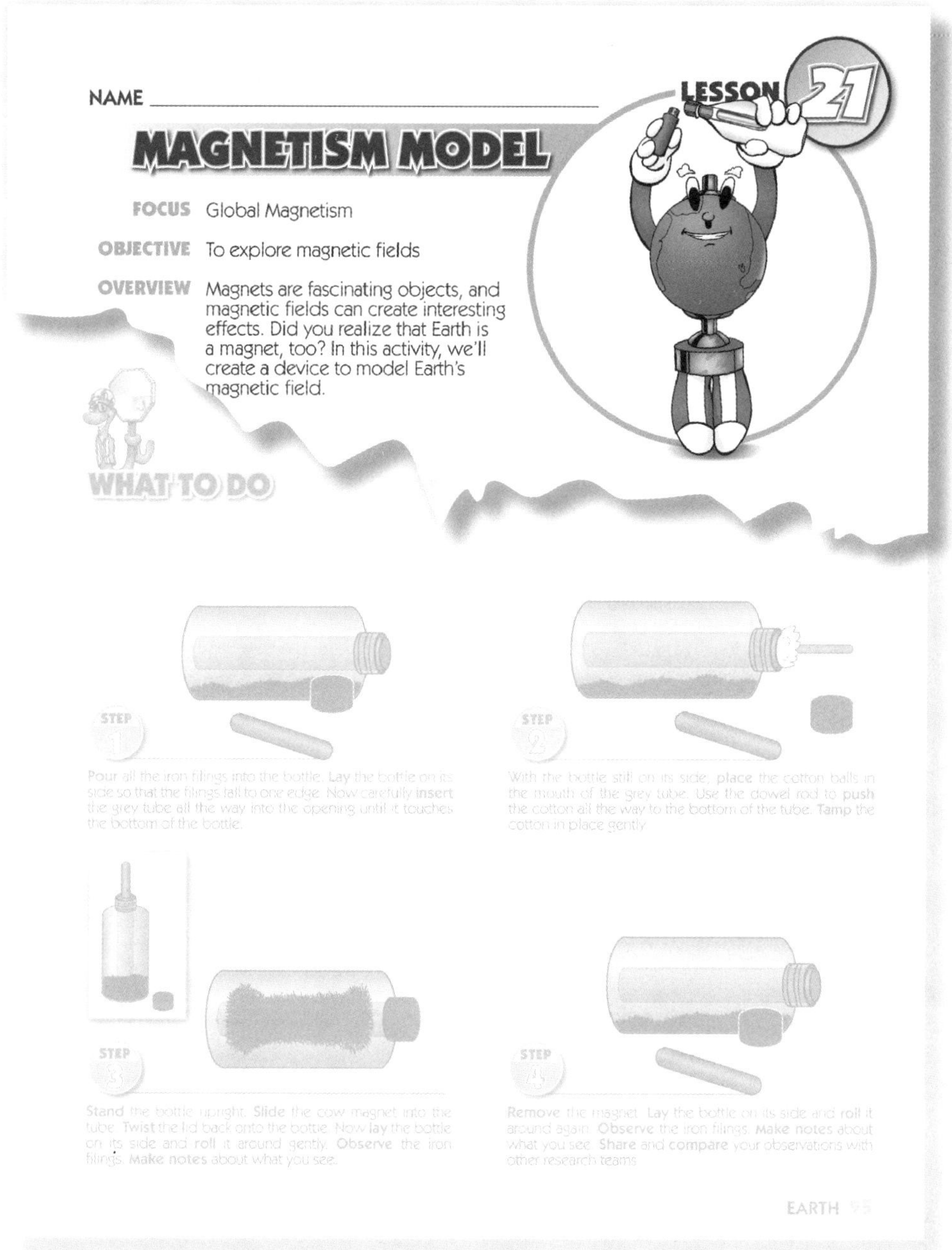
NAME ______________________

LESSON 21

MAGNETISM MODEL

FOCUS Global Magnetism

OBJECTIVE To explore magnetic fields

OVERVIEW Magnets are fascinating objects, and magnetic fields can create interesting effects. Did you realize that Earth is a magnet, too? In this activity, we'll create a device to model Earth's magnetic field.

WHAT TO DO

STEP 1

Pour all the iron filings into the bottle. **Lay** the bottle on its side so that the filings fall to one edge. Now carefully **insert** the grey tube all the way into the opening until it touches the bottom of the bottle.

STEP 2

With the bottle still on its side, **place** the cotton balls in the mouth of the grey tube. Use the dowel rod to **push** the cotton all the way to the bottom of the tube. **Tamp** the cotton in place gently.

STEP 3

Stand the bottle upright. **Slide** the cow magnet into the tube. **Twist** the lid back onto the bottle. Now **lay** the bottle on its side and **roll** it around gently. **Observe** the iron filings. **Make notes** about what you see.

STEP 4

Remove the magnet. **Lay** the bottle on its side and **roll** it around again. **Observe** the iron filings. **Make notes** about what you see. **Share** and **compare** your observations with other research teams.

EARTH 95

Category

Earth Science

Focus

Global Magnetism

Objective

To explore magnetic fields

National Standards

A1, A2, B1, B2, D1, D2, G1, G2

Materials Needed

plastic bottle with lid
PVC tube (grey)
iron filings
cotton balls
dowel rod
cow magnet

Safety Concerns

4. Other
Keep the magnet away from electronic devices.

Additional Comments

Make sure students are using the GREY tube. (The WHITE tubes are for a different activity!) Remind students to keep the cow magnet away from computers, cell phones, and other devices that may be negatively affected by magnets. Also, iron filings can be messy. Monitor students closely to make certain they are being careful as they pour the iron flings into bottle.

Overview

Read the overview aloud to your students. The goal is to create an atmosphere of curiosity and inquiry.

WHAT TO DO

Monitor student research teams as they complete each step.

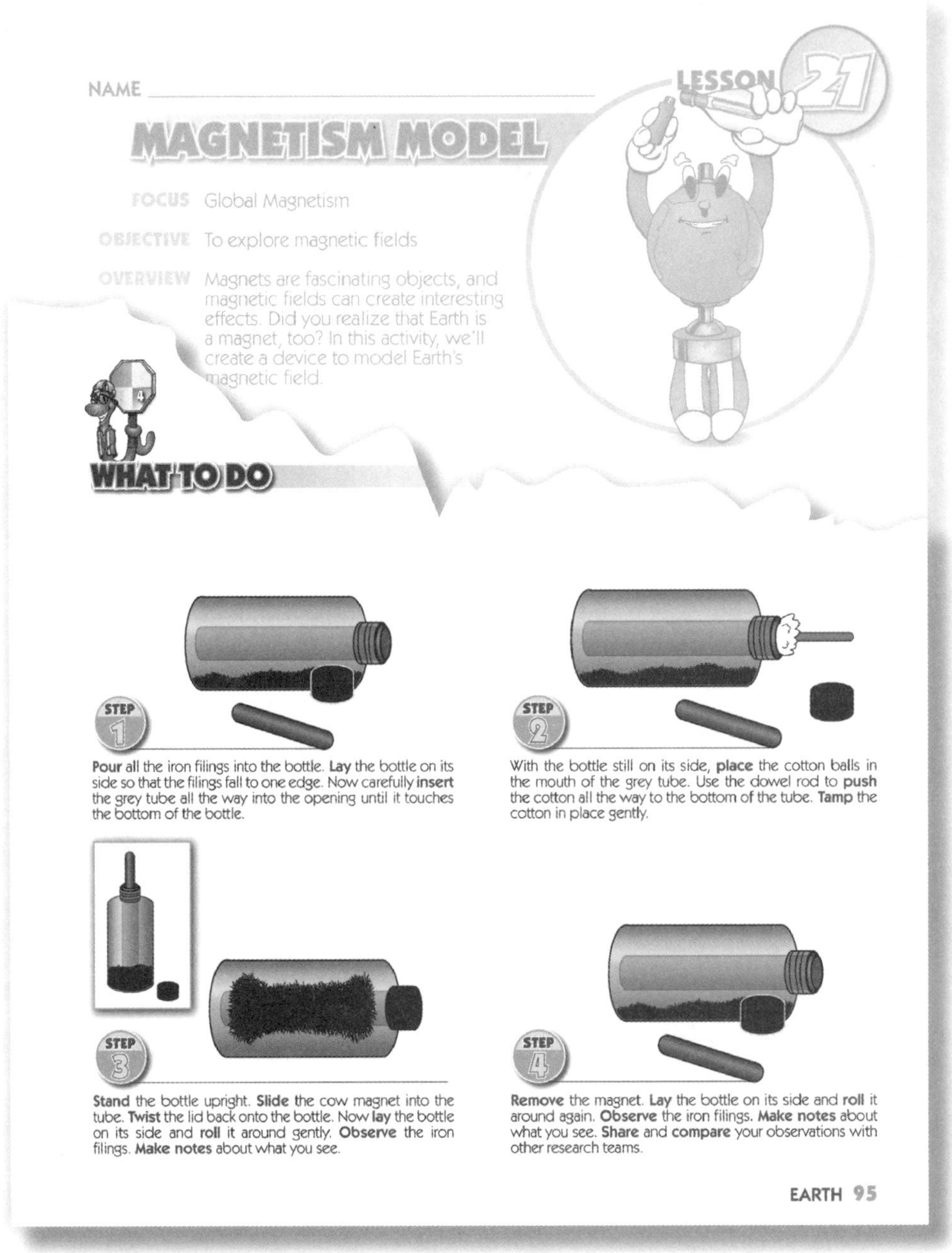

NAME ______________________________ LESSON 21

MAGNETISM MODEL

FOCUS Global Magnetism

OBJECTIVE To explore magnetic fields

OVERVIEW Magnets are fascinating objects, and magnetic fields can create interesting effects. Did you realize that Earth is a magnet, too? In this activity, we'll create a device to model Earth's magnetic field.

WHAT TO DO

STEP 1

Pour all the iron filings into the bottle. **Lay** the bottle on its side so that the filings fall to one edge. Now carefully **insert** the grey tube all the way into the opening until it touches the bottom of the bottle.

STEP 2

With the bottle still on its side, **place** the cotton balls in the mouth of the grey tube. Use the dowel rod to **push** the cotton all the way to the bottom of the tube. **Tamp** the cotton in place gently.

STEP 3

Stand the bottle upright. **Slide** the cow magnet into the tube. **Twist** the lid back onto the bottle. Now **lay** the bottle on its side and **roll** it around gently. **Observe** the iron filings. **Make notes** about what you see.

STEP 4

Remove the magnet. **Lay** the bottle on its side and **roll** it around again. **Observe** the iron filings. **Make notes** about what you see. **Share** and **compare** your observations with other research teams.

EARTH 95

Teacher to Teacher

Like the magnet in this activity, Earth produces a three dimensional magnetic field. This invisible field funnels high-energy solar particles to the north and south poles. The interaction of these particles with Earth's atmosphere creates the Aurora Borealis — the beautiful phenomenon we call the "northern lights." (Note: In the Southern Hemisphere, this phenomenon is known as the Aurora Australus.)

WHAT JUST HAPPENED?

As we've seen in other lessons, **models** are helpful when studying an object or **force**. This model allowed you to observe a **three-dimensional magnetic field**. Although the field was invisible, the iron filings let you see its effects.

The field created by the magnet is a reflection of Earth's magnetic field, complete with **north** and **south poles**. But there's one big difference! The bottle's magnetic field reaches out a couple of inches. Earth's magnetic field reaches far out into space!

Even though scientists know an enormous amount about magnetic fields, magnetism remains one of the big mysteries of science.

MORE ABOUT MAGNETISM . . .

Magnets are all around us. They are used to lock and unlock doors, sort scrap metal in recycling yards, and hold notes on refrigerators. Every electric motor has a set of magnets inside. Even those dark strips you see on the back of credit cards, drivers' licenses, and hotel keys are a type of magnet.

But did you realize that you're *standing* on a magnet? As we discovered in this lesson, Earth itself is a giant magnet whose magnetic field reaches far out into space. A compass can use this magnetic field to help show directions. Its magnetized pointer aligns with Earth's magnetic field, making it point North. For centuries, sailors depended on the compass as a key navigational instrument.

The Earth's magnetic field also protects us from intense solar radiation. As particles shoot out from the Sun, they are trapped by the Earth's magnetic field and travel to the north and south poles. (When these particles interact with Earth's atmosphere above the Arctic, they create the phenomenon we call the "northern lights".)

But since Earth's magnetic field is generated by liquid iron in the Earth's core, the magnetic poles can move around a bit. According to scientists, the magnetic poles have been relatively stable since the late 1600s. But in the last 100 years, the North magnetic pole has moved almost 700 miles out into the Arctic Ocean. At this rate, it could move from northern Canada over to Siberia within the next half-century, taking the northern lights with it!

In earlier times, a shift of the magnetic poles would have created a major dilemma for navigators. Fortunately, however, today's ships and planes rely on Global Positioning Satellites (GPS) to know where they are, so the movement of the magnetic poles will have little effect on navigation.

DIGGING DEEPER:

With your team, research and discuss some aspect of magnetism. Possible topics include how magnets make electric motors run, the frequency and duration of the northern lights, or how Earth's magnetic field keeps us safe from solar winds. Be sure to compare your findings with other teams.

96 EARTH

WHAT WE LEARNED:

1. **Why can't you draw a picture of this magnetic field? What advantage does a 3-D model like this have? How is that helpful?**

   a) it's three dimensional

   b) lets us see the effect from different angles.

   c) creates better understanding

2. **Based on what you've learned, can a magnet affect something without touching it? Why or why not? Explain your answer.**

   a) yes

   b) even though the magnet was inside a heavy plastic tube, it still had an effect on the iron filings; a magnetic field reaches out far beyond the magnet's surface

3. **Describe at least two things that you have learned about Earth's magnetic field.**

   answers will vary, but should reflect logical descriptions and comparisons

EARTH 97

What Just Happened?

Read this section aloud with your students. Be sure to emphasize the bold-face words that identify key concepts and introduce new vocabulary.

As we've seen in other lessons, ***models*** *are helpful when studying an object or* ***force****. This model allowed you to observe a* ***three-dimensional magnetic field****. Although the field was invisible, the iron filings let you see its effects.*

The field created by the magnet is a reflection of Earth's magnetic field, complete with ***north*** *and* ***south poles****. But there's one big difference! The bottle's magnetic field reaches out a couple of inches. Earth's magnetic field reaches far out into space!*

Even though scientists know an enormous amount about magnetic fields, magnetism remains one of the big mysteries of science.

More About . . .

Have students read this section as you would a traditional science text — or use cooperative learning techniques to allow students the opportunity to work on the material collaboratively.

Digging Deeper

(Optional) Challenge teams to reseach and discuss practical applications of the lesson concepts. Encourage them to share their findings with the rest of the class.

What We Learned

Answers will vary. Suggested responses are shown at left.

Conclusion

Read this section aloud to the class to summarize the concepts learned in this activity.

Food for Thought

Read the Scripture aloud to the class. Talk about things that exist but cannot be seen. Discuss how our kindness and caring can help others see God's power and love.

Science Journal

Encourage students to make notes and drawings, recording their impressions about various aspects of the lesson. If time permits, have a group discussion to review responses. Be sure to discuss correct and incorrect predictions, reminding students that the "trial and error" approach is part of the scientific process.

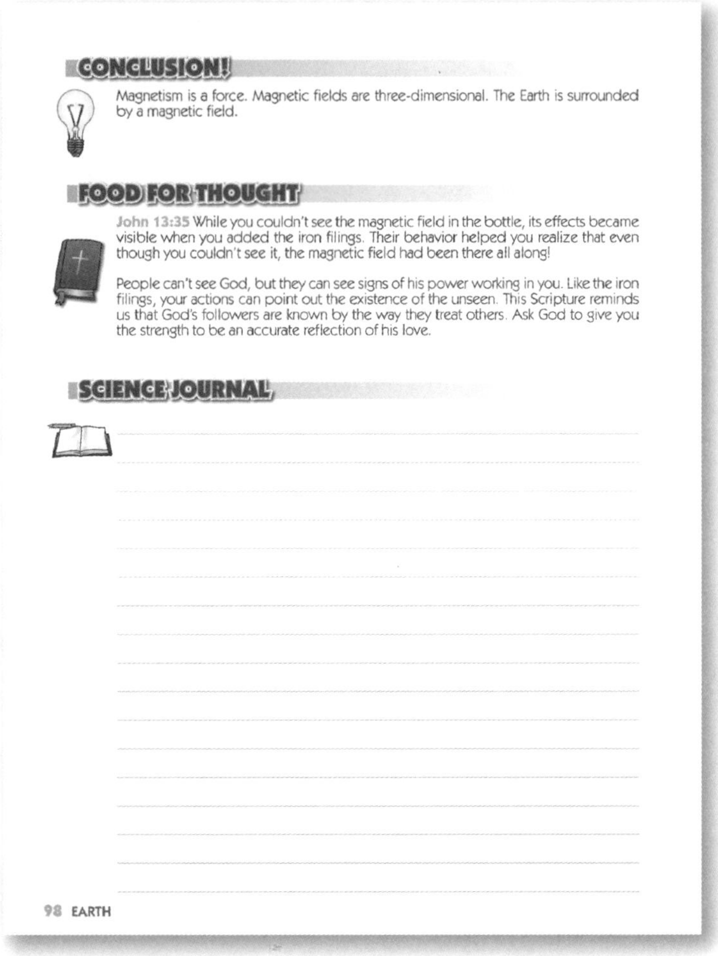

CONCLUSION!

Magnetism is a force. Magnetic fields are three-dimensional. The Earth is surrounded by a magnetic field.

FOOD FOR THOUGHT

John 13:35 While you couldn't see the magnetic field in the bottle, its effects became visible when you added the iron filings. Their behavior helped you realize that even though you couldn't see it, the magnetic field had been there all along!

People can't see God, but they can see signs of his power working in you. Like the iron filings, your actions can point out the existence of the unseen. This Scripture reminds us that God's followers are known by the way they treat others. Ask God to give you the strength to be an accurate reflection of his love.

SCIENCE JOURNAL

98 EARTH

Extended Teaching

1. Repeat this activity placing two smaller magnets inside the tube with like poles touching. Have students compare the results with the original activity. How were they similar? How were they different?

2. Repeat the activity above only this time insert the magnets with opposite poles touching. Have students compare the results with activity 1 and the original activity. How were they similar? How were they different?

3. Invite a veterinarian to visit your classroom. Ask him/her to explain how cow magnets work and how they are used. Have students write a paragraph about one thing they learn.

4. Using the Internet, have teams research pictures and descriptions of the northern (or southern) lights. Challenge each team to contribute materials for a classroom bulletin board on this topic.

5. Take a field trip to a recycling facility. Have the manager demonstrate the huge electromagnets used there. Find out how these are used to sort metal. Have students write a paragraph about one thing they learn.

NAME ______________________________

LESSON 22

STUDENT SATELLITES

FOCUS Geosynchronous Orbit

OBJECTIVE To explore ways objects move in space

OVERVIEW Television, radio, cellular phones, pagers, weather radar — many such devices can link to satellites! In this activity, we'll explore how satellites orbit around the Earth.

WHAT TO DO

STEP 1 Using chalk, **make** a two-foot circle on the pavement. **Ask** one team member (the Earth) to **stand** in this circle holding the end of a rope. The Earth can rotate, but must always stay inside the circle.

STEP 2 **Ask** a second team member (Satellite 1) to **hold** the other end of the rope and **walk** away until it's snug. Have both students face each other. Now have Satellite 1 **walk** around in a circle as the Earth rotates slowly.

STEP 3 **Ask** a third team member (Satellite 2) to **walk** just outside Satellite 1's orbit, but in the opposite direction. **Draw** this in your journal and **make notes** about the relationship of the Earth and its satellites.

STEP 4 **Review** each step in this activity. **Discuss** similarities and differences between the two satellites. **Share** and compare observations with other research teams.

EARTH 99

Category

Earth Science

Focus

Geosynchronous Orbit

Objective

To explore ways objects move in space

National Standards

A1, A2, B1, B2, D3, G1, G2

Materials Needed

chalk
rope

Safety Concerns

none

Additional Comments

The rope not only represents the distance between Earth and a satellite, but also the pull of gravity between the two. Both students can feel the tug of the rope — a great "hands-on" way to understand that forces work both ways.

Overview

Read the overview aloud to your students. The goal is to create an atmosphere of curiosity and inquiry.

WHAT TO DO

Monitor student research teams as they complete each step.

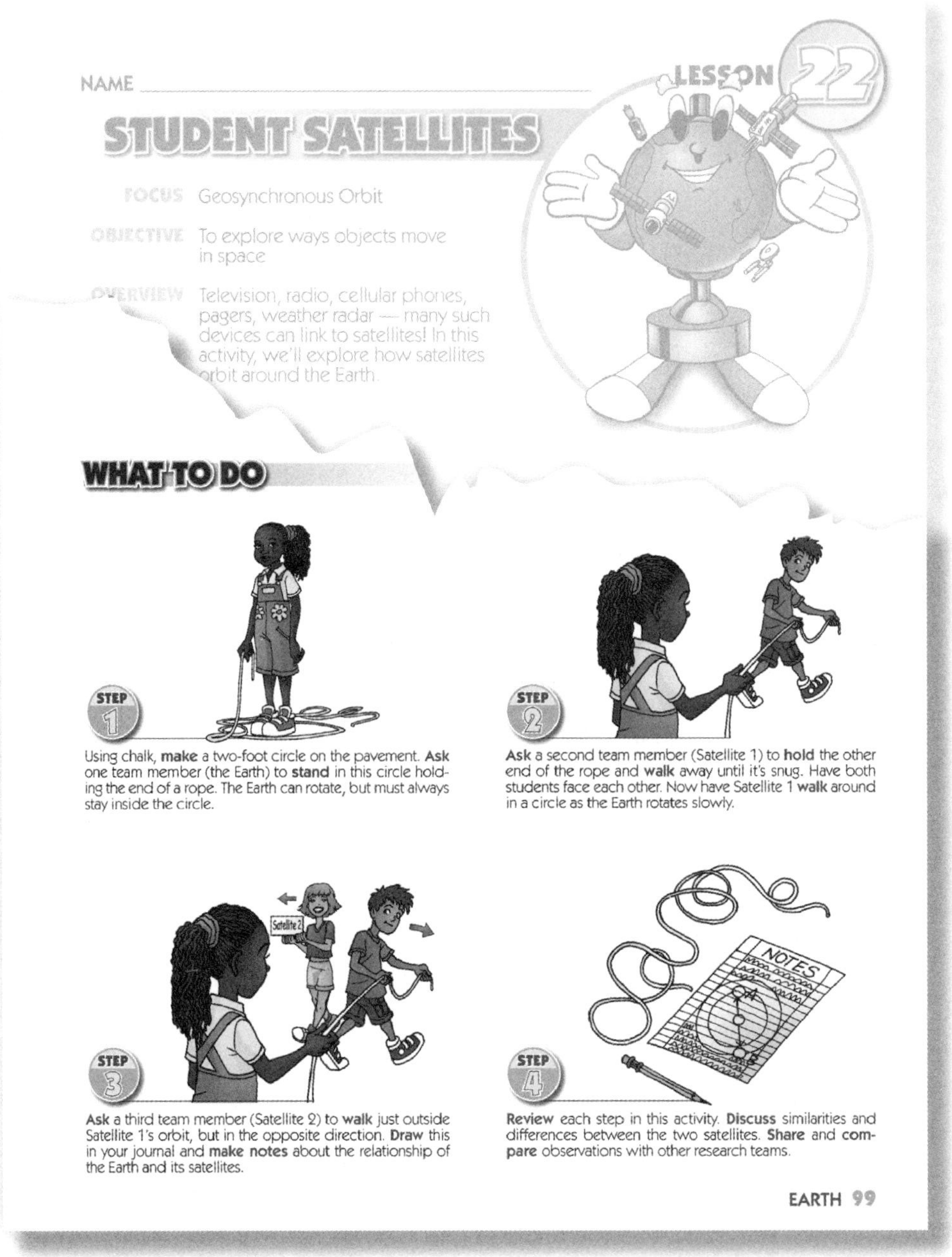

NAME ______________________ LESSON 22

STUDENT SATELLITES

FOCUS Geosynchronous Orbit

OBJECTIVE To explore ways objects move in space

OVERVIEW Television, radio, cellular phones, pagers, weather radar — many such devices can link to satellites! In this activity, we'll explore how satellites orbit around the Earth.

WHAT TO DO

STEP 1 Using chalk, **make** a two-foot circle on the pavement. **Ask** one team member (the Earth) to **stand** in this circle holding the end of a rope. The Earth can rotate, but must always stay inside the circle.

STEP 2 **Ask** a second team member (Satellite 1) to **hold** the other end of the rope and **walk** away until it's snug. Have both students face each other. Now have Satellite 1 **walk** around in a circle as the Earth rotates slowly.

STEP 3 **Ask** a third team member (Satellite 2) to **walk** just outside Satellite 1's orbit, but in the opposite direction. **Draw** this in your journal and **make notes** about the relationship of the Earth and its satellites.

STEP 4 **Review** each step in this activity. **Discuss** similarities and differences between the two satellites. **Share** and **compare** observations with other research teams.

EARTH 99

Teacher to Teacher

Forces always come in pairs. In this activity, gravity is opposed by centripetal force — a force away from the center of the orbit. When you swing a bucket of water, for instance, the water is being pulled down by gravity. But if you swing the bucket fast enough (even over your head), centripetal force keeps you from getting wet!

WHAT JUST HAPPENED?

Assume the center team member's eyes are a point on Earth. Because of their different orbits, one **satellite** remained lined up with that point, but the other satellite went by many different points! Scientists and engineers use these two kinds of orbits for very different purposes.

Surveillance satellites (military, geological, etc.) circle the globe. They send back images as they pass over different regions of Earth. **Communication** satellites (phone, television, etc.) must "park" directly above a specific spot on Earth so signals can be bounced off them. Although these satellites move at tremendous speeds, they stay in the same spot relative to Earth, so they don't seem to move at all. This is called a **geosynchronous** orbit.

MORE ABOUT SATELLITES . . .

Satellites are used for everything from communication, to monitoring weather patterns, to determining a vehicle's location and direction. Research satellites help scientists study the universe. Military satellites help us keep an eye on our enemies. Special satellites help scientists predict crop production, monitor pollution, and study climate change. Television, radio, cell phones, weather forecasts, and GPS devices are just a few ways that the average American relies on the vast network of satellites that now circle the globe.

But it wasn't always that way!

The first satellite, **Sputnik I**, was launched by the Soviet Union in 1957. Millions of older Americans still remember how that event started the great "space race" that eventually led to America landing Neil Armstrong on the Moon. One direct result of the race was that scientists developed the many types of satellites we use today.

But that's not all! As they developed the technology needed for satellites and manned space travel, scientists quickly realized that modified versions of these new products would be useful here on Earth, too.

Here are just a few of the innovations that came out of NASA's space program: medical imaging technology, ear thermometers, smoke detectors, more effective fire-fighting equipment, computer-aided design programs, cordless tools, thermal gloves and boots, pens that write upside down, shock-absorbing helmets, flexible ski boots, invisible braces, joystick controllers, advanced plastics, liquid crystal polymers, disposable diapers . . . and the list goes on.

Next time you look up at the night sky, think about the satellites and how their development and implementation have changed our world.

DIGGING DEEPER:

Interview a grandparent or an older friend (someone at least in their 60s) about his/her memories of the day the Soviet Union announced the launch of Sputnik I. How did Americans feel about this event? What sort of things were being said? What statements were made by the American government over the next few years?

100 EARTH

WHAT WE LEARNED:

1 **What do the students in each step represent? (Be specific.) Why couldn't the student in Step 3 represent a communications satellite?**

a) Step 1 student = Earth; Step 2 student = a communications satellite; Step 3 student = a surveillance satellite

b) it doesn't stay lined up with a specific spot; it is not geosynchronous

2 **Why was there such a big difference between the speed of Satellite 1 and the speed of the Earth?**

because of its distance, it had to go faster to stay even with that spot on Earth

3 **What force did the rope represent in this model? Why would the distance be important with a real satellite?**

a) gravity

b) too close and gravity would pull it back to Earth; too far and gravity couldn't hold it

EARTH 101

What Happened

Review the section with students. Emphasize bold-face words that identify key concepts and introduce new vocabulary.

Assume the center team member's eyes are a point on Earth. Because of their different orbits, one ***satellite*** *remained lined up with that point, but the other satellite went by many different points! Scientists and engineers use these two kinds of orbits for very different purposes.*

Surveillance *satellites (military, geological, etc.) circle the globe. They send back images as they pass over different regions of Earth.* ***Communication*** *satellites (phone, television, etc.) must "park" directly above a specific spot on Earth so signals can be bounced off them. Although these satellites move at tremendous speeds, they stay in the same spot relative to Earth, so they don't seem to move at all. This is called a* ***geosynchronous*** *orbit.*

More About . . .

Have students read this section as you would a traditional science text — or use cooperative learning techniques to allow students the opportunity to work on the material collaboratively.

Digging Deeper

(Optional) Challenge teams to reseach and discuss practical applications of the lesson concepts. Encourage them to share their findings with the rest of the class.

What We Learned

Answers will vary. Suggested responses are shown at left.

Conclusion

Read this section aloud to the class to summarize the concepts learned in this activity.

Food for Thought

Read the Scripture aloud to the class. Talk about how creating and maintaining any kind of relationship takes time. Discuss ways to set aside more time for getting to know God better.

Science Journal

If time permits, have a general class discussion about notes and drawings various students added to their journal pages. Discuss correct and incorrect predictions, and remind students that this "trial and error" process is part of the scientific process.

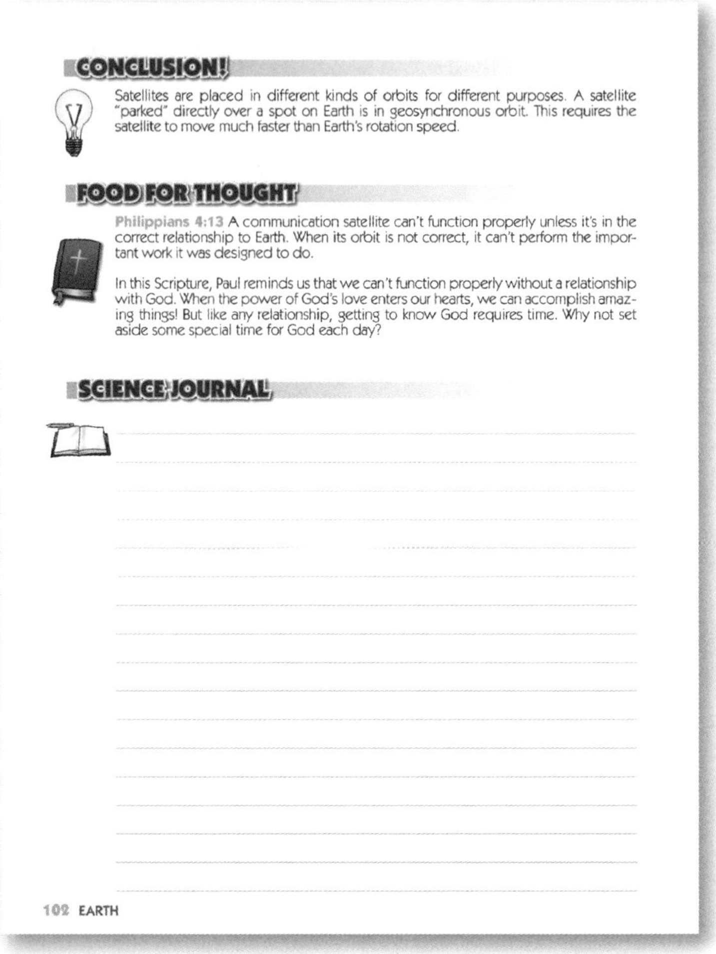

CONCLUSION!

Satellites are placed in different kinds of orbits for different purposes. A satellite "parked" directly over a spot on Earth is in geosynchronous orbit. This requires the satellite to move much faster than Earth's rotation speed.

FOOD FOR THOUGHT

Philippians 4:13 A communication satellite can't function properly unless it's in the correct relationship to Earth. When its orbit is not correct, it can't perform the important work it was designed to do.

In this Scripture, Paul reminds us that we can't function properly without a relationship with God. When the power of God's love enters our hearts, we can accomplish amazing things! But like any relationship, getting to know God requires time. Why not set aside some special time for God each day?

SCIENCE JOURNAL

102 EARTH

Extended Teaching

1. Repeat this activity using longer rope. Have students compare the results to the original activity. How were they similar? How were they different?

2. Invite a surveyor to visit your classroom and bring a GPS device. Ask him/her to explain how it works, and how it makes surveying easier. Have students write a paragraph about one thing they learn.

3. Have students research satellites, their history, and their uses. Challenge each team to create a poster describing and depicting at least one specific satellite.

4. Using the Internet, have teams research the position and number of geosynchronous satellites currently orbiting the Earth. Challenge each team to contribute their findings to a classroom bulletin board on the topic.

5. Take a field trip to an observatory or University astronomy department. Challenge students to discover everything they can about satellites. Have students write a paragraph or two about something they learn.

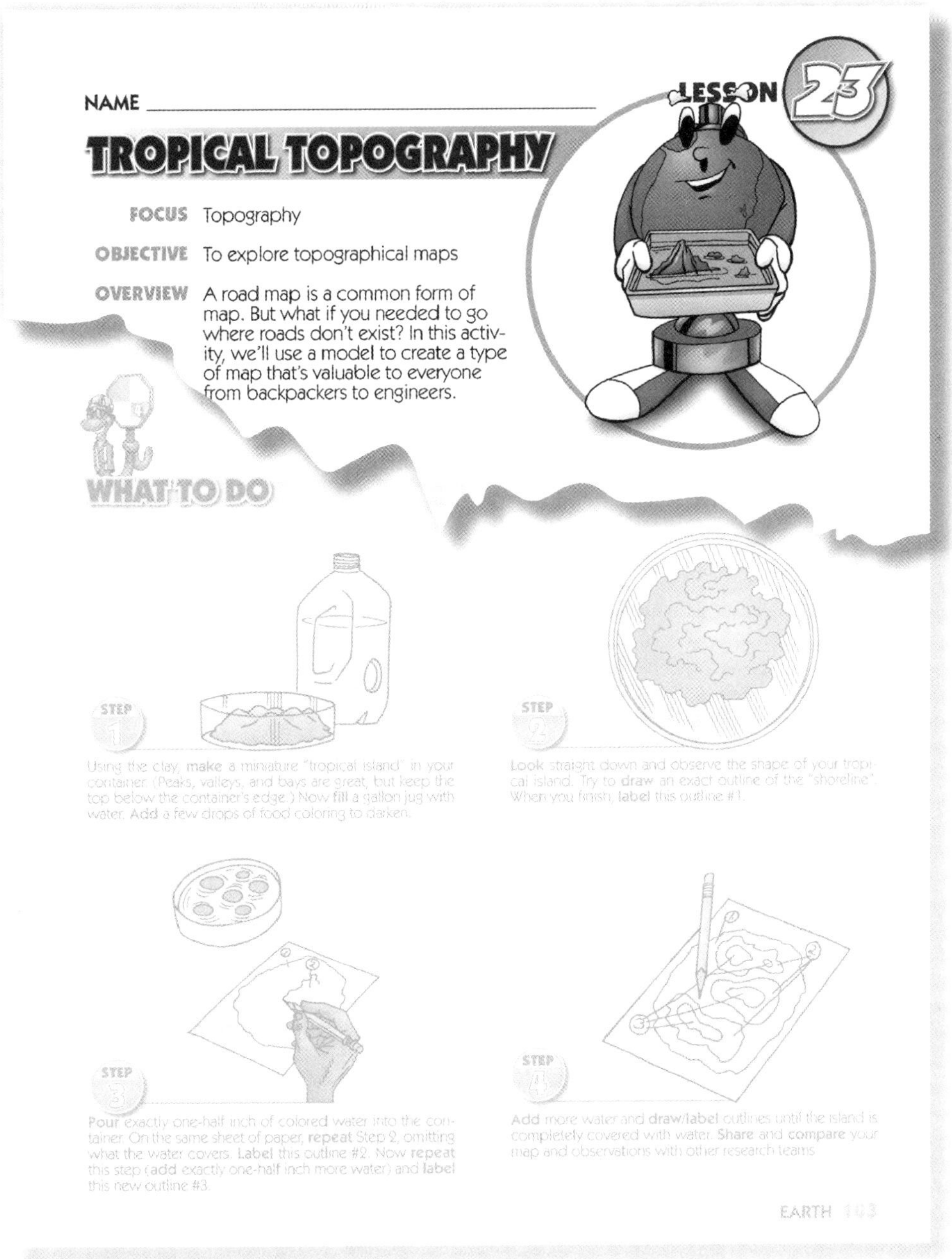
NAME ____________________

LESSON 23

TROPICAL TOPOGRAPHY

FOCUS Topography

OBJECTIVE To explore topographical maps

OVERVIEW A road map is a common form of map. But what if you needed to go where roads don't exist? In this activity, we'll use a model to create a type of map that's valuable to everyone from backpackers to engineers.

WHAT TO DO

STEP 1 Using the clay, **make** a miniature "tropical island" in your container. (Peaks, valleys, and bays are great, but keep the top below the container's edge.) Now **fill** a gallon jug with water. **Add** a few drops of food coloring to darken.

STEP 2 **Look** straight down and observe the shape of your tropical island. Try to **draw** an exact outline of the "shoreline". When you finish, **label** this outline #1.

STEP 3 **Pour** exactly one-half inch of colored water into the container. On the same sheet of paper, **repeat** Step 2, omitting what the water covers. **Label** this outline #2. Now **repeat** this step (**add** exactly one-half inch more water) and **label** this new outline #3.

STEP 4 **Add** more water and **draw/label** outlines until the island is completely covered with water. **Share** and **compare** your map and observations with other research teams

EARTH 103

Category

Earth Science

Focus

Topography

Objective

To explore topographic maps

National Standards

A1, A2, B1, D1, F2, G1, G2

Materials Needed

clay
plastic container
gallon jug
water
food coloring
paper
ruler

Safety Concerns

4. Slipping
There is a potential for spills. Remind students to exercise caution with water.

Additional Comments

Any clear plastic container at least 3 inches deep will work for this activity. Adding the food coloring to the water yourself avoids students getting the water too dark. It only takes a few drops to get the right effect.

Overview

Read the overview aloud to your students. The goal is to create an atmosphere of curiosity and inquiry.

WHAT TO DO

Monitor student research teams as they complete each step.

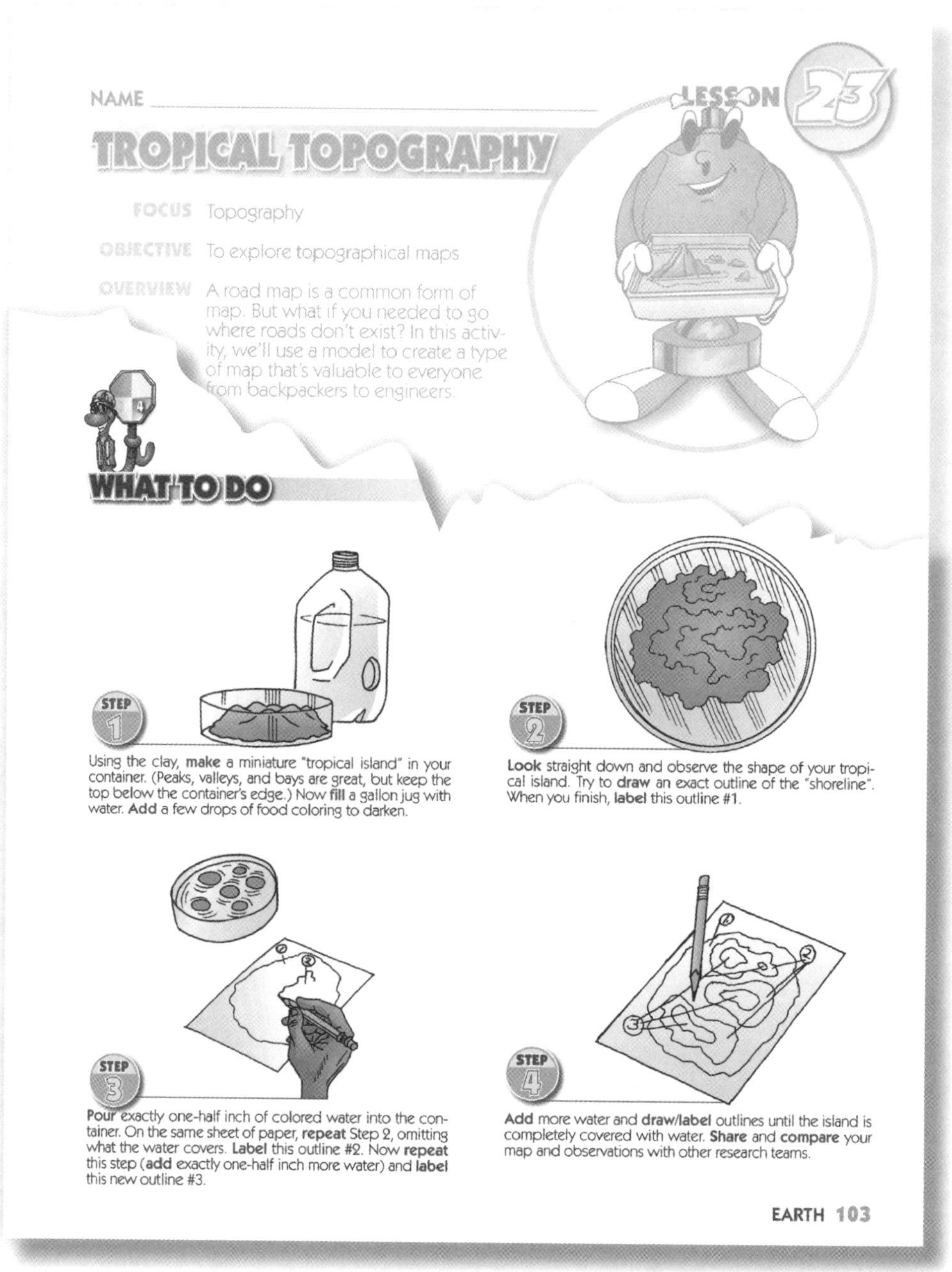

NAME

LESSON 23

TROPICAL TOPOGRAPHY

FOCUS Topography

OBJECTIVE To explore topographical maps

OVERVIEW A road map is a common form of map. But what if you needed to go where roads don't exist? In this activity, we'll use a model to create a type of map that's valuable to everyone from backpackers to engineers.

WHAT TO DO

STEP 1 Using the clay, **make** a miniature "tropical island" in your container. (Peaks, valleys, and bays are great, but keep the top below the container's edge.) Now **fill** a gallon jug with water. **Add** a few drops of food coloring to darken.

STEP 2 **Look** straight down and observe the shape of your tropical island. Try to **draw** an exact outline of the "shoreline". When you finish, **label** this outline #1.

STEP 3 **Pour** exactly one-half inch of colored water into the container. On the same sheet of paper, **repeat** Step 2, omitting what the water covers. **Label** this outline #2. Now **repeat** this step (**add** exactly one-half inch more water) and **label** this new outline #3.

STEP 4 **Add** more water and **draw/label** outlines until the island is completely covered with water. **Share** and **compare** your map and observations with other research teams.

EARTH 103

Teacher to Teacher

Geographical information includes satellite images, aerial photography, ultraviolet light, infrared, and even radar. Combining this information with population data, income, crime rates, and other statistics creates Geographic Information Systems (GIS). Using GIS, computers can rearrange such data to create many kinds of maps.

WHAT JUST HAPPENED?

You just made a **topographical map** — a tool that shows an area's **contour** (shape). Each **contour line** shows the shape of the land at a particular level. Closer contour lines indicate steeper slopes and vice-versa. In the model, water helped us determine level. In the field, surveyors use special equipment to determine **altitude** (height).

Many topographical maps are made by the U.S. Geological Survey (USGS). The most common scale is based on contour intervals of 20 feet.

Topographical maps have hundreds of uses. For instance, a hiker can estimate the best trail, a geologist can locate special surface features, or an engineer can plan the optimum route for a new road.

MORE ABOUT TOPOGRAPHY . . .

Like many scientific terms, the word "**topography**" comes from the ancient languages — in this case, the Greek words "topos" (meaning "place") and "graphia" (meaning "writing"). This "place writing" refers to the study of Earth's surface features like hills, valleys, rivers, and roads.

Having a graphic representation of a place can be very handy! If you're hiking, a topographical map can not only show you the easiest route to walk (through the valley), but also where the best views might be (at the top of the highest hill).

The three-dimensional effect of a topographical map is achieved in a variety of ways. The most common techniques are contour lines, color tints, and relief shading. Maps produced by the USGS often use shades of green for forests, shades of brown for open areas, and shades of blue for water.

Of course, computers have added a whole new dimension to the study of maps. Sites like Topozone.com offer professionals a wide variety of detailed feature maps that can be downloaded for future study. Free programs like Google™ Earth provide an interactive experience based on satellite and aerial images. (Try typing in the address of your school, then zooming in closer and closer until you can see the top of the building or the cars in the parking lot!)

Today's researchers can use the Internet to locate nearly any place on Earth. Not only are they able to print out detailed topographical maps of a site, but they can also search for historical, weather, political, and population maps of the area. And thanks to NASA, there are even detailed topographical maps available for the Moon, various planets, and significant asteroids.

DIGGING DEEPER:

Research and discuss how maps are important to scientists, engineers, farmers, and others. Find a topographical map showing your school. Use the contour lines to determine where floodwaters might collect if there was a heavy rain. (Hint: Water always flows to the lowest places first.)

104 EARTH

WHAT WE LEARNED:

1. Describe how your map changed with each new contour line. Explain how your map could help someone describe the surface features of your island without seeing it.

a) answers will vary

b) shows the general shape of the island and its valleys and peaks

2. Compare your team's topographical map with the maps of other teams. How were they similar? How were they different?

answers will vary, but should reflect logical comparisons

3. Radio towers are often sited on the highest point in an area. Based on what you've learned, explain how a topographical map could help an engineer locate potential sites.

a topographical map would show the highest points in the area

EARTH 105

What Happened

Review the section with students. Emphasize bold-face words that identify key concepts and introduce new vocabulary.

*You just made a **topographical map** – a tool that shows an area's **contour** (shape). Each **contour line** shows the shape of the land at a particular level. Closer contour lines indicate steeper slopes and vice-versa. In the model, water helped us determine level. In the field, surveyors use special equipment to determine **altitude** (height).*

Many topographical maps are made by the U.S. Geological Survey (USGS). The most common scale is based on contour intervals of 20 feet.

Topographical maps have hundreds of uses. For instance, a hiker can estimate the best trail, a geologist can locate special surface features, or an engineer can plan the optimum route for a new road.

More About . . .

Have students read this section as you would a traditional science text — or use cooperative learning techniques to allow students the opportunity to work on the material collaboratively.

Digging Deeper

(Optional) Challenge teams to reseach and discuss practical applications of the lesson concepts. Encourage them to share their findings with the rest of the class.

What We Learned

Answers will vary. Suggested responses are shown at left.

Conclusion

Read this section aloud to the class to summarize the concepts learned in this activity.

Food for Thought

Read the Scripture aloud to the class. Talk about how Scripture can be used as a "road map" for our lives. Discuss specific examples of "directions" Scripture gives.

Science Journal

If time permits, have a general class discussion about notes and drawings various students added to their journal pages. Discuss correct and incorrect predictions, and remind students that this "trial and error" process is part of the scientific process.

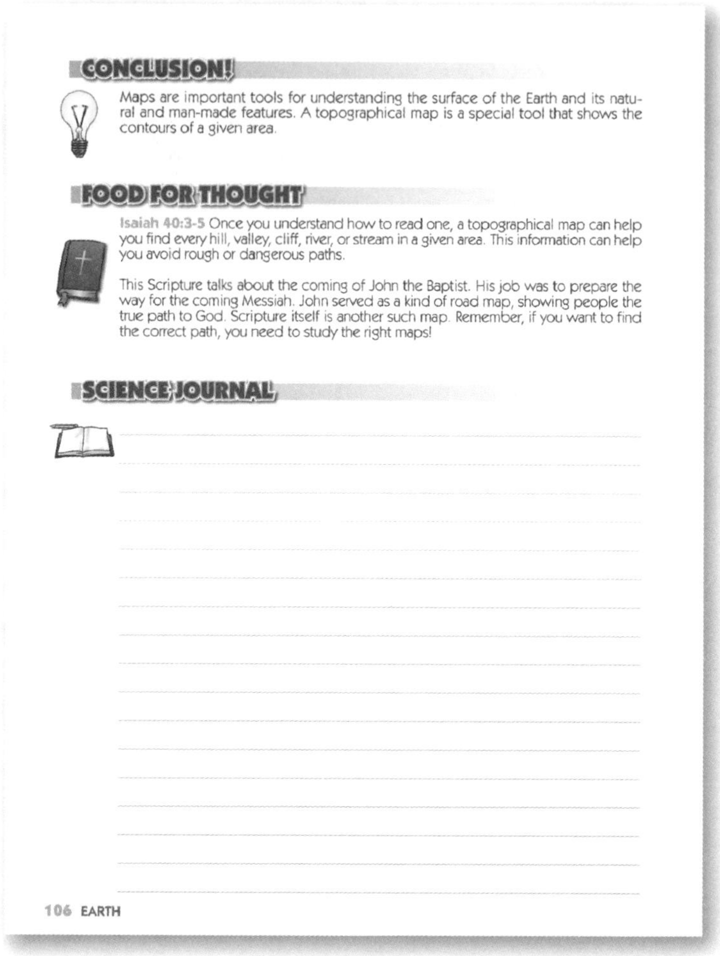
CONCLUSION!

Maps are important tools for understanding the surface of the Earth and its natural and man-made features. A topographical map is a special tool that shows the contours of a given area.

FOOD FOR THOUGHT

Isaiah 40:3-5 Once you understand how to read one, a topographical map can help you find every hill, valley, cliff, river, or stream in a given area. This information can help you avoid rough or dangerous paths.

This Scripture talks about the coming of John the Baptist. His job was to prepare the way for the coming Messiah. John served as a kind of road map, showing people the true path to God. Scripture itself is another such map. Remember, if you want to find the correct path, you need to study the right maps!

SCIENCE JOURNAL

106 EARTH

Extended Teaching

1. Repeat this activity, only this time have students observe and draw from the side instead of the top. Have students compare the results with the original activity. How are they similar? How are they different?

2. Invite an engineer to visit your classroom. Ask him/her to bring topographical maps and models used for planning roads, bridges, dams, tunnels, etc. Have students write a paragraph about one thing they learn.

3. Take a field trip to a construction site. Have a surveyor demonstrate his/her equipment and how the shape of the land is measured. Have students write a paragraph about one thing they learn.

4. Challenge teams to create a topographical map of an area near your school. After drawing their map, have students add buildings, roads, and other features. Post the maps on a bulletin board.

5. Get a topographical map of your area (available through USGS or an outdoor outfitter). Challenge teams to locate prominent geographical features. Have students locate your school, their homes, and other locations.

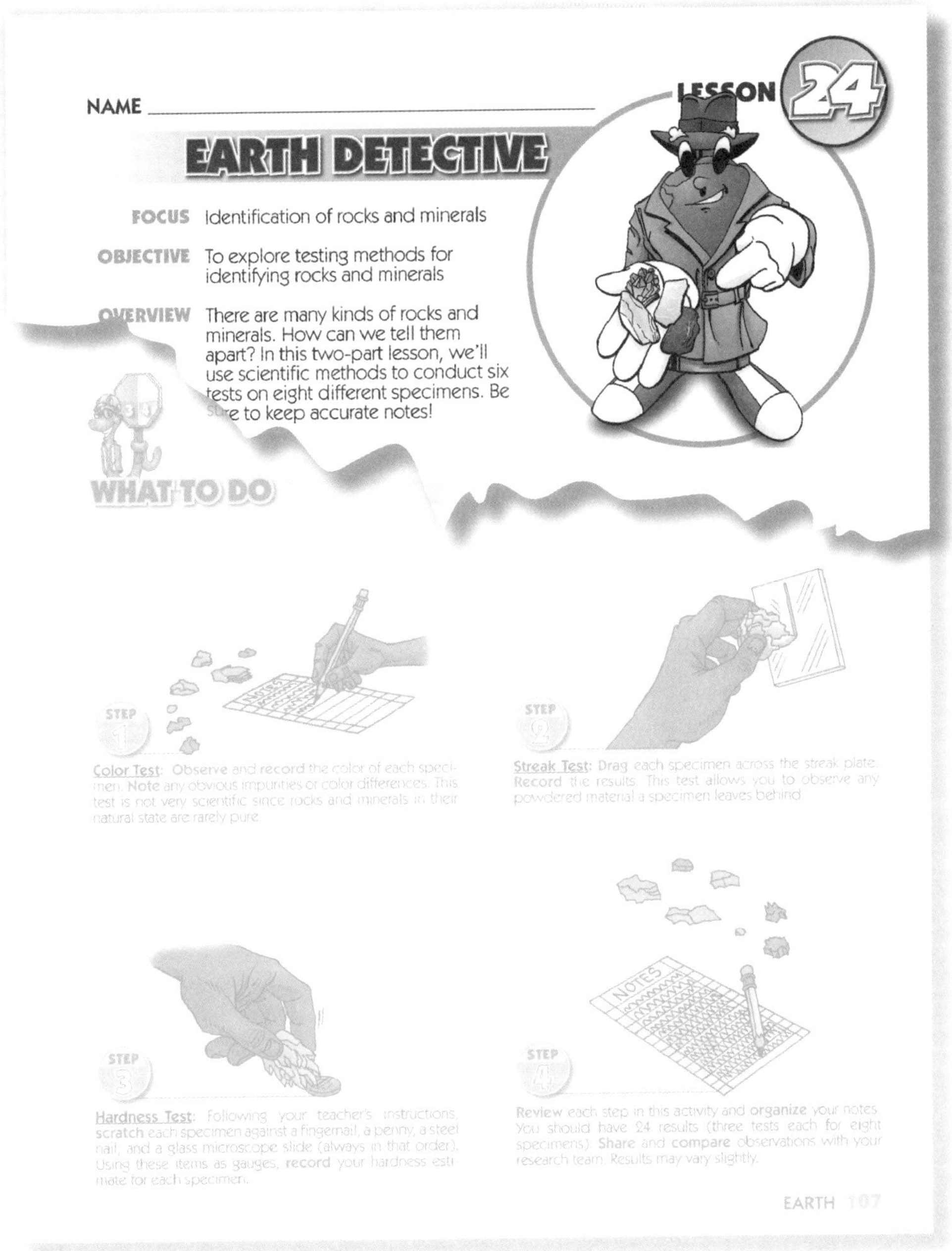
NAME

LESSON 24

EARTH DETECTIVE

FOCUS Identification of rocks and minerals

OBJECTIVE To explore testing methods for identifying rocks and minerals

OVERVIEW There are many kinds of rocks and minerals. How can we tell them apart? In this two-part lesson, we'll use scientific methods to conduct six tests on eight different specimens. Be sure to keep accurate notes!

WHAT TO DO

STEP 1

Color Test: **Observe** and **record** the color of each specimen. **Note** any obvious impurities or color differences. This test is not very scientific since rocks and minerals in their natural state are rarely pure.

STEP 2

Streak Test: **Drag** each specimen across the streak plate. **Record** the results. This test allows you to observe any powdered material a specimen leaves behind.

STEP 3

Hardness Test: Following your teacher's instructions, **scratch** each specimen against a fingernail, a penny, a steel nail, and a glass microscope slide (always in that order). Using these items as gauges, **record** your hardness estimate for each specimen.

STEP 4

Review each step in this activity and **organize** your notes. You should have 24 results (three tests each for eight specimens). **Share** and **compare** observations with your research team. Results may vary slightly.

EARTH 107

Additional Comments

Remind students that these are the same tests geologists use! Results will vary on the color test. In the streak test, focus on the residue (if any). For hardness, introduce the "Mohs scale." (A 10 will scratch anything; a 1 scratches nothing.) Give students the following ratings to help them estimate sample hardness: fingernail = 2, penny = 3, steel nail = 5, glass = 6.

Overview

Read the overview aloud to your students. The goal is to create an atmosphere of curiosity and inquiry.

Category

Earth Science

Focus

Identification of rocks and minerals

Objective

To explore testing methods for identifying rocks and minerals

National Standards

A1, A2, B1, D1, D2, G1, G2

Materials Needed

rock specimens:
- **rose quartz**
- **amethyst**
- **calcite**
- **magnetite**

streak plate
penny
steel nail
microscope slide

Safety Concerns

3. Hygiene
Remind students to wash their hands thoroughly after handling samples.

4. Breakage
Glass microscope slides can break. Remind students to exercise caution.

WHAT TO DO

Monitor student research teams as they complete each step.

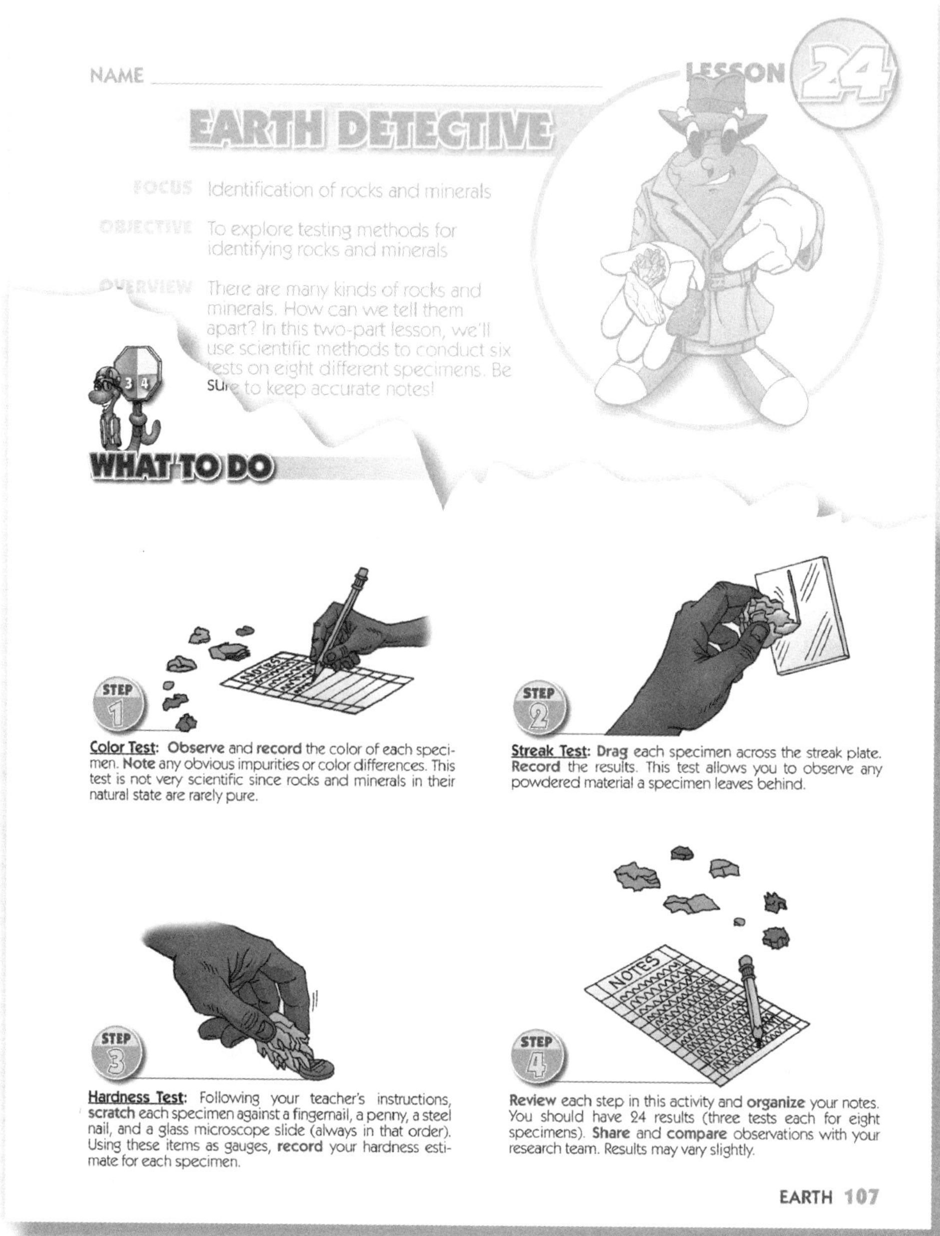

NAME ______________________ LESSON 24

EARTH DETECTIVE

FOCUS Identification of rocks and minerals

OBJECTIVE To explore testing methods for identifying rocks and minerals

OVERVIEW There are many kinds of rocks and minerals. How can we tell them apart? In this two-part lesson, we'll use scientific methods to conduct six tests on eight different specimens. Be sure to keep accurate notes!

WHAT TO DO

Color Test: Observe and **record** the color of each specimen. **Note** any obvious impurities or color differences. This test is not very scientific since rocks and minerals in their natural state are rarely pure.

Streak Test: Drag each specimen across the streak plate. **Record** the results. This test allows you to observe any powdered material a specimen leaves behind.

Hardness Test: Following your teacher's instructions, **scratch** each specimen against a fingernail, a penny, a steel nail, and a glass microscope slide (always in that order). Using these items as gauges, **record** your hardness estimate for each specimen.

Review each step in this activity and **organize** your notes. You should have 24 results (three tests each for eight specimens). **Share** and **compare** observations with your research team. Results may vary slightly.

EARTH 107

Teacher to Teacher

Although the terms "rocks" and "minerals" are often used interchangeably, there are specific differences. Minerals are inorganic solids (carbon is not their main element). Minerals are usually made of one specific compound (not many mixed together). Minerals have characteristics that can be easily tested. By contrast, rocks are usually mixtures of various minerals and elements such as carbon. Rocks also vary enormously from place to place, while minerals are very similar regardless of where they're found.

WHAT JUST HAPPENED?

Your teacher will review specific results from your **Color**, **Streak**, and **Hardness** tests. Here's additional information about the first four specimens:

Specimen #1 - **Rose Quartz**: This beautiful mineral is just one form of quartz. Common forms of quartz are found in sand and gravel. A member of the silicate family, quartz contains the elements silicon and oxygen. **Specimen #2** - **Amethyst** (another form of quartz): "Semi-precious" forms are often used in jewelry. Although this type is mostly purple, amethyst comes in many different colors. **Specimen #3** - **Calcite**: Calcite is primarily the chemical calcium carbonate. Carbonates are common minerals made primarily from the shells of ocean creatures. **Specimen #4** - **Magnetite**: It's magnetic! Ancient cultures called it "lodestone" or "lead stone" since it lined up north/south when suspended. It once was used for making simple navigational devices.

MORE ABOUT ROCKS AND MINERALS . . .

What is the difference between a mineral and a rock?

Minerals are inorganic solids that occur naturally on Earth. A mineral has a characteristic chemical composition and some very specific physical properties. When scientists talk about a mineral, they are usually referring to a pure specimen that can be easily tested. (In this activity, you worked with some samples of the minerals quartz, amethyst, calcite, and magnetite.)

By contrast, rocks are a mixture of two or more minerals. The actual "ingredients" and the amounts may vary widely from rock to rock.

Here's an analogy: To make a cookie, you mix together flour, sugar, butter, and other ingredients. You may decide to add some nuts or raisins or chocolate chips. When all these individual parts are combined and baked, you have a cookie. The finished cookie depends on what was put in, how long it was baked, how much total material was used, and so on. And even though many cookies are similar, each individual cookie is different.

Rocks are a bit like cookies — except they have different ingredients and take a lot longer to make. (And, of course, they're not good to eat!) A particular rock might be a combination of the minerals calcite and quartz with flecks of mica mixed in. The individual pieces are the minerals, but the finished combination is called a rock. And even though many rocks are similar, each individual rock is different.

Once you understand the difference between rocks and minerals, it's easy to see why rocks can vary enormously from place to place (different ingredients), while minerals are very similar regardless of where on Earth they are found.

DIGGING DEEPER:

Research and discuss the four minerals that you tested in this lesson. Find out where they are commonly found, how they are used, and why they are important. Choose one of these minerals and make a poster to share your findings.

108 EARTH

WHAT WE LEARNED:

1. Describe the color test in Step 1. What were the results for each specimen?

   1 = pink/white, 2 = purple/white, 3 = white,
   4 = black/brown, 5 = light brown/white,
   6 = gold, 7 = clear/white, 8 = red/rust

2. Describe the streak test in Step 2. What were the results for each specimen?

   1 = white, 2 = white, 3 = white,
   4 = black/brown, 5 = white, 6 = black/dark,
   7 = colorless (no streak), 8 = white

3. Describe the hardness test in Step 3. What were the results for each specimen?

   1 = 7, 2 = 6, 3 = 3, 4 = 6, 5 = 1, 6 = 6,
   7 = 3, 8 = 7

   (Samples will vary. Allow plus or minus variation of 2).

EARTH 109

What Happened

Review the section with students. Emphasize bold-face words that identify key concepts and introduce new vocabulary.

*Your teacher will review specific results from your **Color**, **Streak**, and **Hardness** tests. Here's additional information about the first four specimens:*

*Specimen #1 - **Rose Quartz**: This beautiful mineral is just one form of quartz. Common forms of quartz are found in sand and gravel. A member of the silicate family, quartz contains the elements silicon and oxygen. Specimen #2 - **Amethyst** (another form of quartz): "Semi-precious" forms are often used in jewelry. Although this type is mostly purple, amethyst comes in many different colors. Specimen #3 - **Calcite**: Calcite is primarily the chemical calcium carbonate. Carbonates are common minerals made primarily from the shells of ocean creatures. Specimen #4 - **Magnetite**: It's magnetic! Ancient cultures called it "lead stone" or "lodestone" since it pointed north/south when suspended. It once was used for making simple navigational devices.*

More About . . .

Have students read this section as you would a traditional science text — or use cooperative learning techniques to allow students the opportunity to work on the material collaboratively.

Digging Deeper

(Optional) Challenge teams to reseach and discuss practical applications of the lesson concepts. Encourage them to share their findings with the rest of the class.

What We Learned

Answers will vary. Suggested responses are shown at left.

Conclusion

Read this section aloud to the class to summarize the concepts learned in this activity.

Food for Thought

Read Matthew 16:18 aloud to the class. Challenge teams to discover stories in Scripture where weak human beings used God's strength to solve a problem.

Science Journal

If time permits, have a general class discussion about notes and drawings various students added to their journal pages. Discuss correct and incorrect predictions, and remind students that this "trial and error" process is part of the scientific process.

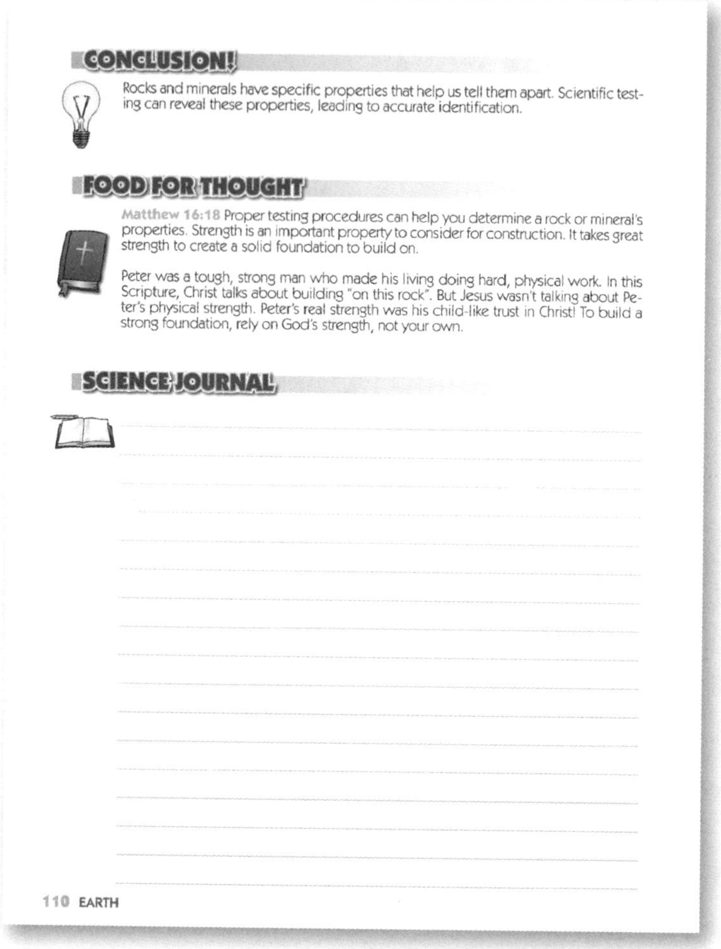

CONCLUSION!

Rocks and minerals have specific properties that help us tell them apart. Scientific testing can reveal these properties, leading to accurate identification.

FOOD FOR THOUGHT

Matthew 16:18 Proper testing procedures can help you determine a rock or mineral's properties. Strength is an important property to consider for construction. It takes great strength to create a solid foundation to build on.

Peter was a tough, strong man who made his living doing hard, physical work. In this Scripture, Christ talks about building "on this rock". But Jesus wasn't talking about Peter's physical strength. Peter's real strength was his child-like trust in Christ! To build a strong foundation, rely on God's strength, not your own.

SCIENCE JOURNAL

110 EARTH

Extended Teaching

1. There are many different types of quartz. Have teams research quartz to discover the various types and their uses. Have students write a paragraph about one thing they learn.

2. Using the Internet, have teams research what rocks and minerals are mined in your region. (Don't forget sand and gravel!) Challenge each team to create a poster about one such location and the material mined there.

3. Invite a "rock hound" to visit your classroom. Ask him/her to bring specimens, and discuss the various types of rocks and minerals. Have students write a paragraph about one thing they learn.

4. Take a field trip to a rock quarry. Find out what kind of rock is being excavated, how it is processed, and how it is used. Have students write a paragraph about one thing they learn.

5. Like the ancients, students are often fascinated by magnetite. Have teams research the history of this interesting mineral and its uses. Challenge each team to contribute material for a magnetite bulletin board.

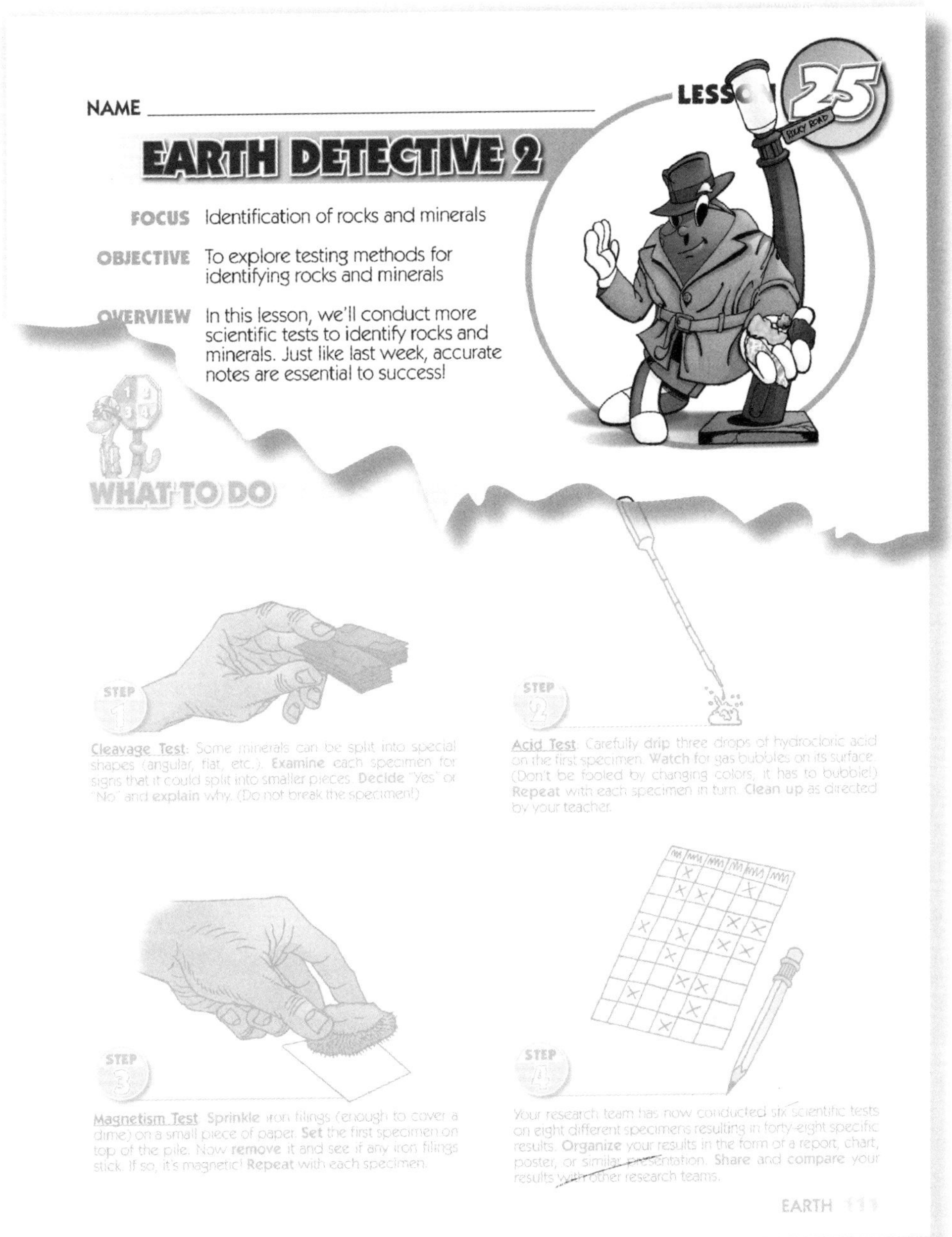
NAME ______________________________

LESSON 25

EARTH DETECTIVE 2

FOCUS Identification of rocks and minerals

OBJECTIVE To explore testing methods for identifying rocks and minerals

OVERVIEW In this lesson, we'll conduct more scientific tests to identify rocks and minerals. Just like last week, accurate notes are essential to success!

WHAT TO DO

STEP 1
Cleavage Test: Some minerals can be split into special shapes (angular, flat, etc.). **Examine** each specimen for signs that it could split into smaller pieces. **Decide** "Yes" or "No" and **explain** why. (Do not break the specimen!)

STEP 2
Acid Test: Carefully **drip** three drops of hydrocloric acid on the first specimen. **Watch** for gas bubbles on its surface. (Don't be fooled by changing colors, it has to bubble!) **Repeat** with each specimen in turn. **Clean up** as directed by your teacher.

STEP 3
Magnetism Test: **Sprinkle** iron filings (enough to cover a dime) on a small piece of paper. **Set** the first specimen on top of the pile. Now **remove** it and see if any iron filings stick. If so, it's magnetic! **Repeat** with each specimen.

STEP 4
Your research team has now conducted six scientific tests on eight different specimens resulting in forty-eight specific results. **Organize** your results in the form of a report, chart, poster, or similar presentation. **Share** and **compare** your results with other research teams.

EARTH 111

Category
Earth Science

Focus
More identification of rocks and minerals

Objective
To explore testing methods for identifying rocks and minerals

National Standards
A1, A2, B1, D1, D2, G1, G2

Materials Needed
rock specimens:
- **talc**
- **pyrite**
- **mica**
- **jasper**

pipette
hydrochloric acid
iron filings
paper
plastic bag (optional)

Safety Concerns
1. Goggles
Always protect eyes when working with chemicals.

2. Corrosion
Avoid direct contact of chemicals with bare skin.

3. Hygiene
Remind students to wash their hands thoroughly after handling samples.

4. Breakage
Remind students they should NOT break the specimens in Step 1.

Additional Comments
Students should wash their hands carefully after each test. You may wish to do Step 2 (hydrochloric acid) as a demonstration.

Overview
Read the overview aloud to your students. The goal is to create an atmosphere of curiosity and inquiry.

WHAT TO DO

Monitor student research teams as they complete each step.

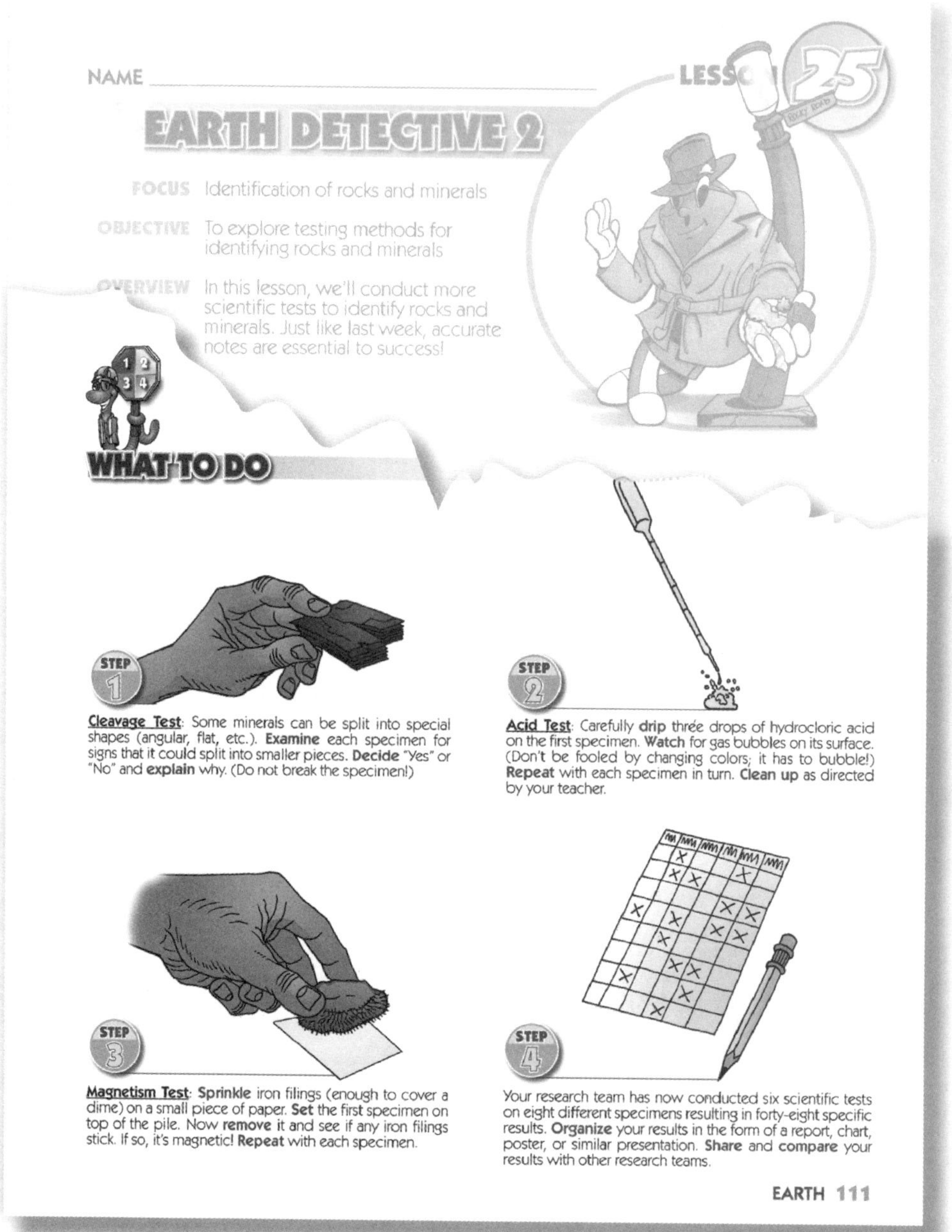

NAME

LESS 25

EARTH DETECTIVE 2

FOCUS Identification of rocks and minerals

OBJECTIVE To explore testing methods for identifying rocks and minerals

OVERVIEW In this lesson, we'll conduct more scientific tests to identify rocks and minerals. Just like last week, accurate notes are essential to success!

WHAT TO DO

STEP 1

Cleavage Test: Some minerals can be split into special shapes (angular, flat, etc.). **Examine** each specimen for signs that it could split into smaller pieces. **Decide** "Yes" or "No" and **explain** why. (Do not break the specimen!)

STEP 2

Acid Test: Carefully **drip** three drops of hydrocloric acid on the first specimen. **Watch** for gas bubbles on its surface. (Don't be fooled by changing colors; it has to bubble!) **Repeat** with each specimen in turn. **Clean up** as directed by your teacher.

STEP 3

Magnetism Test: **Sprinkle** iron filings (enough to cover a dime) on a small piece of paper. **Set** the first specimen on top of the pile. Now **remove** it and see if any iron filings stick. If so, it's magnetic! **Repeat** with each specimen.

STEP 4

Your research team has now conducted six scientific tests on eight different specimens resulting in forty-eight specific results. **Organize** your results in the form of a report, chart, poster, or similar presentation. **Share** and **compare** your results with other research teams.

EARTH 111

Teacher to Teacher

Another simple test is the Luster Test. Luster is the "shininess" of something. Metallic minerals generally show the most luster, but any mineral can have a degree of luster. Like the Color Test, the Luster Test is based on observation. Although terms vary, some typical descriptions are "glassy," "metallic," and "dull."

WHAT JUST HAPPENED?

Your teacher will review specific results from your **Cleavage, Acid**, and **Magnetism** tests. Here's additional information about the last four specimens:

Specimen #5 - Talc: Talc is extremely soft and can be ground into a fine powder. Since "talcum powder" is soft and absorbent, it's often used on babies! Talc is also known as Soapstone. **Specimen #6 - Pyrite**: Pyrite is mostly iron with a metallic, golden color. Because of its appearance, pyrite is sometimes called "fool's gold." **Specimen #7 - Mica**: Mica also belongs to the silicate family, one of the most common minerals on Earth. Mica often looks like glassy sheets stacked in a pile. **Specimen #8 - Jasper**: Jasper is another silicate and also a form of quartz. Although it's a deep red color, it leaves a white streak in the streak test! Jasper is also known as agate.

MORE ABOUT ROCKS AND MINERALS . . .

As we discovered in Lesson 24, "minerals" are inorganic solids that occur naturally on Earth. Every mineral has a characteristic chemical composition and specific physical properties. (In this activity, you worked with some samples of the minerals talc, pyrite, mica, and jasper.) By contrast, "rocks" are a mixture of two or more minerals. The actual ingredients and the amount of mineral content may vary widely from rock to rock.

The scientific study of rocks is called **petrology**. This is the branch of geology that deals with the origin, composition, structure, and alteration of rocks.

Petrologists divide all rocks on Earth into three basic groups: igneous, sedimentary, and metamorphic.

Igneous rocks are formed from melted rock called "magma". (When magma flows onto the Earth's surface, we call it "lava".) Some of these rocks are formed deep inside the Earth. Granite is a good example. Others are formed on the Earth's surface by cooling lava. The lava stone used in landscaping is a good example.

Sedimentary rocks are formed from broken or eroded rock particles. These tiny bits of rock are carried by wind or water and deposited into layers. As these pile up, the pressure and heat from gravity forms them into larger slabs and chunks of rock. Sandstone is a good example of sedimentary rock.

Metamorphic rock is formed from either igenous or sedimentary rock. (The name comes from the Greek word *metamorphosis* which means "to change".) Enormous heat and pressure deep inside the Earth changes igenous or sedimentary rock into a much harder kind of rock. Marble is a good example of metamorphic rock.

DIGGING DEEPER:

Research and discuss the four minerals you tested in this lesson. Find out where they are commonly found, how they are used, and why they are important. Choose one of these minerals and make a poster to share your findings.

112 EARTH

WHAT WE LEARNED:

1. **Describe the cleavage test in Step 1. What were the results for each specimen?**

   1 = none, 2 = none, 3 = none, 4 = none,
   5 = none, 6 = none, 7 = cleavage evident,
   8 = none

2. **Describe the acid test in Step 2. What were the results for each specimen?**

   1 = negative, 2 = negative, 3 = positive,
   4 = negative, 5 = negative, 6 = negative,
   7 = negative, 8 = negative

3. **Describe the magnetism test in Step 3. What were the results for each specimen?**

   1 = negative, 2 = negative, 3 = negative,
   4 = positive, 5 = negative, 6 = negative,
   7 = negative, 8 = negative

EARTH 113

What Happened

Review the section with students. Emphasize bold-face words that identify key concepts and introduce new vocabulary.

*Your teacher will review specific results from your **Cleavage**, **Acid**, and **Magnetism** tests. Here's additional information about the last four specimens:*

*Specimen #5 - **Talc**: Talc is extremely soft and can be ground into a fine power. Since "talcum powder" is soft and absorbent, it's often used on babies! Talc is also known as Soapstone. Specimen #6 - **Pyrite**: Pyrite is mostly iron with a metallic, golden color. Because of its appearance, pyrite is sometimes called "Fool's Gold." Specimen #7 - **Mica**: Mica also belongs to the silicate family, one of the most common minerals on Earth. Mica often looks like glassy sheets stacked in a pile. Specimen #8 - **Jasper**: Jasper is another silicate and also a form of quartz. Although it's a deep red color, it leaves a white streak in the streak test! Jasper is also known as agate.*

More About . . .

Have students read this section as you would a traditional science text — or use cooperative learning techniques to allow students the opportunity to work on the material collaboratively.

Digging Deeper

(Optional) Challenge teams to reseach and discuss practical applications of the lesson concepts. Encourage them to share their findings with the rest of the class.

What We Learned

Answers will vary. Suggested responses are shown at left.

Conclusion

Read this section aloud to the class to summarize the concepts learned in this activity.

Food for Thought

Read the Scripture aloud to the class. Talk about how each one of us is unique, making us ideal for certain tasks. Read Galatians 5:22-23 and Jeremiah 29:11 to the class. Discuss the meaning of these verses.

Science Journal

If time permits, have a general class discussion about notes and drawings various students added to their journal pages. Discuss correct and incorrect predictions, and remind students that this "trial and error" process is part of the scientific process.

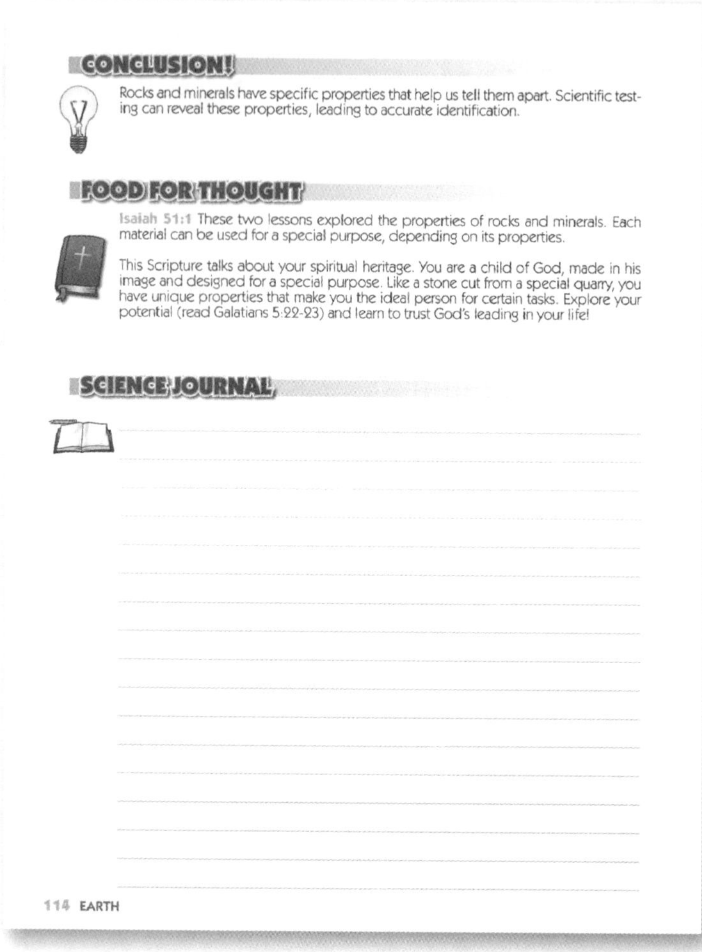
CONCLUSION!

Rocks and minerals have specific properties that help us tell them apart. Scientific testing can reveal these properties, leading to accurate identification.

FOOD FOR THOUGHT

Isaiah 51:1 These two lessons explored the properties of rocks and minerals. Each material can be used for a special purpose, depending on its properties.

This Scripture talks about your spiritual heritage. You are a child of God, made in his image and designed for a special purpose. Like a stone cut from a special quarry, you have unique properties that make you the ideal person for certain tasks. Explore your potential (read Galatians 5:22-23) and learn to trust God's leading in your life!

SCIENCE JOURNAL

114 EARTH

Extended Teaching

1. Continue team research into rocks and minerals mined in your region. Challenge each team to create another poster about a specific location and the material mined there. Add these posters to last week's presentations.

2. Using the Internet, have teams research "fool's gold." (In addition to mineral references, the phrase "fool's gold" is an interesting part of our linguistic culture!) Challenge teams to present their findings to the class.

3. Continue your visit with a local "rock hound". Have him/her bring additional samples to class and continue your discussion. Have students write a paragraph about another thing they learn.

4. Take a field trip to a university geology deparment. Look at the various mineral samples and ask questions. (University collections are often fascinating!) Have students write a paragraph about one thing they learn.

5. Talc is another interesting mineral. Have teams research talc and its uses, both present and historic (talcum powder, etc.). Challenge each team to contribute material for a bulletin board about talc.

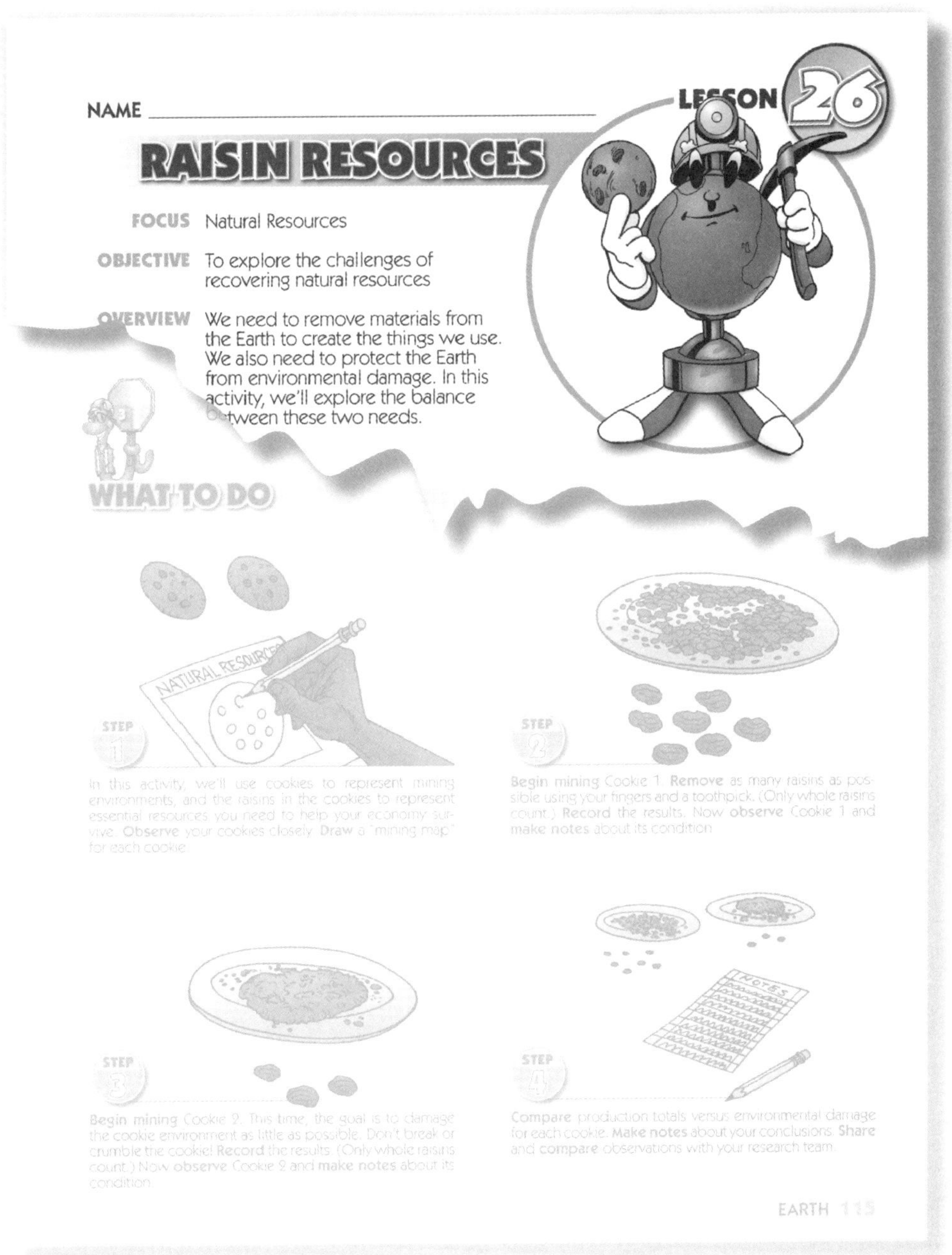
NAME ______________________________

LESSON 26

RAISIN RESOURCES

FOCUS Natural Resources

OBJECTIVE To explore the challenges of recovering natural resources

OVERVIEW We need to remove materials from the Earth to create the things we use. We also need to protect the Earth from environmental damage. In this activity, we'll explore the balance between these two needs.

WHAT TO DO

STEP 1 In this activity, we'll use cookies to represent mining environments, and the raisins in the cookies to represent essential resources you need to help your economy survive. **Observe** your cookies closely. **Draw** a "mining map" for each cookie.

STEP 2 **Begin mining** Cookie 1. **Remove** as many raisins as possible using your fingers and a toothpick. (Only whole raisins count.) **Record** the results. Now **observe** Cookie 1 and **make notes** about its condition.

STEP 3 **Begin mining** Cookie 2. This time, the goal is to damage the cookie environment as little as possible. Don't break or crumble the cookie! **Record** the results. (Only whole raisins count.) Now **observe** Cookie 2 and **make notes** about its condition.

STEP 4 **Compare** production totals versus environmental damage for each cookie. **Make notes** about your conclusions. **Share** and **compare** observations with your research team.

EARTH 115

Category

Earth Science

Focus

Natural Resources

Objective

To explore the challenges of recovering natural resources

National Standards

A1, A2, D1, D2, E1, E2, F2, F4, F5, G1, G2

Materials Needed

toothpicks
raisin cookies
paper plate

Safety Concerns

3. Hygiene
Remind students not to eat the cookies or raisins.

Additional Comments

This activity highlights the difference a specific goal (extracting resources vs. environmental concern) can have on a particular site and its production. Focus on the balance needed to meet society's needs without permanently damaging the environment. Chocolate chip cookies also work well for this activity.

Overview

Read the overview aloud to your students. The goal is to create an atmosphere of curiosity and inquiry.

WHAT TO DO

Monitor student research teams as they complete each step.

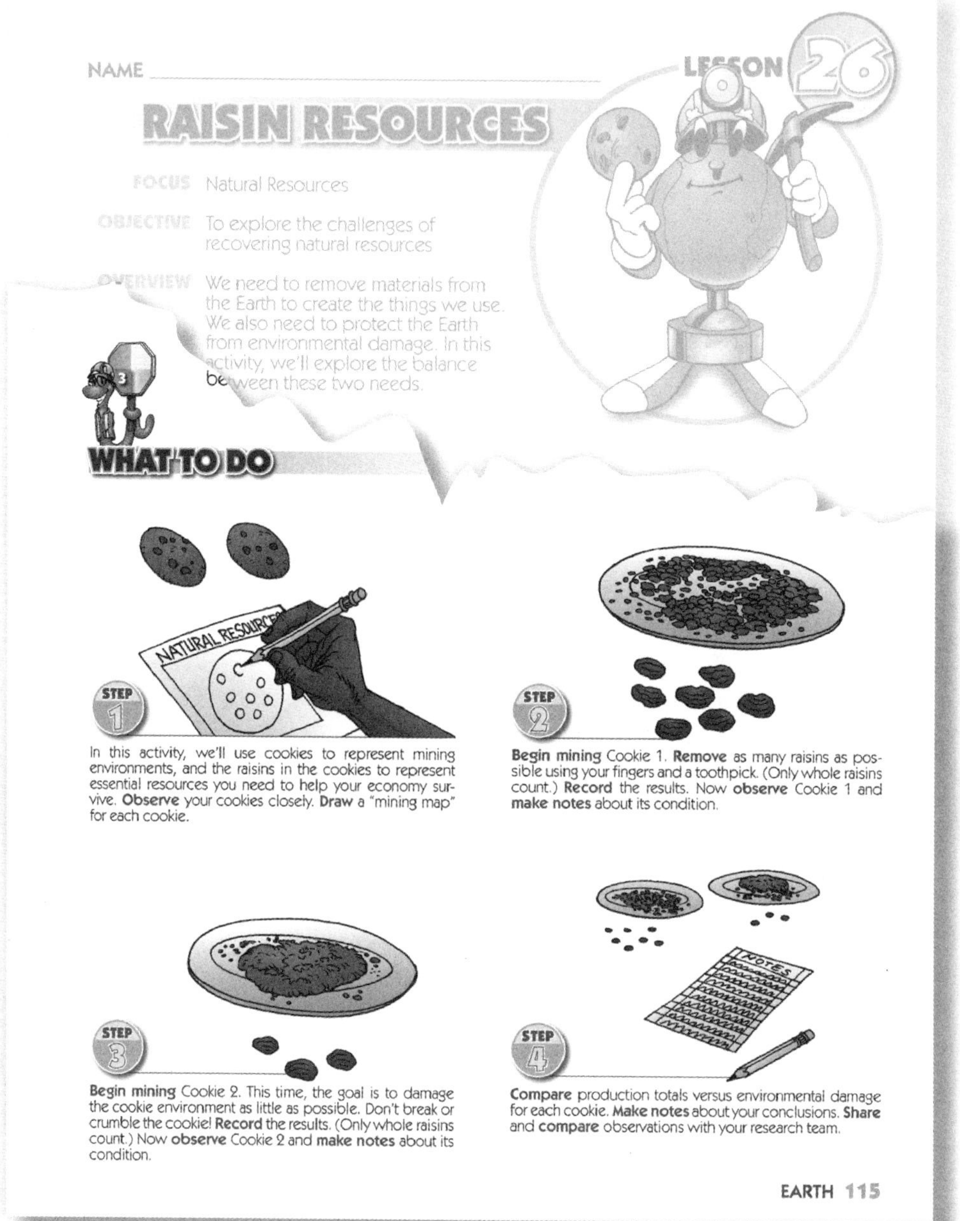

NAME ______________________

LESSON 26

RAISIN RESOURCES

FOCUS Natural Resources

OBJECTIVE To explore the challenges of recovering natural resources

OVERVIEW We need to remove materials from the Earth to create the things we use. We also need to protect the Earth from environmental damage. In this activity, we'll explore the balance between these two needs.

WHAT TO DO

STEP 1 In this activity, we'll use cookies to represent mining environments, and the raisins in the cookies to represent essential resources you need to help your economy survive. **Observe** your cookies closely. **Draw** a "mining map" for each cookie.

STEP 2 **Begin mining** Cookie 1. **Remove** as many raisins as possible using your fingers and a toothpick. (Only whole raisins count.) **Record** the results. Now **observe** Cookie 1 and **make notes** about its condition.

STEP 3 **Begin mining** Cookie 2. This time, the goal is to damage the cookie environment as little as possible. Don't break or crumble the cookie! **Record** the results. (Only whole raisins count.) Now **observe** Cookie 2 and **make notes** about its condition.

STEP 4 **Compare** production totals versus environmental damage for each cookie. **Make notes** about your conclusions. **Share** and **compare** observations with your research team.

EARTH 115

Teacher to Teacher

Even though environmental laws in the U.S. are relatively strict, we still import huge amounts of materials (manganese, cobalt, chronium, etc.) from countries with few such laws. This has a strong effect on the environmental stability of these countries. Thus, in spite of our national standards, many environmentalists believe America's impact on the global environment is quite negative.

WHAT JUST HAPPENED?

Scientists refer to any usable material that comes from the Earth as a **resource**. Resources can be materials (metal, fuel, rock, or mineral), animals (domestic livestock or wild creatures), plants (food crops or native plants), or any other kind of usable item that is on, in, or under the Earth.

Mining is the process of removing something valuable from the Earth. As you saw in Step 2, **extracting** (removing) resources can leave the land completely useless for any other purpose. But Step 3 demonstrated that restrictive mining practices can greatly decrease **production**.

Modern mining operations must balance the two extremes, reclaiming the land by repairing any environmental damage.

MORE ABOUT NATURAL RESOURCES . . .

Our modern world depends on mining raw materials, and then turning these natural resources into usable products. Mining not only gives us simple building materials like sand and gravel, but also fuels like coal, and the minerals and ores to make metals.

But as we saw in this lesson, mining can also do great damage. While we need the raw materials that mining produces, we must not destroy the Earth in order to get them. The challenge of modern mining is to extract and process these key resources with the least possible disruption to the land they lie on or under.

Mine reclamation and similar programs are designed to restore the physical and biological quality of air, land, and water in areas that are disturbed by development. The objective is to prevent (or at least minimize) any adverse long-term environmental impact. These reclamation programs try to establish self-sustaining ecosystems that are as similar to what existed before development began as is practical.

Environmental laws have given companies involved in mining, oil and gas exploration, and similar activities the incentive to develop special environmental technologies to protect the Earth. These technologies are now part of every stage of an operation, from exploration, to drilling and excavation, to processing and manufacturing.

In mining, for instance, reclamation techniques include removing buildings and sheds; closing pits and shafts; stabilizing underground workings, soils, and slopes; treating tailings and waste water; and replanting the land.

Although these activities can be expensive, they are an important part of preserving the balance between our need for raw materials, and the need to carefully protect the Earth's environment for future generations.

DIGGING DEEPER:

Visit one of the many federal and state websites that deal with natural resources and the environment. Research and discuss some of the challenges outlined there. Choose a particular problem and write a short paper describing the solution.

116 EARTH

WHAT WE LEARNED:

1. **Describe the mining of Cookie 1 (Step 2). How many raisins did you recover? What was the condition of the cookie after mining?**

a) answers will vary

b) answers will vary

c) the cookie was destroyed

2. **Describe the mining of Cookie 2 (Step 3). How many raisins did you recover? What was the condition of the cookie after mining?**

a) answers will vary

b) answers will vary

c) holes, but cookie still relatively intact

3. **Based on what you've learned, what are some factors society needs to consider when dealing with natural resources? Why might these factors vary in importance from person to person? Explain.**

a) What are the resources needed? What are the environmental concerns? etc.

b) a miner might see things differently from a farmer or an environmentalist; etc.

EARTH 117

What Happened

Review the section with students. Emphasize bold-face words that identify key concepts and introduce new vocabulary.

*Scientists refer to any usable material that comes from the Earth as a **resource**. Resources can be materials (metal, fuel, rock, or mineral), animals (domestic livestock or wild creatures), plants (food crops or native fauna), or any other kind of usable item that is on, in, or under the Earth.*

***Mining** is the process of removing something valuable from the Earth. As you saw in Step 2, **extracting** (removing) resources can leave the land completely useless for any other purpose. But Step 3 demonstrated that restrictive mining practices can greatly decrease **production**.*

Modern mining operations must balance the two extremes, reclaiming the land by repairing any environmental damage.

More About . . .

Have students read this section as you would a traditional science text — or use cooperative learning techniques to allow students the opportunity to work on the material collaboratively.

Digging Deeper

(Optional) Challenge teams to reseach and discuss practical applications of the lesson concepts. Encourage them to share their findings with the rest of the class.

What We Learned

Answers will vary. Suggested responses are shown at left.

Conclusion

Read this section aloud to the class to summarize the concepts learned in this activity.

Food for Thought

Read the Scripture aloud to the class. Talk about good character traits (kindness, hospitality, cleanliness, etc.) that people often overlook. Discuss how we can learn to look at others through God's eyes.

Science Journal

If time permits, have a general class discussion about notes and drawings various students added to their journal pages. Discuss correct and incorrect predictions, and remind students that this "trial and error" process is part of the scientific process.

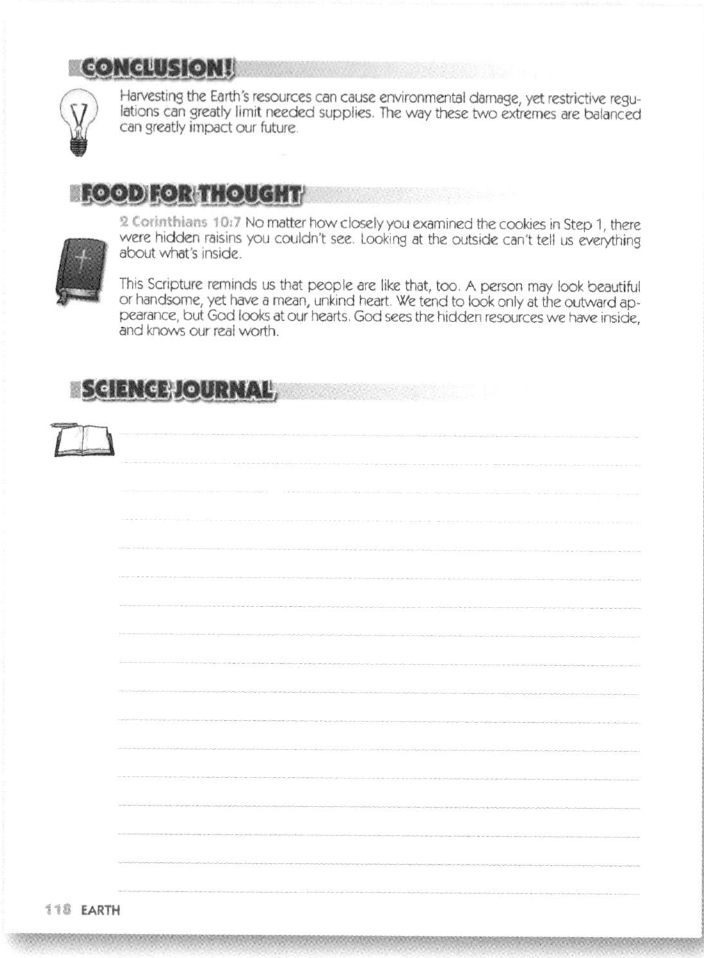

CONCLUSION!

Harvesting the Earth's resources can cause environmental damage, yet restrictive regulations can greatly limit needed supplies. The way these two extremes are balanced can greatly impact our future.

FOOD FOR THOUGHT

2 Corinthians 10:7 No matter how closely you examined the cookies in Step 1, there were hidden raisins you couldn't see. Looking at the outside can't tell us everything about what's inside.

This Scripture reminds us that people are like that, too. A person may look beautiful or handsome, yet have a mean, unkind heart. We tend to look only at the outward appearance, but God looks at our hearts. God sees the hidden resources we have inside, and knows our real worth.

SCIENCE JOURNAL

118 EARTH

Extended Teaching

1. Using the Internet, have teams research various Earth resources, where they are found, and how they are used. Challenge each team to contribute materials for a classroom bulletin board on this topic.

2. Invite someone from the State Department of Natural Resources to visit your classroom. Ask him/her to describe state resources and how they're protected. Have students write a paragraph about one thing they learn.

3. Have students research resources that are recycled and how recycling helps our environment. Challenge each team to create a poster showing examples of items that can be recycled.

4. Invite an environmental scientist to visit your classroom. Ask him/her to discuss the difference between resources and reserves. Have students write a paragraph about one thing they learn.

5. Take a field trip to a recycling center. Find out what materials are recycled, where they come from, how they are processed, and where they go. Have students write a paragraph about one thing they learn.

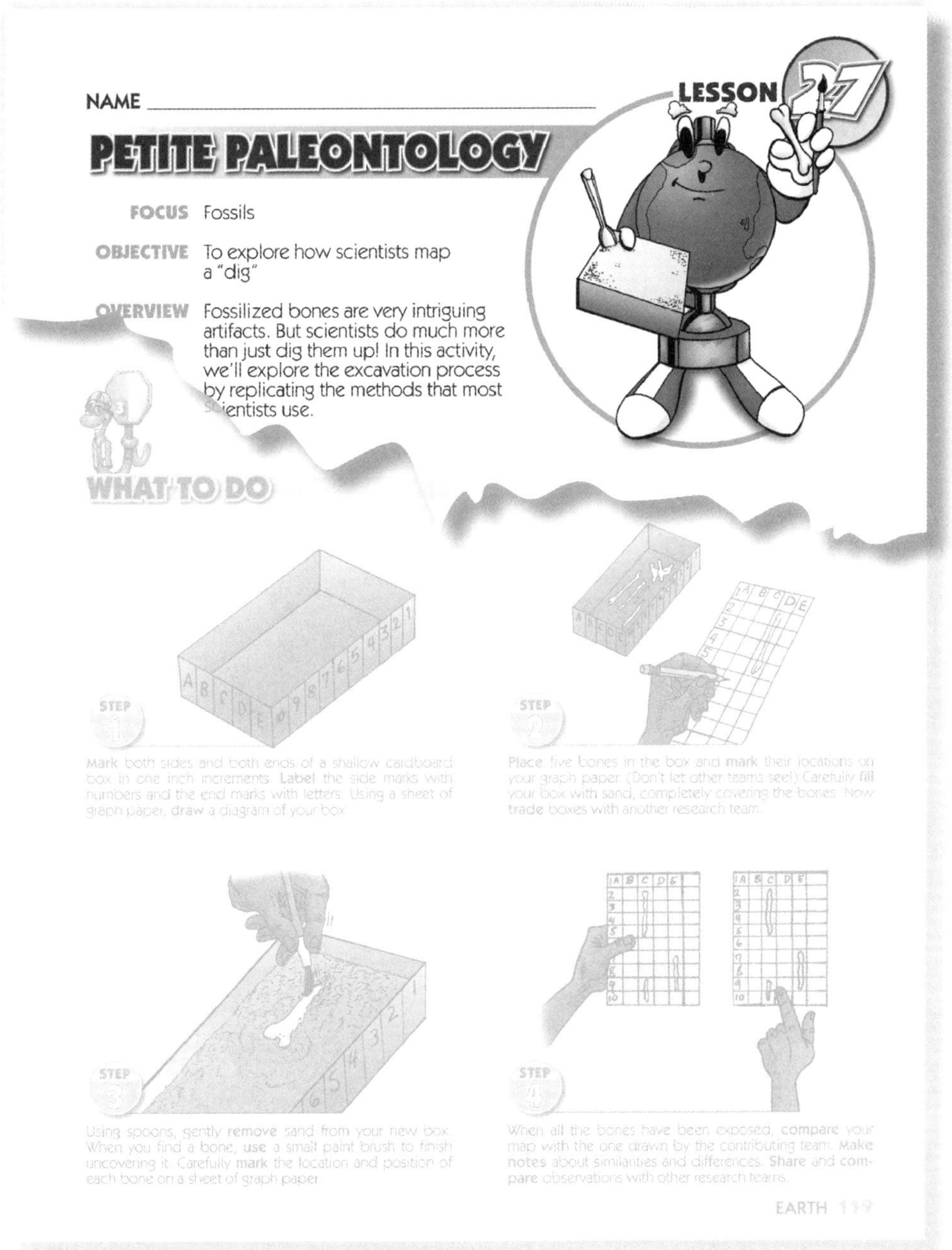

NAME ____________

LESSON 27

PETITE PALEONTOLOGY

FOCUS Fossils

OBJECTIVE To explore how scientists map a "dig"

OVERVIEW Fossilized bones are very intriguing artifacts. But scientists do much more than just dig them up! In this activity, we'll explore the excavation process by replicating the methods that most scientists use.

WHAT TO DO

STEP 1

Mark both sides and both ends of a shallow cardboard box in one inch increments. **Label** the side marks with numbers and the end marks with letters. Using a sheet of graph paper, **draw** a diagram of your box.

STEP 2

Place five bones in the box and **mark** their locations on your graph paper. (Don't let other teams see!) Carefully **fill** your box with sand, completely covering the bones. Now **trade** boxes with another research team.

STEP 3

Using spoons, gently **remove** sand from your new box. When you find a bone, **use** a small paint brush to finish uncovering it. Carefully **mark** the location and position of each bone on a sheet of graph paper.

STEP 4

When all the bones have been exposed, **compare** your map with the one drawn by the contributing team. **Make notes** about similarities and differences. **Share** and **compare** observations with other research teams.

EARTH 119

Category

Earth Science

Focus

Fossils

Objective

To explore how scientists map a "dig"

National Standards

A1, A2, C4, C5, D1, D2, G1, G2

Materials Needed

plastic spoon
small paint brush
paper cup
cardboard box
ruler
graph paper
bones - 5
sand

Safety Concerns

3. Hygiene
Remind students to wash their hands with soap and water after handling materials.

Additional Comments

You can use dog biscuits for the "bones" in this activity, but chicken bones are much more realistic! (Wash bones thoroughly with a bleach solution to disinfect, rinse then dry them thoroughly .) Boxes, sand, and bones can be reused from year to year if cleaned, dried and stored. Graph paper with 1/4" squares works well for this activity.

Overview

Read the overview aloud to your students. The goal is to create an atmosphere of curiosity and inquiry.

WHAT TO DO

Monitor student research teams as they complete each step.

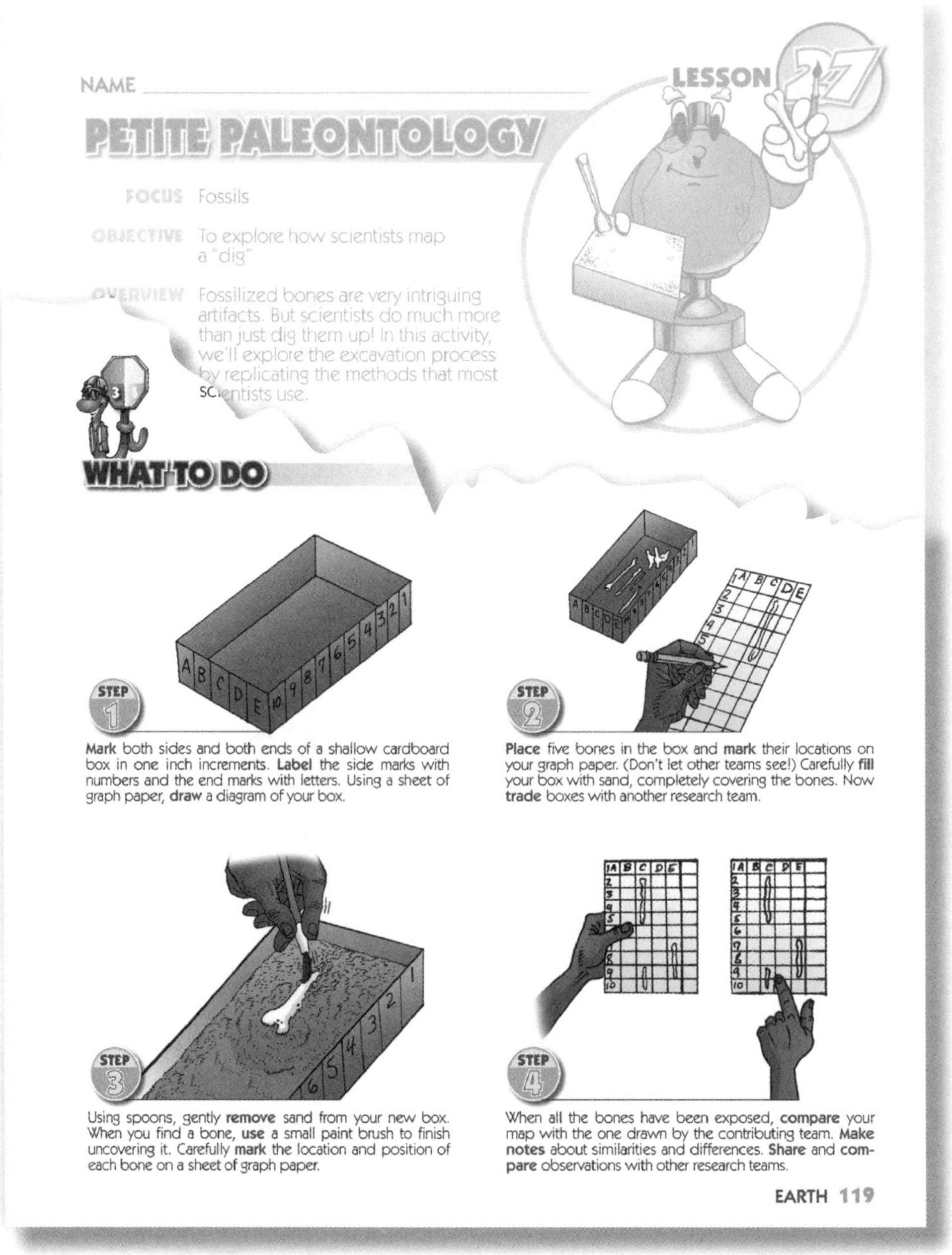

NAME ______________________ LESSON 27

PETITE PALEONTOLOGY

FOCUS Fossils

OBJECTIVE To explore how scientists map a "dig"

OVERVIEW Fossilized bones are very intriguing artifacts. But scientists do much more than just dig them up! In this activity, we'll explore the excavation process by replicating the methods that most scientists use.

WHAT TO DO

STEP 1 **Mark** both sides and both ends of a shallow cardboard box in one inch increments. **Label** the side marks with numbers and the end marks with letters. Using a sheet of graph paper, **draw** a diagram of your box.

STEP 2 **Place** five bones in the box and **mark** their locations on your graph paper. (Don't let other teams see!) Carefully **fill** your box with sand, completely covering the bones. Now **trade** boxes with another research team.

STEP 3 Using spoons, gently **remove** sand from your new box. When you find a bone, **use** a small paint brush to finish uncovering it. Carefully **mark** the location and position of each bone on a sheet of graph paper.

STEP 4 When all the bones have been exposed, **compare** your map with the one drawn by the contributing team. **Make notes** about similarities and differences. **Share** and **compare** observations with other research teams.

EARTH 119

Teacher to Teacher

How old are fossils? A definitive answer is difficult since scientists (both creationist and secular) often disagree about methodologies (sampling, radioactive dating, half-life, etc.). A good comparitive answer, however, is that the deeper the rock layer, the older the fossil. This is called the Law of Superposition.

WHAT JUST HAPPENED?

Scientists who study fossils are called **paleontologists**. Most people associate **fossils** with dinosaurs, even though a fossil is any **preserved** item that suggests an ancient creature or plant existed. The soft body parts (skin, muscle, organs) of ancient creatures **decayed** rapidly and were rarely preserved. The decay-resistant parts (bones, teeth) are much more common.

Once a fossil is found, scientists are very particular about how it is removed and how the surrounding area is explored. They measure and mark each fossil using a method that's very similar to the simple procedure you used in this activity. The distribution of bones can offer information about the creature's **motion**, body **structure**, body **function**, its relationship to other creatures, and even how it died. Modern paleontologists can even create computerized 3-D maps to further enhance their understanding.

MORE ABOUT FOSSILS . . .

Where's the best place to find a fossil? In a museum! Museum exhibits display fossils that have been removed from the field and cleaned for easier study. They often tell the story of the fossil, including where it was found, how it was removed, and the significance of the find. Usually there are even sketches showing what the creature that the fossil came from might have looked like.

Paleontologists and professional fossil collectors use a variety of tools for removing fossils, starting with a professional grade rock hammer. Other tools may include picks, shovels, sledge hammers, pry bars, sifters, and brooms. Fine work may even require devices like dental tools or tiny paint brushes. The big tools are used for removing a fossil from the rock surrounding it. The small tools help clear away dust and rock particles so the outline of the fossil becomes clear.

Collecting fossils can be lots of fun! Many rock shops offer simple fossils at reasonable prices, and some online stores specialize in fossils for beginners. Of course, in some areas of the country you can find fossils yourself. Bluffs, canyons, eroded hillsides, and rocky lake shores are good places to look for fossils. Common fossils like crinoid stems (which look like beads or buttons) are relatively easy to find. The only tools you need are an old butter knife and a toothbrush. Be sure to work slowly and clean each piece carefully as you go. It's also a good idea to keep a "fossil log" by writing down the date and location of each find.

But never go fossil hunting except with a responsible adult! Potential sites can be dangerous — eroded hillsides can crumble away, and flash floods can make a dry stream bed into a death trap. Also, removing some kinds of fossils can destroy the scientific value of a site. Always check with an adult before you begin digging.

DIGGING DEEPER:

Research and discuss some ways fossils are categorized (body fossils, tracks and burrows, casts, molds, etc.). Choose a particular type of fossil, then find out more about it. Make a poster or write a report to share your findings with the class.

WHAT WE LEARNED:

1. **Why are there very few invertebrate fossils (like worms)? What parts of an ancient creature were most likely to become fossils? Why?**

   a) they decompose rapidly

   b) bones, teeth, etc.

   c) they don't decompose as fast

2. **Explain how a grid (like the one you established in Step 1) is an important tool in the study of fossils.**

   it helps scientists record the exact location of each body part; location offers many clues about a creature's motion, body structure, body function, etc.

3. **Based on what you've learned, would a Paleontologist prefer to see a fossil in the lab or in the field? Why? Explain your answer.**

   a) in the field

   b) the location and position of fossil remains can tell a scientist many things (see #2 above)

What Happened

Review the section with students. Emphasize bold-face words that identify key concepts and introduce new vocabulary.

Scientists who study fossils are called ***paleontologists****. Most people associate* ***fossils*** *with dinosaurs, even though a fossil is any* ***preserved*** *item that suggests an ancient creature or plant existed. The soft body parts (skin, muscle, organs) of ancient creatures* ***decayed*** *rapidly and were rarely preserved. The decay-resistant parts (bones, teeth) are much more common.*

Once a fossil is found, scientists are very particular about how it is removed and how the surrounding area is explored. They measure and mark each fossil using a method that's very similar to the simple procedure you used in this activity. The distribution of bones can offer information about the creature's ***motion****, body* ***structure****, body* ***function****, its relationship to other creatures, and even how it died. Modern paleontologists can even create computerized 3-D maps to further enhance their understanding.*

More About . . .

Have students read this section as you would a traditional science text — or use cooperative learning techniques to allow students the opportunity to work on the material collaboratively.

Digging Deeper

(Optional) Challenge teams to reseach and discuss practical applications of the lesson concepts. Encourage them to share their findings with the rest of the class.

What We Learned

Answers will vary. Suggested responses are shown at left.

Conclusion

Read this section aloud to the class to summarize the concepts learned in this activity.

Food for Thought

Read the Scripture aloud to the class. Talk about God's promise that those who love and serve Him will inherit eternal life and live with Him forever.

Science Journal

If time permits, have a general class discussion about notes and drawings various students added to their journal pages. Discuss correct and incorrect predictions, and remind students that this "trial and error" process is part of the scientific process.

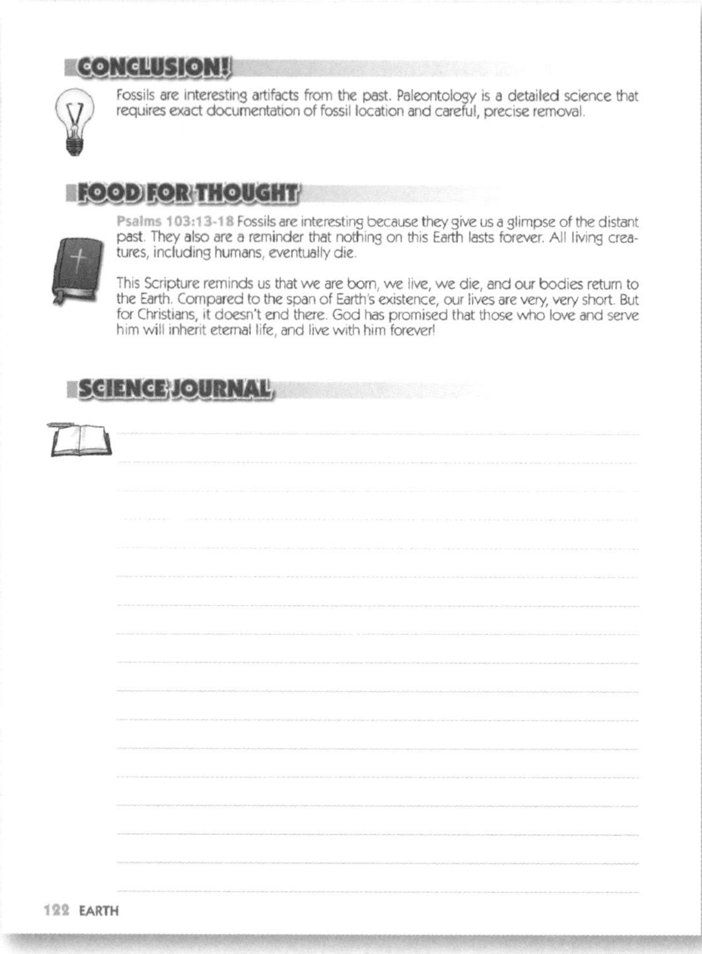

CONCLUSION!

Fossils are interesting artifacts from the past. Paleontology is a detailed science that requires exact documentation of fossil location and careful, precise removal.

FOOD FOR THOUGHT

Psalms 103:13-18 Fossils are interesting because they give us a glimpse of the distant past. They also are a reminder that nothing on this Earth lasts forever. All living creatures, including humans, eventually die.

This Scripture reminds us that we are born, we live, we die, and our bodies return to the Earth. Compared to the span of Earth's existence, our lives are very, very short. But for Christians, it doesn't end there. God has promised that those who love and serve him will inherit eternal life, and live with him forever!

SCIENCE JOURNAL

122 EARTH

Extended Teaching

1. Take a field trip to a museum. Observe the different types of animal and plant fossils. Have students write a paragraph about one thing they learn.

2. Using the Internet, have teams find a current fossil dig website. Find out what is being discovered at this location. Challenge each team to create a poster depicting the site and its findings.

3. Have teams compare a road map with the map they made in this activity. How are they different? How are they similar? (Hint: look for grid locators, scale, etc.)

4. Invite a surveyor to visit your classroom. Ask him/her to explain how grids (quadrangles, section lines, etc.) are used in surveying. Have students write a paragraph about one thing they learn.

5. Have teams research famous American fossil sites (La Brea Tar Pits, California; Dinosaur National Monument, Utah; Mammoth Site, South Dakota; etc.). Challenge each team to create a poster depicting one such site.

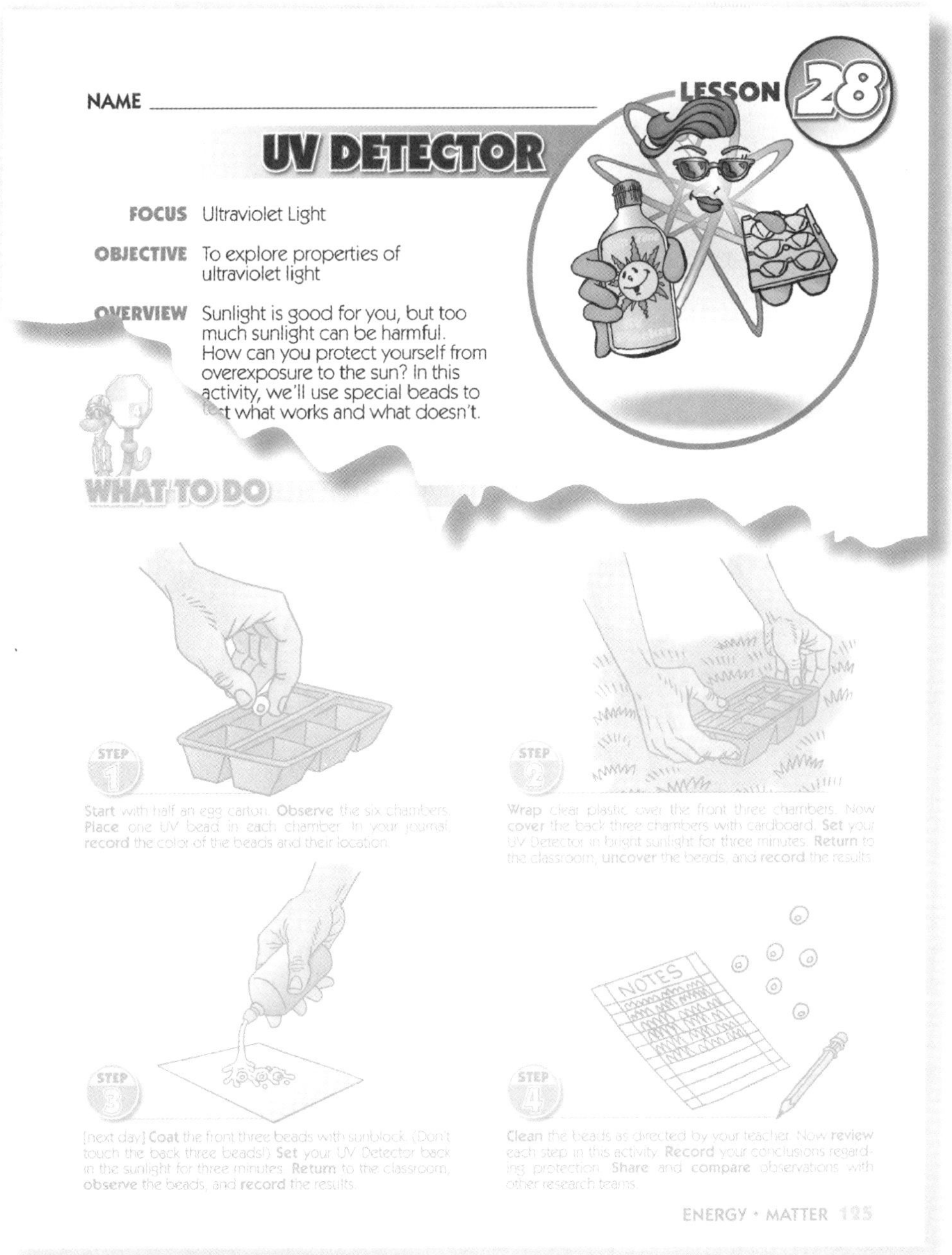

NAME ______________________

LESSON 28

UV DETECTOR

FOCUS Ultraviolet Light

OBJECTIVE To explore properties of ultraviolet light

OVERVIEW Sunlight is good for you, but too much sunlight can be harmful. How can you protect yourself from overexposure to the sun? In this activity, we'll use special beads to test what works and what doesn't.

WHAT TO DO

STEP 1

Start with half an egg carton. **Observe** the six chambers. **Place** one UV bead in each chamber. In your journal, **record** the color of the beads and their location.

STEP 2

Wrap clear plastic over the front three chambers. Now **cover** the back three chambers with cardboard. **Set** your UV Detector in bright sunlight for three minutes. **Return** to the classroom, **uncover** the beads, and **record** the results.

STEP 3

[next day] **Coat** the front three beads with sunblock. (Don't touch the back three beads!) **Set** your UV Detector back in the sunlight for three minutes. **Return** to the classroom, **observe** the beads, and **record** the results.

STEP 4

Clean the beads as directed by your teacher. Now **review** each step in this activity. **Record** your conclusions regarding protection. **Share** and **compare** observations with other research teams.

ENERGY • MATTER 125

Category

Physical Science
Energy/Matter

Focus

Ultraviolet Light

Objective

To explore properties of ultraviolet light

National Standards

A1, A2, B1, B3, E1, E2, F1, F3, F4, F5, G1, G2

Materials Needed

UV beads
egg carton
clear plastic
cardboard
sunblock

Safety Concerns

4. Slipping Hazard
Remind students to exercise caution with sunblock. Clean up spills immediately.

Additional Comments

Results will vary since different beads have various degrees of solar sensitivity. If beads and egg cartons are cleaned and dried carefully, they can be stored and used next year.

Overview

Read the overview aloud to your students. The goal is to create an atmosphere of curiosity and inquiry.

WHAT TO DO

Monitor student research teams as they complete each step.

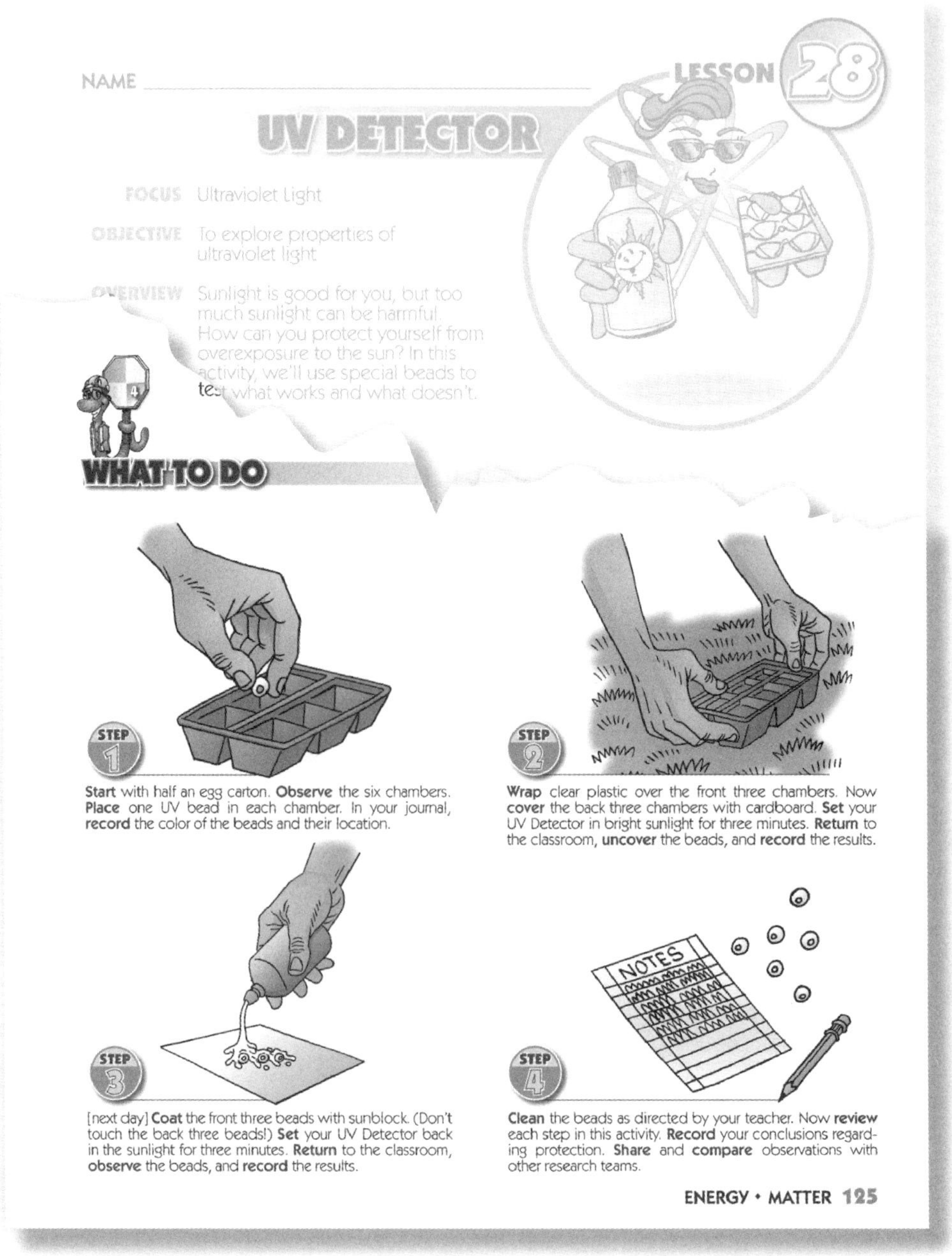

NAME ______________________

LESSON 28

UV DETECTOR

FOCUS Ultraviolet Light

OBJECTIVE To explore properties of ultraviolet light

OVERVIEW Sunlight is good for you, but too much sunlight can be harmful! How can you protect yourself from overexposure to the sun? In this activity, we'll use special beads to test what works and what doesn't.

WHAT TO DO

STEP 1

Start with half an egg carton. **Observe** the six chambers. **Place** one UV bead in each chamber. In your journal, **record** the color of the beads and their location.

STEP 2

Wrap clear plastic over the front three chambers. Now **cover** the back three chambers with cardboard. **Set** your UV Detector in bright sunlight for three minutes. **Return** to the classroom, **uncover** the beads, and **record** the results.

STEP 3

[next day] **Coat** the front three beads with sunblock. (Don't touch the back three beads!) **Set** your UV Detector back in the sunlight for three minutes. **Return** to the classroom, **observe** the beads, and **record** the results.

STEP 4

Clean the beads as directed by your teacher. Now **review** each step in this activity. **Record** your conclusions regarding protection. **Share** and **compare** observations with other research teams.

ENERGY • MATTER 125

Teacher to Teacher

UV-A and UV-B are common forms of ultraviolet light. Tanning booths use UV-A; sunlight is primarily UV-B. It's easy to sunburn with UV-B, but this form rarely penetrates deep into the skin. By contrast, UV-A minimizes the potential for burning, but it penetrates deep into skin and can lead to permanent damage.

WHAT JUST HAPPENED?

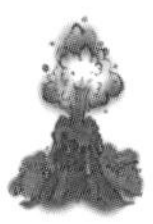

The beads you used in this activity are sensitive to **ultraviolet** (UV) **light**. Ultraviolet light can be dangerous to living things because prolonged exposure to its **energy** damages **skin cells**. Under certain conditions, this can lead to skin **cancer**. Cancer cells reproduce rapidly and this wild growth forces out normal, healthy cells, resulting in severe health problems or even death.

In Step 2, you protected three beads by blocking the sunlight entirely with a **physical barrier** (cardboard). In Step 3, you protected three beads by blocking sunlight with sunblock. Sunblock is also a form of physical barrier, but it's a lot more convenient than holding cardboard over your head!

Different types of sunblock provide different levels of protection, indicated by the SPF (sun protection factor) number on the bottle.

MORE ABOUT ULTRAVIOLET LIGHT . . .

Even though prolonged exposure to ultraviolet light can be dangerous to living things, UV light is not all bad! In fact, proper use of UV light can be quite helpful.

Ultraviolet light can be used to sterilize and disinfect. UV light deactivates the DNA of bacteria, viruses, and other pathogens without the risks associated with chemicals. Hospitals, hotels, laboratories, and other public facilities often use this process to purify everything from drinking water to the air we breathe. Implementation is simple, relatively inexpensive, and requires very little maintenance.

Ultraviolet light can also be used to detect counterfeit money or IDs. Most U.S. currency, international passports, and state driver's licenses now contain security threads that glow when exposed to UV light. This helps various law enforcement agencies reduce dangers to our nation's economy and our national security.

Ultraviolet light can even be used for pest control. House flies, gnats, fruit flies, and other flying insects are attracted to ultraviolet light. This helps lure them into special traps where they are "zapped" with electricity or caught on sticky pads. Many commercial food handling operations depend on such devices to help keep these pests at manageable levels.

Scientists study the ultraviolet light given off by distant objects in space. Doctors use it to treat some kinds of skin diseases. It can be used to extend the shelf life of fruit juices. It is even used in special fire detection devices. And the list goes on.

As you can see, even though we need to take care to minimize our exposure to ultraviolet light, there are many other ways that UV light helps make our lives better.

DIGGING DEEPER:

Research and discuss some of the many uses for ultraviolet light. Choose one specific process (like studying objects in space), then find out more about it. Write a report or make a poster to share your findings with the class.

WHAT WE LEARNED:

1 **Compare Step 2 and Step 3. How were they similar? How were they different? What do cardboard and sunblock have in common?**

a) similar: both exposed to sun, both involved changing only one variable

b) different: one used cardboard to block UV light; the other used sunblock

c) both will block UV light

2 **Why is prolonged exposure to ultraviolet light hazardous? What are some steps you can take to protect yourself?**

a) it could lead to skin cancer

b) use sunscreen, wear protective clothing, minimize time exposed, etc.

3 **Based on what you've learned, is ultraviolet light "good" or "bad"? Explain your answer.**

it can be good or bad: good uses of UV light include sterilizing and disinfecting, detecting counterfeit money, and controlling pests; bad aspects of UV light include sunburn and the potential for skin cancer

What Happened

Review the section with students. Emphasize bold-face words that identify key concepts and introduce new vocabulary.

*The beads you used in this activity are sensitive to **ultraviolet** (UV) **light**. Ultraviolet light can be dangerous to living things because prolonged exposure to its **energy** damages **skin cells**. Under certain conditions, this can lead to skin **cancer**. Cancer cells reproduce rapidly and this wild growth forces out normal, healthy cells, resulting in severe health problems or even death.*

*In Step 2, you protected three beads by blocking the sunlight entirely with a **physical barrier** (cardboard). In Step 3, you protected three beads by blocking sunlight with sunblock. Sunblock is also a form of physical barrier, but it's a lot more convenient than holding cardboard over your head!*

Different types of sunblock provide different levels of protection, indicated by the SPF (sun protection factor) number on the bottle.

More About . . .

Have students read this section as you would a traditional science text — or use cooperative learning techniques to allow students the opportunity to work on the material collaboratively.

Digging Deeper

(Optional) Challenge teams to reseach and discuss practical applications of the lesson concepts. Encourage them to share their findings with the rest of the class.

What We Learned

Answers will vary. Suggested responses are shown at left.

Conclusion

Read this section aloud to the class to summarize the concepts learned in this activity.

Food for Thought

Read the Scripture aloud to the class. Talk about how continued exposure to sin can damage our souls. Discuss how spending more time with God can protect us.

Science Journal

If time permits, have a general class discussion about notes and drawings various students added to their journal pages. Discuss correct and incorrect predictions, and remind students that this "trial and error" process is part of the scientific process.

CONCLUSION!

Ultraviolet light is an invisible part of sunlight that contains a great deal of energy. Ultraviolet light can be dangerous to living things because prolonged exposure damages skin cells.

FOOD FOR THOUGHT

John 17:12 The best way to protect your skin from harmful UV light is to block the sunlight. If left unprotected, your skin can be severely damaged by prolonged exposure to UV light.

There are similarities in the spiritual world. The best way to protect yourself from evil is to block it out. If left unprotected, your soul can be damaged by prolonged exposure to evil! This Scripture reminds us that the ultimate protection lies in a relationship with Jesus. Only he can keep you safe from the damaging effects of sin.

SCIENCE JOURNAL

128 ENERGY • MATTER

Extended Teaching

1. Repeat this activity, only experiment with sunscreens that have different SPF levels. Have students compare the results with the original activity. How were they similar? How were they different?

2. Using the Internet, have students research changes in the ozone layer. What substances do scientists believe are causing the problem? What is being done about it? Challenge teams to present their findings to the class.

3. Invite someone from the American Cancer Society to visit your classroom. Ask him/her to discuss how too much exposure to sunlight can cause cancer. Have students write a paragraph about one thing they learn.

4. Take a field trip to a hospital or medical center. Ask a health care professional to talk about different types of skin cancer and how they are treated. Have students write a paragraph about one thing they learn.

5. Have teams research melanocytes. Challenge each team to create a poster showing how these cells work to protect us from overexposure to the sun.

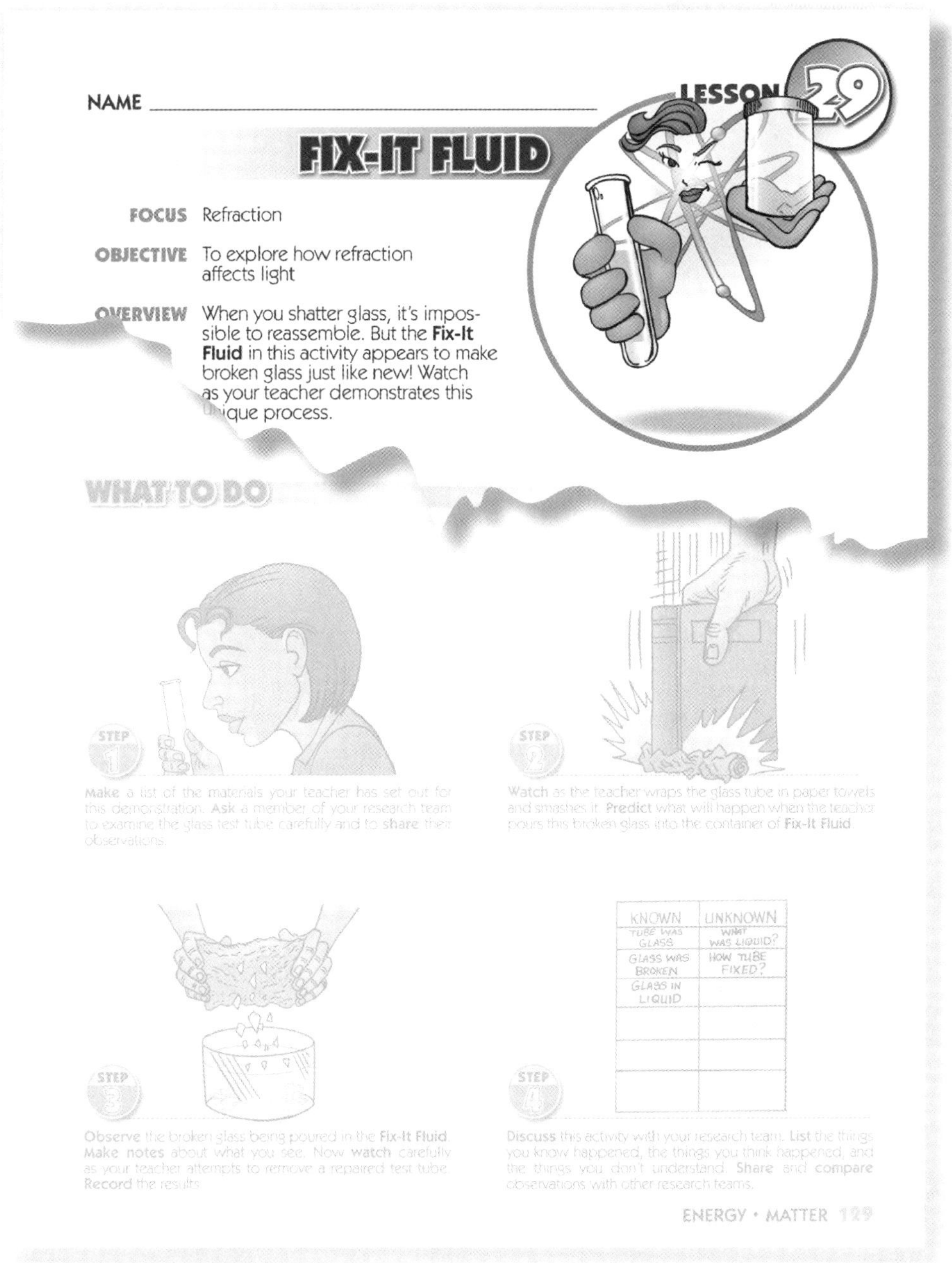

NAME ______

LESSON 29

FIX-IT FLUID

FOCUS Refraction

OBJECTIVE To explore how refraction affects light

OVERVIEW When you shatter glass, it's impossible to reassemble. But the **Fix-It Fluid** in this activity appears to make broken glass just like new! Watch as your teacher demonstrates this unique process.

WHAT TO DO

STEP 1

Make a list of the materials your teacher has set out for this demonstration. **Ask** a member of your research team to examine the glass test tube carefully and to **share** their observations.

STEP 2

Watch as the teacher wraps the glass tube in paper towels and smashes it. **Predict** what will happen when the teacher pours this broken glass into the container of **Fix-It Fluid**.

STEP 3

Observe the broken glass being poured in the **Fix-It Fluid**. **Make notes** about what you see. Now **watch** carefully as your teacher attempts to remove a repaired test tube. **Record** the results.

STEP 4

KNOWN	UNKNOWN
TUBE WAS GLASS	WHAT WAS LIQUID?
GLASS WAS BROKEN	HOW TUBE FIXED?
GLASS IN LIQUID	

Discuss this activity with your research team. **List** the things you know happened, the things you think happened, and the things you don't understand. **Share** and **compare** observations with other research teams.

ENERGY • MATTER 129

Category

Physical Science
Energy/Matter

Focus

Refraction

Objective

To explore how refraction affects light

National Standards

A1, A2, B1, B3, E1, E2, F5, G1, G2

Materials Needed

glass test tubes - 2
test tube holder
paper towels
mineral oil
container

Safety Concerns

none (demonstration only)

Additional Comments

Start with a wide glass container. Prior to class, fill it with heavy mineral oil and place an unbroken test tube on the bottom. Remove all air bubbles from the tube so it becomes invisible. After pouring in the broken glass in Step 2, reach in with a test tube holder and remove the unbroken tube (make sure both tubes are the same size). Surprise! Having a second tube in the oil alows you to "do it again," as the students may request.

Overview

Read the overview aloud to your students. The goal is to create an atmosphere of curiosity and inquiry.

WHAT TO DO

Be sure to do the demonstration *before* students read "What Happened" (page 130)!

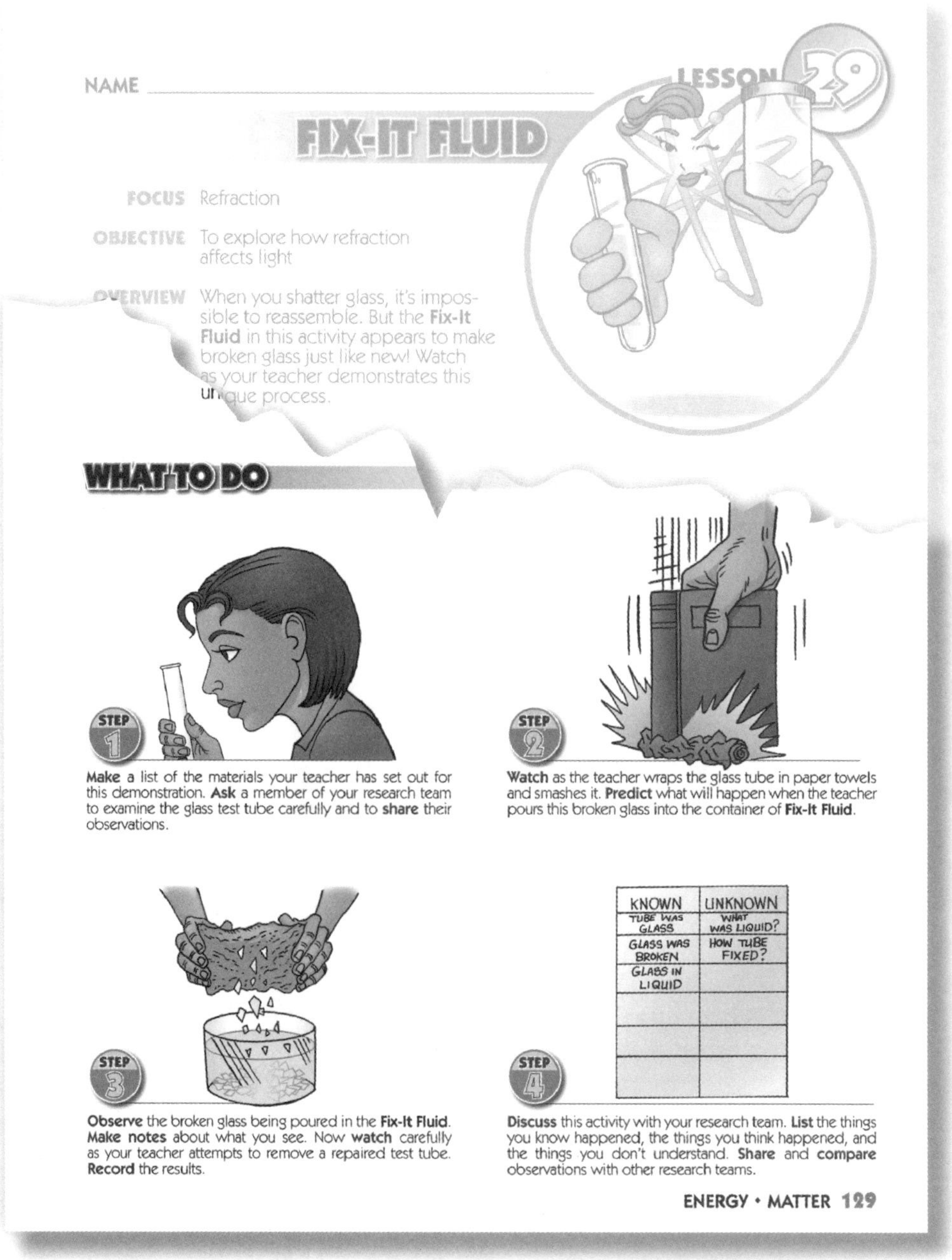

NAME ______________________

LESSON 29

FIX-IT FLUID

FOCUS Refraction

OBJECTIVE To explore how refraction affects light

OVERVIEW When you shatter glass, it's impossible to reassemble. But the **Fix-It Fluid** in this activity appears to make broken glass just like new! Watch as your teacher demonstrates this unique process.

WHAT TO DO

STEP 1 **Make** a list of the materials your teacher has set out for this demonstration. **Ask** a member of your research team to examine the glass test tube carefully and to **share** their observations.

STEP 2 **Watch** as the teacher wraps the glass tube in paper towels and smashes it. **Predict** what will happen when the teacher pours this broken glass into the container of **Fix-It Fluid**.

STEP 3 **Observe** the broken glass being poured in the **Fix-It Fluid**. **Make notes** about what you see. Now **watch** carefully as your teacher attempts to remove a repaired test tube. **Record** the results.

KNOWN	UNKNOWN
TUBE WAS GLASS	WHAT WAS LIQUID?
GLASS WAS BROKEN	HOW TUBE FIXED?
GLASS IN LIQUID	

STEP 4 **Discuss** this activity with your research team. **List** the things you know happened, the things you think happened, and the things you don't understand. **Share** and **compare** observations with other research teams.

ENERGY • MATTER 129

Teacher to Teacher

Our world is full of optical illusions. The "sun" we see at sunset is actually a refracted image of the real thing. A heat mirage is created by light refracted in rising hot air. Even trick mirrors rely on refraction to produce images that aren't actually there. And as we saw in this activity, refraction can have the opposite affect, too!

WHAT JUST HAPPENED?

(Do NOT read this section until instructed by your teacher!) When **light** goes through any material, it slows down. This speed change causes the light to "bend" — a process known as **refraction**. The amount of bending is called the **index of refraction**. When you look into a **liquid**, an object is easy to see when there's a big difference between its index of refraction and the liquid's index of refraction. The opposite is also true.

The **Fix-It Fluid** in this activity was actually heavy mineral oil, a liquid with nearly the same index of refraction as glass. Since the light was bent the same amount, it made it nearly impossible to see the pieces of broken glass.

It also made it nearly impossible to see the unbroken test tube the teacher had hidden in the bottom of the jar. Gotcha!

MORE ABOUT REFRACTION . . .

As you discovered, refraction involves bending light. But bent light can do a lot more than just create optical illusions. Refraction is vital to many of the devices we use every day. In fact, if you're wearing glasses or contact lenses, you're using refraction right now to help you read this sentence!

Lenses are the primary tool we use to refract light. The lenses found in glasses (and telescopes, microscopes, cameras, etc.) are usually made of glass or plastic. These lenses are designed to bend light in very specific ways.

But not all lenses are made of glass or plastic.

According to scientists, the oldest known lens is a curved piece of rock crystal that was found in the ruins of Ninevah. Archeologists say this artifact was used over 600 years before the birth of Christ.

Early lenses were often used to start fires by focusing sunlight on a pile of tinder. Historic writings show that such devices were common in ancient Rome.

Today, scientists classify simple lenses by their surface shapes. Surfaces that bulge out are called "**convex**". Surfaces that depress inward are called "**concave**". Flat surfaces are called "**planar**" (or "plano"). Thus a lens that has one flat surface and one bulging surface would be called a "plano-convex" lens.

Of course, refraction is not just useful. It can also create beautiful images. When sunlight refracts through drops of water, you often get a rainbow. And when light is bent by a crystal or a diamond, it can refract into beautiful bands and sparkles of color.

DIGGING DEEPER:

Research and discuss specific applications of refraction. Write a report or make a poster showing one of these applications in detail. (Possible topics might include "how lenses correct eye problems", "how telescopes use lenses to help us see into space", and so on.)

WHAT WE LEARNED:

1 What was your prediction in Step 2? How did this reflect what actually happened?

answers will vary, but should reflect logical comparisons

2 How did the light's speed change as it passed through the mineral oil? What did this cause the light to do? What is the term that describes the amount light bends?

a) it slowed down

b) bend

c) the index of refraction

3 Based on what you've learned, explain the optical illusion that was produced in this activity. How did it occur?

the oil's refraction index was similar to the refraction index of glass; light was bent almost the same by the oil and glass, making the glass invisible; etc.

What Happened

Review the section with students. Emphasize bold-face words that identify key concepts and introduce new vocabulary.

*(Do NOT read this section until instructed by your teacher!) When **light** goes through any material, it slows down. This speed change causes the light to "bend" – a process known as **refraction**. The amount of bending is called the **index of refraction**. When you look into a **liquid**, an object is easy to see when there's a big difference between its index of refraction and the liquid's index of refraction. The opposite is also true.*

The Fix-It Fluid in this activity was actually heavy mineral oil, a liquid with nearly the same index of refraction as glass. Since the light was bent the same amount, it made it nearly impossible to see the pieces of broken glass.

It also made it nearly impossible to see the unbroken test tube the teacher had hidden in the bottom of the jar. Gotcha!

More About . . .

Have students read this section as you would a traditional science text — or use cooperative learning techniques to allow students the opportunity to work on the material collaboratively.

Digging Deeper

(Optional) Challenge teams to reseach and discuss practical applications of the lesson concepts. Encourage them to share their findings with the rest of the class.

What We Learned

Answers will vary. Suggested responses are shown at left.

Conclusion

Read this section aloud to the class to summarize the concepts learned in this activity.

Food for Thought

Read the Scripture aloud to the class. Talk about how the world's illusions can fool us. Discuss how a close connection with God is the only way to avoid being deceived.

Science Journal

If time permits, have a general class discussion about notes and drawings various students added to their journal pages. Discuss correct and incorrect predictions, and remind students that this "trial and error" process is part of the scientific process.

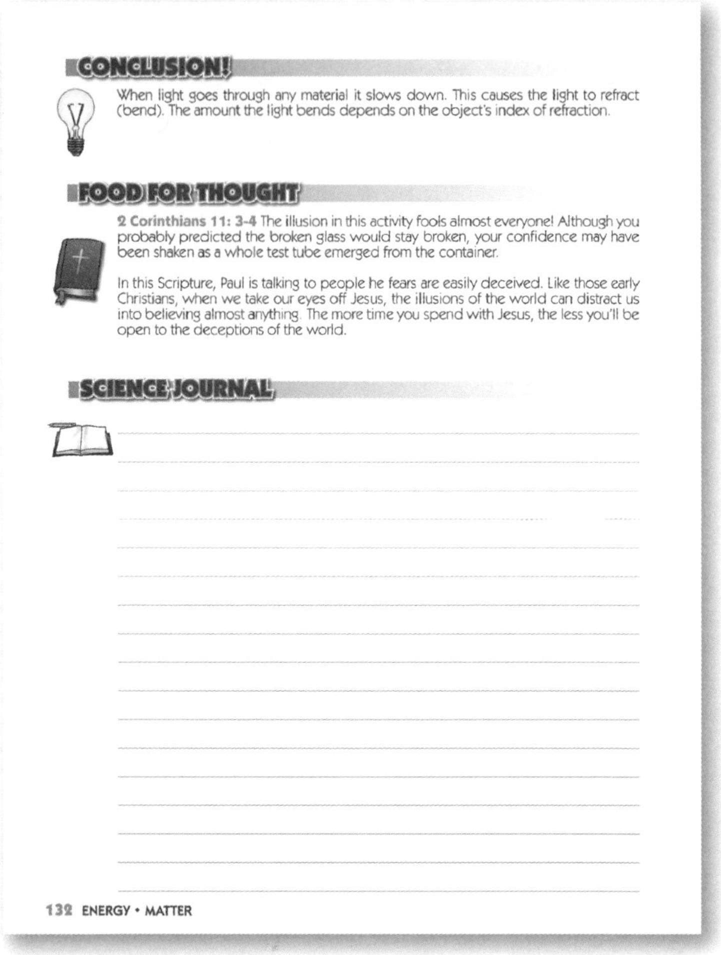

CONCLUSION!

When light goes through any material it slows down. This causes the light to refract (bend). The amount the light bends depends on the object's index of refraction.

FOOD FOR THOUGHT

2 Corinthians 11: 3-4 The illusion in this activity fools almost everyone! Although you probably predicted the broken glass would stay broken, your confidence may have been shaken as a whole test tube emerged from the container.

In this Scripture, Paul is talking to people he fears are easily deceived. Like those early Christians, when we take our eyes off Jesus, the illusions of the world can distract us into believing almost anything. The more time you spend with Jesus, the less you'll be open to the deceptions of the world.

SCIENCE JOURNAL

132 ENERGY • MATTER

Extended Teaching

1. Invite an optometrist to visit your classroom. Ask him/her to explain how lenses bend light, and how this helps correct vision. Have students write a paragraph about one thing they learn.

2. Bring devices with lenses (camera, telescope, microscope, etc.) to class. Have students examine them to see how lenses create images. Challenge each team to make a poster showing how one of these devices works.

3. Take a field trip to a photography studio. Ask the photographer to demonstrate how lenses bend light to make different images. Have students write a paragraph about one thing they learn.

4. Using the Internet, have students research how laser surgeries (like radial keratotomy) help people see without glasses or contacts. Challenge each team to contribute material for a bulletin board on this topic.

5. Have teams discuss what life might be like without sight. Challenge each student to write a story on this theme, focusing on day-to-day activities.

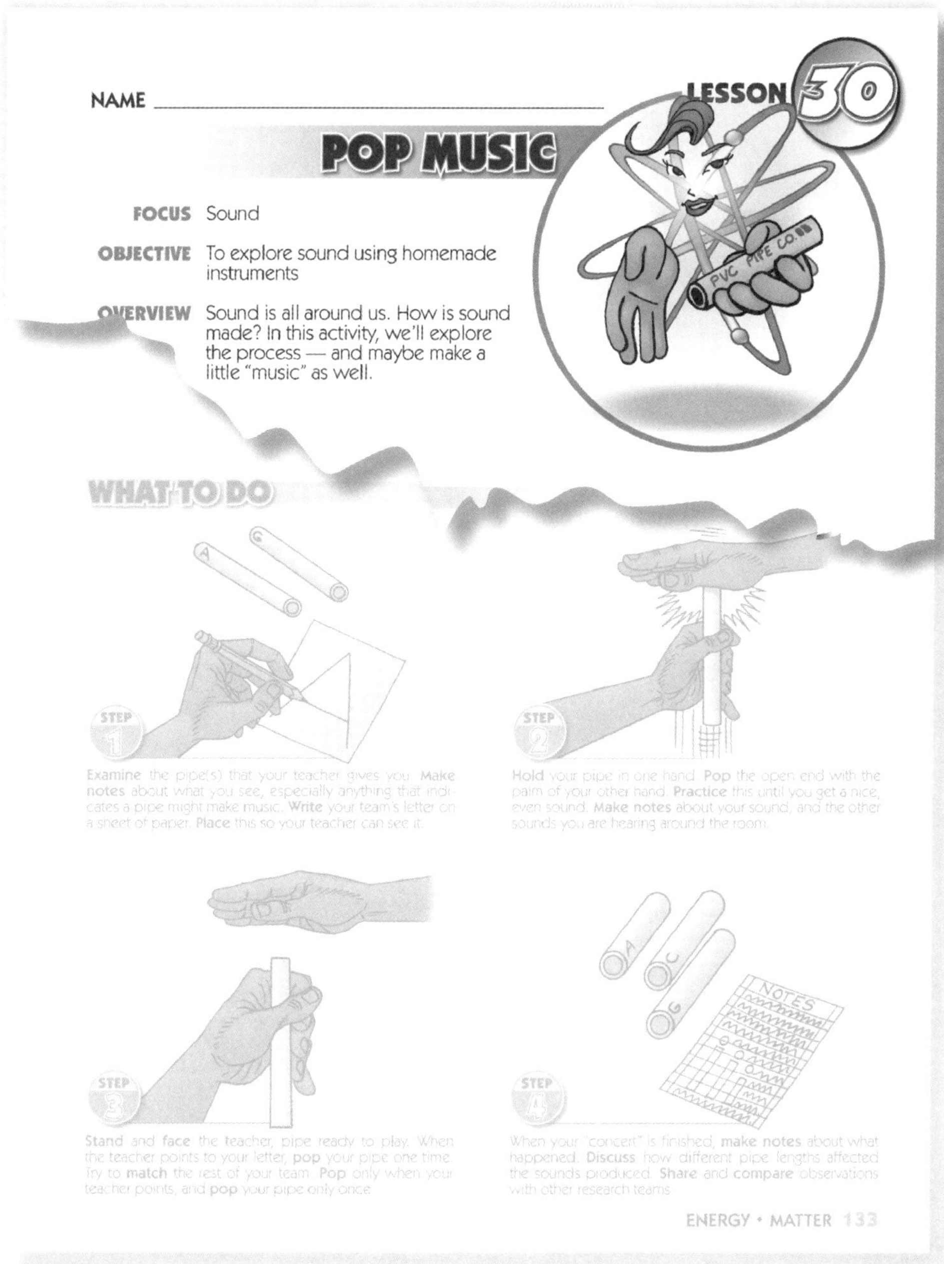
NAME ______________________

LESSON 30

POP MUSIC

FOCUS Sound

OBJECTIVE To explore sound using homemade instruments

OVERVIEW Sound is all around us. How is sound made? In this activity, we'll explore the process — and maybe make a little "music" as well.

WHAT TO DO

STEP 1
Examine the pipe(s) that your teacher gives you. **Make notes** about what you see, especially anything that indicates a pipe might make music. **Write** your team's letter on a sheet of paper. **Place** this so your teacher can see it.

STEP 2
Hold your pipe in one hand. **Pop** the open end with the palm of your other hand. **Practice** this until you get a nice, even sound. **Make notes** about your sound, and the other sounds you are hearing around the room.

STEP 3
Stand and **face** the teacher, pipe ready to play. When the teacher points to your letter, **pop** your pipe one time. Try to **match** the rest of your team. **Pop** only when your teacher points, and **pop** your pipe only once.

STEP 4
When your "concert" is finished, **make notes** about what happened. **Discuss** how different pipe lengths affected the sounds produced. **Share** and **compare** observations with other research teams.

ENERGY • MATTER 133

Category

Physical Science
Energy/Matter

Focus

Sound

Objective

To explore sound using homemade instruments

National Standards

A1, A2, B1, B2, B3, E1, E2, F5, G1, G2

Materials Needed

Pop Music sheet
(teacher only, p. 241)
sound pipes - 7
paper

Safety Concerns

none

Additional Comments

Students should quickly discover the relationship between a tube's length and its pitch. (Longer pipes have a "lower" pitch or frequency.) Be sure to clean and disinfect pipes before storing for next year.

Overview

Read the overview aloud to your students. The goal is to create an atmosphere of curiosity and inquiry.

WHAT TO DO

Monitor student research teams as they complete each step.

Step 3

To conduct your "Pop Music" concert:

1. Collect all the pipes from each team's materials kit.

2. Sort the pipes into groups according to the lettering on each pipe.

3. Divide your class into seven groups. (Keep the groups as equal as possible.)

4. Give Group 1 the "A" pipes, Group 2 the "B" pipes, etc.

5. Using the "Pop Music" sheet (back of this guidebook), point to groups in turn to create a melody.

6. Repeat for different songs, or make up your own melodies!

Note: Each kit comes with 7 pipes lettered A through G. Step 3 requires mixing pipes from different kits. After completion, make sure pipes are returned to their original groupings before placing them back in the kits for storage.

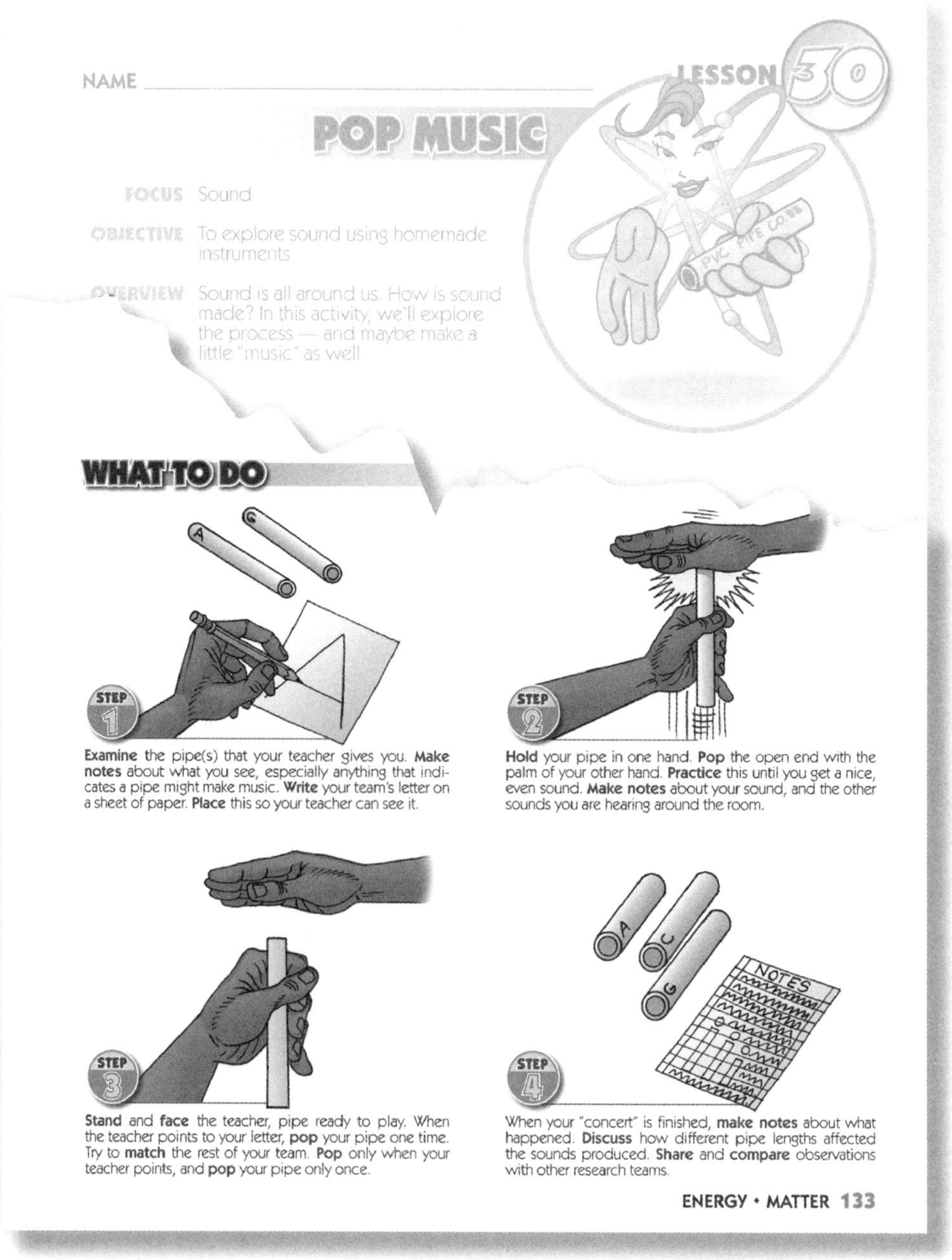
NAME

LESSON 30

POP MUSIC

FOCUS Sound

OBJECTIVE To explore sound using homemade instruments

OVERVIEW Sound is all around us. How is sound made? In this activity, we'll explore the process — and maybe make a little "music" as well

WHAT TO DO

STEP 1 **Examine** the pipe(s) that your teacher gives you. **Make notes** about what you see, especially anything that indicates a pipe might make music. **Write** your team's letter on a sheet of paper. **Place** this so your teacher can see it.

STEP 2 **Hold** your pipe in one hand. **Pop** the open end with the palm of your other hand. **Practice** this until you get a nice, even sound. **Make notes** about your sound, and the other sounds you are hearing around the room.

STEP 3 **Stand** and **face** the teacher, pipe ready to play. When the teacher points to your letter, **pop** your pipe one time. Try to **match** the rest of your team. **Pop** only when your teacher points, and **pop** your pipe only once.

STEP 4 When your "concert" is finished, **make notes** about what happened. **Discuss** how different pipe lengths affected the sounds produced. **Share** and **compare** observations with other research teams.

ENERGY • MATTER 133

Teacher to Teacher

The volume of a sound is related to how much energy is used. The greater the energy, the louder the sound. By contrast, pitch (or frequency) is related to physical shape — primarily length and diameter. That's why the pipes in this activity created different notes. It also explains why an adult has a lower-pitched voice than a child.

WHAT JUST HAPPENED?

Your moving hand had **kinetic** (moving) **energy**. When it hit the pipe, some of this kinetic energy **converted** into **sound**. Sound occurs when something **vibrates** (in this case the air in the pipe). Different pipes made different sounds because the air had different distances to vibrate.

In Step 2, each individual pipe created a specific sound, but these sounds interferred with each other. The result was noise with no pattern or rhythm. In Step 3, however, the vibrations were regular, arranged, and repeatable, creating a simple kind of music.

Scientists call the rate at which air vibrates **frequency**. Musicians call it **pitch** and they assign it letters (A through G) to indicate specific notes. You heard these notes as "music" in your teacher-directed concert!

MORE ABOUT SOUND...

Sound is everywhere. Whenever an object vibrates, it causes air particles around it to bump into each other. Scientists call a group of moving air particles a "**sound wave**".

Sound waves travel away from the source of vibration. Imagine the ripples caused by a rock thrown into a pool. These ripples move outward from the point where the rock hit the water. Sound waves often move in a similar pattern.

Also, you may have seen water ripples slowly smoothing out the farther they get from the source of the disturbance. In the same way, the farther sound waves go the weaker they get (until they eventually run out of energy).

When sound waves are irregular and random, we usually call what we hear "noise". But when somone makes sound waves that are regular, repeating, and pleasant, we often refer to the sounds we hear as "music".

Like other kinds of sound waves, music depends on the kind of material that's vibrating, how fast it's vibrating, and many other factors. For instance, when vibrations are fast, you hear a high note. When vibrations are slow, you hear a low note.

In musical instruments, vibrations are made by blowing across a hole (flute), through a mouthpiece (trumpet), or across a reed (clarinet). They can also be made by plucking a string (guitar), or striking a key that hits a wire (piano). Opening or closing holes, pressing strings, or striking different keys results in different kinds of sound waves that create different kinds of musical notes.

And, of course, skilled musicians in a band or orchestra can mix those special sound waves together to make wonderful music!

DIGGING DEEPER:

Research and discuss a specific type of musical instrument. How does it work? What are the materials it is made from? What part of the instrument creates the vibration? What well-known musicians play this type of instrument? Write a report and share your findings with the class.

WHAT WE LEARNED:

1 **Describe what you heard in Step 3. Compare Step 3 to Step 2. How were they similar? How were they different?**

a) answers will vary

b) they were the same sounds

c) the sounds were much more organized in Step 3; they were more like music; etc.

2 **Explain why different length pipes made different sounds. How did your teacher use these differences to make music?**

a) length changed air vibrations; different length = different pitch; etc.

b) answers will vary but should reflect the process used

3 **Describe a musical instrument and explain how it uses vibration to create sound. Based on what you've learned, what are some ways you might alter that sound?**

answers will vary, but part 2 should reflect the concept of changing length somehow

What Happened

Review the section with students. Emphasize bold-face words that identify key concepts and introduce new vocabulary.

Your moving hand had ***kinetic*** *(moving)* ***energy****. When it hit the pipe, some of this kinetic energy* ***converted*** *into* ***sound****. Sound occurs when something* ***vibrates*** *(in this case the air in the pipe). Different pipes made different sounds because the air had different distances to vibrate.*

In Step 2, each individual pipe created a specific sound, but these sounds interfered with each other. The result was noise with no pattern or rhythm. In Step 3, however, the vibrations were regular, arranged, and repeatable, creating a simple kind of music.

Scientists call the rate at which air vibrates ***frequency****. Musicians call it* ***pitch*** *and they assign it letters (A -G) to indicate specific notes. You heard these notes as "music" in your teacher-directed concert!*

More About . . .

Have students read this section as you would a traditional science text — or use cooperative learning techniques to allow students the opportunity to work on the material collaboratively.

Digging Deeper

(Optional) Challenge teams to reseach and discuss practical applications of the lesson concepts. Encourage them to share their findings with the rest of the class.

What We Learned

Answers will vary. Suggested responses are shown at left.

Conclusion

Read this section aloud to the class to summarize the concepts learned in this activity.

Food for Thought

Read the Scripture aloud to the class. Discuss different kinds of music that are used for worship. Talk about how a joyful heart is "music to God's ears."

Science Journal

If time permits, have a general class discussion about notes and drawings various students added to their journal pages. Discuss correct and incorrect predictions, and remind students that this "trial and error" process is part of the scientific process.

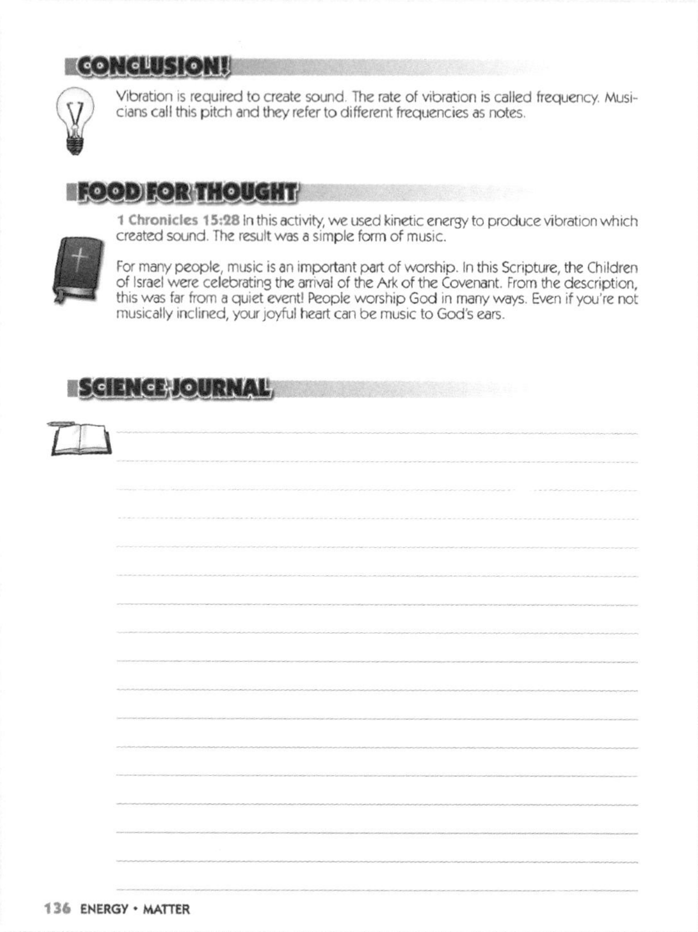

CONCLUSION!

Vibration is required to create sound. The rate of vibration is called frequency. Musicians call this pitch and they refer to different frequencies as notes.

FOOD FOR THOUGHT

1 Chronicles 15:28 In this activity, we used kinetic energy to produce vibration which created sound. The result was a simple form of music.

For many people, music is an important part of worship. In this Scripture, the Children of Israel were celebrating the arrival of the Ark of the Covenant. From the description, this was far from a quiet event! People worship God in many ways. Even if you're not musically inclined, your joyful heart can be music to God's ears.

SCIENCE JOURNAL

136 ENERGY • MATTER

Extended Teaching

1. Take a field trip to visit a college band. Ask the director to explain pitch and demonstrate its effect with different instruments. Have students write a paragraph about one thing they learn.

2. Invite an audiologist to visit your classroom. Ask him/her to demonstrate how hearing is tested. Discuss methods used to help the hearing impaired. Have students write a paragraph about one thing they learn.

3. Using the Internet, have teams research how animals use sound (communication, hunting, etc.). Challenge each team to create a poster showing a specific type of animal and at least one way it uses sound.

4. Have teams research the structure of a human ear. Challenge each team to contribute drawings and descriptions for a classroom bulletin board on this topic.

5. Have teams research famous musicians from the past. Challenge each team to choose one musician, then create a presentation about his/her life and work. If possible, have them include short audio samples.

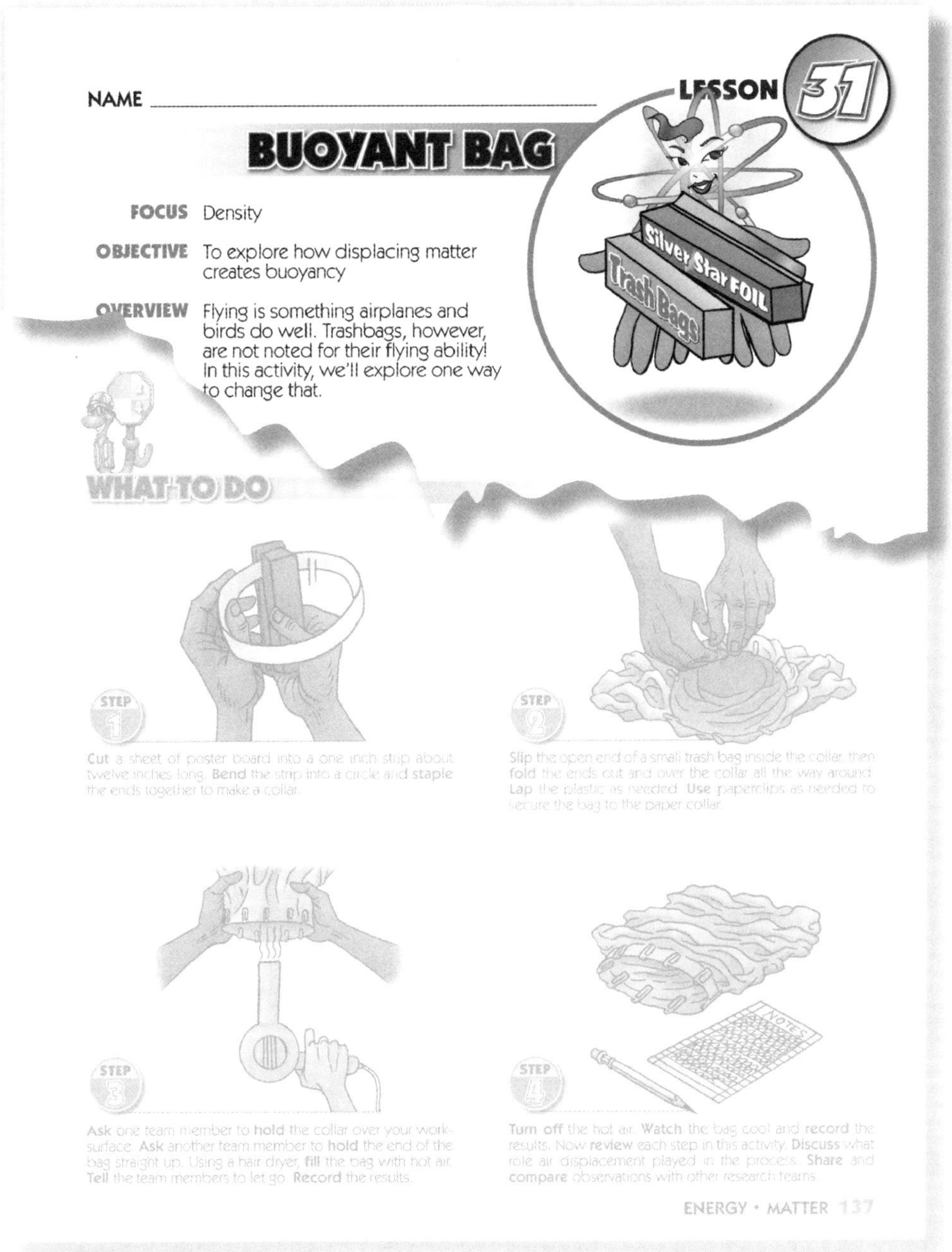
NAME ______________________________

LESSON 31

BUOYANT BAG

FOCUS Density

OBJECTIVE To explore how displacing matter creates buoyancy

OVERVIEW Flying is something airplanes and birds do well. Trashbags, however, are not noted for their flying ability! In this activity, we'll explore one way to change that.

WHAT TO DO

STEP 1 **Cut** a sheet of poster board into a one inch strip about twelve inches long. **Bend** the strip into a circle and **staple** the ends together to make a collar.

STEP 2 **Slip** the open end of a small trash bag inside the collar, then **fold** the ends out and over the collar all the way around. **Lap** the plastic as needed. **Use** paperclips as needed to secure the bag to the paper collar.

STEP 3 **Ask** one team member to **hold** the collar over your work-surface. **Ask** another team member to **hold** the end of the bag straight up. Using a hair dryer, **fill** the bag with hot air. **Tell** the team members to let go. **Record** the results.

STEP 4 **Turn off** the hot air. **Watch** the bag cool and **record** the results. Now **review** each step in this activity. **Discuss** what role air displacement played in the process. **Share** and **compare** observations with other research teams.

ENERGY • MATTER 137

Category

Physical Science
Energy/Matter

Focus

Density

Objective

To explore how displacing matter creates buoyancy

National Standards

A1, A2, B1, B2, B3, E1, E2, F5, G1, G2

Materials Needed

trash bag
paperclips
poster board strips
stapler
hair dryer

Safety Concerns

2. Thermal Burn
Remind students to exercise caution when using the hair dryer.

4. Sharp Objects
Remind students to exercise caution when using scissors.

Additional Comments

This is a great outdoor activity for a windless day. In inclement weather, the school gym is a reasonable substitute. You may need an extension cord for the hair-dryer. Don't put the nose of the dryer in the bag or the thermal safety switch will shut it off. Caution students to be careful chasing flying bags.

Overview

Read the overview aloud to your students. The goal is to create an atmosphere of curiosity and inquiry.

WHAT TO DO

Monitor student research teams as they complete each step.

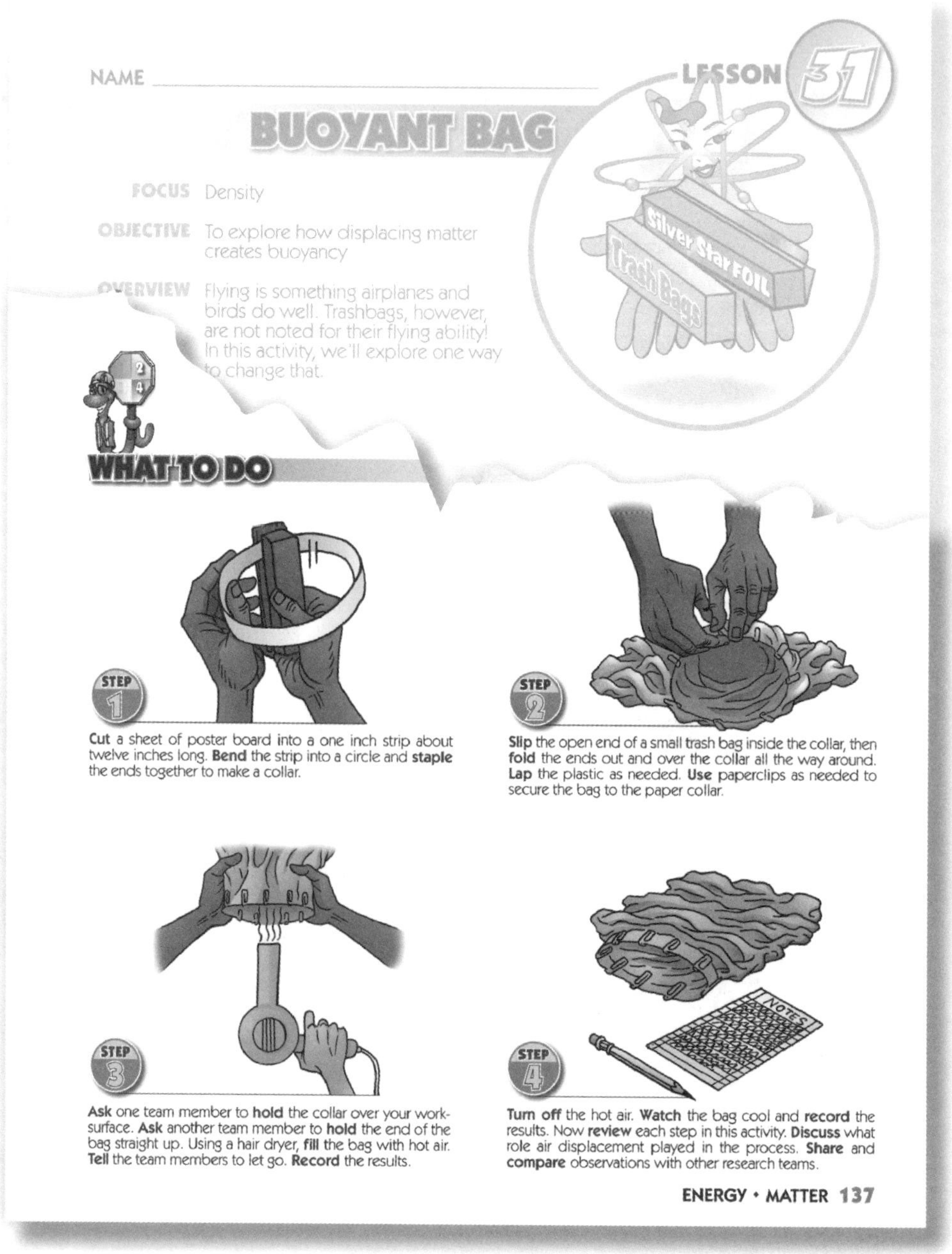

NAME ______________________________ LESSON 31

BUOYANT BAG

FOCUS Density

OBJECTIVE To explore how displacing matter creates buoyancy

OVERVIEW Flying is something airplanes and birds do well. Trashbags, however, are not noted for their flying ability! In this activity, we'll explore one way to change that.

WHAT TO DO

STEP 1: **Cut** a sheet of poster board into a one inch strip about twelve inches long. **Bend** the strip into a circle and **staple** the ends together to make a collar.

STEP 2: **Slip** the open end of a small trash bag inside the collar, then **fold** the ends out and over the collar all the way around. **Lap** the plastic as needed. **Use** paperclips as needed to secure the bag to the paper collar.

STEP 3: **Ask** one team member to **hold** the collar over your work-surface. **Ask** another team member to **hold** the end of the bag straight up. Using a hair dryer, **fill** the bag with hot air. **Tell** the team members to let go. **Record** the results.

STEP 4: **Turn off** the hot air. **Watch** the bag cool and **record** the results. Now **review** each step in this activity. **Discuss** what role air displacement played in the process. **Share** and **compare** observations with other research teams.

ENERGY • MATTER 137

Teacher to Teacher

People usually think of buoyancy in terms of water, but the atmosphere is also a fluid! Either way, buoyancy depends on density. A helium balloon floats because lighter (less dense) helium displaces heavier (more dense) air. A hot air balloon floats because hot air is less dense (and thus lighter) than cold air.

WHAT JUST HAPPENED?

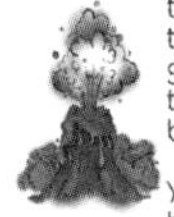

You've heard people say, "hot air rises". While this may be a good general description, the scientific explanation is a bit more complex. Look carefully at what happened to the air inside the bag. As the air was **heated**, its **molecules** started moving faster and getting further apart. Some escaped out the bottom of the bag. This made the air (matter) in the bag less **dense** than the air in the **atmosphere** surrounding it. The difference between the lighter air inside and heavier air outside is what caused the bag to rise.

You may have seen the large burners for hot air balloons. These balloons require very hot air to create much lower **air density** than we used in our activity. This lower density is needed to offset the **weight** of the balloon and its cargo. The massive amount of added **energy** lowers the air's density, letting the balloon rise until it **equalizes** in the less dense air of a higher altitude.

MORE ABOUT DENSITY . . .

As you have seen, changes in density can cause movement. In this activity, heating the air in the bag made it less dense than the air outside the bag, so the bag moved upward. Scientists refer to this upward push of force as "**buoyancy**".

Buoyancy occurs when the fluid in a container is less dense than the fluid surrounding the container. The fluids involved can be either gases (like air) or liquids (like water). Displacement can occur with a different fluid (like water replacing air), or by the same fluid with a different density (like hot air replacing cold air). The important thing is that in order to achieve bouyancy, the fluid in the container must be less dense than the fluid that surrounds it.

Here's an example: Huge ships are buoyant, even though the materials they are made from are much more dense than the water that surrounds them. So why do these ships float? It's because a ship is really a kind of container that displaces water with air. The hull of the ship keeps the water out, allowing air to fill up all the empty spaces in the ship. And since air is less dense than water, the ship floats.

However, if the ship gets a hole in it, then water can rush in and displace the air. The ship begins to lose buoyancy — and if it loses too much, the ship sinks.

Here's something else. We learned in other lessons that all forces come in pairs. When one force pushes or pulls, another force pushes or pulls back. The opposing force for buoyancy is gravity. While buoyancy is pushing up, gravity is pulling down. And in any given situation, density can play a key role in determining which one wins out!

Be sure to look for other examples of the interaction between buoyancy and gravity in the world around you.

DIGGING DEEPER:

Reseach and discuss a device that uses changes in density to cause movement. (Hot air balloons and submarines are good examples.) Describe the role that density plays in its operation. Make a poster that explains how this device works.

138 ENERGY • MATTER

WHAT WE LEARNED:

1. **Explain how air density played a role in this activity. What did density have to overcome to achieve flight? What was the opposing force?**

   a) the hot air in the bag was less dense than the surrounding air

   b) gravity

   c) buoyancy (or lift)

2. **Compare your "buoyant bag" with a hot air balloon. How are they similar? How are they different?**

   a) similar: both use hot air for buoyancy

   b) different: hot air balloon much larger; has a different fuel source; etc.

3. **Based on what you've learned, how would Step 3 be different on a cold day versus a hot day? Explain your answer.**

   a) balloon would rise more quickly on a cold day

   b) colder atmosphere = greater difference in density, thus greater buoyancy

ENERGY • MATTER 139

What Happened

Review the section with students. Emphasize bold-face words that identify key concepts and introduce new vocabulary.

*You've heard people say, "hot air rises." While this may be a good general description, the scientific explanation is a bit more complex. Look carefully at what happened to the air inside the bag. As the air was **heated**, its **molecules** started moving faster and getting further apart. Some escaped out the bottom of the bag. This made the air (matter) in the bag less **dense** than the air in the **atmosphere** surrounding it. The difference between the lighter air inside and heavier air outside is what caused the bag to rise.*

*You may have seen the large burners for hot air balloons. These balloons require very hot air to create much lower **air density** than we used in our activity. This lower density is needed to offset the **weight** of the balloon and its cargo. The massive amount of added **energy** lowers the air's density, letting the balloon rise until it **equalizes** in the less dense air of a higher altitude.*

More About . . .

Have students read this section as you would a traditional science text — or use cooperative learning techniques to allow students the opportunity to work on the material collaboratively.

Digging Deeper

(Optional) Challenge teams to reseach and discuss practical applications of the lesson concepts. Encourage them to share their findings with the rest of the class.

What We Learned

Answers will vary. Suggested responses are shown at left.

Conclusion

Read this section aloud to the class to summarize the concepts learned in this activity.

Food for Thought

Read the Scripture aloud to the class. Talk about ways sins like pride and selfishness, can hold us down. Discuss ways God can lift us up.

Science Journal

If time permits, have a general class discussion about notes and drawings various students added to their journal pages. Discuss correct and incorrect predictions, and remind students that this "trial and error" process is part of the scientific process.

CONCLUSION!

As air is heated, its molecules move faster and get further apart. Thus, hot air is less dense than cold air. In general, balloons fly and ships float because their overall density is less than their surroundings.

FOOD FOR THOUGHT

James 4:10 Whether it's in the air or in the water, an object rises when its density is less than its surroundings. We can use this lifting power to float huge steel boats, raise hot air balloons, and even make trash bags fly!

This Scripture talks about God's lifting power. It reminds us that when we bow down before God, admitting our dependence on him, he will lift us up and surround us with his mighty love. Although many times our pride and selfishness hold us down, God is always ready to lift us up.

SCIENCE JOURNAL

140 ENERGY • MATTER

Extended Teaching

1. Using the Internet, have students research how balloons were used in the Civil War and World War I. Challenge each team to create a poster showing at least one specific use based on their findings.

2. Visit "www.ehotair-ballooning.com" or a similar website. Challenge each team to create a presentation about one aspect of this sport (pilot safety, weather, learning to fly, etc.). Find out about meets in your area.

3. If there's a balloon pilot in your area, invite him/her to bring ballooning equipment to your school. Ask if they will do a "burn" (inflating without lifting off). Have students write a paragraph about one thing they learn.

4. Have teams research long distance ballooning, especially "round the world" attempts. (Check out Steve Fossett, Brian Jones, etc.) Challenge each team to contribute material for a classroom bulletin board on this topic.

5. Have teams research air domes and similar "inflatable" buildings. Find out what role air density plays in these unique structures. Challenge each team to create a poster describing one such building.

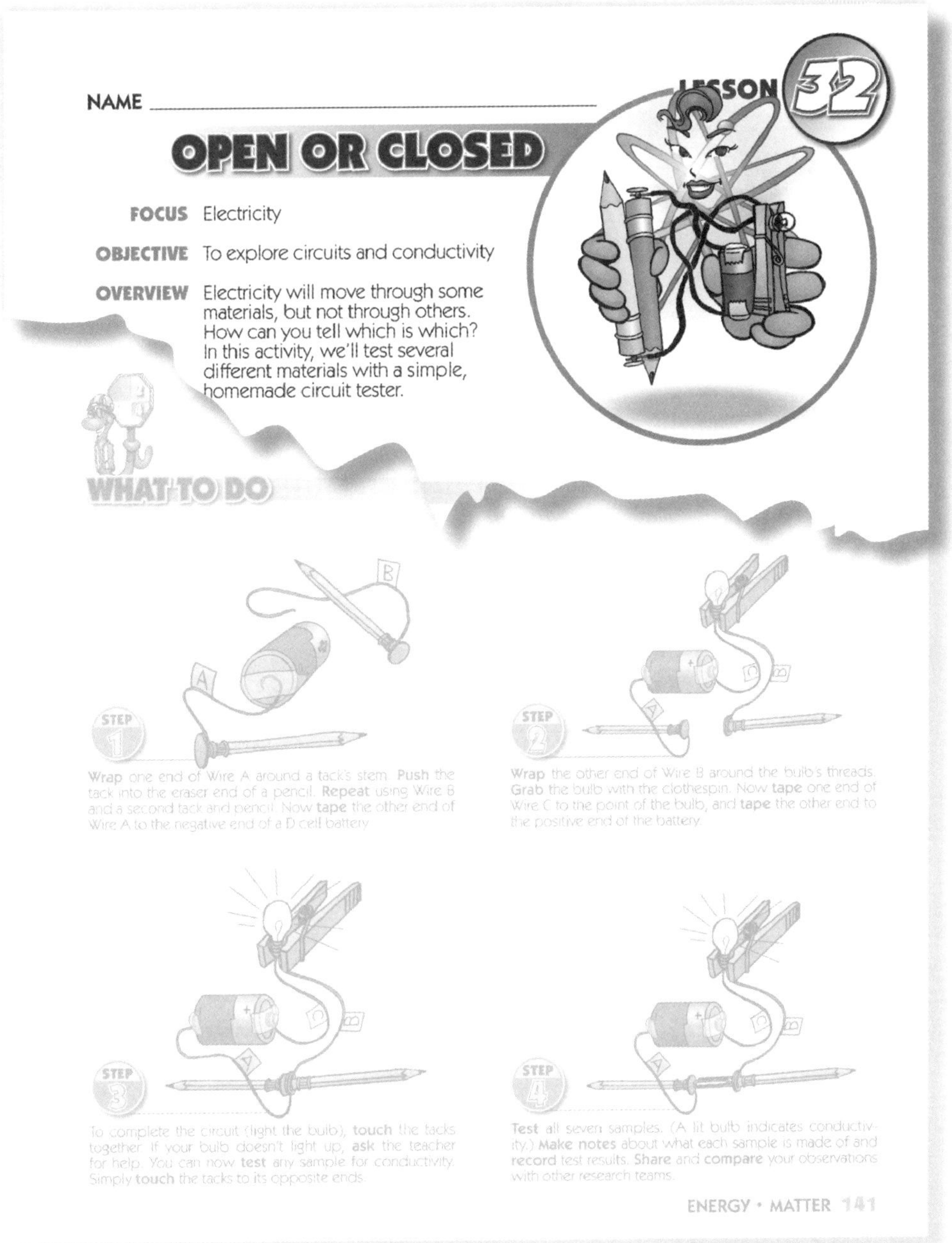
NAME ______________________________

LESSON 32

OPEN OR CLOSED

FOCUS Electricity

OBJECTIVE To explore circuits and conductivity

OVERVIEW Electricity will move through some materials, but not through others. How can you tell which is which? In this activity, we'll test several different materials with a simple, homemade circuit tester.

WHAT TO DO

STEP 1

Wrap one end of Wire A around a tack's stem. **Push** the tack into the eraser end of a pencil. **Repeat** using Wire B and a second tack and pencil. Now **tape** the other end of Wire A to the negative end of a D cell battery.

STEP 2

Wrap the other end of Wire B around the bulb's threads. **Grab** the bulb with the clothespin. Now **tape** one end of Wire C to the point of the bulb, and **tape** the other end to the positive end of the battery.

STEP 3

To complete the circuit (light the bulb), **touch** the tacks together. If your bulb doesn't light up, **ask** the teacher for help. You can now **test** any sample for conductivity. Simply **touch** the tacks to its opposite ends.

STEP 4

Test all seven samples. (A lit bulb indicates conductivity.) **Make notes** about what each sample is made of and **record** test results. **Share** and **compare** your observations with other research teams.

ENERGY • MATTER 141

Additional Comments

This activity introduces students to the concept of separating materials into groups based on properties. Since there are over a dozen pieces involved, a shoebox (with materials list) can help teams keep materials organized. Before beginning, make sure the insulation has been removed from both ends of the wire.

Overview

Read the overview aloud to your students. The goal is to create an atmosphere of curiosity and inquiry.

Category

Physical Science
Energy/Matter

Focus

Electricity

Objective

To explore circuits and conductivity

National Standards

A1, A2, B1, B2, B3, E1, E2, F5, G1, G2

Materials Needed

insulated wire-3
tacks - 2
D cell battery
small bulb
clothespin
samples:
- **nail**
- **paperclip**
- **plastic fork**
- **rubberband**
- **toothpick**
- **washer**

pencils - 2
tape
aluminum foil

Safety Concerns

2. Thermal Burn
Tacks can get hot if held together too long. Remind students to exercise caution.

4. Other
Warning for students: Never use household current for science experiments!

WHAT TO DO

Monitor student research teams as they complete each step.

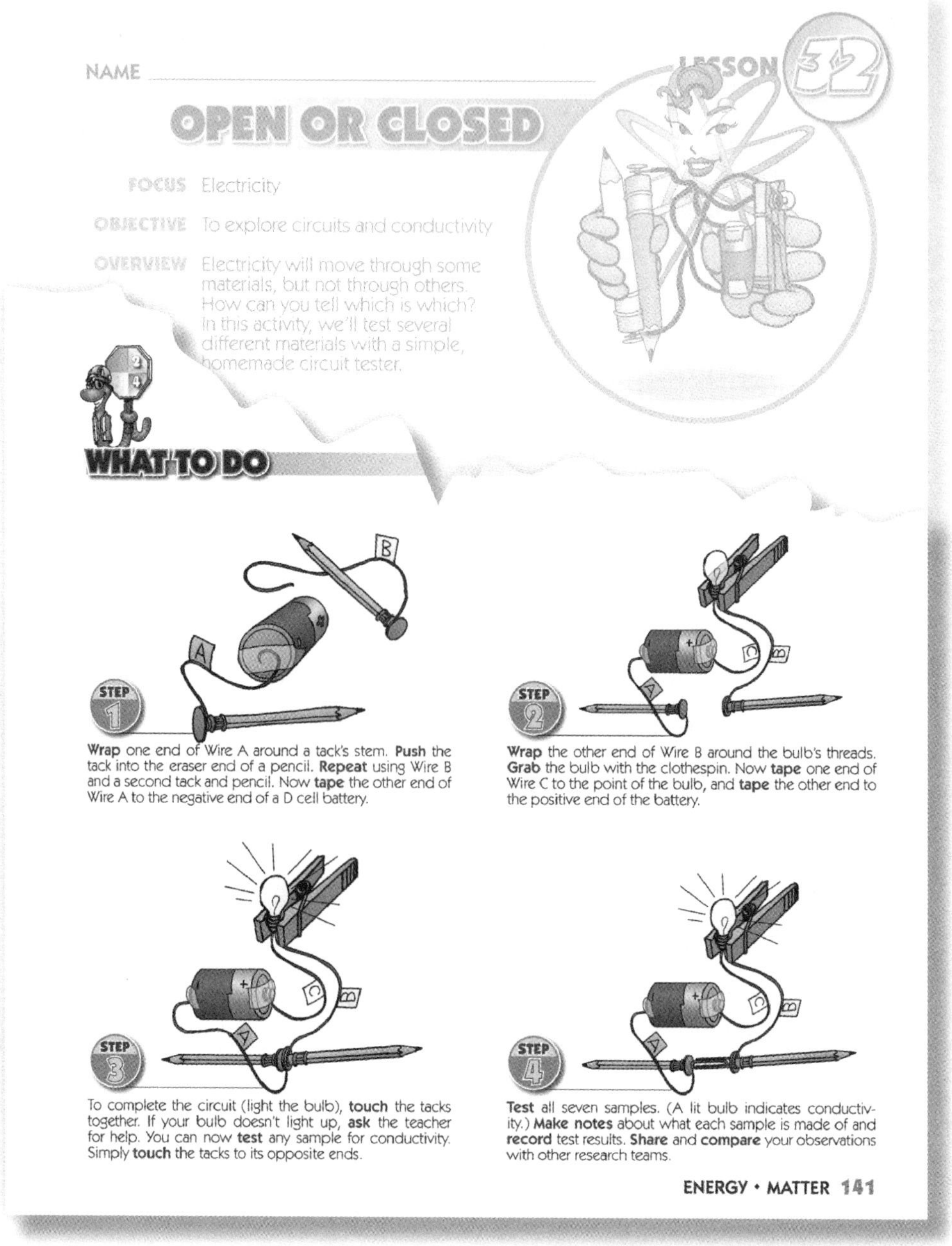

NAME ______________________ LESSON 32

OPEN OR CLOSED

FOCUS Electricity

OBJECTIVE To explore circuits and conductivity

OVERVIEW Electricity will move through some materials, but not through others. How can you tell which is which? In this activity, we'll test several different materials with a simple, homemade circuit tester.

WHAT TO DO

STEP 1: **Wrap** one end of Wire A around a tack's stem. **Push** the tack into the eraser end of a pencil. **Repeat** using Wire B and a second tack and pencil. Now **tape** the other end of Wire A to the negative end of a D cell battery.

STEP 2: **Wrap** the other end of Wire B around the bulb's threads. **Grab** the bulb with the clothespin. Now **tape** one end of Wire C to the point of the bulb, and **tape** the other end to the positive end of the battery.

STEP 3: To complete the circuit (light the bulb), **touch** the tacks together. If your bulb doesn't light up, **ask** the teacher for help. You can now **test** any sample for conductivity. Simply **touch** the tacks to its opposite ends.

STEP 4: **Test** all seven samples. (A lit bulb indicates conductivity.) **Make notes** about what each sample is made of and **record** test results. **Share** and **compare** your observations with other research teams.

ENERGY • MATTER 141

Teacher to Teacher

Of the atom's three basic particles — protons, neutrons, and electrons — only the electrons move easily. (Movement of other particles would involve a nuclear reaction or severe radiation!) This free flow of electrons from one atom to another is what makes electricity possible.

WHAT JUST HAPPENED?

When it comes to **electricity**, most materials can be split into two groups: **conductors**, which allow electricity to flow, and **insulators**, which don't. In fact, one definition of electricity is "the movement of **electrons** through a conductor".

In this activity, you created a simple **circuit** to detect this movement. When you touched the tacks to a conductive material, the circuit was **closed**, electricity flowed, and the bulb lit up. When you touched the tacks to a non-conductive material, nothing happened because the electricity could not flow. This was an **open** circuit.

Conductors allow us to use the power of electricity in everything from lights to hair dryers to water heaters. But since our bodies are mostly water (an excellent conductor), we need insulators to protect us from all this power.

MORE ABOUT ELECTRICITY . . .

Without **conductors** and **insulators**, electricity wouldn't be very helpful. These materials help us control electricity and send it through circuits to do useful work. Because scientists and engineers can control electricity, it has become a convenient form of energy for providing things like power, heat, and light.

Today electricity is so common that we often take it for granted, just like air or water. But people's lives were much different just over 100 years ago. (And that's just a blink of an eye in historical terms!)

Before electricity, people had to use kerosene lamps for light. Before electricity, food was kept cool in "iceboxes" that needed a big block of ice every day or so to work. Before electricity, homes were usually heated by wood or coal burning stoves. Before electricity, people often had to carry all their water from a nearby well or spring. (Imagine how many buckets of water you would have to carry just to take a bath!)

But then, scientists began to understand how electricity worked and how it could be generated. Inventors like Thomas Edison began to create useful devices to use this new source of power. (One of the first was a glass globe with wires inside that lit up when electricity flowed through — the ancestor of the common light bulb.) Soon scientists like Nikola Tesla found ways to generate a better kind of current and transmit it over long distances. That eventually led to the enormous electrical distribution systems that now carry power to every corner of the country.

So the next time you flip on a light switch, talk on the phone, watch TV, or work on a computer, remember how electricity makes each of these conveniences possible, and imagine what your life would be like without electricity. It will give a whole new meaning to the word "powerless".

DIGGING DEEPER:

Research and discuss some kind of device that uses a circuit. What is this device used for? How is it helpful? How would your life change if it were not available? Write a report or make a poster to share your findings with the class.

142 ENERGY • MATTER

WHAT WE LEARNED:

1. **Which of the seven materials were conductors? Which were insulators? How could you tell?**

   a) nail, foil, paperclip

   b) plasticfork, washer, rubber band, toothpick

   c) by how the bulb reacted

2. **Describe the circuit tester you created for this activity. What were its major parts? What role did each part play?**

   a) major parts = battery, wires, tacks, pencils, bulb

   b) answers may vary slightly, but should reflect logical descriptions

3. **Based on what you've learned, why is a bare wire on an appliance dangerous? What do all solutions for fixing this problem have in common?**

   a) The human body is a conductor; electricity can flow through it!

   b) controlling the flow of electrons (electricity) so they go where we want them to, but don't go where we don't want them to

ENERGY • MATTER 143

What Happened

Review the section with students. Emphasize bold-face words that identify key concepts and introduce new vocabulary.

When it comes to ***electricity****, most materials can be split into two groups:* ***conductors,*** *which allow electricity to flow, and* ***insulators*** *which don't. In fact, one definition of electricity is "the movement of* ***electrons*** *through a conductor."*

In this activity, you created a simple ***circuit*** *to detect this movement. When you touched the tacks to a conductive material, the circuit was* ***closed****, electricity flowed, and the bulb lit up. When you touched the tacks to a non-conductive material, nothing happened because the electricity could not flow. This was an* ***open*** *circuit.*

Conductors allow us to use the power of electricity in everything from lights to hair dryers to water heaters. But since our bodies are mostly water (an excellent conductor), we need insulators to protect us from all this power.

More About . . .

Have students read this section as you would a traditional science text — or use cooperative learning techniques to allow students the opportunity to work on the material collaboratively.

Digging Deeper

(Optional) Challenge teams to reseach and discuss practical applications of the lesson concepts. Encourage them to share their findings with the rest of the class.

What We Learned

Answers will vary. Suggested responses are shown at left.

Conclusion

Read this section aloud to the class to summarize the concepts learned in this activity.

Food for Thought

Read the Scripture aloud to the class. Talk about how Jesus is "the light of the world." Discuss ideas on how we can spend more time developing a relationship with God.

Science Journal

If time permits, have a general class discussion about notes and drawings various students added to their journal pages. Discuss correct and incorrect predictions, and remind students that this "trial and error" process is part of the scientific process.

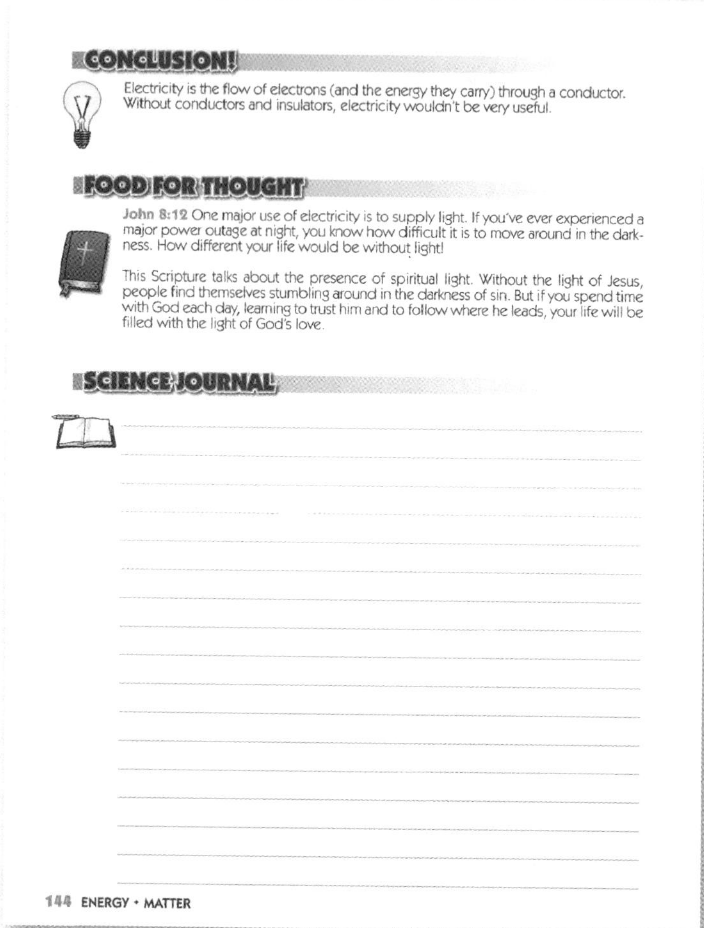

CONCLUSION!

Electricity is the flow of electrons (and the energy they carry) through a conductor. Without conductors and insulators, electricity wouldn't be very useful.

FOOD FOR THOUGHT

John 8:12 One major use of electricity is to supply light. If you've ever experienced a major power outage at night, you know how difficult it is to move around in the darkness. How different your life would be without light!

This Scripture talks about the presence of spiritual light. Without the light of Jesus, people find themselves stumbling around in the darkness of sin. But if you spend time with God each day, learning to trust him and to follow where he leads, your life will be filled with the light of God's love.

SCIENCE JOURNAL

144 ENERGY • MATTER

Extended Teaching

1. Have teams conduct an "Electrical Expedition." Have them locate and list as many electrical devices as possible. Challenge each team to contribute pictures and descriptions to a bulletin board on this topic.

2. Invite an electrician to visit your classroom. Have him/her talk about electricity safety rules, and show different safety devices (lock outs, GFI switches, etc.) Have students write a paragraph about one thing they learn.

3. Have teams research static and current electricity. How are they created? How are they used? How are they similar? How are they different? Challenge each team to create a poster about one thing they learn.

4. Diesel powered locomotives are actually giant electricity plants. Have teams research how they make and use electricity. Challenge each team to create a poster about one thing they learn.

5. Take a field trip to a power plant. Find out how electricity is generated. What is the fuel source? Ask about potential problems and their solutions. Have students write a paragraph about one thing they learn.

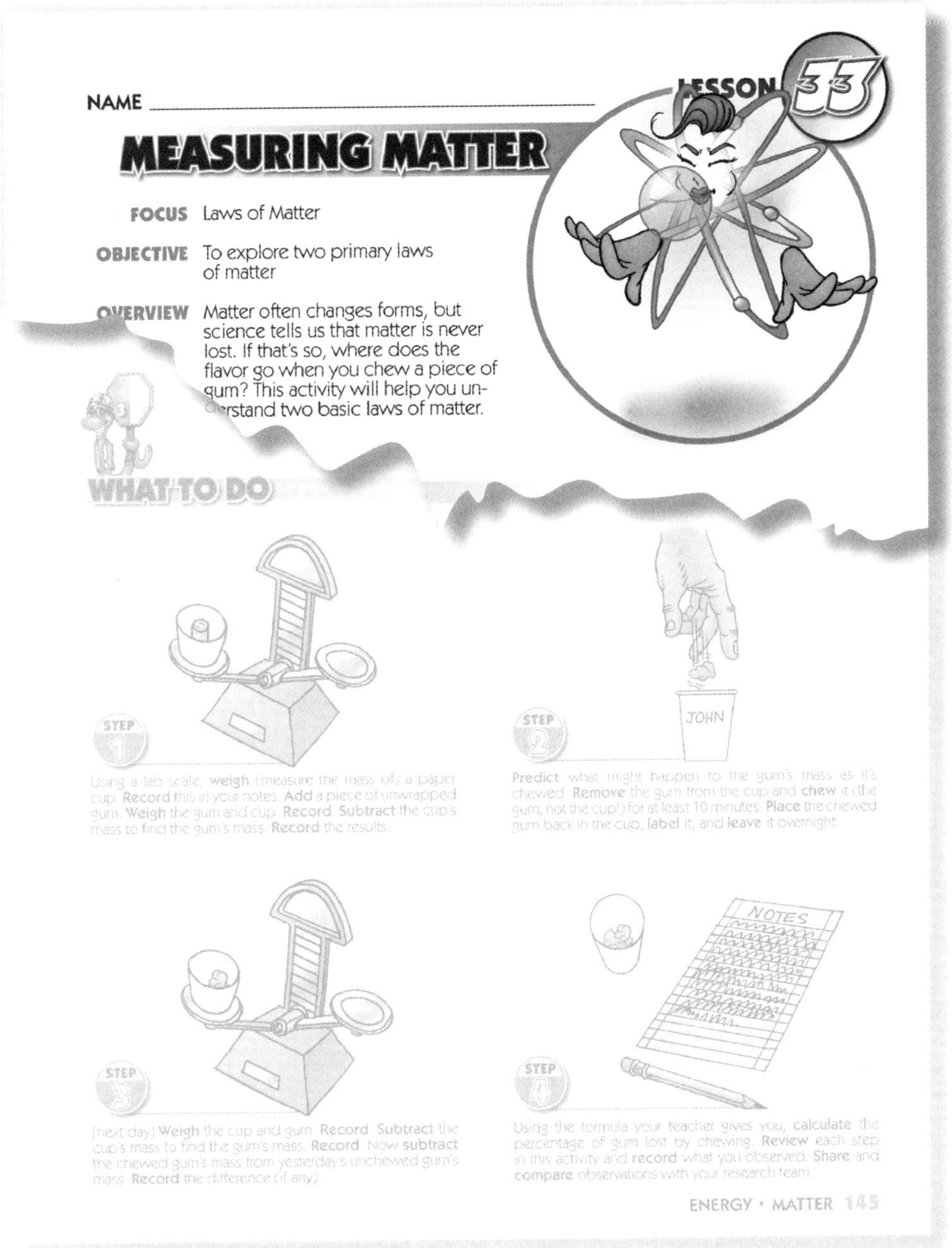

NAME ______________________

LESSON 33

MEASURING MATTER

FOCUS Laws of Matter

OBJECTIVE To explore two primary laws of matter

OVERVIEW Matter often changes forms, but science tells us that matter is never lost. If that's so, where does the flavor go when you chew a piece of gum? This activity will help you understand two basic laws of matter.

WHAT TO DO

STEP 1
Using a lab scale, **weigh** (measure the mass of) a paper cup. **Record** this in your notes. **Add** a piece of unwrapped gum. **Weigh** the gum and cup. **Record. Subtract** the cup's mass to find the gum's mass. **Record** the results.

STEP 2
Predict what might happen to the gum's mass as it's chewed. **Remove** the gum from the cup and **chew** it (the gum, not the cup!) for at least 10 minutes. **Place** the chewed gum back in the cup, **label** it, and **leave** it overnight.

STEP 3
[next day] **Weigh** the cup and gum. **Record**. **Subtract** the cup's mass to find the gum's mass. **Record**. Now **subtract** the chewed gum's mass from yesterday's unchewed gum's mass. **Record** the difference (if any).

STEP 4
Using the formula your teacher gives you, **calculate** the percentage of gum lost by chewing. **Review** each step in this activity and **record** what you observed. **Share** and **compare** observations with your research team.

ENERGY • MATTER 145

Category

Physical Science
Energy/Matter

Focus

Laws of Matter

Objective

To explore two primary laws of matter

National Standards

A1, A2, B1, B2, E1, E2, F5, G1, G2

Materials Needed

lab scale
paper cup
bubble gum

Safety Concerns

3. Hygiene
Don't allow students to chew gum again after Step 2.

Additional Comments

While chewing the gum is an integral part of this activity, remind students that it's bad procedure to put anything in your mouth during a science experiment! If students aren't familiar with a lab scale, you may need to demonstrate its use.

Overview

Read the overview aloud to your students. The goal is to create an atmosphere of curiosity and inquiry.

WHAT TO DO

Monitor student research teams as they complete each step.

A Special Note:
The Student Worktext (page 146) states that *"Any sample of pure water will be 88.8% oxygen and 11.2% hydrogen."*

But wait a minute! Everyone knows that water is H_2O. Doesn't that mean there's twice as much hydrogen as there is oxygen in water?

Actually it's doesn't. The designation H_2O simply tells us the number and type of molecules that are joined together — and all molecules are not created equal!

Oxygen molecules are much LARGER hydrogen molecules. That's why from a percentage standpoint, there's much more oxygen than hydrogen in any sample of pure water.

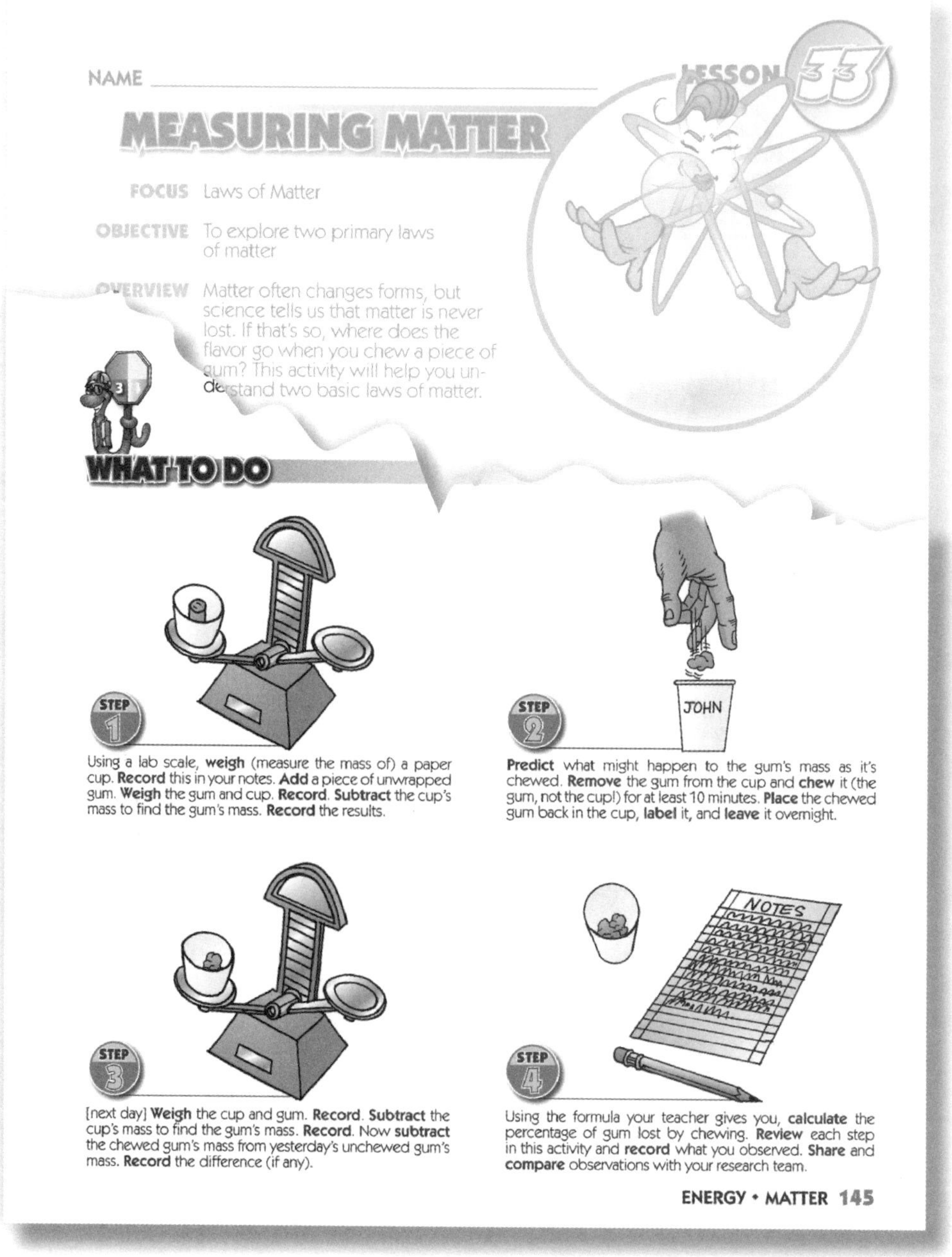

NAME ______________________ LESSON 33

MEASURING MATTER

FOCUS Laws of Matter

OBJECTIVE To explore two primary laws of matter

OVERVIEW Matter often changes forms, but science tells us that matter is never lost. If that's so, where does the flavor go when you chew a piece of gum? This activity will help you understand two basic laws of matter.

WHAT TO DO

STEP 1: Using a lab scale, **weigh** (measure the mass of) a paper cup. **Record** this in your notes. **Add** a piece of unwrapped gum. **Weigh** the gum and cup. **Record**. **Subtract** the cup's mass to find the gum's mass. **Record** the results.

STEP 2: **Predict** what might happen to the gum's mass as it's chewed. **Remove** the gum from the cup and **chew** it (the gum, not the cup!) for at least 10 minutes. **Place** the chewed gum back in the cup, **label** it, and **leave** it overnight.

STEP 3: [next day] **Weigh** the cup and gum. **Record**. **Subtract** the cup's mass to find the gum's mass. **Record**. Now **subtract** the chewed gum's mass from yesterday's unchewed gum's mass. **Record** the difference (if any).

STEP 4: Using the formula your teacher gives you, **calculate** the percentage of gum lost by chewing. **Review** each step in this activity and **record** what you observed. **Share** and **compare** observations with your research team.

ENERGY • MATTER 145

Teacher to Teacher

There is one exception to the "Law of Conservation of Matter" — a nuclear reaction! In a nuclear weapon, this reaction instantly converts matter into massive amounts of energy. As this energy is released, destruction follows.

By contrast, a nuclear power plant uses a slow, continuous reaction. Although this reaction also converts matter directly into energy, the process is controlled, allowing us to harness the energy to help generate electricity.

WHAT JUST HAPPENED?

Based on your measurements, some of the gum appeared to vanish. But science tells us this "missing" **matter** has to be somewhere. That's the **Law of Conservation of Matter**. In this case, you simply chewed out the mass that made up the flavor material and the sugar in the gum, and you *swallowed* it!

When you compared notes with other research teams, you probably discovered that the **percentage** of mass left over was about the same. That's because the company that makes the gum uses the same recipe (**proportions**) every time.

Chemical compounds always have the same formula, too. For instance, a sample of pure water will always contain the same percent of hydrogen and oxygen by weight. That's the **Law of Definite Proportions**. And like a good recipe, if it's followed perfectly using identical ingredients, the results are always the same.

MORE ABOUT LAWS OF MATTER . . .

As you have seen, matter can change into different forms, but it is not destroyed by these changes. The atoms that matter is made from never wear out and they never break down. (Of course, atoms can be "split" in a nuclear reaction, converting matter into energy — but even this process doesn't *destroy* the atoms.)

The "**Law of Conservation of Matter**" reflects the concept that the atoms that make up our world and everything in it are recycled over and over again. Even though countless physical and chemical changes are happening all around us all the time, the matter involved can never be used up.

Here's an example. When you burn a log in the fireplace, it seems as though the log has been destroyed. Often all that's left behind is a small pile of ash. But if you could measure the log's original mass and compare that to the mass of the carbon dioxide and water released by the burning, plus the mass of the soot and ash left behind, plus the mass of all the other by-products of the burning, you'd soon find that the matter from the original log has been completely accounted for.

In addition, the "**Law of Definite Proportion**" states that a chemical compound always contains exactly the same proportion of elements by mass. For example, any sample of pure water will be 88.8% oxygen and 11.2% hydrogen. This built-in consistency is what makes scientific research possible. If a scientist doing an experiment takes good notes and makes accurate observations, then another scientist should be able to duplicate the results.

Knowing about these two laws of matter can help you better understand what's really happening as matter changes forms.

DIGGING DEEPER:

Research and discuss some kind of physical or chemical change. What did the object look like before the change? What did it look like after the change? If possible, duplicate this change for the class and explain what happened to the matter involved.

WHAT WE LEARNED:

1. What is the "Law of Conservation of Matter"?

   matter is never destroyed; "missing" matter always has to be somewhere

2. What is the "Law of Definite Proportions"?

   a chemical compound always contains exactly the same proportion of elements by mass

3. Why is the Law of Definite Proportions important in scientific research?

   if a scientist doing an experiment takes good notes and makes accurate observations, then another scientist should be able to duplicate the results

What Happened

Review the section with students. Emphasize bold-face words that identify key concepts and introduce new vocabulary.

Based on your measurements, some of the gum appeared to vanish! But science tells us this "missing" ***matter*** *has to be somewhere! That's the* ***Law of Conservation of Matter****. In this case, you simply chewed out and swallowed the flavor material and the sugar in the gum.*

When you compared notes with other research teams, you probably discovered that the ***percentage*** *of mass left over was about the same. That's because the gum company uses the same recipe (proportions) every time.*

Chemical compounds *always have the same formula, too. For instance, a sample of pure water will always contain the same percent of hydrogen and oxygen by weight. That's the* ***Law of Definite Proportions****. And like a good recipe, if it's followed perfectly using identical ingredients, the results are always the same.*

More About . . .

Have students read this section as you would a traditional science text — or use cooperative learning techniques to allow students the opportunity to work on the material collaboratively.

Digging Deeper

(Optional) Challenge teams to reseach and discuss practical applications of the lesson concepts. Encourage them to share their findings with the rest of the class.

What We Learned

Answers will vary. Suggested responses are shown at left.

Conclusion

Read this section aloud to the class to summarize the concepts learned in this activity.

Food for Thought

Read the Scripture aloud to the class. Talk about how things can change in our lives. Discuss how developing and maintaining a relationship with God can keep us anchored when times get tough.

Science Journal

If time permits, have a general class discussion about notes and drawings various students added to their journal pages. Discuss correct and incorrect predictions, and remind students that this "trial and error" process is part of the scientific process.

CONCLUSION!

Although matter often changes forms, it is never lost. This is the "Law of Conservation of Matter." The "Law of Definite Proportions" explains why specific compounds are always identical.

FOOD FOR THOUGHT

2 Timothy 1:12 The Law of Conservation of Matter states that although matter often changes forms, it is never destroyed. Sometimes those changes are massive (like an ice sculpture turning into a mud puddle). But the basic matter involved is still there.

Over time, your life may take different forms. You may move, your family situation may change, you may grow taller, learn new things, or even experience hardships and tragedies. But as long as you maintain your relationship with Jesus, he'll keep your soul safe from harm — and that's what really matters.

SCIENCE JOURNAL

148 ENERGY • MATTER

Extended Teaching

1. Repeat this activity, only this time use sugarless gum. Have students compare the results with the original activity. How were they similar? How were they different? What may have contributed to changes?

2. Individually weigh ingredients for a loaf of bread, then mix them up and put them in a bread machine. After baking, weigh the loaf. Challenge students to explain the difference in mass.

3. Invite a baker to visit your classroom. Ask him/her to bring samples showing major variations in the proportion of yeast added. Discuss what happened to each. Have students write a paragraph about one thing they learn.

4. Take a field trip to a concrete batch plant. Ask about variations in the mix and why they are needed. Find out about "psi" ratings. Have students write a paragraph about one thing they learn.

5. Bring old recipe books to class. Have teams compare the same dish from different books. How are the recipes similar? How are they different? Challenge each team to make a presentation about one thing they learn.

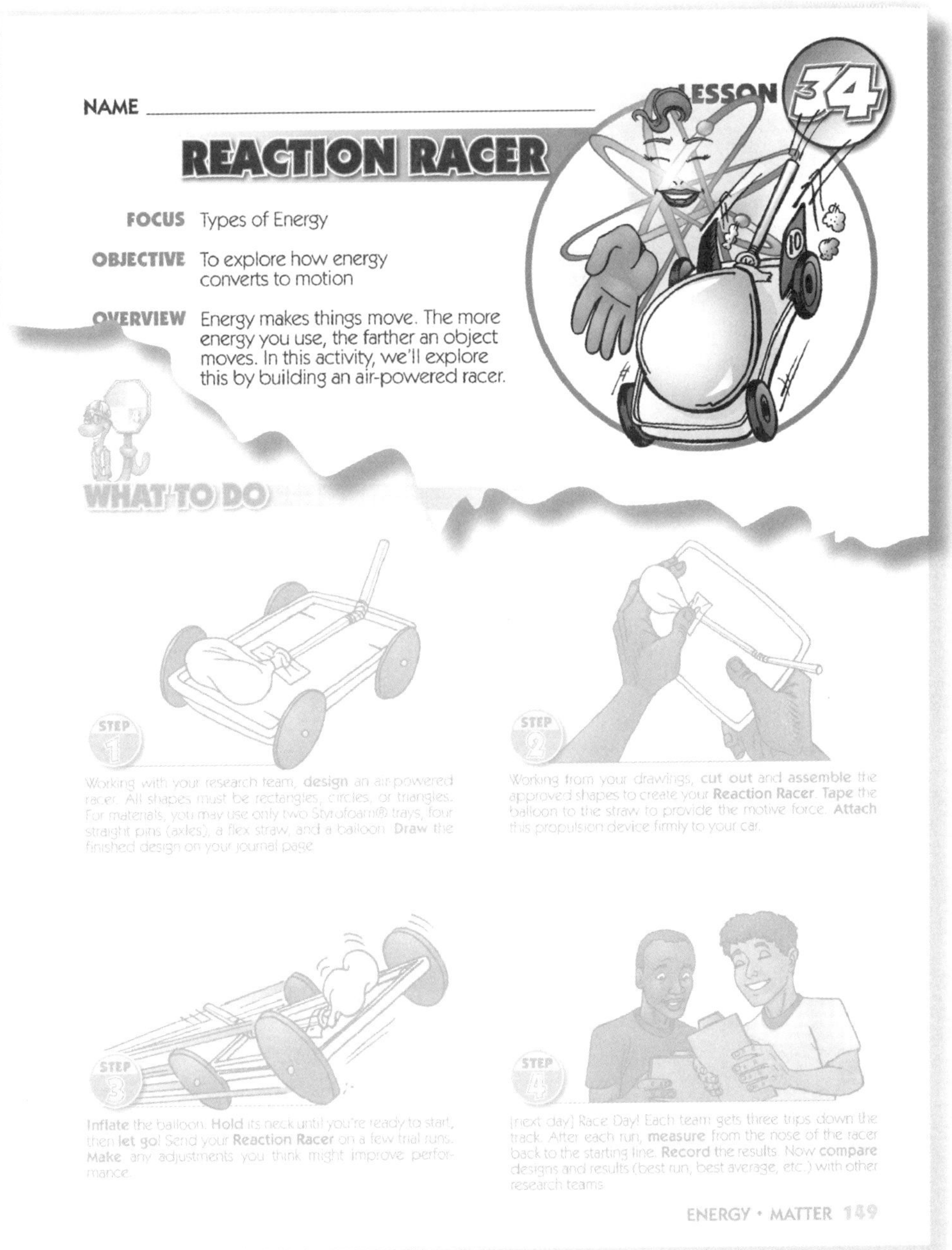

NAME ______________________________

LESSON 34

REACTION RACER

FOCUS Types of Energy

OBJECTIVE To explore how energy converts to motion

OVERVIEW Energy makes things move. The more energy you use, the farther an object moves. In this activity, we'll explore this by building an air-powered racer.

WHAT TO DO

STEP 1 Working with your research team, **design** an air-powered racer. All shapes must be rectangles, circles, or triangles. For materials, you may use only two Styrofoam® trays, four straight pins (axles), a flex straw, and a balloon. **Draw** the finished design on your journal page.

STEP 2 Working from your drawings, **cut out** and **assemble** the approved shapes to create your **Reaction Racer**. **Tape** the balloon to the straw to provide the motive force. **Attach** this propulsion device firmly to your car.

STEP 3 **Inflate** the balloon. **Hold** its neck until you're ready to start, then **let go**! Send your **Reaction Racer** on a few trial runs. **Make** any adjustments you think might improve performance.

STEP 4 [next day] Race Day! Each team gets three trips down the track. After each run, **measure** from the nose of the racer back to the starting line. **Record** the results. Now **compare** designs and results (best run, best average, etc.) with other research teams.

ENERGY • MATTER 149

Category

Physical Science
Energy/Matter

Focus

Types of Energy

Objective

To explore how energy converts to motion

National Standards

A1, A2, B1, B2, B3, E1, E2, F5, G1, G2

Materials Needed

Styrofoam® tray
straight pins - 4
flex straw
balloon
ruler
scissors
tape

Safety Concerns

4. Sharp Objects
Remind students to exercise caution with scissors and pins.

Additional Comments

Occasionally the pins need some kind of "hubcap" to keep them from slipping into or through the Styrofoam®. A tiny bit of plastic cut from a soda straw works well for this. Monitor teams to make sure this remains a group project.

Overview

Read the overview aloud to your students. The goal is to create an atmosphere of curiosity and inquiry.

WHAT TO DO

Monitor student research teams as they complete each step.

NAME ____________________

LESSON 34

REACTION RACER

FOCUS Types of Energy

OBJECTIVE To explore how energy converts to motion

OVERVIEW Energy makes things move. The more energy you use, the farther an object moves. In this activity, we'll explore this by building an air-powered racer.

WHAT TO DO

STEP 1

Working with your research team, **design** an air-powered racer. All shapes must be rectangles, circles, or triangles. For materials, you may use only two Styrofoam® trays, four straight pins (axles), a flex straw, and a balloon. **Draw** the finished design on your journal page.

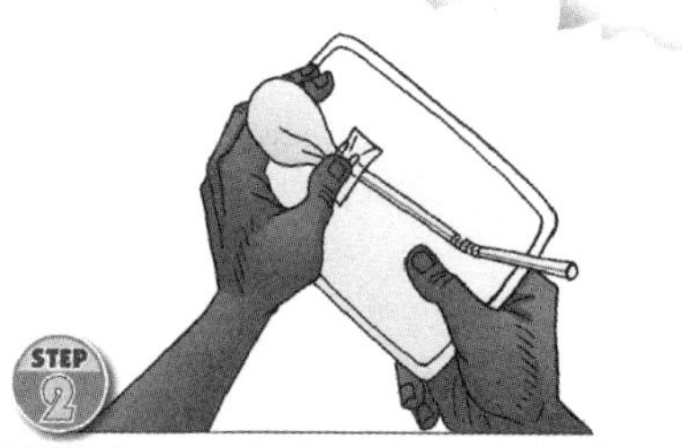

STEP 2

Working from your drawings, **cut out** and **assemble** the approved shapes to create your **Reaction Racer**. **Tape** the balloon to the straw to provide the motive force. **Attach** this propulsion device firmly to your car.

STEP 3

Inflate the balloon. **Hold** its neck until you're ready to start, then **let go**! Send your **Reaction Racer** on a few trial runs. **Make** any adjustments you think might improve performance.

STEP 4

[next day] Race Day! Each team gets three trips down the track. After each run, **measure** from the nose of the racer back to the starting line. **Record** the results. Now **compare** designs and results (best run, best average, etc.) with other research teams.

ENERGY • MATTER 149

Teacher to Teacher

This activity is rich in concepts!

First, it demonstrates all three of Newton's Laws.

Second, it supports the concept of trial and error design.

Third, it offers inherent lessons about the relationship of form and function.

Opportunities to expand these concepts are almost limitless.

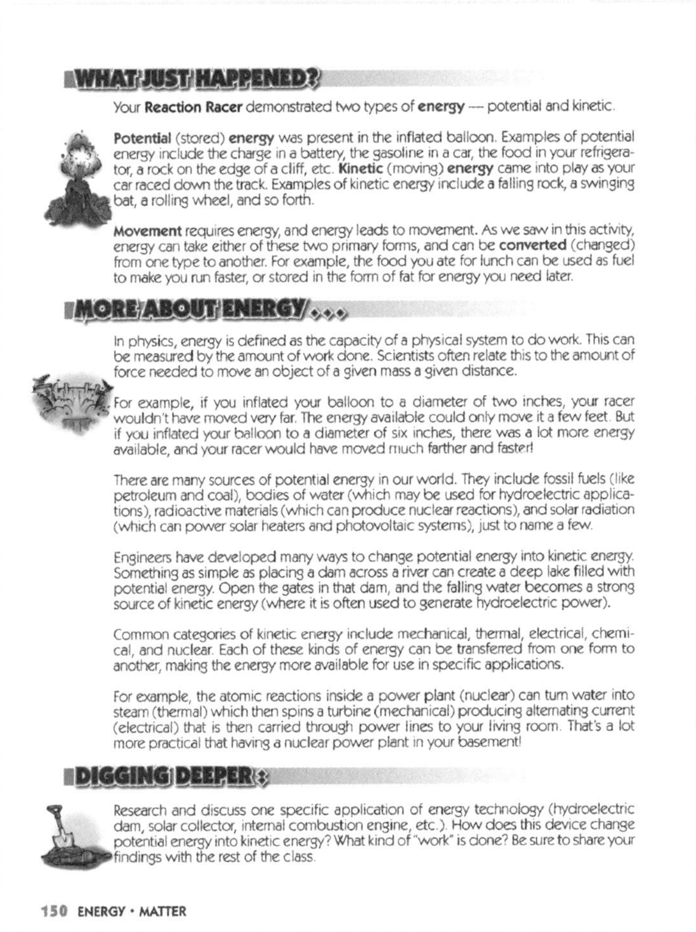

WHAT JUST HAPPENED?

Your **Reaction Racer** demonstrated two types of **energy** — potential and kinetic.

Potential (stored) **energy** was present in the inflated balloon. Examples of potential energy include the charge in a battery, the gasoline in a car, the food in your refrigerator, a rock on the edge of a cliff, etc. **Kinetic** (moving) **energy** came into play as your car raced down the track. Examples of kinetic energy include a falling rock, a swinging bat, a rolling wheel, and so forth.

Movement requires energy, and energy leads to movement. As we saw in this activity, energy can take either of these two primary forms, and can be **converted** (changed) from one type to another. For example, the food you ate for lunch can be used as fuel to make you run faster, or stored in the form of fat for energy you need later.

MORE ABOUT ENERGY . . .

In physics, energy is defined as the capacity of a physical system to do work. This can be measured by the amount of work done. Scientists often relate this to the amount of force needed to move an object of a given mass a given distance.

For example, if you inflated your balloon to a diameter of two inches, your racer wouldn't have moved very far. The energy available could only move it a few feet. But if you inflated your balloon to a diameter of six inches, there was a lot more energy available, and your racer would have moved much farther and faster!

There are many sources of potential energy in our world. They include fossil fuels (like petroleum and coal), bodies of water (which may be used for hydroelectric applications), radioactive materials (which can produce nuclear reactions), and solar radiation (which can power solar heaters and photovoltaic systems), just to name a few.

Engineers have developed many ways to change potential energy into kinetic energy. Something as simple as placing a dam across a river can create a deep lake filled with potential energy. Open the gates in that dam, and the falling water becomes a strong source of kinetic energy (where it is often used to generate hydroelectric power).

Common categories of kinetic energy include mechanical, thermal, electrical, chemical, and nuclear. Each of these kinds of energy can be transferred from one form to another, making the energy more available for use in specific applications.

For example, the atomic reactions inside a power plant (nuclear) can turn water into steam (thermal) which then spins a turbine (mechanical) producing alternating current (electrical) that is then carried through power lines to your living room. That's a lot more practical that having a nuclear power plant in your basement!

DIGGING DEEPER:

Research and discuss one specific application of energy technology (hydroelectric dam, solar collector, internal combustion engine, etc.). How does this device change potential energy into kinetic energy? What kind of "work" is done? Be sure to share your findings with the rest of the class.

150 ENERGY • MATTER

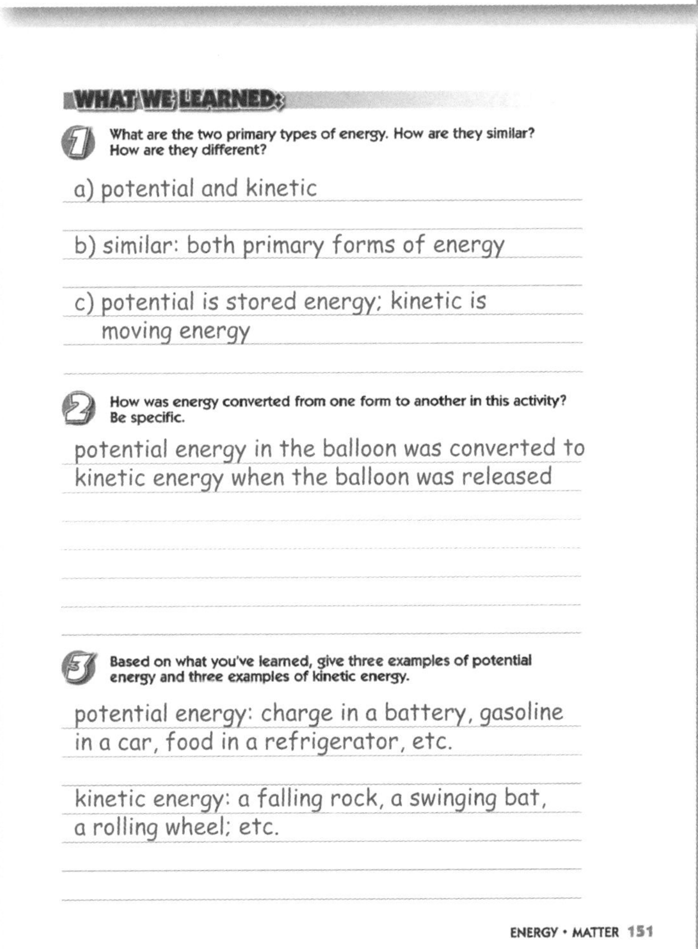

WHAT WE LEARNED:

1. **What are the two primary types of energy. How are they similar? How are they different?**

   a) potential and kinetic

   b) similar: both primary forms of energy

   c) potential is stored energy; kinetic is moving energy

2. **How was energy converted from one form to another in this activity? Be specific.**

   potential energy in the balloon was converted to kinetic energy when the balloon was released

3. **Based on what you've learned, give three examples of potential energy and three examples of kinetic energy.**

   potential energy: charge in a battery, gasoline in a car, food in a refrigerator, etc.

   kinetic energy: a falling rock, a swinging bat, a rolling wheel; etc.

ENERGY • MATTER 151

What Happened

Review the section with students. Emphasize bold-face words that identify key concepts and introduce new vocabulary.

*Your Reaction Racer demonstrated two types of **energy** – potential and kinetic.*

***Potential** (stored) **energy** was present in the inflated balloon. Examples of potential energy include the charge in a battery, the gasoline in a car, the food in your refrigerator, a rock on the edge of a cliff, etc. **Kinetic** (moving) **energy** came into play as your car raced down the track. Examples of kinetic energy include a falling rock, a swinging bat, a rolling wheel, and so forth.*

***Movement** requires energy, and energy leads to movement. As we saw in this activity, energy can take either of these two primary forms, and can be **converted** (changed) from one type to another. For example, the food you ate for lunch can be used as fuel to make you run faster, or stored in the form of fat for energy you need later.*

More About . . .

Have students read this section as you would a traditional science text — or use cooperative learning techniques to allow students the opportunity to work on the material collaboratively.

Digging Deeper

(Optional) Challenge teams to reseach and discuss practical applications of the lesson concepts. Encourage them to share their findings with the rest of the class.

What We Learned

Answers will vary. Suggested responses are shown at left.

Conclusion

Read this section aloud to the class to summarize the concepts learned in this activity.

Food for Thought

Read the Scripture aloud to the class. Talk about times when we are emotionally and mentally drained. Discuss how God provides a never-ending source of power for our lives.

Science Journal

If time permits, have a general class discussion about notes and drawings various students added to their journal pages. Discuss correct and incorrect predictions, and remind students that this "trial and error" process is part of the scientific process.

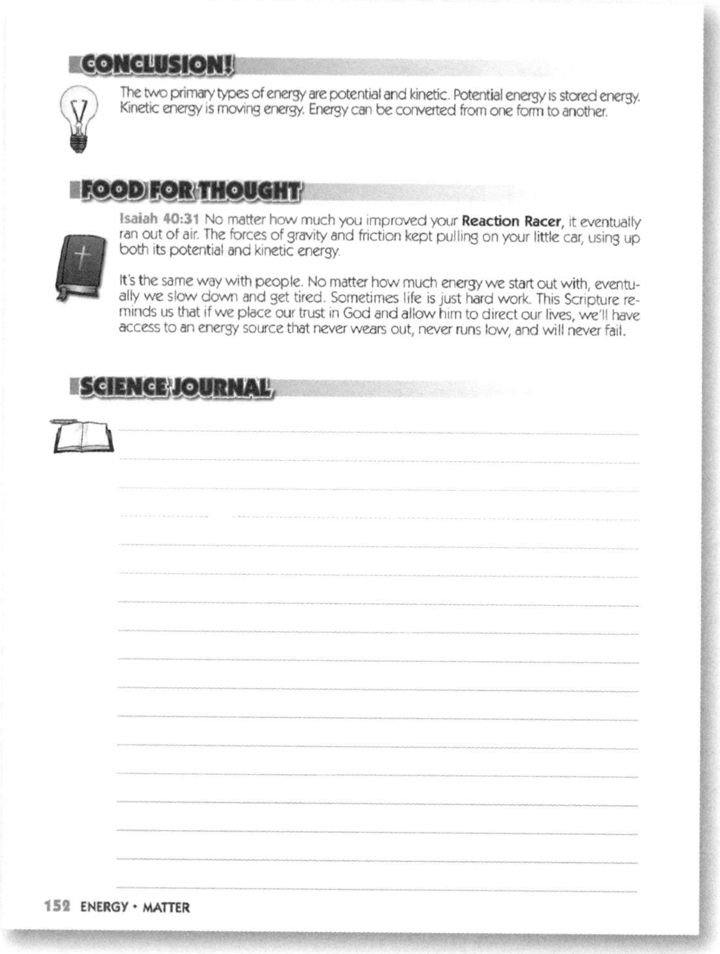
CONCLUSION!

The two primary types of energy are potential and kinetic. Potential energy is stored energy. Kinetic energy is moving energy. Energy can be converted from one form to another.

FOOD FOR THOUGHT

Isaiah 40:31 No matter how much you improved your **Reaction Racer**, it eventually ran out of air. The forces of gravity and friction kept pulling on your little car, using up both its potential and kinetic energy.

It's the same way with people. No matter how much energy we start out with, eventually we slow down and get tired. Sometimes life is just hard work. This Scripture reminds us that if we place our trust in God and allow him to direct our lives, we'll have access to an energy source that never wears out, never runs low, and will never fail.

SCIENCE JOURNAL

152 ENERGY • MATTER

Extended Teaching

1. Repeat this activity using different size racers and balloons. Have students compare the results with the original activity. How were they similar? How were they different?

2. Discuss ways friction might be reduced to make a Reaction Racer go further. Think in terms of the racing surface, axle lubricants, wheel thickness, etc. Have students test their hypotheses.

3. Using the Internet, have teams research how the shape of a race car affects its speed and efficiency. Challenge each team to create a poster showing a specific car and how this principle is applied.

4. Take a field trip to a racing shop. Find out how vehicles are designed to work with or overcome various forces (gravity, friction, wind resistance, etc.). Have students write a paragraph about one thing they learn.

5. Invite a motorcross racer to visit your classroom. Ask him/her to bring equipment, and to discuss the physical forces that affect this sport. Have students write a paragraph about one thing they learn.

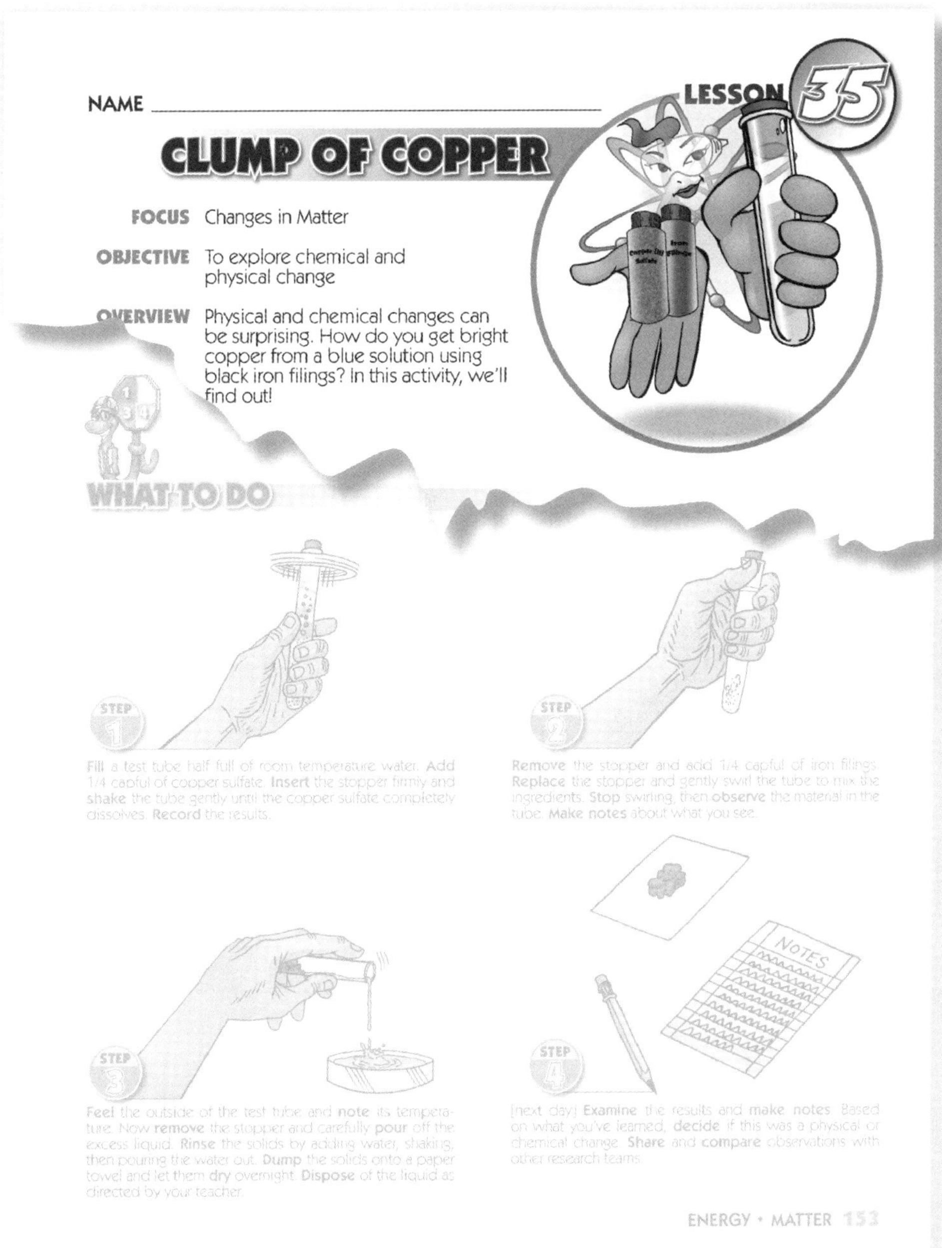

NAME ______________________

LESSON 35

CLUMP OF COPPER

FOCUS Changes in Matter

OBJECTIVE To explore chemical and physical change

OVERVIEW Physical and chemical changes can be surprising. How do you get bright copper from a blue solution using black iron filings? In this activity, we'll find out!

WHAT TO DO

STEP 1
Fill a test tube half full of room temperature water. **Add** 1/4 capful of copper sulfate. **Insert** the stopper firmly and **shake** the tube gently until the copper sulfate completely dissolves. **Record** the results.

STEP 2
Remove the stopper and add 1/4 capful of iron filings. **Replace** the stopper and gently swirl the tube to mix the ingredients. **Stop** swirling, then **observe** the material in the tube. **Make notes** about what you see.

STEP 3
Feel the outside of the test tube and **note** its temperature. Now **remove** the stopper and carefully **pour** off the excess liquid. **Rinse** the solids by adding water, shaking, then pouring the water out. **Dump** the solids onto a paper towel and let them **dry** overnight. **Dispose** of the liquid as directed by your teacher.

STEP 4
[next day] **Examine** the results and **make notes**. Based on what you've learned, **decide** if this was a physical or chemical change. **Share** and **compare** observations with other research teams.

ENERGY • MATTER 153

Additional Comments

A great way to introduce this activity is to hold up a penny and a test tube of blue copper sulfate. Ask the students what they think the two have in common. The answer (both contain copper) is not apparent, so challenge the students by saying, "Well, let's do this activity to see if we can find out!"

Overview

Read the overview aloud to your students. The goal is to create an atmosphere of curiosity and inquiry.

Category

Physical Science
Energy/Matter

Focus

Changes in Matter

Objective

To explore chemical and physical change

National Standards

A1, A2, B1, E1, E2, F5, G1, G2

Materials Needed

test tube
copper sulfate
solid stopper
iron filings
paper towel
water

Safety Concerns

1. Goggles
Since chemicals are used in this activity, goggles are recommended.

3. Skin Contact
Remind students to avoid skin contact with the copper sulfate.

4. Slipping
There is a potential for spills. Remind students to exercise caution.

WHAT TO DO

Monitor student research teams as they complete each step.

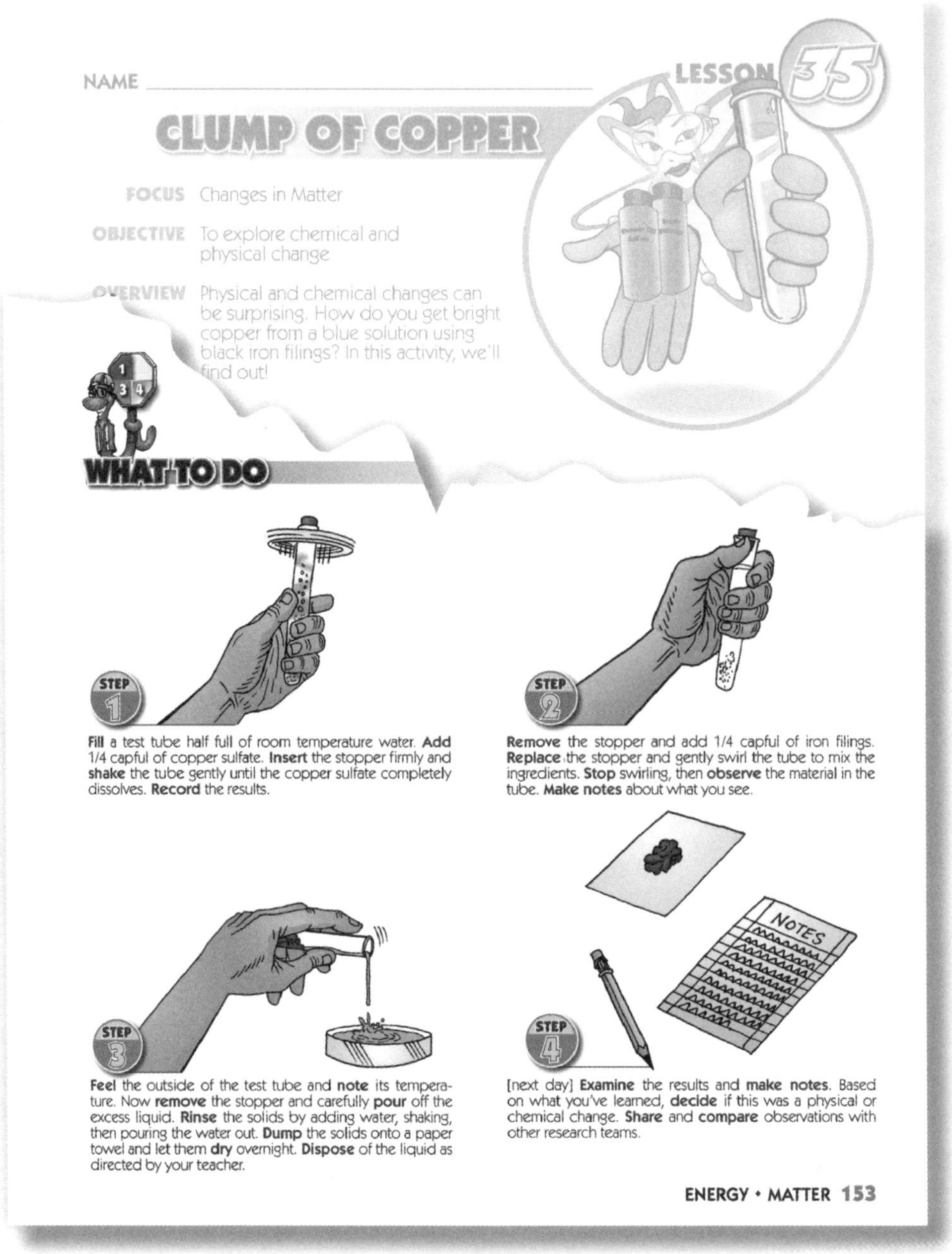

NAME ____________________ LESSON 35

CLUMP OF COPPER

FOCUS Changes in Matter

OBJECTIVE To explore chemical and physical change

OVERVIEW Physical and chemical changes can be surprising. How do you get bright copper from a blue solution using black iron filings? In this activity, we'll find out!

WHAT TO DO

STEP 1

Fill a test tube half full of room temperature water. **Add** 1/4 capful of copper sulfate. **Insert** the stopper firmly and **shake** the tube gently until the copper sulfate completely dissolves. **Record** the results.

STEP 2

Remove the stopper and add 1/4 capful of iron filings. **Replace** the stopper and gently swirl the tube to mix the ingredients. **Stop** swirling, then **observe** the material in the tube. **Make notes** about what you see.

STEP 3

Feel the outside of the test tube and **note** its temperature. Now **remove** the stopper and carefully **pour** off the excess liquid. **Rinse** the solids by adding water, shaking, then pouring the water out. **Dump** the solids onto a paper towel and let them **dry** overnight. **Dispose** of the liquid as directed by your teacher.

STEP 4

[next day] **Examine** the results and **make notes**. Based on what you've learned, **decide** if this was a physical or chemical change. **Share** and **compare** observations with other research teams.

ENERGY • MATTER 153

Teacher to Teacher

Scientists call the chemical reaction in this activity a "single replacement reaction." This means that one atom of an element replaces one ion of another element. Since this turns the ion into an atom, it results in a different substance.

WHAT JUST HAPPENED?

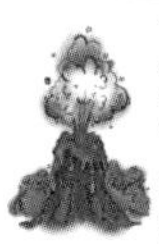

To create **physical change**, we break, grind, boil, freeze, or otherwise modify the appearance of a substance — but it's the same material, just a different form. For example, when you **dissolved** the copper sulfate in water, it was still copper sulfate even though it was now in the form of a **solution**. This is a physical change.

But when we create **chemical change**, we end up with a completely different substance. In this case, the **iron atoms** became iron **ions** as they dissolved. These iron ions reacted with the **copper ions** already dissolved in the water. This created copper **atoms**, which then clumped together as **gravity** pulled them to the bottom of the test tube.

Chemical changes often give off **energy** (as you saw from the heat you felt in Step 3).

MORE ABOUT CHANGES IN MATTER . . .

As you discovered, this activity included both a physical change (copper sulfate into copper sulfate solution) and a chemical change (copper sulfate into iron sulfate and copper). The physical change was fairly simple. You only changed the *form* of the matter from a solid into a liquid. But the chemical change was more complex. Here's how it worked:

Copper sulfate is made of two different "ions" — copper ion and sulfate ion. (Ions are atoms or groups of atoms that have a positive or negative charge.) The iron filings you used were made of iron atoms with no charge.

So when you mixed the neutral iron filings with the charged copper sulfate solution, something had to happen to equalize the imbalance in the charges. In this case, the iron atoms swapped places with the copper ions, resulting in iron ions and copper atoms! And in this form, they became a lump of copper.

A chemist would describe this "charge swap" with the following notation:

$$Fe + CuSO_4 \Rightarrow Cu \text{ and } FeS0_4$$

Or to put it into language that you and I understand, when you mix iron and copper sulfate together, you end up with iron sulfate and copper.

Chemists also call this a "single replacement reaction", since only one element is replaced. These reactions can be used to make pure metals from the ores found naturally in the Earth. Atoms from an inexpensive material are often used for this kind of swap, changing the ions of an expensive material (like copper) into atoms.

DIGGING DEEPER:

Research and discuss other examples of physical and chemical change. Make a poster labeled "Physical Changes". Describe at least three examples of physical change, and illustrate these changes with clippings from old magazines. Repeat the process to make a second poster labeled "Chemical Changes".

154 ENERGY • MATTER

WHAT WE LEARNED:

1. Describe what happened in Step 1. Was this a chemical or a physical change? Why?

a) copper sulfate dissolved

b) physical

c) still copper sulfate, only now in liquid form

2. Describe what happened in Step 2. Was this a chemical or a physical change? Why?

a) material began to clump at bottom, and change color

b) chemical

c) a different substance was created

3. Based on what you've learned, is burning firewood a chemical or physical change? Explain your answer.

a) chemical change

b) ashes and wood are different substances

ENERGY • MATTER 155

What Happened

Review this section with your students. Emphasize bold-face words that identify key concepts, and introduce new vocabulary.

*To create **physical change,** we break, grind, boil, freeze, or otherwise modify the appearance of a substance — but it's the same material, just a different form. For example, when you **dissolved** the copper sulfate in water, it was still copper sulfate, even though it was now in the form of a **solution**. This is a physical change.*

*But when we create **chemical change**, we end up with a completely different substance. In this case, the **iron atoms** became iron **ions** as they dissolved. These iron ions reacted with the **copper ions** already dissolved in the water. This created copper **atoms**, which then clumped together as **gravity** pulled them to the bottom of the test tube.*

*Chemical changes often give off **energy** (as you saw from the heat you felt in Step 3).*

More About . . .

Have students read this section as you would a traditional science text — or use cooperative learning techniques to allow students the opportunity to work on the material collaboratively.

Digging Deeper

(Optional) Challenge teams to reseach and discuss practical applications of the lesson concepts. Encourage them to share their findings with the rest of the class.

What We Learned

Answers will vary. Suggested responses are shown at left.

Conclusion

Read this section aloud to the class to summarize the concepts learned in this activity.

Food for Thought

Read the Scripture aloud to the class. Talk about how God has a plan for all of us. (See also Jeremiah 29:11.) Discuss why it is so important to trust God to direct our lives.

Science Journal

Encourage students to make notes and drawings, recording their impressions about various aspects of the lesson. If time permits, have a group discussion to review responses. Be sure to discuss correct and incorrect predictions, reminding students that the "trial and error" approach is part of the scientific process.

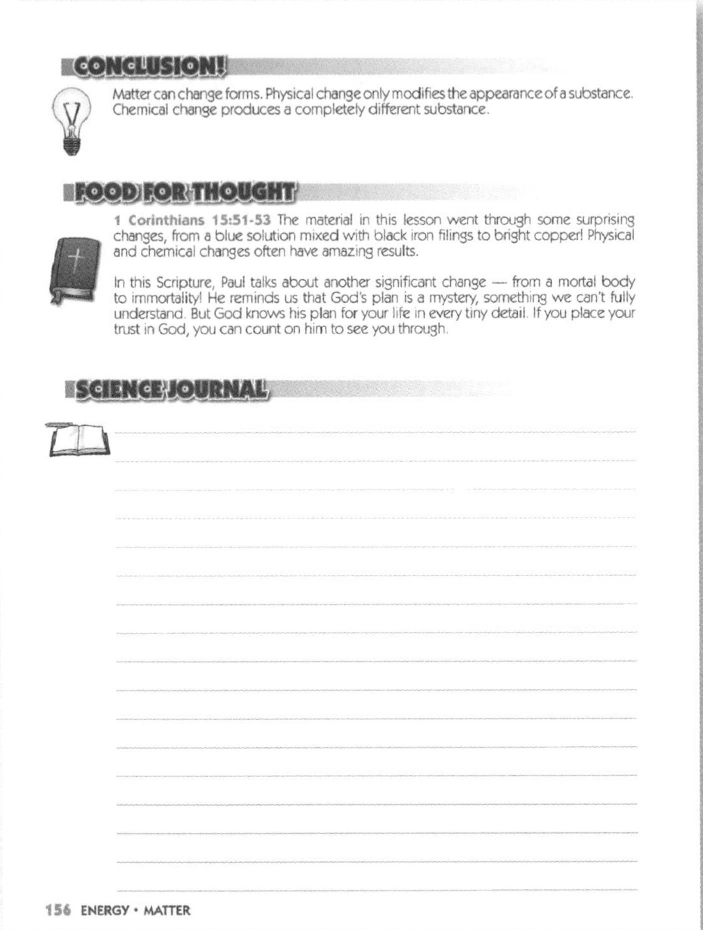

CONCLUSION!

Matter can change forms. Physical change only modifies the appearance of a substance. Chemical change produces a completely different substance.

FOOD FOR THOUGHT

1 Corinthians 15:51-53 The material in this lesson went through some surprising changes, from a blue solution mixed with black iron filings to bright copper! Physical and chemical changes often have amazing results.

In this Scripture, Paul talks about another significant change — from a mortal body to immortality! He reminds us that God's plan is a mystery, something we can't fully understand. But God knows his plan for your life in every tiny detail. If you place your trust in God, you can count on him to see you through.

SCIENCE JOURNAL

156 ENERGY • MATTER

Extended Teaching

1. Have teams place their copper samples in a safe outdoor location. After two weeks, retrieve samples and examine them. Challenge students to write a paragraph explaining how and why samples have changed.

2. Invite a coppersmith to visit your classroom. Ask him/her to bring samples and discuss copper working techniques. Have students write a paragraph about one thing they learn.

3. Using the Internet, have teams locate American copper mines — current and past. Challenge each team to contribute material for a bulletin board on copper mines. (An excellent source for environmental maps is: www.nationalatlas.gov.)

4. Continue by finding out about environmental problems connected with these mines. What are they and how are they being addressed? Challange each team to make a presentation to the class on their findings.

5. If one is in your area, arrange a field trip to a mine. Have teams discover everything they can about its history, function, and environmental impact. Challenge each team to create a poster about one aspect of this mine.

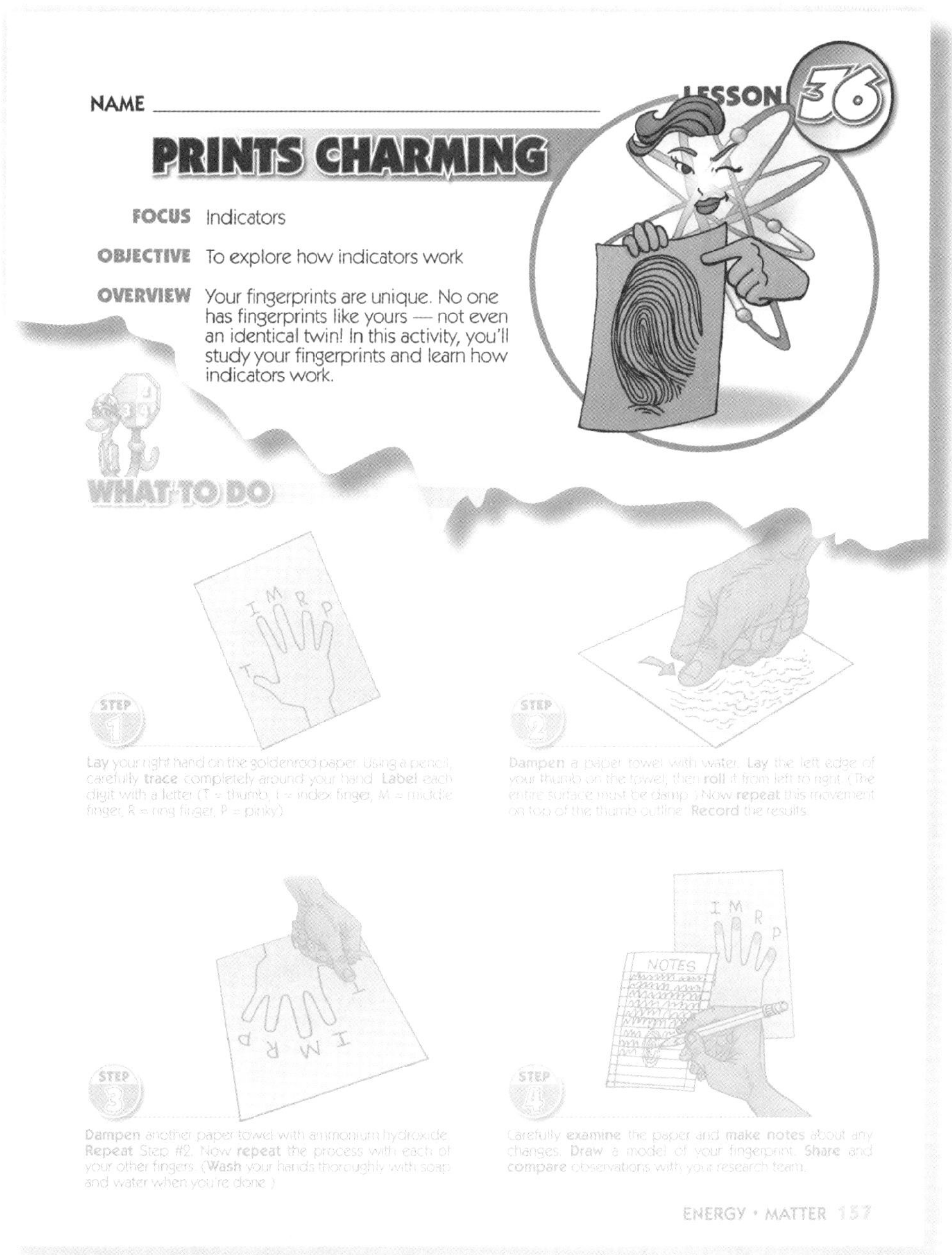

NAME ______________________

LESSON 36

PRINTS CHARMING

FOCUS Indicators

OBJECTIVE To explore how indicators work

OVERVIEW Your fingerprints are unique. No one has fingerprints like yours — not even an identical twin! In this activity, you'll study your fingerprints and learn how indicators work.

WHAT TO DO

STEP 1
Lay your right hand on the goldenrod paper. Using a pencil, carefully **trace** completely around your hand. **Label** each digit with a letter (T = thumb, I = index finger, M = middle finger, R = ring finger, P = pinky).

STEP 2
Dampen a paper towel with water. **Lay** the left edge of your thumb on the towel, then **roll** it from left to right. (The entire surface must be damp.) Now **repeat** this movement on top of the thumb outline. **Record** the results.

STEP 3
Dampen another paper towel with ammonium hydroxide. **Repeat** Step #2. Now **repeat** the process with each of your other fingers. (**Wash** your hands thoroughly with soap and water when you're done.)

STEP 4
Carefully **examine** the paper and **make notes** about any changes. **Draw** a model of your fingerprint. **Share** and **compare** observations with your research team.

ENERGY • MATTER 157

Category

Physical Science
Energy/Matter

Focus

Indicators

Objective

To explore how indicators work

National Standards

A1, A2, B1, E1, E2, F1, F5, G1, G2

Materials Needed

goldenrod paper
ammonium hydroxide
pencil
paper towels
water

Safety Concerns

2. Corrosion
Remind students to exercise caution when using ammonium hydroxide.

3. Hygiene
Remind students to wash hands thoroughly after Step 3.

4. Other
During Step 3, caution students to keep fingers away from eyes or mouth.

Additional Comments

Since students will be touching the ammonium hydroxide, begin this activity with a discussion of its safe use. Even though it is a common household chemical, students should still exercise caution. In addition, too much ammonium hydroxide on fingers will cause fingerprints to smear!

Overview

Read the overview aloud to your students. The goal is to create an atmosphere of curiosity and inquiry.

WHAT TO DO

Monitor student research teams as they complete each step.

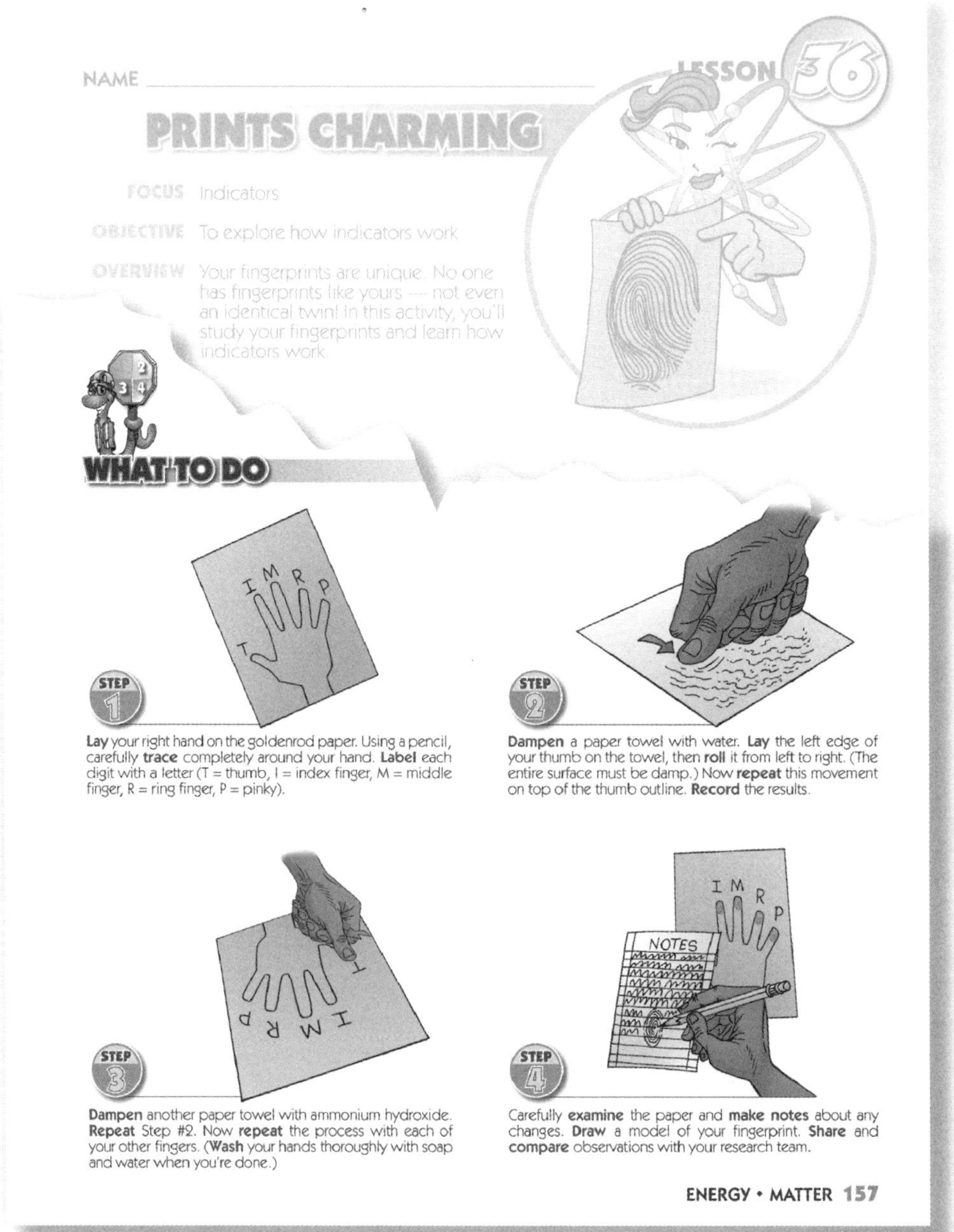

NAME ______________________ LESSON 36

PRINTS CHARMING

FOCUS Indicators

OBJECTIVE To explore how indicators work

OVERVIEW Your fingerprints are unique. No one has fingerprints like yours — not even an identical twin! In this activity, you'll study your fingerprints and learn how indicators work.

WHAT TO DO

STEP 1

Lay your right hand on the goldenrod paper. Using a pencil, carefully **trace** completely around your hand. **Label** each digit with a letter (T = thumb, I = index finger, M = middle finger, R = ring finger, P = pinky).

STEP 2

Dampen a paper towel with water. **Lay** the left edge of your thumb on the towel, then **roll** it from left to right. (The entire surface must be damp.) Now **repeat** this movement on top of the thumb outline. **Record** the results.

STEP 3

Dampen another paper towel with ammonium hydroxide. **Repeat** Step #2. Now **repeat** the process with each of your other fingers. (**Wash** your hands thoroughly with soap and water when you're done.)

STEP 4

Carefully **examine** the paper and **make notes** about any changes. **Draw** a model of your fingerprint. **Share** and **compare** observations with your research team.

ENERGY • MATTER 157

Teacher to Teacher

Fingerprints are just one more example of the effect of DNA on living things. Everyone's DNA is unique, so everyone's fingerprint is unique. There's one notable twist, however. The DNA of identical twins is . . . well, identical. But because of various "outside" forces, their fingerprints are still unique.

WHAT JUST HAPPENED?

The color change you saw was the result of an **indicator**. Indicators are chemicals which change color when an **acid** or **base** is present. The indicator in this special paper wasn't affected by the water since water is **neutral** (neither acid or base). But when you used **ammonium hydroxide** (a base), it made the indicator in the paper turn bright red.

Everyone's fingerprint is unique (a valuable fact in forensics work), but there are some basic patterns many people have in common. The most easily observed patterns are the loop, the arch, and the whorl. A **loop** is a hump like an upside down U. An **arch** is a loop with a floor to it. A **whorl** is like a loop leaning to one side or the other. If you're interested in fingerprints and fingerprinting, an encyclopedia or the Internet can help you explore this area further.

MORE ABOUT INDICATORS...

Indicators are usually made from chemicals that are weak acids or weak bases. These weak chemicals change colors when exposed to various pH conditions.

The term "pH" refers to a scale that scientists use to measure whether a solution is more acid or more alkaline (base). The pH scale ranges from 0 to 14, with a rating of 7 considered neutral. The lower the number, the more acidic a substance is. The higher the number, the more alkaline the substance is.

Indicators can be very helpful tools. They are a vital part of processes like soil testing, medical testing, and environmental monitoring.

Indicators in soil testing make for better crops. For example, suppose you want to plant blueberries in your backyard. Since blueberries prefer soil that is somewhat acid (a pH between 4 and 5), a soil test can tell you what is needed to raise or lower the soil's pH and create the ideal blueberry bed. This is much faster and more efficient than just planting the blueberries and waiting to see what happens!

Indicators in medical testing help doctors diagnose problems. For example, body fluids like urine or saliva can be checked for pH levels, identifying potential acid-base imbalances in the body. Specific pH numbers help doctors identify a wide variety of medical concerns from acid reflux to kidney stones.

Indicators can also help scientists monitor the environment. Chemical spills, fertilizer run-off, and other man-made pollutants sometimes get into streams and rivers, altering the pH of the water and killing fish. Scientists can regularly check the pH of a suspect area to determine the impact of environmental contaminants and suggest solutions.

DIGGING DEEPER:

Research and discuss the many ways that indicators can be used. Choose a particular application, then write a report describing the process. Share this with the class. If possible, give a demonstration that shows how this type of indicator works.

158 ENERGY • MATTER

WHAT WE LEARNED:

1 **What is an indicator? What do indicators do? Name at least one way that indicators can be helpful.**

a) a special kind of chemical

b) change colors when an acid or base is present

c) soil testing, medical testing, environmental monitoring, etc.

2 **Compare Step 2 with Step 3. How were they similar? How were they different?**

a) similar: same procedure, same paper, etc.

b) different liquid, paper turned red, etc.

3 **Choose five classmates from other teams and list their names. Try to match their fingerprints with common patterns. For fingerprints that don't match, carefully describe the pattern.**

answer should be in sets (name and fingerprint type or description)

ENERGY • MATTER 159

What Happened

Review the section with students. Emphasize bold-face words that identify key concepts and introduce new vocabulary.

*The color change you saw was the result of an **indicator**. Indicators are chemicals which change color when an **acid** or **base** is present. The indicator in this special paper wasn't affected by the water since water is **neutral** (neither acid or base). But when you used **ammonium hydroxide** (a base), it made the indicator in the paper turn bright red.*

*Everyone's fingerprint is unique (a valuable fact in forensics work), but there are some basic patterns many people have in common. The most easily observed patterns are the loop, the arch, and the whorl. A **loop** is a hump like an upside down U. An **arch** is a loop with a floor to it. A **whorl** is like a loop leaning to one side or the other. If you're interested in fingerprints and fingerprinting, an encyclopedia or the Internet can help you explore this area further.*

More About . . .

Have students read this section as you would a traditional science text — or use cooperative learning techniques to allow students the opportunity to work on the material collaboratively.

Digging Deeper

(Optional) Challenge teams to reseach and discuss practical applications of the lesson concepts. Encourage them to share their findings with the rest of the class.

What We Learned

Answers will vary. Suggested responses are shown at left.

Conclusion

Read this section aloud to the class to summarize the concepts learned in this activity.

Food for Thought

Read the Scripture aloud to the class. Talk about how we can make lasting changes in our lives when we spend time developing a relationship with God.

Science Journal

If time permits, have a general class discussion about notes and drawings various students added to their journal pages. Discuss correct and incorrect predictions, and remind students that this "trial and error" process is part of the scientific process.

CONCLUSION!

Indicators are chemicals that change color when exposed to an acid or a base. A paper containing an indicator can be used to collect and study fingerprints. Fingerprints are a unique identification tool.

FOOD FOR THOUGHT

Matthew 7:16 Thanks to the chemical indicator in the paper, your fingerprints were no longer hidden. Once they appeared, everyone could see them in great detail.

Regardless of how nice someone looks, you don't really know what a person is like until you see how they act. Jesus reminds us of that in this Scripture by saying that thornbushes don't bear grapes, and figs aren't found on thistles! The only way to really change your outward behavior is to change what's inside — and that can happen only by spending quality time with God.

SCIENCE JOURNAL

160 ENERGY • MATTER

Extended Teaching

1. Repeat the activity using the opposite hand. Have students compare their thumbprint with the thumbprint from the original activity. How were they similar? How were they different?

2. Invite a police officer to visit your classroom. Ask him/her to explain how fingerprints are taken at a crime scene and how they are used to solve crimes. Have students write a paragraph about one thing they learn.

3. Review the basic fingerprint patterns (loop, arch, whorl). Have teams examine each other's fingers, then list the pattern each team member matches. Compare lists to discover which pattern is most common in your class.

4. Secretly take thumbprints from five volunteers. Enlarge these several times, then post them on a bulletin board. Challenge teams to discover the volunteers by examining each other's thumbs.

5. Have teams research the Human Genome Project. Challenge each team to find some interesting information we've learned about genetics as a result of the project. Create a bulletin board based on their findings.

ASSESSMENT

Read this first . . .

The following pages contain Black Line Masters designed to be used with the *A Reason For® Science* Student Worktexts.

NAME________________________________ DATE ______________

LESSON 1

YEASTY BEASTY

True/False (Circle T for true, F for false.)

T F **1.** A controlled experiment compares an experimental environment with a controlled environment.

T F **2.** In a controlled experiment, two or more variables are changed each time.

T F **3.** A controlled experiment starts with a theory about a hypothesis.

T F **4.** A living thing must be able to respond to its environment.

T F **5.** A variable is the thing that stays the same each time you run an experiment.

Multiple Choice (Fill in the circle beside the best answer.)

6. A hypothesis that seems true and could be tested further is called . . .

- ○ **a.** an experiment
- ○ **b.** a control
- ○ **c.** a theory
- ○ **d.** a variable

7. Living things are "born," grow, mature, reproduce, and die. This is called a . . .

- ○ **a.** lifetime
- ○ **b.** life cycle
- ○ **c.** life circle
- ○ **d.** lifeline

8. In this activity, the bottle that received only yeast and sugar was the . . .

- ○ **a.** control
- ○ **b.** variable
- ○ **c.** theoretical
- ○ **d.** experimental

9. In this activity, the bottle that received yeast, sugar, and water was the . . .

- ○ **a.** control
- ○ **b.** variable
- ○ **c.** theoretical
- ○ **d.** experimental

10. Every living thing can do all of the following except . . .

- ○ **a.** take in nutrients
- ○ **b.** eliminate waste products
- ○ **c.** reproduce
- ○ **d.** think

NAME______________________________ DATE____________

LESSON 2

PRESERVED PLANTS

True/False (Circle T for true, F for false.)

T F **1.** Preserving something means to keep it from decomposing or rotting.

T F **2.** A good reference book can help you identify (and avoid) poisonous plants.

T F **3.** In this activity, the cardboard and newspaper provided moisture for the plants.

T F **4.** A "plant press" is a place where books and papers about flowers are printed.

T F **5.** Sketches and field notes help researchers learn more about plants.

Multiple Choice (Fill in the circle beside the best answer.)

6. All of the following are good rules for plant collecting except . . .

○ **a.** respect parks and private property
○ **b.** carry a reference book and avoid poisonous plants
○ **c.** look for rare plants in a wildlife refuge
○ **d.** make notes about when/where each plant is collected

7. Scientists call the process of removing water from something . . .

○ **a.** condensation
○ **b.** dehydration
○ **c.** composition
○ **d.** decomposition

8. Scientists call the process of water changing into a gas . . .

○ **a.** condensation
○ **b.** composition
○ **c.** evaporation
○ **d.** decomposition

9. How does increasing surface area affect the dehydrating process?

○ **a.** The greater the surface area, the slower the dehydration.
○ **b.** The greater the surface area, the faster the dehydration.
○ **c.** The amount of surface area has no effect on dehydration.
○ **d.** The greater the dehydration, the slower the surface area.

10. Removing water from a plant specimen helps . . .

○ **a.** the plant decompose more rapidly
○ **b.** the plant maintain moisture
○ **c.** the microorganisms in the plant thrive
○ **d.** slow the work of microorganisms significantly

a reason for Science

NAME________________________________ DATE ____________

LESSON 3

CLEVERLY CLASSIFIED

True/False (Circle T for true, F for false.)

T F **1.** Scientists arrange all living things into groups based on characteristics.

T F **2.** Using different "yes/no" questions will result in different groupings.

T F **3.** Good scientists don't use "yes / no" questions to separate living things into groups.

T F **4.** Only major animals and plants can be grouped using scientific classification.

T F **5.** The terms "classification" and "taxonomy" both describe the same process.

Multiple Choice (Fill in the circle beside the best answer.)

6. The process of grouping objects into similar types based on characteristics is called . . .

○ **a.** classification
○ **b.** taxonomy
○ **c.** both of the above
○ **d.** neither of the above

7. When you separate your laundry into "darks" and "lights" you are using a form of . . .

○ **a.** regimentation
○ **b.** classification
○ **c.** incorporation
○ **d.** decomposition

8. Which of the following would a scientist ignore in classifying a group of dogs?

○ **a.** hair length
○ **b.** size
○ **c.** age
○ **d.** eye color

9. Which of the following would a scientist ignore in classifying a group of plants?

○ **a.** general leaf shape
○ **b.** comparative stem thickness
○ **c.** type of seeds
○ **d.** nursery that grows them

10. How often do scientists use identical "yes/no" questions when classifying living things?

○ **a.** never
○ **b.** almost never
○ **c.** once in a very great while
○ **d.** always

NAME______________________________ DATE ____________

LESSON 4

DNA DIFFERENCE

True/False (Circle T for true, F for false.)

T F **1.** Although people look very different, their DNA is identical.

T F **2.** DNA contains the "blueprints" for making and running a living thing.

T F **3.** All DNA is made from the same molecules.

T F **4.** The pattern of DNA molecules is different for every creature.

T F **5.** Because all DNA is the same, it is of no value in criminal investigations.

Multiple Choice (Fill in the circle beside the best answer.)

6. DNA stands for . . .

○ **a.** Denatured Neutral Antibodies
○ **b.** Ribonucleic Acid
○ **c.** Di-ribonucleic Acid
○ **d.** Deoxyribonucleic Acid

7. Since DNA is different for every creature . . .

○ **a.** it is of no use to science
○ **b.** different creatures can all look the same
○ **c.** every creature is unique
○ **d.** it is too complex to study

8. Very simple forms of DNA can be extracted . . .

○ **a.** only by using complex chemicals
○ **b.** only with multi-million dollar equipment
○ **c.** using simple tools and denatured alcohol
○ **d.** It is impossible to extract DNA.

9. DNA research helps scientists in the study of . . .

○ **a.** genetics
○ **b.** geriatrics
○ **c.** gymnastics
○ **d.** none of the above

10. All DNA is made from . . .

○ **a.** the same molecules, but uses different patterns
○ **b.** complex carbohydrates
○ **c.** the same patterns, but uses different molecules
○ **d.** spirals of denatured protein

NAME________________________________ DATE______________

LESSON 5

MITOSIS MYSTERY

True/False (Circle T for true, F for false.)

T F **1.** A normal human cell has 46 chromosomes.

T F **2.** Chromosomes contain specific DNA data that makes everyone unique.

T F **3.** Your chromosomes are identical to those of everyone in your family.

T F **4.** Daughter cells have the same number of chromosomes as mother cells.

T F **5.** During mitosis, the number of chromosomes in certain cells temporarily changes.

Multiple Choice (Fill in the circle beside the best answer.)

6. When cells divide during mitosis, the resulting cells are called . . .

○ **a.** mother cells
○ **b.** daughter cells
○ **c.** meiosis
○ **d.** chromosomes

7. The process of a cell dividing into two new cells is called . . .

○ **a.** mitosis
○ **b.** meiosis
○ **c.** cell multiplication
○ **d.** cell modeling

8. Before a mother cell divides, what happens to the chromosomes?

○ **a.** the number of chromosomes is halved
○ **b.** the number of chromosomes doubles
○ **c.** chromosomes divide into six equal groups
○ **d.** there is no change in chromosomes

9. How many chromosomes do human beings receive from each parent?

○ **a.** 23
○ **b.** 46
○ **c.** 92
○ **d.** 4

10. Compared to mother cells, how many chromosomes do daughter cells normally have?

○ **a.** the same number
○ **b.** half as many
○ **c.** twice as many
○ **d.** It is impossible to tell.

NAME________________________________ DATE ____________

LESSON 6

MARVELOUS MEIOSIS

True/False (Circle T for true, F for false.)

T F **1.** The term "gender" refers to whether you are male or female.

T F **2.** There is no difference in chromosomes between males and females.

T F **3.** Gender is determined by a particular combination of three different chromosomes.

T F **4.** Females have two "Y" chromosomes and males have two "X" chromosomes.

T F **5.** Females do not have any "Y" chromosomes.

Multiple Choice (Fill in the circle beside the best answer.)

6. Scientists call a sex cell . . .

- ○ **a.** an "X" chromosome
- ○ **b.** a "Y" chromosome
- ○ **c.** a gamete
- ○ **d.** meiosis

7. The sex cells created during meiosis have ____ chromosomes as regular cells.

- ○ **a.** twice as many
- ○ **b.** half as many
- ○ **c.** one-fourth as many
- ○ **d.** the same number of

8. In sexual reproduction, each parent supplies ____ the number of chromosomes needed.

- ○ **a.** twice
- ○ **b.** half
- ○ **c.** four times
- ○ **d.** one fourth

9. The scientific term referring to whether a creature is male or female is . . .

- ○ **a.** meiosis
- ○ **b.** gamete
- ○ **c.** gender
- ○ **d.** mitosis

10. The process of splitting the number of chromosomes in a cell in half is called . . .

- ○ **a.** mitosis
- ○ **b.** meiosis
- ○ **c.** conception
- ○ **d.** reproduction

NAME________________________________ DATE______________

LESSON 7

GENERATING GENDER

True/False (Circle T for true, F for false.)

T F **1.** The term "zygote" means the same thing as "gamete".

T F **2.** Males and females have one sex chromosome that is the same.

T F **3.** Human beings have a total of 46 sex chromosomes.

T F **4.** Fertilization restores the correct number of chromosomes.

T F **5.** A human zygote has the same number of chromosomes as other human cells.

Multiple Choice (Fill in the circle beside the best answer.)

6. Compared to a zygote, how many chromosomes does a gamete have?

- ◯ **a.** the same number
- ◯ **b.** half as many
- ◯ **c.** twice as many
- ◯ **d.** four times as many

7. How many chromosomes does a human zygote have?

- ◯ **a.** 1
- ◯ **b.** 2
- ◯ **c.** 23
- ◯ **d.** 46

8. What affect does fertilization have on the number of chromosomes?

- ◯ **a.** cuts them in half
- ◯ **b.** reduces the number by one
- ◯ **c.** brings them back to normal
- ◯ **d.** doubles them

9. The combination of a sperm and an egg cell is called . . .

- ◯ **a.** meiosis
- ◯ **b.** mitosis
- ◯ **c.** chromosome division
- ◯ **d.** fertilization

10. Which of the following chromosome combinations is correct?

- ◯ **a.** boy = XX; girl = YY
- ◯ **b.** boy = YY; girl = XY
- ◯ **c.** boy = XY; girl = XX
- ◯ **d.** boy = YY; girl = XX

a reason for Science

NAME________________________________ DATE ____________

LESSON 8

FASCINATING FINGERPRINTS

True/False (Circle T for true, F for false.)

T F **1.** When scientists make observations, they look for patterns.

T F **2.** Fingerprints are a very accurate way of identifying people.

T F **3.** Brothers and sisters always have identical fingerprints.

T F **4.** Since DNA testing began, fingerprints are no longer admissible in court as evidence.

T F **5.** Fingerprinting is the process of making an image of a person's fingertips.

Multiple Choice (Fill in the circle beside the best answer.)

6. Which of the following is not a common fingerprint pattern?

○ **a.** dip
○ **b.** arch
○ **c.** whorl
○ **d.** loop

7. The "high" places on your fingerprints are called . . .

○ **a.** whorls
○ **b.** ridges
○ **c.** loops
○ **d.** dips

8. Which of the following fingerprint patterns is like an upside-down U?

○ **a.** whorl
○ **b.** ridge
○ **c.** loop
○ **d.** arch

9. Which of the following fingerprint patterns is like a loop with a floor in it?

○ **a.** whorl
○ **b.** ridge
○ **c.** loop
○ **d.** arch

10. The low spots on your fingerprints are called . . .

○ **a.** whorls
○ **b.** ridges
○ **c.** valleys
○ **d.** loops

NAME______________________ DATE __________

LESSON 9

CREATE A KID

True/False (Circle T for true, F for false.)

T F **1.** Due to genetic composition, humans come in many different shapes and sizes.

T F **2.** All members of an immediate family have identical genes.

T F **3.** People who are related often appear similar since they have some genes in common.

T F **4.** If a person has damaged genes, their children could have birth defects.

T F **5.** Every gene has an equal chance at being dominant.

Multiple Choice (Fill in the circle beside the best answer.)

6. The chemical that stores our body's essential information is called . . .

○ **a.** RNA
○ **b.** ATA
○ **c.** DNA
○ **d.** IOU

7. Long strings of attached genes are called . . .

○ **a.** chromosomes
○ **b.** a DNA chain
○ **c.** a meiosis link
○ **d.** a mitosis chain

8. Which characteristic appears if one gene is dominant and one recessive?

○ **a.** the recessive gene
○ **b.** the dominant gene
○ **c.** a "blending" of the two genes
○ **d.** none of the above

9. Which characteristic appears if both genes are recessive?

○ **a.** the recessive
○ **b.** the dominant
○ **c.** both of the above
○ **d.** neither of the above

10. Some of the characteristics you studied were "blended." This means . . .

○ **a.** only recessive characteristics appear
○ **b.** only dominant characteristics appear
○ **c.** a combination of dominant and recessive characteristics appear
○ **d.** nothing happens at all

NAME________________________ DATE ____________

LESSON 10

ATOM ANCESTORS

True/False (Circle T for true, F for false.)

T F **1.** The Rutherford model is the oldest known model of the atom.

T F **2.** The Bohr model shows electrons orbiting a central nucleus.

T F **3.** John Dalton believed atoms were solid particles.

T F **4.** The charge cloud model represents the final step in creating atom models.

T F **5.** As scientists gain new understanding, scientific models tend to change.

Multiple Choice (Fill in the circle beside the best answer.)

6. The steel wool in the charge cloud model represents . . .

- ○ **a.** the nucleus of an atom
- ○ **b.** a solid "chunk" of atomic material
- ○ **c.** the electron "cloud"
- ○ **d.** gas

7. "Splitting" atoms most closely relates to . . .

- ○ **a.** electronic energy
- ○ **b.** solid particles
- ○ **c.** atomic energy
- ○ **d.** It is not possible to split an atom

8. The Greek word used to create the word "atom" means . . .

- ○ **a.** indivisible
- ○ **b.** divisible
- ○ **c.** indestructable
- ○ **d.** destructable

9. The "plum pudding" model of the atom was created by . . .

- ○ **a.** John Dalton
- ○ **b.** Neils Bohr
- ○ **c.** Ernest Rutherford
- ○ **d.** J. J. Thomson

10. Atoms contain . . .

- ○ **a.** positive electrons and negative protons
- ○ **b.** negative electrons and positive protons
- ○ **c.** only positive protons
- ○ **d.** only negative electrons

a reason for Science

NAME______________________________ DATE ______________

LESSON 11

ATTRACTIVE ELEMENT

True/False (Circle T for true, F for false.)

T F **1.** Water is a combination of hydrogen and oxygen.

T F **2.** A "bubble" of water can act as a kind of lens.

T F **3.** Surface tension causes water molecules to repel one another.

T F **4.** Surface tension is created when hydrogen and copper interact.

T F **5.** Ordinary detergent can interfere with the bonding of water molecules.

Multiple Choice (Fill in the circle beside the best answer.)

6. The bonding elements in water that creates surface tension are . . .

○ **a.** hydrogen and copper
○ **b.** hydrogen and oxygen
○ **c.** oxygen and copper
○ **d.** none of the above

7. A bubble of water can sometimes . . .

○ **a.** act as a kind of magnifier
○ **b.** reduce the size of an image
○ **c.** increase the surface tension of copper
○ **d.** decrease the surface tension of copper

8. When it's added to water, detergent . . .

○ **a.** bonds with copper molecules
○ **b.** increases surface tension
○ **c.** breaks surface tension
○ **d.** has little or no effect

9. A drop of water is most similar to a . . .

○ **a.** concave lens
○ **b.** convex lens
○ **c.** convex bond
○ **d.** none of the above

10. Falling flat on the surface of a swimming pool hurts because . . .

○ **a.** a smaller portion of your body repels the water
○ **b.** a larger portion of your body attracts the water
○ **c.** a small portion of your body must break the surface tension
○ **d.** a large portion of your body must break the surface tension

a reason for Science

NAME________________________ DATE ____________

LESSON 12

ICE SLICER

True/False (Circle T for true, F for false.)

T F **1.** The downward pull of gravity can be converted into heat energy.

T F **2.** When you lift something, you are assisting the force of gravity.

T F **3.** Opposing the force of gravity can create potential energy.

T F **4.** Adding heat can change water from a liquid form to a solid form.

T F **5.** Kinetic energy is moving energy.

Multiple Choice (Fill in the circle beside the best answer.)

6. In this activity, the purpose of the wire was to . . .

○ **a.** transfer force from the weights to the surface of the ice
○ **b.** turn potential energy into kinetic energy
○ **c.** turn potential energy into heat energy
○ **d.** all of the above

7. The downward pull of gravity can create . . .

○ **a.** heat
○ **b.** pressure
○ **c.** both of the above
○ **d.** neither of the above

8. Heat is a form of . . .

○ **a.** potential (stored) energy
○ **b.** potential (moving) energy
○ **c.** kinetic (stored) energy
○ **d.** kinetic (moving) energy

9. In general, the more force applied to an area . . .

○ **a.** the more pressure produced
○ **b.** the more pressure relieved
○ **c.** the more heat removed
○ **d.** none of the above

10. A weighted wire cutting ice is an example of a . . .

○ **a.** liquid changing to a solid
○ **b.** solid changing to a liquid
○ **c.** solid changing to a gas
○ **d.** gas changing to a solid

NAME________________________________ DATE ______________

LESSON 13

BOUNCE BACK BALL

True/False (Circle T for true, F for false.)

T F **1.** It takes energy to make something move.

T F **2.** Energy can be converted from one form into another.

T F **3.** An efficient machine is one that absorbs all the energy put into it.

T F **4.** Increasing efficiency is one major goal of engineering.

T F **5.** When energy is put into something, it is always completely absorbed.

Multiple Choice (Fill in the circle beside the best answer.)

6. The amount of energy put into something compared to what we get back is called . . .

○ **a.** the engineering ratio
○ **b.** the efficiency ratio
○ **c.** the absorption ratio
○ **d.** none of the above

7. If a ball fell 10 inches and bounced back eight, its efficiency rating would be . . .

○ **a.** 8%
○ **b.** 10%
○ **c.** 80%
○ **d.** 18%

8. When a ball hits the floor and bounces back, some of its energy is absorbed by . . .

○ **a.** friction
○ **b.** air resistance
○ **c.** flexing
○ **d.** all of the above

9. What does an "efficiency rating" on an appliance mean?

○ **a.** The higher the rating, the more energy used.
○ **b.** The higher the rating, the less energy used.
○ **c.** The lower the rating, the less energy used.
○ **d.** Efficiency ratings have nothing to do with energy consumption.

10. An very good furnace could have an efficiency rating of . . .

○ **a.** 100 %
○ **b.** 90%
○ **c.** 30 %
○ **d.** 10 %

NAME________________________________ DATE ______________

LESSON 14

KINETIC CAN

True/False (Circle T for true, F for false.)

T F **1.** Friction absorbs energy.

T F **2.** Scientists refer to moving energy as "potential" energy.

T F **3.** Kinetic energy can be converted into potential energy (and vice-versa).

T F **4.** Stored energy is known as "kinetic" energy.

T F **5.** A well-designed machine can give back more energy than is put into it.

Multiple Choice (Fill in the circle beside the best answer.)

6. When energy is converted from one form to another . . .

○ **a.** some energy is always absorbed
○ **b.** more energy is always produced
○ **c.** energy available remains exactly the same
○ **d.** Energy forms cannot be converted

7. One kind of force . . .

○ **a.** can never affect the action of another kind of force
○ **b.** can oppose the action of another kind of force
○ **c.** can exist by itself without any opposing forces
○ **d.** none of the above

8. The rubber band/bolt arrangement was designed to . . .

○ **a.** store kinetic energy
○ **b.** store potential energy
○ **c.** generate electricity
○ **d.** generate kinetics

9. A rolling can is a good example of . . .

○ **a.** potential energy
○ **b.** kinetic energy
○ **c.** electrical energy
○ **d.** absorption energy

10. Energy can be . . .

○ **a.** stored
○ **b.** converted
○ **c.** absorbed
○ **d.** all of the above

a reason for Science

NAME________________________ DATE____________

LESSON 15

GRAVITY GRABBER

True/False (Circle T for true, F for false.)

T F **1.** Gravity is a force.

T F **2.** An object's center of gravity is always its exact center.

T F **3.** The location of its center of gravity can affect an object's behavior.

T F **4.** Scientists refer to a twisting force as "torque."

T F **5.** Center of gravity is based on mass, not shape.

Multiple Choice (Fill in the circle beside the best answer.)

6. For an object to balance . . .

- ◯ **a.** there must be more force in one direction
- ◯ **b.** there must be no force in any direction
- ◯ **c.** there must be equal force in both directions
- ◯ **d.** Balance is not related to force

7. Which of the following is most similar to mass?

- ◯ **a.** center of gravity
- ◯ **b.** weight
- ◯ **c.** torque
- ◯ **d.** friction

8. A baseball bat's center of gravity would be found . . .

- ◯ **a.** in its exact center
- ◯ **b.** close to the handle
- ◯ **c.** close to the heavy end
- ◯ **d.** none of the above

9. Torque is identical to . . .

- ◯ **a.** gravity
- ◯ **b.** friction
- ◯ **c.** weight
- ◯ **d.** none of the above

10. The "floating hammer" in this lesson demonstrates . . .

- ◯ **a.** unbalanced forces
- ◯ **b.** balanced forces
- ◯ **c.** movement and torque
- ◯ **d.** weight and friction

NAME________________________ DATE ____________

LESSON 16

DIET DILEMMA

True/False (Circle T for true, F for false.)

T F **1.** An object's density affects its buoyancy.

T F **2.** The more dense an object is, the better it floats.

T F **3.** Buoyancy and gravity are opposing forces.

T F **4.** Buoyancy pulls down; gravity pushes up.

T F **5.** Similar looking materials may have different densities.

Multiple Choice (Fill in the circle beside the best answer.)

6. Density compares the weight of a material to the weight of . . .

◯ **a.** another material having the same volume
◯ **b.** another material having a different volume
◯ **c.** the same material having a different volume
◯ **d.** none of the above

7. Two objects made of different materials will likely . . .

◯ **a.** have the same density
◯ **b.** have the same volume
◯ **c.** have different densities
◯ **d.** have different volumes

8. Gravity creates a greater pull on . . .

◯ **a.** objects that are less dense
◯ **b.** objects that are more dense
◯ **c.** objects that float in the water
◯ **d.** both a and c above

9. If two objects have the same volume, but different weights . . .

◯ **a.** the objects have different densities
◯ **b.** the objects have identical densities
◯ **c.** the heavier object is less dense
◯ **d.** the lighter object is more dense

10. Life vests should be made of . . .

◯ **a.** a very dense material for optimum protection
◯ **b.** a very dense material for optimum buoyancy
◯ **c.** a very light material that increases gravity
◯ **d.** a very light material that increases buoyancy

a reason for Science

NAME________________________________ DATE ____________

LESSON 17

STRUCTURAL STRENGTH

True/False (Circle T for true, F for false.)

T F **1.** Structure affects the ability of a material to transfer forces.

T F **2.** Proper design allows lighter structures to support heavier loads.

T F **3.** Good bridges are designed to oppose the force of gravity.

T F **4.** A material must be heavier than the object it supports.

T F **5.** Forces can be transferred from one place to another.

Multiple Choice (Fill in the circle beside the best answer.)

6. Making a sheet of paper into a series of folds can . . .

○ **a.** help it support weight in any direction
○ **b.** help it support weight in one specific direction
○ **c.** make it easier to write on
○ **d.** all of the above

7. The structure of a bridge must be designed to hold . . .

○ **a.** the weight of anything crossing it
○ **b.** the land attached to its ends
○ **c.** the weight of the bridge itself
○ **d.** both a and c above

8. For a structure to stand, it must be able to . . .

○ **a.** transfer forces
○ **b.** eliminate forces
○ **c.** transfer material
○ **d.** eliminate weight

9. Since paper is made from wood fibers, folding a sheet of paper . . .

○ **a.** breaks the fibers, making the paper weaker
○ **b.** breaks the fibers, making the paper stronger
○ **c.** helps the fibers repel each other
○ **d.** helps the fibers support each other

10. Good structural design requires knowing how to . . .

○ **a.** eliminate weight
○ **b.** eliminate forces
○ **c.** transfer forces
○ **d.** transfer funds

a reason for Science

NAME______________________________ DATE ______________

INCREDIBLE EGGMOBILE

LESSON 18

True/False (Circle T for true, F for false.)

T F **1.** An object in motion stays in motion unless a force acts on it.

T F **2.** A motionless object stays motionless unless a force acts on it.

T F **3.** In a car crash, passengers must absorb all the forces to avoid injury.

T F **4.** Wearing a seat belt to keep you attached to the car is an example of inertia.

T F **5.** A ball sitting at the top of a ramp is an example of kinetic energy.

Multiple Choice (Fill in the circle beside the best answer.)

6. Releasing a ball so it rolls down a ramp converts . . .

- ◯ **a.** kinetic energy into potential energy
- ◯ **b.** potential energy into kinetic energy
- ◯ **c.** gravity into potential energy
- ◯ **d.** kinetic energy into gravity

7. Wearing a seatbelt is a good idea because . . .

- ◯ **a.** when you stop, the vehicle stops
- ◯ **b.** when you stop, the vehicle continues to move
- ◯ **c.** when the vehicle stops, you stop
- ◯ **d.** when the vehicle stops, you continue to move

8. In this activity, the packing material was designed to . . .

- ◯ **a.** transfer energy from the impact
- ◯ **b.** eliminate energy from the impact
- ◯ **c.** absorb energy from the impact
- ◯ **d.** none of the above

9. A rapidly moving vehicle demonstrates . . .

- ◯ **a.** kinetic energy
- ◯ **b.** potential energy
- ◯ **c.** gravitational energy
- ◯ **d.** none of the above

10. What do a football helmet, knee pads, and shoulder pads have in common?

- ◯ **a.** They are designed to eliminate forces.
- ◯ **b.** They are designed to eliminate energy.
- ◯ **c.** They are designed to absorb gravity.
- ◯ **d.** They are designed to absorb forces.

NAME________________________ DATE ____________

LESSON 19

AIR ELEVATOR

True/False (Circle T for true, F for false.)

T F **1.** Since it can not be seen, air is not matter.

T F **2.** When oxygen is removed from an enclosed space, air pressure falls.

T F **3.** Combustion can create differences in air pressure.

T F **4.** Air pressure changes can create movement.

T F **5.** Movement cannot occur when forces are unbalanced.

Multiple Choice (Fill in the circle beside the best answer.)

6. Scientists refer to burning as . . .

○ **a.** condensation
○ **b.** combustion
○ **c.** pressure
○ **d.** equilibrium

7. Movement occurs when . . .

○ **a.** forces are perfectly balanced.
○ **b.** equilibrium is achieved
○ **c.** forces are unbalanced
○ **d.** there are no forces present

8. In relationship to an enclosed space . . .

○ **a.** low pressure pushes, high pressure pulls
○ **b.** low pressure pulls, high pressure pushes
○ **c.** both high and low pressure pull
○ **d.** both high and low pressure push

9. Creating an opening in an enclosed space allows . . .

○ **a.** air pressure only to rise
○ **b.** air pressure only to fall
○ **c.** air pressure to equalize
○ **d.** none of the above

10. Air pressure is best described as a kind of . . .

○ **a.** oxygen
○ **b.** equilibrium
○ **c.** combustion
○ **d.** force

a reason for Science

NAME________________________ DATE__________

LESSON 20

TEST TUBE MOSQUITO

True/False (Circle T for true, F for false.)

T F **1.** Heating water causes its molecules to condense.

T F **2.** The term "equilibrium" means unbalanced forces.

T F **3.** Unbalanced forces can create movement.

T F **4.** Heat can create differences in air pressure.

T F **5.** Air pressure seeking equilibrium can create movement.

Multiple Choice (Fill in the circle beside the best answer.)

6. When water is heated, it can turn from a . . .

○ **a.** gas into a liquid
○ **b.** liquid into a gas
○ **c.** solid into a liquid
○ **d.** solid into a gas

7. When water in an enclosed space is heated . . .

○ **a.** air pressure increases
○ **b.** air pressure decreases
○ **c.** air pressure equalizes
○ **d.** none of the above

8. When heated water in an enclosed space cools . . .

○ **a.** air pressure increases
○ **b.** air pressure decreases
○ **c.** air pressure equalizes
○ **d.** none of the above

9. The process of heating . . .

○ **a.** removes force
○ **b.** removes energy
○ **c.** adds energy
○ **d.** none of the above

10. Increasing heat energy can . . .

○ **a.** create unbalanced forces
○ **b.** cause movement
○ **c.** change air pressure
○ **d.** all of the above

a reason for Science

NAME________________________________ DATE ______________

LESSON 21

MAGNETISM MODEL

True/False (Circle T for true, F for false.)

T F **1.** Magnetism is a kind of force.

T F **2.** The area around a magnet is called a magnetic field.

T F **3.** Magnetic fields are usually two-dimensional.

T F **4.** The Earth is surrounded by a magnetic field.

T F **5.** Scientists completely understand magnetism.

Multiple Choice (Fill in the circle beside the best answer.)

6. Magnetic fields . . .

○ **a.** are made of iron filings
○ **b.** are easily visible
○ **c.** are three dimensional
○ **d.** all of the above

7. A magnet can affect something . . .

○ **a.** only by touching it
○ **b.** only by not touching it
○ **c.** without touching it
○ **d.** none of the above

8. A well-designed model can help a scientist . . .

○ **a.** see things that are invisible
○ **b.** better understand complex forces
○ **c.** create a 3-D representation
○ **d.** all of the above

9. The Earth has . . .

○ **a.** a two-dimensional magnetic field with north and south poles
○ **b.** a three-dimensional magnetic field with north and south poles
○ **c.** a three-dimensional magnetic filed with no poles
○ **d.** no magnetic field due to its size and intense gravity

10. Which of the following would be affected by a magnet?

○ **a.** packing pellets
○ **b.** cellulose materials like wood
○ **c.** silicate materials like glass
○ **d.** ferrous materials like iron

NAME________________________________ DATE ____________

LESSON 22

STUDENT SATELLITES

True/False (Circle T for true, F for false.)

T F **1.** The path a satellite travels around Earth is called its "orbit."

T F **2.** Surveillance satellites need a geosynchronous orbit.

T F **3.** Communication and surveillance satellites maintain similar orbits.

T F **4.** All satellites move at the same speed.

T F **5.** Orbiting satellites must maintain a balance in relationship to gravity.

Multiple Choice (Fill in the circle beside the best answer.)

6. Which of the following does not use satellites?
- ◯ **a.** television
- ◯ **b.** cell phones
- ◯ **c.** radio
- ◯ **d.** electricity

7. Surveillance satellites are designed to . . .
- ◯ **a.** keep an eye on other satellites
- ◯ **b.** park directly above specific spots on Earth
- ◯ **c.** pass over different regions of Earth
- ◯ **d.** send back images of other planets

8. Communication satellites are used primarily for . . .
- ◯ **a.** observing different regions of the Earth
- ◯ **b.** observing different planets
- ◯ **c.** communicating with other satellites
- ◯ **d.** relaying radio, television, and cell phone signals

9. A satellite in geosynchronous orbit . . .
- ◯ **a.** stays in the same spot in relationship to Earth
- ◯ **b.** passes over many different countries each day
- ◯ **c.** heads directly away from Earth into space
- ◯ **d.** can be used to track international terrorists

10. A satellite in geosynchronous orbit . . .
- ◯ **a.** must move much slower than the Earth rotates
- ◯ **b.** must move much faster than the Earth rotates
- ◯ **c.** uses Earth's rotation to "slingshot" into space
- ◯ **d.** has no relationship to Earth's rotation

NAME________________________________ DATE ____________

LESSON 23

TROPICAL TOPOGRAPHY

True/False (Circle T for true, F for false.)

T F **1.** Maps are important tools for understanding Earth's surface.

T F **2.** Scientists refer to road maps as "topographical maps."

T F **3.** A topographical map shows the contour of a given area.

T F **4.** The U.S. Geological Survey makes detailed topographical maps.

T F **5.** A contour line shows the shape of the land at a particular level.

Multiple Choice (Fill in the circle beside the best answer.)

6. On a topographical map, the closer the lines are . . .

- ◯ **a.** the flatter the land
- ◯ **b.** the steeper the land
- ◯ **c.** the easier it is to farm
- ◯ **d.** the more houses you can build

7. A common topographical map scale has contour intervals of . . .

- ◯ **a.** 20 feet
- ◯ **b.** 200 feet
- ◯ **c.** 2000 feet
- ◯ **d.** none of the above

8. Surveyors use special equipment to determine the land's . . .

- ◯ **a.** attitude
- ◯ **b.** azimuth
- ◯ **c.** altitude
- ◯ **d.** models

9. On a topographical map, a large flat area would be shown by . . .

- ◯ **a.** contour lines close together
- ◯ **b.** contour lines far apart
- ◯ **c.** contour lines that vary in width
- ◯ **d.** the word "plain" in capital letters

10. A topographical map could help . . .

- ◯ **a.** a hiker estimate the best trail
- ◯ **b.** a geologist locate special surface features
- ◯ **c.** an engineer plan the best route for a road
- ◯ **d.** all of the above

NAME____________________________ DATE____________

LESSON 24

EARTH DETECTIVE

True/False (Circle T for true, F for false.)

T F **1.** One way to identify minerals is by their characteristics.

T F **2.** All rocks are essentially the same.

T F **3.** Scientists refer to scratching a material as a "toughness" test.

T F **4.** The color of a material can be affected by impurities.

T F **5.** A penny is harder to scratch than a microscope slide.

Multiple Choice (Fill in the circle beside the best answer.)

6. Quartz is commonly found in . . .

○ **a.** diamonds
○ **b.** roses
○ **c.** sand
○ **d.** coal

7. Another name for "magnetite" is . . .

○ **a.** quartz
○ **b.** amethyst
○ **c.** carbonate
○ **d.** lodestone

8. To perform a streak test, scientists . . .

○ **a.** observe the material closely for its color
○ **b.** drag the material across a piece of tile
○ **c.** scratch the material against a microscope slide
○ **d.** all of the above

9. Calcite is also known as . . .

○ **a.** sodium chloride
○ **b.** calcium carbonate
○ **c.** calcium silicate
○ **d.** amethyst

10. Scientists need to know the properties of rocks and minerals . . .

○ **a.** to help identify these materials accurately
○ **b.** to find new uses for rocks and minerals
○ **c.** both of the above
○ **d.** neither of the above

a reason for Science

NAME________________________ DATE ____________

EARTH DETECTIVE 2

LESSON 25

True/False (Circle T for true, F for false.)

T F **1.** A cleavage test helps determine a material's magnetic characteristics.

T F **2.** Most rocks and minerals are magnetic.

T F **3.** Talc is mostly iron with a metallic, golden color.

T F **4.** Jasper is also known as agate.

T F **5.** Jasper leaves a red streak in the streak test.

Multiple Choice (Fill in the circle beside the best answer.)

6. In an acid test, scientists watch for . . .

○ **a.** color changes
○ **b.** bubbles
○ **c.** iron filings
○ **d.** splitting

7. In a cleavage test, scientists watch for . . .

○ **a.** color changes
○ **b.** bubbles
○ **c.** iron filings
○ **d.** splitting

8. Another name for pyrite is . . .

○ **a.** amethyst
○ **b.** talc
○ **c.** fool's gold
○ **d.** soapstone

9. Talc is also known as . . .

○ **a.** pyrite
○ **b.** soapstone
○ **c.** amethyst
○ **d.** agate

10. Mica is a . . .

○ **a.** silicate
○ **b.** carbonate
○ **c.** magnetite
○ **d.** none of the above

NAME________________________________ DATE ____________

LESSON 26

RAISIN RESOURCES

True/False (Circle T for true, F for false.)

T F **1.** Harvesting Earth's resources can cause environmental damage.

T F **2.** Restrictive mining regulations can greatly limit supplies of raw materials.

T F **3.** It is not possible to balance production and environmental issues.

T F **4.** Scientists refer to any usable material that comes from Earth as a "resource."

T F **5.** Anything that leads to increased production is good.

Multiple Choice (Fill in the circle beside the best answer.)

6. Which of the following is an example of a resource?

○ **a.** rocks and minerals
○ **b.** livestock and wild creatures
○ **c.** food crops and native plants
○ **d.** all of the above

7. Removing resources from the Earth through mining is also called . . .

○ **a.** extraction
○ **b.** adaption
○ **c.** environmentalism
○ **d.** recycling

8. Unrestricted mining can . . .

○ **a.** increase production without harming the environment
○ **b.** increase production, but damage the environment
○ **c.** decrease production, but protect the environment
○ **d.** decrease production, but damage the environment

9. Tightly controlled mining can . . .

○ **a.** increase production without harming the environment
○ **b.** increase production, but damage the environment
○ **c.** decrease production, but protect the environment
○ **d.** decrease production, but damage the environment

10. What should society consider when dealing with natural resources?

○ **a.** the need for natural resources
○ **b.** the potential damage to the environment
○ **c.** neither a nor b
○ **d.** both a and b

a reason for Science

NAME________________________________ DATE ____________

LESSON 27

PETITE PALEONTOLOGY

True/False (Circle T for true, F for false.)

T F **1.** Only dinosaur bones are called fossils.

T F **2.** Distribution of bones can offer clues about how a creature died.

T F **3.** Scientists who study fossils are called paleontologists.

T F **4.** Paleontology requires exact documentation of fossil location.

T F **5.** Soft body parts of ancient creatures were rarely preserved.

Multiple Choice (Fill in the circle beside the best answer.)

6. A fossil is . . .

- ○ **a.** a preserved plant
- ○ **b.** a preserved animal
- ○ **c.** evidence a living thing existed
- ○ **d.** all of the above

7. A fossil may offer clues about all of the following except . . .

- ○ **a.** a creature's structure
- ○ **b.** a creature's color
- ○ **c.** a creature's function
- ○ **d.** how a creature died

8. Distribution of bones can offer clues about a creature's . . .

- ○ **a.** motion
- ○ **b.** death
- ○ **c.** relationship with other creatures
- ○ **d.** all of the above

9. A pattern of lines used as a reference for locating points is called a . . .

- ○ **a.** procedure
- ○ **b.** grid
- ○ **c.** distribution
- ○ **d.** none of the above

10. Modern paleontologists can create . . .

- ○ **a.** exact representations of all ancient creatures' body structures
- ○ **b.** detailed descriptions of all ancient creatures' soft body parts
- ○ **c.** computerized three-dimensional maps
- ○ **d.** all of the above

a reason for Science

NAME________________________________ DATE ____________

LESSON 28

UV DETECTOR

True/False (Circle T for true, F for false.)

T F **1.** Ultraviolet light is invisible to human eyes.

T F **2.** Prolonged exposure to ultraviolet light can be dangerous.

T F **3.** All forms of sunlight are harmful to humans.

T F **4.** Sunblock forms a physical barrier to UV light.

T F **5.** All sunblocks provide the same level of protection.

Multiple Choice (Fill in the circle beside the best answer.)

6. Prolonged exposure to ultraviolet light . . .

○ **a.** can help heal skin diseases
○ **b.** can cause diabetes
○ **c.** can cause a form of cancer
○ **d.** all of the above

7. All of the following could be physical barriers to UV light except . . .

○ **a.** cardboard
○ **b.** sunblock
○ **c.** a tree
○ **d.** air

8. SPF stands for . . .

○ **a.** Solar Polarization Factor
○ **b.** Safe Physical Factor
○ **c.** Sun Protection Factor
○ **d.** none of the above

9. Skin cancer occurs when . . .

○ **a.** rapidly growing cancer cells crowd out healthy cells
○ **b.** rapidly growing healthy cells attract cancer cells
○ **c.** slowly growing cancer cells replace cartilage
○ **d.** skin cells grow too slowly

10. Which of the following contributes to skin cancer?

○ **a.** skin cells that grow too slowly
○ **b.** prolonged exposure to UV light
○ **c.** using products with high SPF numbers
○ **d.** all of the above

NAME______________________________ DATE ____________

LESSON 29

FIX-IT FLUID

True/False (Circle T for true, F for false.)

T F **1.** Mineral oil can be used to repair broken glass.

T F **2.** When light goes through any material, it slows down.

T F **3.** When light slows down, it bends.

T F **4.** Scientists refer to light's ability to bend as "reflection."

T F **5.** The amount light bends depends on an object's "index of reflection."

Multiple Choice (Fill in the circle beside the best answer.)

6. When light passes through eyeglasses or contacts, it . . .

○ **a.** speeds up
○ **b.** is reflected
○ **c.** is refracted
○ **d.** none of the above

7. The greater the "index of refraction" . . .

○ **a.** the more light is bent
○ **b.** the less light is bent
○ **c.** the more light reflects
○ **d.** none of the above

8. An object is easy to see in a liquid if there is . . .

○ **a.** a big difference in their index of reflection
○ **b.** a big difference in their index of refraction
○ **c.** almost no difference in their index of reflection
○ **d.** almost no difference in their index of refraction

9. The amount that light bends depends on an object's . . .

○ **a.** ratio of reflection
○ **b.** ratio of refraction
○ **c.** index of reflection
○ **d.** index of refraction

10. How are glass and heavy mineral oil similar?

○ **a.** They always have the same temperature.
○ **b.** They have a very similar index of refraction.
○ **c.** They are made from identical molecules.
○ **d.** none of the above

NAME________________________________ DATE ______________

LESSON 30

POP MUSIC

True/False (Circle T for true, F for false.)

T F **1.** Scientists refer to moving energy as "kinetic" energy.

T F **2.** Vibration is required to create sound.

T F **3.** Different vibrations usually create the same sound.

T F **4.** The terms "frequency" and "pitch" describe the same thing.

T F **5.** Musicians refer to different frequencies as "notes."

Multiple Choice (Fill in the circle beside the best answer.)

6. Hitting a pipe produces a sound. The longer the pipe . . .

○ **a.** the lower the pitch
○ **b.** the higher the pitch
○ **c.** the higher the frequency
○ **d.** none of the above

7. To create music, sounds are usually . . .

○ **a.** regular
○ **b.** arranged
○ **c.** repeatable
○ **d.** all of the above

8. Another name for pitch is . . .

○ **a.** amplitude
○ **b.** wavelength
○ **c.** frequency
○ **d.** none of the above

9. The rate at which something vibrates is called its . . .

○ **a.** amplitude
○ **b.** wavelength
○ **c.** frequency
○ **d.** none of the above

10. When energy creates a vibration, the result is . . .

○ **a.** kinetic
○ **b.** sound
○ **c.** conversion
○ **d.** rhythm

NAME________________________________ DATE ______________

LESSON 31

BUOYANT BAG

True/False (Circle T for true, F for false.)

T F **1.** As air is heated, its molecules slow down and clump together.

T F **2.** Warm molecules generally contain less energy than cold molecules.

T F **3.** Hot air is less dense than cold air.

T F **4.** Balloons fly because their density is less than their surroundings.

T F **5.** Displacing matter can cause buoyancy.

Multiple Choice (Fill in the circle beside the best answer.)

6. The greater the amount of air displaced, the greater the . . .

- ◯ **a.** density
- ◯ **b.** buoyancy
- ◯ **c.** mass
- ◯ **d.** weight

7. The density of hot air is . . .

- ◯ **a.** greater than cold air
- ◯ **b.** less than cold air
- ◯ **c.** the same as cold air
- ◯ **d.** Temperature does not affect density.

8. A hot-air balloon will rise until the density of the surrounding air is . . .

- ◯ **a.** equal to the density of the air in the balloon
- ◯ **b.** less than the density of the air in the balloon
- ◯ **c.** more than the density of the air in the balloon
- ◯ **d.** none of the above

9. Adding energy (like heat) to air will . . .

- ◯ **a.** lower its density
- ◯ **b.** raise its density
- ◯ **c.** lower its mass
- ◯ **d.** none of the above

10. Generally, the warmer a material is . . .

- ◯ **a.** the greater its density
- ◯ **b.** the greater its mass
- ◯ **c.** the lower its density
- ◯ **d.** the lower its energy

a reason for Science

NAME________________________________ DATE ______________

LESSON 32

CIRCUIT TESTER

True/False (Circle T for true, F for false.)

T F **1.** Electricity involves the flow of electrons and the energy they carry.

T F **2.** Electricity can flow through any kind of material.

T F **3.** All materials respond in a similar fashion to the flow of electricity.

T F **4.** An open circuit means electricity can flow freely.

T F **5.** Turning a light switch off creates an open circuit.

Multiple Choice (Fill in the circle beside the best answer.)

6. All of the following could be conductors except . . .

- ◯ **a.** a paperclip
- ◯ **b.** a nail
- ◯ **c.** a piece of glass
- ◯ **d.** a piece of bare wire

7. All of the following could be insulators except . . .

- ◯ **a.** plastic
- ◯ **b.** wood
- ◯ **c.** rubber
- ◯ **d.** aluminum

8. When electricity flows through a circuit, the circuit is . . .

- ◯ **a.** closed
- ◯ **b.** open
- ◯ **c.** lit
- ◯ **d.** none of the above

9. Turning on a light creates . . .

- ◯ **a.** an open circuit
- ◯ **b.** a closed circuit
- ◯ **c.** a recessed circuit
- ◯ **d.** none of the above

10. Electricity is the flow of electrons through . . .

- ◯ **a.** an insulator
- ◯ **b.** a conductor
- ◯ **c.** an open circuit
- ◯ **d.** both b and c

NAME______________________________ DATE ____________

LESSON 33

MEASURING MATTER

True/False (Circle T for true, F for false.)

T F **1.** Although it often changes forms, matter is never lost.

T F **2.** Chemical compounds always have the same formula.

T F **3.** Pure water always contains three different elements.

T F **4.** Tiny amounts of matter are lost in any physical change.

T F **5.** Tiny amounts of matter are lost in any chemical change.

Multiple Choice (Fill in the circle beside the best answer.)

6. The "Law of Conservation of Matter" states that . . .

○ **a.** when matter changes forms, only small amounts are los
○ **b.** when matter changes forms, no matter is lost
○ **c.** specific compounds are always identical
○ **d.** specific compounds vary only slightly

7. The "Law of Definite Proportions" states that . . .

○ **a.** when matter changes forms, only small amounts are lost
○ **b.** when matter changes forms, no matter is lost
○ **c.** specific compounds are always identical
○ **d.** specific compounds vary only slightly

8. An example of the "Law of Conservation of Matter" is . . .

○ **a.** the number of times a student chews a piece of gum
○ **b.** the recipe a company uses to make peanut butter
○ **c.** that only a limited number of cars will fit in a parking lot
○ **d.** that trash isn't really "thrown away," just redistributed

9. An example of the "Law of Definite Proportions" is . . .

○ **a.** the number of times a student chews a piece of gum
○ **b.** the recipe a company uses to make peanut butter
○ **c.** that only a limited number of cars will fit in a parking lot
○ **d.** that trash isn't really "thrown away," just redistributed

10. A minor change in the proportion of ingredients will always result in . . .

○ **a.** a change in the product's color
○ **b.** a change in the product's texture
○ **c.** some degree of change in the product
○ **d.** no change in the product at all

a reason for Science

NAME________________________________ DATE ______________

LESSON 34

REACTION RACER

True/False (Circle T for true, F for false.)

T F **1.** Potential energy is moving energy.

T F **2.** Kinetic energy is stored energy.

T F **3.** Energy can be converted from one form to another.

T F **4.** Movement requires energy, and energy leads to movement.

T F **5.** Applying more energy usually makes an object move farther.

Multiple Choice (Fill in the circle beside the best answer.)

6. Which of the following is an example of potential energy?

○ **a.** a charged battery
○ **b.** gas in a car
○ **c.** food in a refrigerator
○ **d.** all of the above

7. Which of the following is an example of kinetic energy?

○ **a.** a frozen wheel
○ **b.** a rock in a field
○ **c.** a swinging bat
○ **d.** all of the above

8. All of the following are examples of energy conversion except . . .

○ **a.** running up a hill
○ **b.** charging a battery
○ **c.** digesting your lunch
○ **d.** a can of gasoline

9. Holding a rock very still over a bucket of water is an example of . . .

○ **a.** potential energy
○ **b.** kinetic energy
○ **c.** moving energy
○ **d.** reaction energy

10. Scientists refer to a change in energy as . . .

○ **a.** connection
○ **b.** conversion
○ **c.** combustion
○ **d.** comparison

NAME________________________________ DATE ______________

LESSON 35

CLUMP OF COPPER

True/False (Circle T for true, F for false.)

T F **1.** Matter is always the same and never changes forms.

T F **2.** Physical change only modifies the appearance of something.

T F **3.** Chemical change produces a completely different substance.

T F **4.** Physical changes almost always give off energy (like heat).

T F **5.** Dissolving a material in water is a physical change.

Multiple Choice (Fill in the circle beside the best answer.)

6. Which of the following is an example of a physical change?

- ○ **a.** grinding
- ○ **b.** burning
- ○ **c.** freezing
- ○ **d.** all of the above

7. When a material is dissolved in water, the result is a . . .

- ○ **a.** substance
- ○ **b.** solution
- ○ **c.** chemical change
- ○ **d.** none of the above

8. When iron atoms react with copper ions they can produce . . .

- ○ **a.** iron atoms
- ○ **b.** copper atoms
- ○ **c.** blue ions
- ○ **d.** bronze atoms

9. Iron atoms reacting with copper ions is an example of . . .

- ○ **a.** physical change
- ○ **b.** chemical change
- ○ **c.** chemical solution
- ○ **d.** substance abuse

10. When iron atoms react with copper ions, the matter in the iron . . .

- ○ **a.** is completely destroyed
- ○ **b.** is partially destroyed as the iron becomes a new substance
- ○ **c.** remains the same substance
- ○ **d.** is changed into a different substance

a reason for Science

NAME________________________________ DATE ______________

LESSON 36

PRINTS CHARMING

True/False (Circle T for true, F for false.)

T F **1.** Indicators change color when exposed to an acid or base.

T F **2.** Indicator paper is helpful in collecting and identifying fingerprints.

T F **3.** Only identical twins have identical fingerprints.

T F **4.** Ammonium hydroxide is a weak form of acid.

T F **5.** Although all fingerprints are unique, similar patterns are common.

Multiple Choice (Fill in the circle beside the best answer.)

6. The pH of pure water is usually . . .

◯ **a.** a base
◯ **b.** an acid
◯ **c.** neutral
◯ **d.** none of the above

7. Which of the following is a common fingerprint pattern?

◯ **a.** loop
◯ **b.** arch
◯ **c.** whorl
◯ **d.** all of the above

8. The goldenrod paper used in this activity contained . . .

◯ **a.** a strong acid
◯ **b.** a strong base
◯ **c.** a neutral
◯ **d.** an indicator

9. The "arch" fingerprint pattern is . . .

◯ **a.** a hump like an upside down U
◯ **b.** a loop with a floor to it
◯ **c.** a loop leaning to one side or the other
◯ **d.** a hump in a spinning pattern

10. The "whorl" fingerprint pattern is . . .

◯ **a.** a hump like an upside down U
◯ **b.** a loop with a floor to it
◯ **c.** a loop leaning to one side or the other
◯ **d.** a hump in a spinning pattern

a reason for Science

Assessment Answer Key

LIFE

Lesson 1
Yeasty Beasty

1. T
2. F
3. F
4. T
5. F
6. c
7. b
8. a
9. d
10. d

Lesson 2
Preserved Plants

1. T
2. T
3. F
4. F
5. T
6. c
7. b
8. c
9. b
10. d

Lesson 3
Cleverly Classified

1. T
2. T
3. F
4. F
5. T
6. c
7. b
8. c
9. d
10. d

Lesson 4
DNA Difference

1. F
2. T
3. T
4. T
5. F
6. d
7. c
8. c
9. a
10. a

Lesson 5
Mitosis Mystery

1. T
2. T
3. F
4. T
5. T
6. b
7. a
8. b
9. a
10. a

Lesson 6
Marvelous Meiosis

1. T
2. F
3. F
4. F
5. T
6. c
7. b
8. b
9. c
10. b

Lesson 7
Generating Gender

1. F
2. T
3. F
4. T
5. T
6. b
7. d
8. c
9. d
10. c

Lesson 8
Fascinating Fingerprints

1. T
2. T
3. F
4. F
5. T
6. a
7. b
8. c
9. d
10. c

Lesson 9
Create a Kid

1. T
2. F
3. T
4. T
5. F
6. c
7. a
8. b
9. a
10. c

Assessment Answer Key
FORCES

Lesson 10
Atom Ancestors

1. F
2. T
3. T
4. F
5. T
6. c
7. c
8. a
9. d
10. b

Lesson 11
Attractive Element

1. T
2. T
3. F
4. F
5. T
6. b
7. a
8. c
9. b
10. d

Lesson 12
Ice Slicer

1. T
2. F
3. T
4. F
5. T
6. d
7. c
8. d
9. a
10. b

Lesson 13
Bounce Back Ball

1. T
2. T
3. F
4. T
5. F
6. b
7. c
8. d
9. b
10. b

Lesson 14
Kinetic Can

1. T
2. F
3. T
4. F
5. F
6. a
7. b
8. b
9. b
10. d

Lesson 15
Gravity Grabber

1. T
2. F
3. T
4. T
5. T
6. c
7. b
8. c
9. d
10. b

Lesson 16
Diet Dilemma

1. T
2. F
3. T
4. F
5. T
6. a
7. c
8. b
9. a
10. d

Lesson 17
Structural Strength

1. T
2. T
3. T
4. F
5. T
6. b
7. d
8. a
9. d
10. c

Lesson 18
Incredible Eggmobile

1. T
2. T
3. F
4. T
5. F
6. b
7. c
8. c
9. a
10. d

Lesson 19
Air Elevator

1. F
2. T
3. T
4. T
5. F
6. b
7. c
8. b
9. c
10. d

Lesson 20
Test Tube Mosquito

1. F
2. F
3. T
4. T
5. T
6. b
7. a
8. b
9. c
10. d

Lesson 21
Magnetism Model

1. T
2. T
3. F
4. T
5. F
6. c
7. c
8. d
9. b
10. d

Lesson 22
Student Satellites

1. T
2. F
3. F
4. F
5. T
6. d
7. c
8. d
9. a
10. b

Lesson 23
Tropical Topography

1. T
2. F
3. T
4. T
5. T
6. b
7. a
8. c
9. b
10. d

Lesson 24
Earth Detective

1. T
2. F
3. F
4. T
5. F
6. c
7. d
8. b
9. b
10. c

Lesson 25
Earth Detective 2

1. F
2. F
3. F
4. T
5. F
6. b
7. d
8. c
9. b
10. a

Lesson 26
Raisin Resources

1. T
2. T
3. F
4. T
5. F
6. d
7. a
8. b
9. c
10. d

Lesson 27
Petite Paleontology

1. F
2. T
3. T
4. T
5. T
6. d
7. b
8. d
9. b
10. c

Assessment Answer Key
ENERGY/MATTER

Lesson 28
UV Detector

1. T
2. T
3. F
4. T
5. F
6. c
7. d
8. c
9. a
10. b

Lesson 29
Fix-It Fluid

1. F
2. T
3. T
4. F
5. F
6. c
7. a
8. b
9. d
10. b

Lesson 30
Pop Music

1. T
2. T
3. F
4. T
5. T
6. a
7. d
8. c
9. c
10. b

Lesson 31
Buoyant Bag

1. F
2. F
3. T
4. T
5. T
6. b
7. b
8. a
9. a
10. c

Lesson 32
Circuit Tester

1. T
2. F
3. F
4. F
5. T
6. c
7. d
8. a
9. b
10. b

Lesson 33
Measuring Matter

1. T
2. T
3. F
4. F
5. F
6. b
7. c
8. d
9. b
10. c

Lesson 34
Reaction Racer

1. F
2. F
3. T
4. T
5. T
6. d
7. c
8. d
9. a
10. b

Lesson 35
Clump Of Copper

1. F
2. T
3. T
4. F
5. T
6. d
7. b
8. b
9. b
10. d

Lesson 36
Prints Charming

1. T
2. T
3. F
4. F
5. T
6. c
7. d
8. d
9. b
10. c

a reason for Science

Shopping List

This **"Shopping List"** is provided for your convenience. It contains all the items that are not common classroom supplies (paper, pencil, scissors, etc.) or components found in your Materials Kit. Please note that there are a few items (like tissue paper rolls) that require advance planning for effective collection.

Lesson 1
20 oz soft drink bottles (2)
Teaspoon

Lesson 2
Plant indentification book
Heavy cardboard
String or cord
Newspaper

Lesson 4
Denatured alcohol
Distilled water
Clear shampoo
Kiwi
Measuring cup

Lesson 8
Magnifying glass (optional)

Lesson 11
Liquid soap
Paper towels

Lesson 12
Block of ice
Weights (2)
Pan

Lesson 14
Plastic lid
Coffee can

Lesson 15
Hammer

Lesson 16
Can diet cola
Can regular cola
Bucket

Lesson 18
Egg

Lesson 19
Matches
Aluminum pie pan

Lesson 20
Red food coloring
Matches

Lesson 22
Chalk
Rope

Lesson 23
Clay
Plastic container
Gallon jug
Food coloring

Lesson 25
Plastic bag (optional)

Lesson 26
Raisin cookies
Papcr platc

Lesson 27
Cardboard box
Graph paper
Bones (5)
Sand

Lesson 28
Egg carton
Clear plastic
Cardboard
Sunblock

Lesson 29
Paper towels
Mineral oil
Container

Lesson 31
Poster board strips
Hair dryer

Lesson 32
Aluminum foil

Lesson 33
Paper cup
Bubble gum

Lesson 35
Paper towels

Lesson 36
Paper towels

LESSON 30

POP MUSIC

Musical Scales

A B C D E F G A

G F E D C B A

A C E G E C A

America

F	F	G	E	F	G	A	A	B	A	G	F
My	Coun-	try	'tis	of	thee	sweet	land	of	lib-	er-	ty...

G	F	E	F
of	thee	I	sing

Twinkle, Twinkle Little Star

F	F	C	C	D	D	C	B	B	A	A	G	G	F
Twin-kle	Twin-kle	lit-	tle	star	how	I	won-	der	what	you	are		

C	C	B	B	A	A	G
Up	a-	bove	the	world	so	high

C	C	B	B	A	A	G
Like	a	dia-	mond	in	the	sky

F	F	C	C	D	D	C	B	B	A	A	G	G	F
Twin-kle	Twin-kle	lit-	tle	star	how	I	won-	der	what	you	are		